MW01591000

Forays into Contemporary South African Theatre

Cross/Cultures

READINGS IN POST/COLONIAL
LITERATURES AND CULTURES IN ENGLISH

Edited by

Bénédicte Ledent and Delphine Munos

Founding Editors

Gordon Collier
Geoffrey Davis†
Hena Maes-Jelinek†

Advisory Board

David Callahan (*University of Aveiro*) – Stephen Clingman (*University of Massachusetts*) – Marc Delrez (*Université de Liège*) – Gaurav Desai (*University of Michigan*) – Russell McDougall (*University of New England*) – John McLeod (*University of Leeds*) – Irikidzayi Manase (*University of the Free State*) – Caryl Phillips (*Yale University*) – Diana Brydon (*University of Manitoba*) – Pilar Cuder-Dominguez (*University of Huelva*) – Wendy Knepper (*Brunel University*) – Carine Mardorossian (*University of Buffalo*) – Maria Olaussen (*University of Gothenburg*) – Chris Prentice (*Otago University*) – Cheryl Stobie (*University of KwaZulu-Natal*) – Daria Tunca (*Université de Liège*)

VOLUME 211

The titles published in this series are listed at *brill.com/cc*

Forays into Contemporary South African Theatre

Devising New Stage Idioms

Edited by

Marc and Jessica Maufort

BRILL
RODOPI

LEIDEN | BOSTON

Cover illustration: courtesy of Annick Englebert.

The Library of Congress Cataloging-in-Publication Data is available online at http://catalog.loc.gov

Typeface for the Latin, Greek, and Cyrillic scripts: "Brill". See and download: brill.com/brill-typeface.

ISSN 0924-1426
ISBN 978-90-04-41445-7 (hardback)
ISBN 978-90-04-41446-4 (e-book)

Copyright 2020 by Koninklijke Brill NV, Leiden, The Netherlands.
Koninklijke Brill NV incorporates the imprints Brill, Brill Hes & De Graaf, Brill Nijhoff, Brill Rodopi,
Brill Sense, Hotei Publishing, mentis Verlag, Verlag Ferdinand Schöningh and Wilhelm Fink Verlag.
All rights reserved. No part of this publication may be reproduced, translated, stored in a retrieval system,
or transmitted in any form or by any means, electronic, mechanical, photocopying, recording or otherwise,
without prior written permission from the publisher.
Authorization to photocopy items for internal or personal use is granted by Koninklijke Brill NV provided
that the appropriate fees are paid directly to The Copyright Clearance Center, 222 Rosewood Drive, Suite
910, Danvers, MA 01923, USA. Fees are subject to change.

This book is printed on acid-free paper and produced in a sustainable manner.

Printed by Printforce, the Netherlands

In memoriam
Geoffrey V. Davis
(1943–2018)

∴

Contents

PART 3
Female Playwriting

PART 4

Creolization: From the Cape to Transnational Vistas

Acknowledgments

This project originated in an international conference, "New Stage Idioms: South African Drama, Theatre and Performance in the Twenty-first Century," held at the Université Libre de Bruxelles (ULB), Belgium, from May 11–13, 2017. Most of the essays collected in this anthology were first presented at the conference while others were subsequently commissioned especially for this volume. As the co-organizers of this conference, we would like to thank the following funding agencies for their support: the National Fund for Scientific Research-Belgium (F.R.S.-FNRS), the "Faculté de Lettres, Traduction et Communication" of the Université Libre de Bruxelles (ULB), the Department of Languages and Literatures of the Université Libre Bruxelles (ULB), the "Philixte" Research Centre, as well as the Weisgerber Foundation. We also extend our thanks to Eveline Haberfeld and Vanessa Demeuldre, who carefully took care of the conference logistics. Annick Englebert admirably devised the conference poster, which she subsequently developed into this book's cover. We are indebted to Greg Homann for his valuable scholarly advice in the compilation of this anthology. We are very grateful to Samuel Pauwels for his meticulous editorial assistance. We also wish to thank the two anonymous readers for their insightful comments, which helped us strengthen this book's arguments. Ms Christa Stevens, our acquisitions editor at Brill, efficiently guided us through the production process. This project would never have reached the publication stage without Geoffrey V. Davis's enthusiastic response to the conference, which he attended as a South African literature scholar. He strongly encouraged us to submit the volume for possible publication in his "Cross/Culture. Readings in Post/colonial Literatures and Cultures in English" series. Geoff unexpectedly passed away at the end of 2018. This book is naturally dedicated to his memory.

Marc and Jessica Maufort
Brussels, June 2019

Notes on Contributors

Veronica Baxter

(PhD) has taught at South African and UK universities over the past thirty years. She currently teaches and supervises students in the Centre for Theatre, Dance and Performance Studies, University of Cape Town. Her research is mainly concerned with applied/social theatre in health, education and social justice contexts. Her most recent publications are *Applied Theatre: Performing Health and Wellbeing*, (co-edited and written with Katharine E Low, Bloomsbury 2017), chapters in *Methuen Drama Guide to South African Theatre* (Middeke, Schnierer and Homann, 2015) and *New Territories: Reconfiguring Theatre and Drama in Post-apartheid South Africa*; (Maufort and Homann, 2015).

Marcia Blumberg

is an Associate Professor at York University in the faculty of Liberal Arts and Professional Studies, where she was appointed to the English department and is also cross appointed to the Theatre and Performance Program. She has published widely, presented papers at many international conferences, and been invited to participate in panels and conduct talkbacks. She teaches undergraduate drama from the Ancient Greeks to international contemporary plays and performances, and graduate courses specializing in South African theatre and other contemporary issues such as the theatre of 9/11.

Petrus du Preez

graduated from the University of the Free State and received his doctorate at Stellenbosch University, where he is currently an Associate Professor and chair at the Drama Department. He is involved in theatre making as an actor, director and author. He has performed extensively on the arts festival circuit in South Africa. In the past year he expanded his practical work to include television and film performances.

Paula Fourie

is a writer living in Stellenbosch, South Africa. She holds a BMus and MMus from the University of Pretoria and a PhD from Stellenbosch University. She currently works as research fellow at Africa Open: Institute for Music, Research and Innovation at Stellenbosch University where she is completing a monograph based on her doctoral research, a biography of South African musician and musical theatre composer Taliep Petersen. Paula is also active in professional theatre, having worked alongside her husband, South African playwright Athol Fugard, since 2012 in the capacities of associate director and co-director.

Craig Higginson

is an internationally acclaimed playwright and novelist who lives in Johannesburg. His plays have been produced in a number of venues, including the National Theatre in London, the Royal Shakespeare Company, the Traverse Theatre and the Trafalgar Studios in London's West End. His novels include *Last Summer, The Landscape Painter, The Dream House* and *The White Room.* He has won several awards, including the Sony Gold Award for the Best Radio Drama in the UK, an Edinburgh Fringe First, the UJ Award for South African Literature in English (twice) and the Naledi Award for Best South African play.

Greg Homann

is an independent academic, theatre director, playwright, and dramaturg. He has headed up theatre and performance departments in The Wits School of Arts and at AFDA (The South African School of Motion Picture & Live Performance). He co-edited *The Methuen Drama Guide to Contemporary South African Theatre* (2015) and *New Territories: Theatre, Drama, and Performance in Post-apartheid South Africa* (2015), and is the editor of *At This Stage: Plays from Post-apartheid South Africa* (2009). His multiple awards for his work include the prestigious Standard Bank Young Artist Award for Theatre in 2014.

Vicki Briault Manus

who recently retired from the University Grenoble-Alpes, has published numerous articles on Southern African literature, stylistics and language issues and a monograph in English entitled *Emerging Traditions: Toward a Postcolonial Stylistics of Black South African Literature in English* (Lanham, MD: Lexington Books, 2011).

Jessica Maufort

specialises in postcolonial ecocriticism, ecopoetics, and magic realism examined in Indigenous and non-Indigenous fiction from Australasia and Canada. With support from a research fellowship of the Belgian Fund for Scientific Research (F.R.S.-FNRS), Jessica is currently pursuing postdoctoral research at the Université Libre de Bruxelles (ULB), investigating the ecopoetics of trauma in the Anthropocene. She has published essays in *Ecozon@: European Journal of Literature, Culture and Environment* and *AJE: Australasian Journal of Ecocriticism and Cultural Ecology.*

Marc Maufort

is Professor of Anglophone literatures at the Université Libre de Bruxelles (ULB), Belgium. He is the current editor of *Recherche littéraire/Literary Research*, the bilingual state of art journal of the International Comparative Literature Association (ICLA). He has written and (co)-edited several books on Eugene O'Neill as well as postcolonial and multi-ethnic drama. His most recent book publication is *New Territories. Theatre, Drama, and Performance in Post-apartheid South Africa* (co-edited with Greg Homann, 2015).

Omphile Molusi

has been writing, directing and acting for theatre since 2001 and is an alumnus of the Market Theatre Laboratory. In 2007 he became the first recipient of the Brett Goldin Bursary Award, which gave him an opportunity to further refine his craft at the Royal Shakespeare Company. He was awarded Scotsman Fringe First Award 2008 at the Edinburgh Fringe Festival and won the Andre Deshields award for best performance at the Black theatre alliance awards 2010 in Chicago. He also runs a playwriting course and is the founder and Artistic Director of TsaMmu Theatre.

Jessica Murray

is a full Professor in the Department of English Studies at UNISA. As a Commonwealth scholar, she obtained her PhD at York University, Canada. Her research explores representations of violence and gender in Southern African writing. She is an NRF-rated scholar and she was awarded the UNISA Chancellor's Prize for Excellence in Research in 2012.

Jill Planche

(BA Hons. York University, Toronto, MA University of Toronto, PhD York University) is an academic with a professional background in building audiences and fundraising for the arts in Canada. Her article "'A community of storytellers and translators.' *Ubu and the Truth Commission* seen through Deleuze's language of emergence" was published in the *JCDE* (*Journal of Contemporary Drama in English*). She continues her research on South African culture as a doctoral candidate in Brock University's Interdisciplinary Humanities PhD Program, investigating the space of South African theatre and its role in the contemporary socio-political-cultural discourse.

Ksenia Robbe

is an Assistant Professor of African and Comparative Literature at the University of Leiden. Her research focuses on South African literature, theatre and visual art, in particular women's writing and the politics of memory. She is the author of *Conversations of Motherhood: South African Women's Writing across Traditions* (UKZN Press, 2015). Her current research explores practices of re-membering the "transitional period" in post-apartheid cultural production.

Mathilde Rogez

is a Senior Lecturer at the Université de Toulouse, France (CAS – EA801), spe-cializing in South African literature. She is the Commonwealth editor for *Miranda* and a member of the editorial board of *Etudes littéraires africaines*, and co-edited a special issue of *ELA* on South African literature in 2014. She is cur-rently co-editing four books, on contemporary South African theatre, on the representation of South African cities, on the suburbs in literature and the arts in the English-speaking world, and on commemorative politics in South Africa in the 21st century.

Chris Thurman

is an Associate Professor in the English Department at the University of the Witwatersrand. He is the editor of *South African Essays on 'Universal' Shake-speare* (2014) and *Sport versus Art: A South African Contest* (2010). His other books are the monograph *Guy Butler: Reassessing a South African Literary Life* (2010); *Text Bites*, a literary anthology for high schools (2009); and two collec-tions of his arts writing and journalism, *At Large: Reviewing the Arts in South Africa* (2012) and *Still at Large: Dispatches from South Africa's Frontiers of Poli-tics and Art* (2017).

Mike van Graan

is the President of the African Cultural Policy Network, a member of UNESCO's Technical Facility on the 2005 Convention on the Protection and Promotion of the Diversity of Cultural Expressions, and an award-winning playwright. After South Africa's first democratic elections, he played an influential role in shap-ing post-apartheid cultural policies He is the 2018 recipient of the Sweden-based Hiroshima Foundation for Peace and Culture Award in recognition of his contribution to the fight against apartheid, to building a post-apartheid society and to the interface of peace and culture both in South Africa and across the African continent.

Ralph Yarrow

is Emeritus Professor of Drama and Comparative Literature, UEA, Norwich, UK. His career spans an engagement with language and cultural produc-tion from Europe to India, from comparative criticism to postcolonial theory, from teaching innovations to directing practice; theatre and performance in France, Germany, Poland, the UK, India and Asia, South Africa. He regularly co-operated with India's leading Forum Theatre/Theatre of the Oppressed organisation, Jana Sanskriti (JS). His books include *Improvisation in Drama, Theatre and Performance* (with Anthony Frost); *Indian Theatre: Theatre of Origin, Theatre of Freedom*; and the co-written *Sacred Theatre* (with Carl Lavery *et al.*).

CHAPTER 1

A Fraught Process: Devising New Stage Idioms for Post-apartheid South Africa

Marc and Jessica Maufort

The vibrant political plays written in the mode of the "workshop theatre" and "protest theatre" of the apartheid era, many of which were produced at some stage at Johannesburg's progressive "Market Theatre," have been collected in numerous anthologies of South African drama. Let it suffice to mention some of the most memorable among these works: Athol Fugard's "township plays," including *Sizwe Bansi Is Dead* (1972) and *The Island* (1973) (devised with John Kani and Winston Ntshona); Barney Simon's *Born in the* RSA (1985); Percy Mtwa, Mbongeni Ingema and Barney Simon's *Woza Albert!*; Zakes Mda's *And the Girls in their Sunday Dresses* (1988): Junction Avenue Theatre Company's *Sophiatown* (1986); Maishe Maponya's *The Hungry Earth* (1979); Paul Slabolepszy's *Mooi Street Moves* (1992); and, Matsemela Manaka's *Goree* (1989).

In the years that followed the end of apartheid, South African theatre was characterized by a remarkable productivity, which resulted in a process of constant aesthetic reinvention. It was nevertheless a fraught process, because, as Greg Homann has indicated, the years of transition into a new democracy entailed a complicated search for a new national identity, fuelled by two major political events. First, this quest seemed to be encapsulated in Desmond Tutu's and Nelson Mandela's dream of a "rainbow nation," in which people from diverse ethnic constituencies would live in harmony.[1] Further, the proceedings of the Truth and Reconciliation Commission, the first hearings of which started in 1996, sought to address the ways in which the traumas of apartheid could be laid to rest.[2] This encouraged playwrights to devise works attempting to heal such traumas, as is the case in Yael Farber's *Theatre as Witness. Three Testimonial Plays from South Africa* (1999–2002). However, as many critics have pointed

---

1 Greg Homann, "Claiming Western Texts for Contemporary South African Theatre. Issues of Relevance and the Dead-end Pursuit of National Identity," in *New Territories: Theatre, Drama, and Performance in Post-apartheid South Africa*, ed. Greg Homann and Marc Maufort (Brussels: Peter Lang, 2015), 123.

2 Greg Homann, "Preamble," in *At This Stage. Plays from Post-apartheid South Africa*, ed. Greg Homann (Johannesburg: Wits University Press, 2009), 9–11.

© KONINKLIJKE BRILL NV, LEIDEN, 2020 | DOI:10.1163/9789004414464_002

out, including Homann,[3] the dream of unity in diversity of what came to be called "Rainbow Nation(ism)" turned into a mere illusion as the post-apartheid government proved incapable of avoiding massive corruption. It is yet to be seen if the newly elected President, Cyril Ramaphosa, will manage to improve this unfortunate predicament.[4] Moreover, the TRC seemed to favour some kind of national amnesia instead of truly confronting past traumas. These memory issues are often addressed in recent playwriting, as the essays collected in this volume indicate.

After 1994, the "protest" theatre template of the apartheid years morphed into a wealth of diverse forms of stage idioms, detectable in the works of Greg Homann, Mike van Graan, Craig Higginson, Lara Foot, Omphile Molusi, Nadia Davids, Magnet Theatre, Allan Kolski Horwitz, Rehane Abrahams, Amy Jephta, and Reza de Wet, to cite only a few prominent examples. Defining these idioms is a fraught task indeed, considering the multifaceted features of post-apartheid dramaturgies. This multivocal volume seeks to document some of the various ways in which the "rainbow" nation has forged these new stage idioms, through theatrical modes of expression. Judging from the various pieces collected here, this process of aesthetic reconfiguration seems to mirror the multicultural diversity of South Africa, with its 11 official languages. At the outset, we would wish to acknowledge our awareness of the many ambivalences characterizing the contemporary South African stage. As the editors of the *Methuen Drama Guide to Contemporary South African Theatre* point out in their introduction, African dramaturgies are typified by an often problematic divide between African-based traditions of orality and European text-centered realist aesthetics.[5] Moreover, as these editors also stress, "From around 1970 a tension has existed in South Africa between the practice of writing a play as a solo playwright and the workshop tradition of play making. The latter arguably became the dominant mode of play creation"[6] by the end of the apartheid era. Although this workshop template was progressively replaced by more experimental idioms in the post-apartheid period, as the essays collected here will show, the contemporary stage still reflects the racialized conflicts underpinning the new democracy. Let it suffice to provide two examples of this contentious state of affairs. Yael Faber's *Mies Julie*, a rewriting of Strindberg's

---

3 Greg Homann, "Claiming Western Texts," 123.

4 Ramaphosa was appointed interim President in 2018. His position was confirmed in the May 2019 elections.

5 Greg Homann, Martin Middeke and Peter Paul Schnierer, "Introduction," in *The Methuen Drama Guide to Contemporary South African Theatre*, ed. Martin Middeke, Peter Paul Schnierer and Greg Homann (London: Bloomsbury Methuen Drama, 2017), 11.

6 *Ibid.*, 1.

eponymous play from a South African perspective, foregrounds the racial tension that opposes black and white communities in the country, as the black servant eventually rapes the white mistress.[7] Brett Bailey's installation piece, *Exhibit B*, in which real human beings are exhibited as living testimonials of colonial slavery and torture, was received controversially in London as a potential re-inscription of colonial practices.[8]

Further, the legacy of European theatre and cultural practices has proved a thorny issue in recent years. While the higher education student protests of 2015–2016 called for a more democratic access to tertiary education, they also demanded a thorough revision of the school curriculum, deemed too Eurocentric.[9] As Chris Thurman has argued, it might not even be possible to continue to teach Shakespeare in South African high schools and even universities.[10] Given the apparently dominant white perspective of this volume, which also includes an essay on transnational Shakespeare, how do we really position ourselves towards these issues? Like Anton Krueger, we feel uncomfortable about the renewed racial oppositions that have characterized stage practices in South Africa since 2010 or so. Krueger documented this phenomenon in a recent review essay about the 2017 National Arts Festival in Grahamstown As he claims: "We need celebration of diversity instead of censure, polyphony instead of drone. [...] The new ethos of an identity staked mainly in terms of antagonism could promote an increasing racial polarization and divisiveness, rather than alleviating the wounds of the past, rather than nurturing grounds for positive recovery and growth."[11] Like Krueger, then, we think that a celebration of cultural polyphony is in order. Because of the logistics of the conference from which this book developed, we admit that our claims to such comprehensiveness are limited. While we would have wished to be able to invite to Belgium more speakers from South Africa, such as the renowned playwrights Zakes Mda or Paul Grootboom, this proved a technical impossibility. The works of

---

7   For a detailed analysis of the reception of *Mies Julie*, see Marisa Keuris, "'*Restitutions of Body and Soil*' in *Mies Julie* (2012): South African Theatre Audience Reception of Yael Farber's Adaptation of Strindberg's *Miss Julie* within a Post-apartheid South African Political Landscape," *South African Theatre Journal* 29, nos. 1–3 (2016): 49–52.

8   Greg Homann, Martin Middeke and Peter Paul Schnierer, "Introduction," 11.

9   For a detailed discussion of these protests, the reader could turn to Elmarie Costandius et al., "#Feesmustfall and Decolonizing the Curriculum: Stellenbosch University Students' and Lecturers' Reactions," *South African Journal of Higher Education* 32, no. 2 (2018): 65–85.

10 Chris Thurman, "Shakespeare in South African Schools: to Die, to Sleep – or Perchance to Dream," *The Conversation*, March 29, 2017, http://theconversation.com/shakespeare-in-south-african-schools-to-die-to-sleep-or-perchance-to-dream-75314

11 Anton Krueger, "Revolutionary Trends at the National Arts Festival 2017 (an overview)," *South African Theatre Journal* 31, nos. 2–3 (2018): 209.

Zakes Mda and Paul Grootboom have received significant critical attention in earlier publications, such as Patrick Ebewo's recent monograph.[12] Further, we made a definite attempt to focus on young black voices from the townships, particularly that of Omphile Molusi. As Molusi seeks to favour writing in African Indigenous languages, the inclusion of his piece gave us a chance to question the English-centred underpinnings of postcolonial studies. This being said, we remain conscious of our position as "outsiders inside," given that the entire spectrum of South African ethnic voices simply could not be addressed. We attempted to compensate this by including essays on a considerable range of different stage practitioners, structuring this anthology as a mosaic design of varied perspectives. This is further underlined by a focus on the dynamic process of creolization, understood in the sense of cultural multiplicities. The illustration we chose for the book's cover precisely invites the reader to discover the enmeshment of the scholarly voices gathered in this collection.

The multi-layered aspect of South African society, particularly noticeable in the coloured population of the Cape area, calls to mind the notion of creolization. Kamau Brathwaite (in "Creolization and Jamaica") and Stuart Hall (in "Cultural Identity and Diaspora") had already suggested the potential benefits of using this concept in New World contexts, in view of its celebration of the "impure."[13] However, creolization was more fully theorized in the works of Édouard Glissant. Glissant first identified this phenomenon in the Caribbean region but later considered it as a characteristic of the world at large. Although the term has enjoyed much recognition among Caribbean theorists and writers, some critics have questioned its usefulness outside the Caribbean basin. Robert Baron and Ana C. Cara have summarized these objections in their introduction to their edited book, *Creolization as Cultural Creativity*. As they indicate, "too often, Creole expressions have been viewed as manifestations of fragmentation and degeneration."[14] Further, some scholars initially felt reluctant to use this term, which originated in linguistics, in the realm of cultural studies.[15] Some commentators also regarded creolization as an "emic

---

12   Patrick J. Ebewo, *Explorations in Southern African Drama, Theatre and Performance* (Newcastle upon Tyne: Cambridge Scholars Publishing, 2017), 48–66, 102–121 (Mda), 121–140 (Grootboom).

13   Edward Kamu Brathwaite, "Creolization in Jamaica," in *The Postcolonial Studies Reader*, ed. Bill Ashcroft, Gareth Griffith, and Helen Tiffin (London: Routledge, 2005), 152–154; Stuart Hall, "Cultural Identity and Diaspora," in *The Postcolonial Studies Reader*, 435–438.

14   Robert Baron and Ana C. Cara, "Introduction: Creolization as Cultural Creativity," in *Creolization as Cultural Creativity*, ed. Robert Baron and Ana C. Cara (Jackson: U of Mississippi P, 2011), 4.

15   *Ibid.*, 10–11.

phenomenon," analyzing cultures "from below," which limited its wider application as "an analytic category."[16] Perhaps surprisingly so for a concept that thrives on heterogeneity, some detractors argued that "creolization is an elite phenomenon, promulgated and promoted by an elite literati and intelligentsia (notably in purportedly decreolized Martinique), rather than a multi-layered, dialogic, widespread phenomenon that serves the interest of a range of cultural communities."[17] Finally, in "Creolization. Definition and Critique," Dominique Chancé deplored Glissant's failure to clearly identify the components of creolization: "It would be surprising if creolization, a phenomenon that is increasingly universal according to critics and sociologists, were to remain unexplained, and if the laws that regulate the interaction of its components were to continue to be mysterious."[18] However, one could arguably counter that, if its components were to be defined as discrete entities, creolization in a truly Glissantian sense would cease to exist. Despite these reservations, we follow in the wake of Baron and Cara in our belief that creolization can shed significant light on the material examined in this book. Like them, we consider creolisation as "cultural creativity in process."[19] We regard it as a multivocal heuristic device that has relevance "anywhere cultures encounter one another," especially in contexts where one comes across "resistance to domination and asymmetrical power relations."[20] Creolization privileges the unfixed or, as Baron and Cara argue, "creative disorder [...], thereby challenging simplistic or static notions of center and periphery."[21] Further, as Elisabeth Mudimbe-Boyi contends in her introduction to her edited *Beyond Dichotomies*, the notion of creolization has the distinct advantage of moving beyond "the binaries colonizers/colonized, center/periphery, Empire/its others, local/global."[22] Such binaries have frequently been identified by critics as flaws inherent in the Western model of postcolonial studies, too often predicated on "the inadequacy of rigid dichotomies."[23]

---

16   *Ibid.*, 11.

17   *Ibid.*, 12.

18   Dominique Chancé, "Creolization. Definition and Critique," in Françoise Lionnet & Shu-mei Shih, eds. *The Creolization of Theory* (Durham and London: Duke University Press, 2011), 267.

19   Robert Baron and Ana C. Cara, "Creolization as Cultural Creativity," 3.

20   *Ibid.*, 3.

21   *Ibid.*, 4.

22   Elisabeth Mudimbe-Boyi, "Preface," in *Beyond Dichotomies. Histories, Identities, Cultures, and the Challenge of Globalization*, ed. Elisabeth Mudimbe-Boyi (Albany: SUNY P, 2002), xiii.

23   *Ibid.*, xiv. Like creolization, Homi Bhabha's notion of hybridity, involving a "third space" of cross-pollination, celebrates the impure. However, some critics, including John F. Szwed, consider that the concept of hybridity masks "a crude duality" (27) and retains "the

Before examining how the concept of creolization can usefully be applied to a South African context, let us first review the main tenets of Glissant's theories. For Glissant, creolization is a continual process of relations, which rejects homogenization and neat binaries. In his *Poétique de la relation* [*Poetics of Relation*], Glissant explicitly links creolization with a rhizomatic vision of the world:

> Gilles Deleuze and Felix Guattari criticized notions of the root and, even perhaps, notions of being rooted. The root is unique, a stock taking all upon itself and killing all around it. In opposition to this, they propose the rhizome, an enmeshed root system, a network spreading either in the ground or in the air, with no predatory rootstock taking over permanently. The notion of the rhizome maintains, therefore, the idea of rootedness but challenges that of a totalitarian root. Rhizomatic thought is the principle behind what I call the Poetics of Relation, in which each and every identity is extended through a relationship with the Other.[24]

In "The Unforeseeable Diversity of the World," Glissant argues that "[i]n composite cultures, creolization is happening before our eyes. These cultures do not lead to a creation of the world; they do not have such a foundation myth. They begin in what I call a digenesis."[25] Moreover, Glissant focuses on nomadism or errantry: "The thought of errantry is a poetics, which always infers that at some moment it is told. The tale of errantry is the tale of Relation."[26] He further emphasizes the lack of fixity embedded in the process of creolization: "if we posit *métissage* as, generally speaking, the meeting and synthesis of two differences, creolization seems to be a limitless *métissage*, its elements diffracted and its consequences unforeseeable. Creolization diffracts, whereas certain

---

assumption of an essentially pure past for all parties before encounter. In spite of the progressive intentions of its users, hybridity is too often the controlling metaphor of a rather shallow and ahistorical analysis" (28). See John F. Szwed, "Metaphors of Incommensurability," in *Creolization as Cultural Creativity*, ed. Robert Baron and Ana C. Cara, 20–31. Likewise, Denis Constant-Martin considers that Homi Bhabha excessively relies on metaphors of location, which does not lead to "a conceptualization of the intertwined, the enmeshed, and the intermixed nature of culture" (169). See Denis-Constant Martin, "A Creolizing South Africa? Mixing, Hybridity, and Creolisation: (Re)imagining the South African Experience," *International Social Science Journal* 58, no. 187 (2006): 165–176.

24   Édouard Glissant, *Poetics of Relation*, trans. Betsy Wing (Ann Arbor: University of Michigan Press, 1997), 11.

25   Édouard Glissant, "The Unforeseeable Diversity of the World," in *Beyond Dichotomies*, ed. Elisabeth Mudimbe-Boyi, 290–291.

26   Édouard Glissant, *Poetics of Relation*, 18

forms of *métissage* can concentrate one more time."[27] In other words, "Relation identity exults the thought of errantry [...]."[28] Glissant elsewhere stresses the fact that "Relation is movement."[29] Consequently, "Relation [...] does not act upon prime elements that are separable or reducible."[30] The "opacity" of the Other can thus be preserved.[31] Along similar lines, he defines the imaginary as "work[ing] in a spiral: from one circularity to the next, it encounters new spaces and does not transform them into either depths or conquests."[32] In *Traité du Tout-Monde*, Glissant further argues that creolization favours fluidity in an era of globalization: "I call creolization the encounter, the interference, the shock, the harmonies and the disharmonies among cultures, in the achieved totality of the *monde-terre* [earth-world] ... My proposition is that today the entire world is becoming archipelized and creolized."[33] A number of scholars have argued that using the concept of creolization in an African or South African context would indeed prove beneficial.

As early as in 1987, Ulf Hannerz claimed, in his essay "The World in Creolisation," that Glissant's concept could productively be applied to the study of Nigerian cultures and literatures in an age of globalization.[34] In an essay more specifically related to South Africa, "'Surviving the Future': Towards a South African Cultural Studies," Natasha Distiller argues that "South Africa's population, with its (many different) black Africans, its coloured Africans, its Indian and Chinese, and other South East Asian and Asian communities, its different communities of white Africans" can hardly be homogenized.[35] She insists on the necessity of acknowledging the constructedness of identities inherent in apartheid's obsession with racial categorizing.[36] She considers that Glissant's notion of creolization facilitates this undertaking. Likewise, Sarah Nuttall, in "City Forms and Writing the 'Now' in South Africa," regards creolization as

---

27   Édouard Glissant, *Poetics of Relation*, 34.
28   *Ibid.*, 144.
29   *Ibid.*, 171.
30   *Ibid.*, 172.
31   Édouard Glissant, *L'intention poétique. Poétique II* (Paris : Gallimard, 1997), 24.
32   Édouard Glissant, *Poetics of Relation*, 199.
33   Édouard Glissant, *Traité du Tout-Monde. Poétique IV* (Paris: Gallimard, 1997), 194. As *Traité du Tout-Monde* has not, to our knowledge, been translated in full, we have used Julin Everett's English translation, in Dominique Chancé's "Creolization. Definition and Critique." In Françoise Lionnet & Shu-mei Shih, eds. *The Creolization of Theory*, 265.
34   Ulf Hannerz, "The World in Creolisation," *Africa: Journal of the International African Institute* 57, no. 4 (1987): 546–559.
35   Natasha Distiller, "'Surviving the Future:' Towards a South African Cultural Studies," *Cultural Studies* 22, no. 2 (2008): 275.
36   *Ibid.*, 280.

apropriate term to describe South African society. As she states, "Given [South Africa's] tri-centric location between the Indian and Atlantic worlds as well as the landmass of the African interior, further readings of this space" demand a "*créolité* hypothesis."[37] Nuttall prefers creolization to the concepts of hybridity and syncretism, in view of the violence inscribed in the slave past of the Cape region and further enhanced by the apartheid system.[38] However, she does not limit the notion of creolization to strictly geographical parameters, but extends it to matters of race, class and the urban environment. From this point of view, she claims, the cultural entanglements generated by migrancy have transformed Johannesburg into a creolized city.[39] As she points out: "The figure of the migrant is central to South African history, a deeply embedded topos, which now takes on new configurations because the country is more open, with fewer forbidden places: space has expanded. [...] The city [...] is also a space of creolisation."[40] Following in similar footsteps, Robin Cohen, in "Creolization and Cultural Globalization: The Soft Sounds of Fugitive Power," compares aspects of creolization in the wake of globalization in Brazil, South Africa and the U.S. Globalization, he contends, enables a "fugitive power," which "stresses the hidden, subtle, sub-rosa, elusive [...] forms of power found in collective shifts of attitudes and social behaviour."[41] This elusiveness is best captured, he continues, in Glissant's notion of creolization, which favours rhizomatic identities.[42] Through creolization, the "fugitive power" of new ethnic formations counters the homogenizing tendencies of globalization.[43] Further, Denis-Constant Martin concludes his essay on the benefits of using a creolization model in a South African context as follows: "Applying the theory of creolization to South Africa would permit a re-foundation of its history, making it clear that the country as it stands today is the momentary outcome of protracted processes of conflicting and creative blending and mixing; [...] it has been creolizing for several centuries; [...] it still is a focus of creolisation."[44] Finally, this survey of the relevance of creolization for South Africa would not be

---

37   Sarah Nuttall, "City Forms and Writing the 'Now' in South Africa," *Journal of Southern African Studies* 30, no. 4 (2004): 734.

38   *Ibid.*, 735.

39   *Ibid.*, 748.

40   *Ibid.*, 734.

41   Robin Cohen, "Creolization and Cultural Globalization: The Soft Sounds of Fugitive Power," *Globalizations* 4, no. 3 (2007): 370.

42   *Ibid.*, 379.

43   *Ibid.*, 382.

44   Denis-Constant Martin, "A Creolizing South Africa? Mixing, Hybridity, and Creolisation: (Re)imagining the South African Experience," 173.

complete without an examination of the situation in Afrikaaner culture, which is so deeply linked to that of English-speaking communities. Such perspective is provided in C.S. van der Waal's "Creolisation and Purity: Afrikaans Language Politics in Post-Apartheid Times." In the years that followed the demise of apartheid, the Afrikaans community felt prompted to renounce the myth of the purity of the white Afrikaans language. As a result, it opted for "the strategic inclusion" of the Cape Afrikaans spoken by former coloureds.[45] This new linguistic consciousness, the critic comments, calls to mind Glissant's notion of creolization.[46] As the above review of recent scholarship indicates, there exists a significant tendency to link Glissant's notion of creolization with the South African context.

Thus, this volume's underlying assumption is that creolization, as described by Glissant, reflects the process of identity renegotiation South African society has undergone since the end of apartheid. Likewise, forms inherited from the apartheid period contribute to fertilizing, indeed to creolizing post-apartheid stage aesthetics. In its ideal manifestation, creolization echoes Nelson Mandela's deferred rainbow dream, freed from its fixed features in favour of a permanently renewed dialogue between its constituents. The well-known rainbow metaphor, Greg Homann reminds us, received early criticism from such prominent playwrights as Zakes Mda.[47] It was generally regarded by commentators as a trope inviting the amalgamation of homogenized identities rather than real diversity.[48] Instead of adopting this bleak view, this book suggests that the full creolization potential of the rainbow metaphor did not immediately manifest itself. It still continues to develop today, as the increasing heterogeneity of contemporary South African theatre indicates. The metaphor of a progressively creolizing rainbow can be used to describe the ever-evolving search for new aesthetic idioms characterizing the South African stage. Moreover, several essays in this book, including Maufort's, Briault Manus's, and Fourie's, explicitly foreground creolization issues. Paula Fourie underlines how fraught the process of South African creolization proved to be, as it was historically rooted in violence and oppression. She cites Breyten Breytenbach on the topic of creolization in the Cape region: "We are a bastard people with a bastard language. Our nature is one of bastardy. It is good and beautiful thus. We

---

45   C.S. van der Waal, "Creolisation and Purity: Afrikaans Language Politics in Post-Apartheid Times," *African Studies* 71, no. 3 (2012): 451.

46   *Ibid.*, 458, 460.

47   Greg Homann, "Preamble," 6.

48   Greg Homann, "Claiming Western Texts," 124. See also Homann's contribution to this volume (23–42).

must be compost, disintegrating to once more integrate into forms."[49] Creolization, this quote indicates, is akin to the ecological concept of the compost,
which suggests that both the old and the new continuously enrich one another
and transform into an innovative, heterogeneous, and hopefully thought-
provoking mixture.[50] This anthology thus explores some of the ways in which
the rainbow vision is slowly coming into its own.[51]

Scholarship on South African drama includes such seminal books as Anne
Fuchs, *Playing the Market. The Market Theatre. Johannesburg 1976–1986* (1990);
Geoffrey V. Davis & Anne Fuchs, eds. *Theatre and Change in South Africa* (1996);
Temple Hauptfleisch, *Theatre & Society in South Africa* (1997); Marcia Blumberg
& Dennis Walder, eds. *South African Theatre As/And Intervention* (1999); and,
Loren Kruger, *The Drama of South Africa. Plays, Pageants and Publics since 1910*
(1999). More recently, a number of studies have focused on new developments
on the South African stage. These works comprise: Anton Krueger, *Experiments
in Freedom; Explorations of Identity in New South African Drama* (2010); Yvette
Hutchison, *South African Performance and Archives of Memory* (2013); Martin
Middeke, Peter Paul Schnierer, Greg Homann, eds. *The Methuen Drama Guide
to Contemporary South African Theatre* (2015); Greg Homann & Marc Maufort,
eds. *New Territories. Theatre, Drama, and Performance in Post-apartheid South
Africa* (2015); Megan Lewis & Anton Krueger, eds. *Magnet Theatre. Three Decades of Making Space* (2016); and, Patrick J. Ebewo, *Explorations in Southern
African Drama, Theatre and Performance* (2017). The diversity of contemporary
theatre and drama in post-apartheid South Africa is such, however, that the
above-mentioned volumes could not possibly provide an exhaustive account
of this ever-evolving artistic field. Nor is it the purpose of this anthology, which
nonetheless intends to offer significant glimpses into the complex creolization
process of contemporary South African stage idioms. In attempting to do so,
this volume offers an arc of reflection straddling the perspectives of playwrights, dramatic and performance strategies, female playwriting as well as

---

49   Breyten Breytenbach, *Parool/Parole: Versamelde Toesprake/collected Speeches* (London:
      Penguin Random House, 2015), 12.
50   The reader wishing to find more theoretical material on the compost and its aesthetic
      potentialities should turn to Jed Rasula's seminal (and experimental) book entitled *This
      Compost*.
51   At least one earlier scholarly study has already suggested that the representation of iden-
      tities on the South African Stage could be described as "rhizomatic," a concept related to
      Glissant's creolization. See Anton Krueger, *Experiments in Freedom. Explorations of Iden-
      tity in New South African Drama* (Newcastle-upon-Tyne: Cambridge Scholars Publishing,
      2010), 37–46 (Chapter Seven, Rhizomatic Identities).

transnational aspects in the wake of the increasing globalization of South African society.

The opening cluster of essays, "Playwrights' Perspectives," includes discussions by Greg Homann, Craig Higginson, Mike van Graan, and Omphile Molusi about their works and the dynamics of the contemporary South African stage. In the opening essay, "On Black and White: Staging South African Identities after Apartheid," Greg Homann distinguishes three types of plays articulating contemporary South African identities: the "Them-Us Play," the "Restorative Nostalgia Play" and the "Rainbow Nation Play." The "Them-Us Play" relies on the rigid racial codes inherited from the apartheid era, inspiring "no strategy.... to progress through the dichotomy of violence" (29). Examples of such plays are Mpumelelo Paul Grootboom and Aubrey Sekhabi's *Inter-racial* (2007), Yaël Farber's *Mies Julie* (2012), Mike van Graan's *When Swallows Cry* (2017). By contrast, the "Restorative Nostalgia Play," such as Lara Foot's *Solomon and Marion* (2007) and Craig Higginson's *Dream of the Dog* (2007), focuses on characters who can move beyond their "preconceived ideas of a closed interaction" (31) towards "an aesthetics of hope and transformation" (34). The third type of play, the "Rainbow Nation Play," usually extolls the ideal of Mandela's rainbow dream. Homann puts it in contrast with what he calls the anti-rainbow play, which "challenges notions of national identity" (34). These plays offer a rhizomatic vision of South African identity, as is the case in *Oedipus @ Koö-Nú* (2015). In his own contribution, "Being in Two Places at the Same Time," playwright Craig Higginson first evokes an anecdote from his childhood, as his mother had an epileptic fit when driving. The young boy eventually saw the incident from a distance, moving "deeper into what I have later come to recognize as my imagined land – the landscape out of which a storyteller can begin to speak and make sense of the world that he or she has successfully escaped" (46). Such sublimation, Higginson argues, stands at "the beginning of all art" (47) and underpins his works to date, including *Dream of the Dog* (of which two versions exist) and the related novel *The Dream House*. Indeed, "the central relationship in the anecdote, the plays and the novel is between an older woman and a younger man and in each the younger man is rejecting the older woman as maternal figure" (50). He further comments on his craft: "I write in order to dissociate myself from what I am and what surrounds me and sublimate myself into something else" (54). He concludes that "we need ... this capacity for being in more than one place at the same time" (54). In "Theatre of the Native Tongue," Omphile Molusi, a young African playwright, writes about the difficulties of writing authentically about African experience in English. For instance, township characters are difficult to depict in English. African languages, like Setswana, project a different world view and thus offer more cultural nuances. Molusi then explains how he first struggled to write in his native Setswana. A decisive experience was his participation as an actor in a production of a play entitled *Lepatata*, written entirely in Setswana by Moagi Modise. Molusi then started writing in his native tongue. His first play written in this mode, *Mogatapele*, was a resounding success. The fact that other playwrights also start writing in African languages is a positive sign of cultural decolonization. In the essay of this initial cluster, entitled "Transformation and the Post-apartheid Condition: The Collision of Policy and Imagination in South African Theatre," Mike van Graan sheds light on the current funding policies in South Africa from his unique perspective as a playwright, director and activist. These policies, he argues, have failed "to make the arts accessible to all through a lack of vision and poor implementation of policy" (69). As a result, theatre "remains largely an elite practice" (69) in contemporary South Africa. Van Graan concludes his essay with an outline of the ways in which these funding policies could be improved.

A second cluster of academic articles, "Dramatic, Theatrical and Performance Reconfigurations," comprises contributions by Marcia Blumberg, Mathilde Rogez, Ralph Yarrow, Vicky Briault Manus and Marc Maufort. In "Performing Athol Fugard's Outsider Art in *The Road to Mecca* and *The Painted Rocks at Revolver Creek*: Transformative Art Defies Percepticide," Marcia Blumberg compares the role of the outsider artist in works from the early and the late career of Athol Fugard, *The Road to Mecca* (1984) and *The Painted Rocks at Revolver Creek* (2015). The first play focuses on the vision of Mecca outsider artist Helen Martins expressed in the Owl House and Camel Yard she devised in the Karoo village of Nieu Bethesda. In the second play, the painted rocks of outsider artist Nukain Mabuza are restored in the post-apartheid era by Jonathan, which enables Afrikaner Elmarie to understand the otherness of black people. This evokes the possibility of reconciliation through the transformative role of the arts. Petrus du Preez, in "Alluring Voices from the Page to Stage: Literary Characters and the Question of the 'Real' in Reza de Wet's *Verleiding*," examines the neglected work of a major South African playwright, Reza de Wet, who wrote both in Afrikaans and in English: i.e. her one-woman show entitled *Verleiding*, first performed in 2005. The play is deeply metafictional, in that it is structured as an academic lecture. Simultaneously, "it expands the genre of the one-person show" (118) and thus could be described as a polyphonic monologue. Focusing on a graduate student's fascination with the life of Eugène Marais, the father of Afrikaans poetry, this work contains allusions to the mystical and the magical, which blurs the boundaries between illusion and reality. The strange disappearance of the student, Lizelle Van Breda, after visiting Marais's house, contains gothic elements. As du Preez concludes, "Van

Breda identifies with the innocent virgin that must be seduced to surrender to the magical male figure, albeit through death" (113). In "From the Stage to the Page: Trauma, Reconciliation and Remembering in Craig Higginson's *Dream of the Dog* and *The Dream House*," Mathilde Rogez offers a close-reading analysis of how Craig Higginson's two versions of his play *Dream of the Dog* and its novelistic version, *The Dream House*, seek to come to terms with the traumas of apartheid. Her approach is inspired by Pierre Rosanvallon's notion of "narrative democracy" (122). Unlike the Truth and Reconciliation Commission, which focused on "gross violations of human rights" (122), Higginson's works rather concentrate on what Njabulo Ndebele calls "the rediscovery of the ordinary," i.e. in this case private griefs. Higginson's work "favours and enables embodied interpersonal relations, which Coetzee would call a 'poetics of reciprocity'" (136). As Rogez concludes, "Higginson's rewriting of his play in a novelistic form thus allows him to explore further the concepts of foldedness and entanglement [...] which are necessary for any true form of dialogue or attempt at reconciliation" (139). In "South African Theatre and the Politics of the Improvisatory," Ralph Yarrow looks at how the improvisatory can contribute to "the possibility of reconfiguring the parameters of identity and community" (144) in the post-apartheid era, characterized by an "*anxiety* about role" (150). The "physical immediacy" of the improvisatory plays a decisive role in this process (157). In dealing with this "ecology of performance" (161), Yarrow examines a wide range of plays, including Mike van Graan's *Green Man Flashing* (2004), John Kani's *Nothing But the Truth* (2002), the collective play *Ubu and the Truth Commission* (1997), Brett Bailey's *Ipi Zombi?* (1997), Nadia Davids's *Cissie* (2002), as well as works by The Magnet Theatre, *Önnest'Bo* and *Cargo*. In "The Faultlines of Idiom: New Thematic and Stylistic Trends in the Plays of Allan Kolski Horwitz," Vicki Briault Manus analyses Allan Kolski Horwitz's five plays to date from a linguistic perspective: *The Pump Room* (2009), *Comrade Babble* (2012), *Boykie and Girlie* (2014), *Jerico* (2015), and *Book Marks* (2016). She pays particular attention to language variety, indeed creolization, in *The Pump Room* and *Comrade Babble*, which hail respectively from the Cape Town region and Gauteng. In "Revisiting the Past, Imagining the Future: Aesthetic of Creolization in Post-apartheid South African Drama," Marc Maufort examines how the colours of Mandela's rainbow dream are reconfigured through what Édouard Glissant would call the process of creolization in four contemporary South African plays. Creolization's rejection of homogenization, for which Mandela's rainbow vision has often been criticized, is manifest in works by Omphile Molusi (*Itsoseng*), Greg Homann (*Oedipus @ Koö-Nú*), Craig Higginson (*The Imagined Land*), and Mike van Graan (*When Swallows Cry*), in which creolization merges with globalization. However, Maufort concludes, creolization is a process more conducive to the creation of new stage idioms than to the advent of the cultural harmony inscribed in Mandela's dream.

A third cluster of essays, "Female Playwriting," explores works created by the many female dramatic voices that have emerged on contemporary South African stage in the twenty-first century.[52] In "Intimate Exposure: Solo Women Performing in Post-apartheid South Africa," Veronica Baxter analyses the work of South African women performers in "monopolylogue or polycharacter monodramas through the lens of Bystrom and Nuttall's 'intimate exposure' and Jill Dolan's discussion of the monopolylogue's potential for intercultural exchange" (210). She considers works by Rehane Abrahams (*What the Water Gave Me*), Nadia Davids (*At Her Feet*), Motshobi Tyelele (*Shwele Bawo!*), Magona, Honeyman and Mtshali-Jones (*Mother to Mother*), and Jennie Reznek (*I Turned Away and She Was Gone*). Baxter argues that these post-apartheid plays reflect Ndebele's plea for a "rediscovery of the ordinary" (212) and "embraced individual interiority" (212). Rehane Abrahams' *What the Water Gave Me* provides a good example of "shift away from the spectacular narratives of the apartheid towards the intimate" (214). All these plays, Baxter continues, enact "a cautionary tale about South Africa's post-apartheid pathology – abduction, abuse, neglect …" (225). They dramatize what Jill Dolan terms the "utopian performative," characterizing the period of transition the new democracy is still going through. In "Recuperating Historical Narratives of Violence and Dislocation in Rehane Abrahams' *What the Water Gave Me*," Jill Planche offers a close-reading analysis of the "recuperation of the buried histories of a Malaysian slave past" in Rehane Abrahams' *What the Water Gave Me* (229). She regards this work as an instance of "minor" theatre. Her examination of it differs from Baxter's in her use of Gilles Deleuze's "concept of affirmative and dynamic processes creating new political subjects; processes of 'becoming' that break from the fixed, prescribed 'being,' that in the context of South Africa has been molded by colonial and state-imposed racial construction" (234). Further, Planche notes: "the concept of the minor embraces subjectivity, space, politics and language in the process of negating or challenging the framework of what Deleuze variously refers to as the State apparatus, or capitalism …" (234). Planche extends this concept to the oppressive nature of the South African State. Jessica Murray prolongs this feminist project in her

---

52   It would be beyond the scope of this book to explore the whole spectrum of gendered
      identities in South African drama, which would necessarily include a survey of the large
      body of works by queer and LGBT artists. Readers interested in further details about these
      gender issues could profitably turn to Anton Krueger, *Experiments in Freedom*, 49–88
      (Part 3, Gendered Identities).

article "Female Interventions in Contemporary South African Drama and Performance: An Analysis of Selected Work by Women Artists." She focuses on how violence against women and even the rape of babies is recorded in a number of works by female artists. She first examines Zanele Muholi's visual and performative work, exposing the "victimisation of black lesbianism" (255). Through the insertion of the "queer, naked, black female body" (256) into her photographic exhibitions, the artist undoubtedly moves towards performance art. Murray subsequently turns towards more purely textual material, i.e. Lara Foot's plays, *Tshepang: The Third Testament*, and *Karoo Moose*, which dramatize "the larger context of structural gender oppression in a community characterized by the sexual abuse of women and girl children" (262). Both plays feature the rape of a female baby, but *Karoo Moose* offers a broader approach, showing "how normalised sexual assault has become ..." (265). However, the female protagonist of *Karoo Moose*, Thozama, experiences some form of liberation by identifying "with the incongruous figure of a moose in the Karoo" (266). These works thus subversively counter the power of patriarchy. In "An Unfinished Homecoming: Postmemory, Place and New Practices of Politicisation in the Plays of Nadia Davids and Amy Jephta," Ksenia Robbe analyses the difficulties inherent in homecoming, in reclaiming confiscated space, especially in the Cape region. Nadia Davids's *Cissie* and Amy Jephta's *All Who Pass* "re-open archives – through the media of oral history and photography – to speak to the present in a consciously active and activist way. Both plays engage with the processes of spatialisation in Cape Town, and particularly with the spaces of District Six ..." (274). The two plays chronicle the lives of members of District Six families forcibly removed from their homes. Robbe draws from Marianna Hirsch's notion of postmemory as "describ[ing] the relationship that the generation after those who witnessed cultural or collective trauma bears to the experience of those who came before, experiences that they 'remember' only by means of the stories, images, or behaviors among which they grew up (277). In both plays, "intimate conversations between mothers and daughters" ... "exemplify what Hirsch calls 'feminist postmemory'" (281). Robbe concludes in insisting on the performative, embodied aspect of these "reanimations" of the past (283).

A final cluster of essays, "Creolization: From the Cape to Transnational Vistas," amplifies earlier considerations about creolization in the Cape region, as Fourie's article evidences, to encompass transnational perspectives, as Thurman argues in his contribution. In her performance-oriented essay, "'Dis Nie Myne Nie, Dis Nie Joune Nie' or Kramer and Petersen's *Ghoema*: Inscribing the Past, Claiming the Present?," Paula Fourie focuses on the notion of creolization in a musical, David Kramer and Taliep Petersen's *Ghoema*. As Fourie claims:

"the agenda of *Ghoema* is ... to explore the past of South Africa's coloured population ... Central to this agenda is the evocation of the ghoema drum and its eponymous rhythm, unique South African musical creations formed in the cultural melting pot that was colonial Cape Town" (294). The ghoema drum has become a signifier of Cape Town's "creole unifying pulse" (294). The result of a collaboration between English-speaker librettist David Kramer and Afrikaans Cape Malay speaker Talipe Petersen, the musical was first produced in 2005. As a blend of Afrikaans folksongs, dance, dialogue and rap, *Ghoema* emphasizes the creolization inherent in the region, which the Afrikaner population denied in order to protect racial purity. On the contrary, *Ghoema* affirms the compost-like nature, in the words of Breyten Breytenbach, of the Afrikaans people and language. Thus, the Afrikaans used in the musical is no longer perceived as the oppressor's language only, as Cape Malay communities also spoke it: "the Afrikaans language is one the legacies of creolization at the Cape of Good Hope" (304). However, Paula Fourie regrets that the musical does not sufficiently emphasize the violence at the core of creolization. The comfortable experience the musical generates tends to soften trauma, "servicing the amnesia craved by the beneficiaries of apartheid" (310). Fourie deplores the musical's "failure to translate its inscription of the past into a meaningful claiming of its present" (310), thereby coming short of realizing Mandela's rainbow dream. Also concentrating on performance, the collection's final essay, Chris Thurman's "Shakespeare versus Shakespeare: Notes on Theatre-making from Belgium to South Africa" examines creolization from a transnational perspective, thus echoing Glissant's equation of creolization and globalization. In order to address the nexus between the local and the universal in productions of Shakespeare in South Africa, Thurman turns to Flemish theatre practice. How can Shakespeare's presumed "universal" message be creolized in specific cultural contexts? To demonstrate how this could be achieved, Thurman first documents how *Ten Oorlog*, Tom Lanoye and Luk Perceval's 1997 adaptation of Shakespeare's history plays, managed to address a contemporary Belgian audience. Tom Lanoye, it should be noted, lives both in Antwerp and Cape Town, which makes him aware of the "urgent sense of political engagement among South African writers ..." (316). *Ten Oorlog* displays "linguistic heterogeneity, a kind of hip-hop 'street' Dutch infused with bursts of English that could variously be described as scat, patter or patois" (318). Lanoye also alludes to the contemporary Belgian political scene, drawing an analogy between Henry VI and King Baudouin/Boudewijn as weak monarchs as well as to the pedophile scandal that took Belgium by storm in that decade. Nonetheless, *Ten Oorlog* managed to strike a balance between the local and the universal. The multilingual context of South Africa offers similar challenges for theatre-makers. Thurman alludes to Sol Plaatje's translation of Shakespeare into Setswana. A production of *Julius Kesara*, "a multilingual adaptation of Plaatje's translation" (327) for a cast of six women, was considered at The Artscape theatre in Cape Town but abandoned for commercial reasons. Thurman praises the use of contemporary language in the theatrical version of *Shakespeare in Love* at the Fugard Theatre; it was restaged there in 2018 with a black actor in the lead role. Thurman also discusses the 2018 production of *The Taming of the Shrew* at Cape Town's open-air theatre, Maynardville, which used a completely female cast, comprising women from different racial and linguistic backgrounds. Thurman comes to the conclusion that "the relationship between the local and the universal is not, after all, one of opposition but one of intersection" (340). He underlines "the insights that connecting Shakespeare in Belgium to Shakespeare in South Africa might bring; the boldness of attending to the local without shying away from the permutations of 'universality'" (340). These permutations are precisely what characterizes Édouard Glissant's notion of creolization. Thurman's contribution thus suggests that a wealth of new stage idioms must be forged, if the "rainbow" dream is to materialize in South African theatres. This fraught task will undoubtedly mobilize the artistic energies of theatre-practitioners for years to come.

Works Cited

Baron, Robert and Ana C. Cara, "Introduction: Creolization as Cultural Creativity." In *Creolization as Cultural Creativity*, edited by Robert Baron and Ana C. Cara. 3–19. Jackson: U of Mississippi P, 2011.

Blumberg, Marcia and Dennis Walder, eds. *South African Theatre As/And Intervention*. Amsterdam: Rodopi, 1999.

Brathwaite, Edward Kamu. "Creolization in Jamaica." In *The Postcolonial Studies Reader*, edited by Bill Ashcroft, Gareth Griffith, and Helen Tiffin. 152–154. London: Routledge, 2005.

Breytenbach, Breyten. *Parool/Parole: Versamelde Toesprake/collected Speeches*. London: Penguin 2015.

Davis, Geoffrey V. and Anne Fuchs, eds. *Theatre and Change in South Africa*. Amsterdam: Harwood, 1996.

Chancé, Dominique. "Creolization. Definition and Critique." Translated by Julin Everett. In *The Creolization of Theory*, edited by Françoise Lionnet and Shu-mei Shih, 262–267. Durham & London: Duke UP, 2011.

Cohen, Robin. "Creolization and Cultural Globalization: The Soft Sounds of Fugitive Power." *Globalizations* 4, no. 3 (2007): 369–384.

Costandius, Elmarie et al. "#Feesmustfall and Decolonizing the Curriculum: Stellenbosch University Students' and Lecturers' Reactions." *South African Journal of Higher Education* 32, no. 2 (2018): 65–85.

Distiller, Natasha. "'Surviving the Future:' Towards a South African Cultural Studies." *Cultural Studies* 22, no. 2 (2008): 273–283.

Ebewo, Patrick J. *Explorations in Southern African Drama, Theatre and Performance.* Newcastle upon Tyne: Cambridge Scholars Publishing, 2017.

Farber, Yael. *Theatre as Witness. Three testimonial Plays from South Africa.* London: Oberon Books, 2000.

Fuchs, Anne. *Playing the Market. The Market Theatre. Johannesburg 1976–1986.* Amsterdam: Harwood. 1990.

Fugard, Athol, John Kani and Winston Ntshona. *Sizwe Bansi Is Dead.* In *Athol Fugard. The Township Plays.* Oxford: Oxford UP, 1993.

Fugard, Athol, John Kani and Winston Ntshona. *The Island.* In *Athol Fugard. The Township Plays.* Oxford: Oxford UP, 1993.

Glissant, Édouard. *L'intention poétique. Poétique* II. Paris : Gallimard, 1997.

Glissant, Édouard. *Poetics of Relation.* Translated by Betsy Wing. Ann Arbor: University of Michigan Press, 1997.

Glissant, Édouard. *Traité du Tout-Monde. Poétique* IV. Paris: Gallimard, 1997.

Glissant, Édouard. "The Unforeseeable Diversity of the World." In *Beyond Dichotomies. Histories, Identities, Cultures, and the Challenge of Globalization*, edited by Elisabeth Mudimbe-Boyi. 287–295. Albany: SUNY P, 2002.

Hall, Stuart. "Cultural Identity and Diaspora." In *The Postcolonial Studies Reader*, edited by Bill Ashcroft, Gareth Griffith, and Helen Tiffin. 435–438. London: Routledge, 2005.

Hannerz, Ulf. "The World in Creolisation." *Africa: Journal of the International African Institute* 57, no. 4 (1987): 546–559.

Hauptfleisch, Temple. *Theatre & Society in South Africa. Reflections in a Fractured Mirror.* Pretoria: J.L. van Schaik, 1997.

Homann, Greg. "Claiming Western Texts for Contemporary South African Theatre. Issues of Relevance and the Dead-end Pursuit of National Identity." In *New Territories: Theatre, Drama, and Performance in Post-apartheid South Africa*, edited by Greg Homann and Marc Maufort, 105–127. Brussels: Peter Lang, 2015.

Homann, Greg. "Preamble." In *At This Stage. Plays from Post-apartheid South Africa*, edited by Greg Homann, 1–16. Johannesburg: Wits UP, 2009.

Homann, Greg and Marc Maufort, eds. *New Territories. Theatre, Drama, and Performance in Post-apartheid South Africa.* Brussels: Peter Lang, 2015.

Homann, Greg, Martin Middeke and Peter Paul Schnierer. "Introduction." In *The Methuen Drama Guide to Contemporary South African Theatre*, edited by Martin

Middeke, Peter Paul Schnierer and Greg Homann, 1–14. London: Bloomsbury Methuen Drama, 2015.

Hutchison, Yvette. *South African Performance and Archives of Memory*. Manchester: Manchester UP, 2013.

Keuris, Marisa. "'*Restitutions of Body and Soil*' in *Mies Julie* (2012): South African Theatre Audience Reception of Yael Farber's Adaptation of Strindberg's *Miss Julie* within a Post-apartheid South African Political Landscape." *South African Theatre Journal* 29, nos. 1–3 (2016): 44–55.

Krueger, Anton. *Experiments in Freedom; Explorations of Identity in New South African Drama.* Newcastle upon Tyne: Cambridge Scholars Publishers, 2010.

Krueger, Anton. "Revolutionary Trends at the National Arts Festival 2017 (an overview)." *South African Theatre Journal* 31, nos. 2–3 (2018): 202–210.

Kruger, Loren. *The Drama of South Africa. Plays, Pageants and Publics since 1910*. London: Routledge, 1999.

Lewis, Megan and Anton Krueger, eds. *Magnet Theatre. Three Decades of Making Space*. Bristol & Chicago: Intellect, 2016.

Manaka, Matsemela. *Goree*. In *Beyond the Echoes of Soweto. Five Plays by Matsemela Manaka*, edited by Geoffrey V. Davis, 173–191. Amsterdam: Harwood, 1997.

Maponya, Maishe. "The Hungry Earth." In *Doing Plays for a Change*. Johannesburg: Wits UP, 2001. 1–24.

Martin, Denis-Constant. "A Creolizing South Africa? Mixing, Hybridity, and Creolisation: (Re)imagining the South African Experience." *International Social Science Journal* 58, no. 187 (2006): 165–176.

Mda, Zakes. *And the Girls in their Sunday Dresses*. In *And the Girls in their Sunday Dresses. Four Works*. Johannesburg: Wits UP, 1993.

Middeke, Martin, Peter Paul Schnierer and Greg Homann, eds. *The Methuen Drama Guide to Contemporary South African Theatre*. London: Bloomsbury, 2015.

Mtwa, Percy, Mbongeni Ingema and Barney Simon. *Woza Albert!* (1981). London: Methuen Drama, 1983.

Mudimbe-Boyi, Elisabeth. "Preface." In *Beyond Dichotomies. Histories, Identities, Cultures, and the Challenge of Globalization*, edited by Elisabeth Mudimbe-Boyi. xi–xxv. Albany: SUNY P, 2002.

Nuttall, Sarah. "City Forms and Writing the 'Now' in South Africa." *Journal of Southern African Studies* 30, no. 4 (2004): 731–748.

Orkin, Martin, ed. *Sophiatown*. In *At the Junction. Four Plays by the Junction Avenue Theatre Company*. Johannesburg: Wits UP, 2001.

Rasula, Jed. *This Compost: Ecological Imperatives in American Poetry*. Athens, GA: U of Georgia P, 2002.

Simon, Barney. "Born in the RSA" (1985). In *Born in the RSA. Four Workshopped Plays*, Johannesburg: Wits UP, 2001.

Slabolepszy, Paul. "Mooi Street Moves." In *Mooi Street and Other Moves*. Johannesburg: Wits UP, 2001.

Szwed, John F. "Metaphors of Incommensurability." In *Creolization as Cultural Creativity*, edited by Robert Baron and Ana C. Cara. 20–31. Jackson: U of Mississippi P, 2011.

Thurman, Chris. "Shakespeare in South African Schools: to Die, to Sleep – or Perchance to Dream." *The Conversation*, March 29, 2017. http://theconversation.com/shakespeare-in-south-african-schools-to-die-to-sleep-or-perchance-to-dream-75314.

van der Waal, C.S. "Creolisation and Purity: Afrikaans Language Politics in Post-Apartheid Times," *African Studies* 71, no. 3 (2012): 446–463.

PART 1

Playwrights' Perspectives

∵

CHAPTER 2

On Black and White: Staging South African Identities after Apartheid

Greg Homann

Abstract

This essay explores the allusions and illusions of identity construction that are evident in contemporary South African drama. Homann reflects on three political actions that he proposes are the fertile ground from which dramatic characters emerge in post-apartheid South African playwriting. To make his case he draws on what Njabulo Ndebele has called the *"them-us" polarity*, Derek Hook's unpacking of the psychoanalytic term *restorative nostalgia*, and ideas of *Rainbow Nation-ism* that were solidified through the efforts of Nelson Mandela. Homann aligns these three ideas to contemporary South African drama as a means to test whether we might be able to speak of the formulation of the them-us play, the restorative nostalgia play, and the Rainbow Nation play.

Ivor Chipkin, in his influential study *Do South Africans Exist?*, shares a story told in 1963 by the famous South African black intellectual and journalist, Nat Nakasa:

> I remember having dinner with a friend in one of the less prosperous white suburbs. One of the guests that night was a talented Afrikaner painter ... My host had hinted earlier that the painter was a Nationalist [i.e. National Party supporter], a supporter of Dr. Verwoerd's apartheid policy. The same man had spent much of his afternoon trying to keep alive a newborn African baby which had been abandoned on a pavement. ... Having talked about his *paintings and jazz* we gravitated inevitably to the colour question. I wanted to know if he really was a Nationalist, and he said yes. We had by now warmed to each other, lighting cigarettes for one and all, sharing the same concern about the food which seemed to take a long time getting ready. "But what kind of a Nationalist are you?" I asked.
> "But why?"

"How can you vote for apartheid and then come and drink brandy with me?"

"But there is nothing wrong in drinking brandy with you. I would like to drink with you anywhere. At my place or yours, for that matter."

"What if I told you that I have no place?"

"What do you mean?"

"Just that, I have no place and that's because of the laws you vote for."

"What? Where are you going to sleep tonight, for instance?"

"I don't know. I may sleep here; wherever I can find a bed tonight."

The painter was moved. I liked seeing his puzzled face.

"Well, if … you mean what you've said, you can come and live with me. We have a whole empty room in that house."

Now I stopped being amused. Something was wrong somewhere.

"But the party you vote for has passed the law which says that's illegal, too," I said.

Now the painter was blushing. He looked the other way and picked up his glass. I became more and more irritated.

"Why are you a Nationalist if you are willing to stay with me? Don't you want the races to be separated?"

Suddenly, the painter took off his glasses and looked at me appealingly: "You see," he said, "I am an Afrikaner. The Nationalist Party is my people's party. That's why I vote for it"[1]

A few year's ago, in my naiveté, I would write quite confidently about the topic, South African Theatre. I would say things like "The mode of representation has shifted and the monological form we came both to loathe and love has dissipated to match a democratic society grappling with multiple points of view"[2] or "The long-standing routine of creating protest-styled work was no longer relevant,"[3] and I would think that these statements were true because they were my lived experience, and they reflected the limited sphere that I worked in. Subsequently I have co-edited two books on South African theatre[4] and

---

1   Ivor Chipkin, *Do South Africans Exist? Nationalism, Democracy and the Identity of "The People"* (Johannesburg: Wits University Press, 2007), 215–216.

2   Greg Homann (ed.), *At This Stage: Plays from post-apartheid South Africa* (Johannesburg: Wits Press, 2009), 2.

3   *Ibid.*, 3.

4   See (1) *The Methuen Drama Guide to Contemporary South African Theatre* edited by Martin Middeke, Peter Paul Schnierer, and Greg Homann, and (2) *New Territories: Theatre, Drama, and Performance in Post-apartheid South Africa* edited by Greg Homann and Marc Maufort.

I have started to pursue, more boldly than before, my own playwriting.[5] These recent experiences – the work on these books, my playwriting, and my on go- ing teaching in a time where students are signalling loud and clear a desire for a decolonised education – have all contributed to illuminating me a little more on my privileged position, my whiteness, and my maleness. So then, as a white male writing about a subject as big and contradictory as South African theatre, performance, and drama, I have to begin by acknowledging my subjective posi- tion. It is this position that makes me question; "How can I write black charac- ters?," "Can I only write white characters?," "How can I, with all my subjective conditioning, begin to tell a story of South African people?," "Should I only be writing my lived experience?," and "Is it wrong for me to try and depict lived experiences that are distant to my own?"

So, with these questions, and many more, in mind, I'm interested in explor- ing the allusions and illusions of identity construction that I see as evident in recent dramatic texts, and that I am thinking about when I put pen to paper. I want to unpack some speculative thinking on the kinds of characters that are imagined for the stage in South Africa's post-apartheid period. To do this, I wish to consider three political actions that I propose have been the fertile ground from which dramatic characters have emerged, and lastly, I want to reflect on the preamble to The Constitution of South Africa, this being the guiding visionary document, based on the Freedom Charter of 1955, that fo- cuses a South African democratic imaginary.

Let us start by naming these three occurrences that loom large in the psyche, consciousness, and imagination of South African society. The first is undoubt- edly apartheid, birthing a vast and oppressive historical framework onto the landscape of the country. Njabulo Ndebele in his seminal collection of essays, *Rediscovery of the Ordinary,* concisely captures the remnants (too small a word to express its scale) of this period. To illustrate his point he relays an analogy of 23, 000 miners who were dismissed from their jobs, describing a scenario of what he calls, the "'them-us' polarity."[6] Here the oppressed and the oppressor, be that about "wealth and poverty, of power and powerlessness, of knowledge and ignorance, of form and formlessness" result in "the simplification and triv- ialisation of moral perception."[7] He states, the consequence of this politically

---

5 Plays by Greg Homann include *Previously Owned* (2009) discussed briefly within this essay, *One Woman Farce* (2012) co-written with Louise Saint-Claire, *Oedipus @ Koö-Nú!* (2014) dis- cussed briefly within these pages, and *A Voice I Cannot Silence* (2015) co-written with Ralph Lawson.

6 Njabulo S Ndebele, *Rediscovery of the Ordinary. Essays on South African Culture* (Scottsville: UKZN Press, 2006), 57.

7 *Ibid.,* 59.

institutionalised "them-us" formation is that "the oppressed need only cast their eyes around to see a universal confirmation of their status."[8] What Ndebele is drawing is a picture in this *them-us* world that traps its characters, oppressor and oppressed, into an unreflective rhetoric that purely sets out to confirm what said characters already know (but more about that later).

The second event is the Truth & Reconciliation Commission (TRC). I have written elsewhere,[9] as have many others,[10] about the significance of this period on identity formation, but to summarise briefly, this was a time that cemented, within a landscape of trauma, identities of the victim, perpetrator, and hero. Although still a vastly limiting formation, identity construction stemming from the TRC discourse is ever so slightly more nuanced than that from the *them-us* polarity. This TRC period, that encouraged remembering (and forgetting), was coupled with the project of reconciliation, leading to what Achille Mbembe has called, "a mode of erasure … accomplished against the duties to memory."[11] To try and capture, under a fitting heading, what this period imaginatively embodies for us today, I have turned to the field of psychoanalysis which gives us the term *restorative nostalgia*. This is useful as it defines, according to Boym, an act of "transhistorical reconstruction of the lost home,"[12] which is an act in close association with the pursuits of the TRC project. We know that ideas of home are deeply connected to a sense of self. Furthermore, Boym explains that "restorative nostalgia does not think of itself as nostalgia, but rather as truth and tradition."[13] Hook summarises Boym in stating that restorative nostalgia is "about communal identity and national metanarratives" and as such, it is of hegemonic character.[14] I assert then, that this idea of *restorative nostalgia* neatly encapsulates the pervasive thinking that arose from the TRC period.

The third event is the now famous, some might say (in)famous, statement by Archbishop Desmond Tutu in which he coined the illusion of the rainbow

---

8   *Ibid.*
9   See *At This Stage, The Methuen Drama Guide to Contemporary South African Theatre*, and *New Territories: Theatre, Drama & Performance in Post-apartheid South Africa*.
10   See, amongst others, Anton Krueger (2010), Ivor Chipkin (2007), Dave Steward, Annie Coombes (2003), Rory Bester (2002), Ashraf Jamal (2005), and Sarah Nuttall & Cheryl Ann Michael (2001).
11   Derek Hook, *(Post)Apartheid Conditions: Psychoanalysis and Social Formation* (Cape Town: HSRC Press, 2014), 176.
12   *Ibid.*, 172.
13   *Ibid.*
14   *Ibid.*, 173.

nation.[15] Rainbow Nation-ism was solidified through the efforts of Nelson Mandela, instilling a power that resided in a broadly accessible image that is idyllic and sentimental. On one level this produced a vision of national identity that was optimistic and hopeful, but on another it was the panacea that has allowed the country to deflect the matter of justice. That said, its affirming power has infiltrated the imaginations of the less critical and less cynical.

So, this gives us three ideas to explore: the *them-us polarity, restorative nostalgia*, and *Rainbow Nation-ism*. My hypothesis is that these three allusions are evidenced in the construction of characters in new South African plays. To develop this speculation I want to attempt to align the *them-us polarity, restorative nostalgia*, and *Rainbow Nation-ism* to drama as a means to test whether we might be able to speak of the formulation of the *them-us play*, the *restorative nostalgia play*, and the *Rainbow Nation play*. Through a critical analysis of some selected examples, I aim to unpack how a politics of identity, as witnessed through dramatic characters, is connected to a politics of state, and in so doing, I hope to refine the definition of these three tropes.

I should add, I am not asserting that these are the only frames from which characters emerge, but I do believe that the tropes we will consider here are three that permeate South African society, and in so doing, they are present in a broad and significant selection of drama, reflecting the complex place we call South Africa.

1   In Pursuit of Defining the "Them-Us Play"

Ndebele, originally writing in the early 90s, stated that South Africans have a manner of thinking about socio-political realities "purely in terms of a total polarity of absolutes."[16] In *Rediscovery of the Ordinary*, he calls for a radical rearrangement of the dialectical poles, which he viewed as important if artists were to avoid the trappings of the apartheid condition, i.e. avoid allowing apartheid conditioning to play out unproductively in a democratic imaginary. It is nevertheless unsurprising that the them-us polarity is still immeasurably embodied in the post-apartheid condition, and, in theatre, in a way that, as the formulation implies, continues the tradition of a trope rooted in an after apartheid imaginary. And of course we must still talk about black and white because

---

15   Rainbow Nation is a phrase that can be traced back to Archbishop Emeritus Desmond Tutu's use of it as early as 1991, generally in the phrase "the rainbow people of God." It was a way to describe the diversity of the people that live in South Africa.

16   Njabulo S Ndebele, *Rediscovery of the Ordinary*, 55.

South Africans still live in a racialised economy, state, and society. Not talking in these terms would be a denial of the very manner of thinking that Ndebele drew our attention to over twenty years ago. So for that reason, the *them-us play* is an important trope – it affords time and an audience to a still much-needed conversation that can potentially work to bring to self-consciousness that which exists subjectively. But what does a *them-us play* look like and, to stick to the topic at hand, how are dramatic characters constituted in these plays?

To unpack a working definition, here are three examples of plays that at first glance seem to align with what we are discussing: Mpumelelo Paul Grootboom and Aubrey Sekhabi's *Inter-racial* (2007), Yaël Farber's reworking of Strindberg's *Miss Julie* into *Mies Julie* (2012), and Mike van Graan's *When Swallows Cry* (2017). These three plays place race relations at the centre of the drama. The characters' primary character trait is that they are black, or white, or, in the case of *Inter-racial*, black trying to depict white. The characters are in high conflict situations. In *Inter-racial* – a them-us play within a them-us play – a cast and director try to stage a play about black and white characters in a clash over events stemming from acts of rape, murder, and adultery. In *Mies Julie*, John, a black Xhosa farm laborer, and Julie, the white Afrikaans daughter of the *Baas* engage in a visceral battle resulting in what Marcia Blumberg has called "extremes of emotions between love and hate, desire and repulsion, and vengeance and forgiveness."[17] Farber couples John and Julie's sexual relationship with the contentious issue of land ownership and ancestral rights – this serving as fuel to the flames. In *When Swallows Cry*, Van Graan uses a trilogy of playlets interweaved with each other to explore three harrowing and life-threatening scenarios in which, in each, two black characters find themselves with a white character. In Playlet One, "Charles Stevenson, a Canadian, travels to an African country to 'make a difference' as a teacher."[18] He is kidnapped and held ransom by two roving bandits that aim to sell him to be used "for propaganda purposes, or to gain more money and arms in exchange for Charles' life."[19] In Playlet Two Amiir, "a Somalian man, fleeing the violence of his own country, and the poverty and difficulties on his continent, arrives at an airport in the USA. His surname appears on Homeland Security's computers as an 'undesirable.' He is thoroughly – and humiliatingly – interrogated by the security

---

17   Martin Middeke, Peter Schnierer and Greg Homann (eds.), *The Methuen Drama Guide to Contemporary South African Theatre* (London: Methuen, 2015), 315.
18   Mike van Graan, *When Swallows Cry* (Personal file, Johannesburg, 2017), 2.
19   *Ibid.*

officials."[20] And in Playlet Three Riason and Josh, "two Zimbabweans – both former teachers – are held in a detention centre in Australia, having arrived there illegally on a boat transporting Africans to Vanuatu. They overpower (Clark) the white officer in the detention centre, and debate plans to escape in order to make new lives for themselves in Australia."[21] The overarching theme of the trilogy is migration in, around, and out of Africa.

In his analysis of *Inter-racial*, Anton Krueger begins by asking "Can one, does one, *perform* race?"[22] He prefigures the question by offering the example of how "psycho-social roles..., such as...being a husband or a father" can be qualified and quantified by the role being performed.[23] What he is essentially reminding his reader of is the Aristotelian notion that character is action, and it is through the performance of an action that character is seen. He states that with a character that is defined by its race, "the criteria which defines the role is not an action but a visual cue." "Race," he says, "is an image rather than a metaphor; the colour interpreted to represent race is the racial qualification itself. One might not be playing the role of the father very explicitly while one is at work, or while driving on the highway toward home, and yet, any audience watching would most likely be able to identify one in a racial capacity."[24] And this is really the crux of the matter. The characters of the them-us play are symbols, objects of separatist discourse. Their primary actions are to *be* black or to *be* white, and in performing these roles as kinds of racial objects, the audience see at work the rigidity of an apartheid informed paradoxical structure. There is no strategy offered through the plays to progress beyond the dichotomy of violence – Julie dies by pushing a sickle into her body to do away with John's baby that she is carrying; Clark shoots Riaison in the chest and Josh in the head; Amiir puts a gun inside his mouth and kills himself rather than return to South Africa where xenophobia based attacks have led to the death of Somalian's like him; Soldier releases Charles under the promise of him sending a ransom when he returns to Canada; and Klaas delivers a lengthy tirade on racial injustice that ultimately ends the play with:

> Fuck this shit man!...Fuck white people!...Fuck them!... Why the fuck did God have to make us "different" from each other?...Why the fuck do we even have to make such a play?...Look, sorry guys, let's go home...I don't

20   *Ibid.*, 3.
21   *Ibid.*
22   Anton Krueger, *Experiments in Freedom. Explorations of Identity in New South African Drama* (Newcastle upon Tyne: Cambridge Scholars Publishing, 2010), 199.
23   *Ibid.*
24   *Ibid.*

wanna have to make such a story, such a play...Fuck white people, man!...
(*The song goes up* – OOM ZIK *starts for the exit but then comes back again in anger*) You know if these motherfuckers find it difficult to co-exist with us, then why don't they go back to England and the Netherlands?...Fuck it!...I'm cancelling guys, it's final!...Let's go home...(*He storms out of the rehearsal room, shouting*) Fuck these white people man!...Fuck white people!...Fuck them!...Fuck them!...Fuck these motherfuckers!!...[25]

Mike van Graan considers the action of his three playlets and their respective endings in *When Swallows Cry* as an invitation to South African audiences to "view the play beyond the limiting lens of 'race,' and to evaluate the human and structural impulses that drives the resolutions."[26] He has written an article in response to audience members and the media who perceived *When Swallows Cry* to be pessimistic in its ending. In this article entitled, *A Response To Those Who Had Difficulty With How "When Swallows Cry" Ends*, he unpacks his intentions as a playwright and argues against any superficial reading of the play, stating that in all his writing he sets out to challenge intellectual and political superficiality, and "to invite audiences to think more, to analyse deeper and to reflect longer on what they have experienced."[27] He has undoubtedly achieved his goal in creating a play that creates debate and dialogue, but I disagree with him that this work, within itself, supersedes a limiting lens of "race." The respective racial identities of van Graan's characters are his dramatic cache, and the choices the characters make, although varied, are reactionary and are acutely rooted in their locked and rigid understanding of those who are othered around them. The play however does expose for its audience the results of such a limited and limiting understanding of identity, and through the bleakness (I will avoid calling it pessimism) of its ending, which does not transcend into a space of hope or optimism, we find van Graan's call to action, debate, and change.

These Them-Us Plays are polemic drama that stage high conflict situations in which characters go at each other. The characters' encounters produce very little in the way of productive modes of living together. Characters appear in the form of racialised identities with rigid notions of self, and the action plays out in a way that confirms what the characters already know. The characters

---

25   Mpumelelo Paul Grootboom and Aubrey Sekhabi, "Inter-racial," in *Reading the Palms of the Times*, ed. Monageng Motshabi (Johannesburg: diartskonageng, 2017), 190–191.

26   Mike Van Graan, "A Response To Those Who Had Difficulty With How 'When Swallows Cry' Ends" (Personal file, Johannesburg, 2017), 4.

27   *Ibid.*, 5.

are void of changing perspectives. If any understanding or common ground is won, then this progress is usually severed at the end through some irreconcilable action, including death. By staging such interactions the impact on the audience could lead to further perpetuating limited and closed understanding of the other, or revealing to the audience their own prejudices, or to problematising such encounters, leaving the audience thinking, "This is no way to live. What can be done about it?" The trappings of the prejudice and / or apartheid condition are the subject of these plays, although, as we can see from the examples discussed, a sub-theme (land, migration, violence, colonialism) works as the frame for the play's action.

2   **Viewing the Restorative Nostalgia Play**

The act of nostalgia expresses a longing for something that is no more, evoking a period, place, or time that was full of happiness. But South Africa's historical landscape is surely not something to long for or romanticise.

With the Restorative Nostalgia play, the historical landscape of apartheid serves as a counterpoint to the action, creating a socio-political tension for the characters. The nostalgia is connected to a meaningful and loving relationship that is now gone, lost. In dramatic writing terms, the characters' primary obstacle to regaining such a relationship is their apartheid conditioning. They are either oblivious to this, and through interaction, become conscious of it, or they are already aware of their conditioning and are trying to do something about their present state of unhappiness. The action challenges the characters to discover that their preconceived ideas of a closed interaction can in fact be open – as characters, they are first identified as objects of separatist discourse (White, Black, Afrikaner, Xhosa, etc.) and later become like mother and son, like sisters, like best friends.

To extend on these thoughts, let us consider Lara Foot's *Reach!* (later revised and produced as *Solomon and Marion*) and Craig Higginson's *Dream of the Dog* as examples. Both of which happen to be plays first performed in 2007 (a good year for restorative nostalgia).

In my introduction to *At This Stage: Plays from Post-apartheid South Africa*, I argued that *Reach!*:

> ...is the story of trying to connect, of trying to narrow the divide between differing histories, generations and racial lines in an attempt to accept, acknowledge and reconcile the traumatic past shared by Marion Banning and Solomon Xaba. ... (Marion's) son Jonathan has been murdered by a

gang of thugs. .... Motivated by his cultural beliefs, Solomon arrives at
Marion's ageing Victorian house to tell the story of what he witnessed the
day Jonathan was killed. Lessons are learnt when Marion gains insight
into Solomon's heritage and conversely, Solomon is able to relieve some
of the grief Marion has lived with by helping her process the murder of
her son.[28]

The characters try to understand each other's subjective positions through being given greater context for the lives they lead, and through this understanding they restore an aspect of their lost self. Solomon is able to complete his
right of passage to becoming a man, and Marion receives the information she
needs to get closure on what happened to her son.

In *Dream of the Dog*, Looksmart arrives at the white owned farm that he
grew up on. He knows that Patricia and Richard Wiley, who own the farm, are
about to move away to a retirement home, but before they do, Looksmart
wants to find out the truth of what really happened to Grace, the girl he wanted to marry. The action centres around the relationship between Patricia and
Looksmart who were once like mother and son, but time, and Looksmart's
memory of the violent dog attack that killed Grace, has tainted their relationship. Looksmart has questions. He is now looking for justice, but Patricia is
interested in a different kind of remembering. She speaks of fishing and clay
animals. Her nostalgia is for a trouble-free time gone by, whereas Looksmart's
nostalgia is menacing. Derek Hook, discussing restorative nostalgia in psycho-
analytic terms, describes that nostalgia can be "the result of something threatening and debilitating; it results in the attempt to freeze change; it is a mode of
erasure operating against an obligation to remember; it entails the role of a
type of hallucinatory comfort in the face of something that has been lost."[29]
Hooks cites Jacob Dlamini's reading of Boym stating that "a re-thinking of the
relations between past, present and future," can create an awareness that "the
past is not merely that which doesn't exist anymore, but...[something that]
might *act*...by inserting itself into a present sensation."[30] What Hooks unpacks
is how remembering gives the past agency in the present. Looksmart, grew up
happy on the farm, but the death of Grace and the events that surrounded that
incident have made him question his entire relationship with that place and
time. His memory of the event is literally acting on him, and it is driving his

---

28   Greg Homann (ed.), *At This Stage: Plays from post-apartheid South Africa* (Johannesburg:
      Wits Press, 2009), 18.
29   Derek Hook, *(Post)Apartheid Conditions*, 177.
30   *Ibid.*, 176. (my emphasis)

desire to get to the truth. The act of remembering and reflecting has destabilised his understanding of his identity as a boy, threatening and debilitating his sense of self as a man. So what Higginson has constructed with Looksmart is a character that represents the South African dilemma, which is to allow a history, and more specifically, memory, to act on you and, as a result, objectify you in terms of race. In an article in the Mail & Guardian, psychologist and academic, Rafael Winkler wrote:

> What we are witnessing today is a contestation between the multiple histories and narratives that constitute the collective memory of South African society. There is a growing need, felt especially by young adults...to address the problem of the histories and narratives that are to have an authoritative status in our collective memory and that are to be passed down as a legacy. It is a struggle whose aim is to claim ownership of the past and lay the foundations of a new beginning and destiny for South Africa.[31]

Winkler calls this an objectifying attitude, and it is this condition that we see in Looksmart's actions and pursuits. He doesn't want Patricia's version of events, but he does want her to confirm his version.

Looksmart leaves Patricia on good terms, restoring to some extent their past relationship but not without acknowledging its flaws.

> LOOKSMART: Ah, Madam – this is a strange land we live in. For your generation, you white people, you still want to be the mothers, the fathers, and we – we must be something like the children. But that relationship can have no place in the future of this country.
> PATRICIA: Yet you were like my son, Looksmart. At least as close as I ever got to having one. (*Off his look*) And I'll be lonely there, in my house by the sea. I really would like you to visit. Even if it is just to humour an old *gogo* with one or two marbles still rolling around inside her head.
> LOOKSMART: If I come, I can come with clay animals I've made so you can look at them and think – it's art![32]

---

31   Rafael Winkler, "Who has authority to talk about identity?," *Mail & Guardian* (Johannesburg), Feb 7, 2017, accessed February 7, 2017, https://mg.co.za/article/2017-02-07-00-who-has-authority-to-talk-about-identity.
32   Craig Higginson, "Dream of the Dog," 60–61.

I am offering then, that the Restorative Nostalgia Play is a sub-category of the Memory Play. The characters' actions are driven by a deep personal need to remember. At the outset, their ethnic identities are set within a national meta-narrative. As the action unfolds, which always entails sharing one's story, or personal truth, the characters identities shift. The denouement, which is often cathartic, leads the characters to reconciliation, as in *Solomon and Marion*, or at least, towards it, as in the case of *Dream of the Dog*, with the frame of trauma and loss slowly receding – an aesthetics of hope and transformation.

3   The Problems of the Rainbow Nation Play

I set out to argue that the Rainbow Nation Play is uncritical of the post-apartheid state and condition. It smooths over conflict points and contested histories, and, as a result, stunts transformation, avoids contradiction. Like the period it stems from, it is usually celebratory in tone, affirming a particular ethnic or cultural identity through the lens of a single perspective. Embracing the rainbow analogy as Temple Hauptfleisch described it with all the various bands in its spectrum secure in their own identity – exploring only one colour in the rainbow.[33] And although I think there are examples of plays like this, I have come to the position, at least for now, that in fact there are far more examples of plays being critical of Rainbow Nation-ism. Playwrights, theatre-makers, and humanities scholarship have resisted the rainbow; rainbows, as we know, are illusions, see-through, tricks of light and water, and any search for a pot-of-gold will only lead to disappointment.

In *Experiments in Freedom*, Anton Krueger makes a fleeting mention of the rainbow play trope. He also avoids naming any specific plays that align with rainbow nation ideals and instead focuses on a few plays that work in opposition and critique of such politics, naming Mike van Graan's *Green Man Flashing*, *Hostile Takevover*, and *Die Generaal*, along with the plays of Reza de Wet as some examples. So in a sense, Krueger's short chapter entitled *Over the Rainbow?* addresses the anti-rainbow play, which is one that critiques government policy and institutions, challenges notions of national identity, and aims to debunk rigid or constrictive designs of self. To frame his points, Krueger summarises key scholarship, stating:

> Criticism of the rainbow nation trope has been made by a number of academics, most notably Bhekizizwe Peterson, Ashraf Jamal, Leon de Kock

---

33   Anton Krueger, *Experiments in Freedom*, 207.

and Gugu Hlongwane. Although they may disagree as to how the metaphor operates and why it is less than helpful, they all seem to agree that one of the reasons why it is dangerous is because it seeks to flatten out differences and simplify complexity. For example, Ashraf Jamal says that "in glossing difference it has failed to address radicality or heterogeneity that subsists at the core of South Africa's differential condition. The problem lies first in the elision and suppression of the incommensurability of difference." De Kock refers to the trope as an "imagined singularity" which is, in fact, a "tatty patchwork." Bhekizizwe Peterson says that the "nebulous celebrations" of the rainbow nation are "suffocating the arts," claiming that this is a result of a reluctance to deal with the "complexities of identity." And finally, Gugu Hlongwane sees the analogy as faulty since whites are still "the social and economic beneficiaries of an Apartheid regime that supported a lopsided accumulation of wealth and social power" and therefore, whites cannot claim to share a national identity with blacks.[34]

So, in this vein, and notwithstanding my initial impulse, I would prefer to speak of the anti-Rainbow play. To unpack a definition, I would like to reflect briefly on my own playwriting as well as Mongiwekhaya's award-winning play, *I See You*.[35]

My play, *Previously Owned*,[36] tells the story of four twenty-something year olds who have found temporary employment in a second-hand bookshop in Melville.[37] Will is a wannabe filmmaker. Britney is a struggling actress who can't get work because she sounds too British to be on South African TV. When Mohau arrives to take on a weekends only job to please his family, his affluence and upbringing soon destabilizes the weekly routine Will and Britney have come to accept. Adrienne Sichel in *The Star Tonight* called *Previously Owned* "a wickedly observant post-democratic whiplash comedy ... potent, yet

---

34   *Ibid.*, 208.
35   *I See You* won Best New South African Script at the Fleur du Cap Awards 2016 and Best Production of a Play at the Naledi Theatre Awards 2016. Its premiere performance was at The Royal Court in London, having been developed through a Royal Court/British Council new writing project in South Africa which began in 2013.
36   The play premiered at the Setkani/Encounter Festival in Brno (Czech Republic) on 1 April 2009. It then returned to South Africa for a short season at The Wits Downstairs Theatre from 14 to 25 April of the same year and was followed by a tour to the National Arts Festival Fringe in Grahamstown.
37   A trendy suburb a few kilometres from the Johannesburg city centre – a cultural melting pot for tertiary educated 20 something year olds. It is a place of coffeehouses, antique stores, vintage shops, restaurants, bars, and music clubs.

non-didactic, messages about seeing the package beyond the wrapping and how disposable a very painful history is to a new generation, are contained in fast-paced scenes which ring true."[38] Robyn Sassen on *Artslink* stated that "The drama gets electric when colonial heritage and erotic assumptions slip into the mêlée of conversation which begins to verge on the intimate."[39] The play, inspired in part by Chipkin's book, is a playful exploration probing a simple question, "What is a South African?"

In an early scene, Britney tries to describe Will's accent to Mo:

> BRITNEY: English speaking atheist liberal artist public school type bi-sexual accent. And now we have just added to it. An English speaking atheist liberal artist public school type bisexual stereotype of a cliché sit-com accent. It's all about building a complex identity.
> MOHAU: That's contradictory.
> BRITNEY: No it's not.
> MOHAU: Well first you say he's this mix of different, what do you call them?
> BRITNEY: Types?
> MOHAU: Yes, and then you say it's all about building a complex identity. Aren't they two different things? I mean either you're a type or you're... what?
> BRITNEY: Fully rounded.
> MOHAU: Exactly.
> BRITNEY: I haven't a clue. I'm just an actress trying to get work. All I know is that I need to start sounding more South African. However I do that, I don't care.[40]

My aim with this narrative thread, which plays out in multiple moments in the play, was to complicate notions of a South African identity. This thematic line works against the rigid classification of identity types imposed under apartheid, or what Gilles Deleuze might call arboreal identity,[41] favouring rather his rhizomatic classification of identity which aligns well with a blending of the proverbial identity-rainbow instead of highlighting a particular band within it. This strategy extended further with the character of Mo or Mohau, whom Will treats with a preconceived racist subtext, later to discover that Mo is adopted

---

38   Adrienne Sichel, "Potent Post-Democratic Whiplash Play," *The Star: Tonight*, April 21, 2009.
39   Robyn Sassen, "Review: Previously Owned," *Artslink*, April 17, 2009.
40   Greg Homann, *Previously Owned* (Personal file, Johannesburg, 2009), 19.
41   As explained in: Anton Krueger, *Experiments in Freedom*, 37–46.

by white parents. This revelation destabilizes Will's easily-boxed understanding of who Mo might be. I should add that this strategy to write Mo as adopted served a double-function. Other than its useful thematic purpose, it also helped address, to a degree, the question of "Can I write black characters?" And it is interesting to note that Neil Coppen, a few years later in his play, *Abnormal Loads,* made use of a similar device with his protagonist, Vincent, as did Mike van Graan in *Rainbow Scars* with a character called Lindiwe who was adopted by a white middle class family.

The use of rhizomatic identity as fluid and slippery proved useful to me in another play too, *Oedipus @ Koö-Nú!* – the title designed to playfully evoke Mandela's birth home, Qunu! Oedipus embodies all three of the identity types installed by the TRC – the victim, the perpetrator, and the hero. He is also an exile, a refugee, a father. The identity mash up was followed through in the style, a postmodern take on *Oedipus at Colonus.* One big intervention on the original text was a satirical song and dance number using the theme music to the Rugby World Cup of 1995, which South Africa hosted and won – an historical moment that is broadly accepted as the pinnacle of Rainbow Nation(ism) and arguably the closest the country has come to a felt sense of oneness (at least white folk would like to think so). In this number, Theseus, who is a woman, lip-syncs poorly to a musical track of the theme song, as the cast, who in this moment represent different national identities, dance in an eclectic muddle of local and international styles. A rainbow fills the stage and rugby balls rain from the sky.

Rainbow imagery, with all its New South Africa resonances, is present in Mongiwekhaya's *I See You* too. The play is set in Johannesburg on a Friday night moving into Saturday morning. It begins by foregrounding Rainbow Nation symbols. The opening stage directions indicate: "The moon slowly rises up, cutting the darkness into the horizon of Johannesburg city in the distance. The key feature is the Nelson Mandela Bridge, lit up with all the colours of the rainbow..."[42] A moment later DJ Mavovo is described as "...a shamanistic presence, personification of the Nelson Mandela Bridge...,"[43] and then we hear a series of short news reports that further establish a historical frame detailing the big political moments in the country including, Mandela's hospitalisation (i.e. the death of the Rainbow Nation's ultimate hero is imminent), Desmond Tutu

42   Mongiwekhaya, *I See You* (London: Bloomsbury, 2016), 3.
43   *Ibid.*

speaking of Ubuntu,[44] and reports of the Marikana Massacre.[45] In scene six the rainbow imagery returns, "...the Nelson Mandela Bridge burns with all the colours of the rainbow in the midst of the fallen stars that is the city of Johannesburg."[46]

Against this historic and symbolic backdrop, we watch the story of two young South Africans whose fun night-out turns into a harrowing and unjust interrogation by the police. Ben and Skinn are products of a new South Africa. Ben is a born-free[47] but raised in America. He no longer uses his African given Xhosa name, Somandla, nor can he speak his mother's tongue – only English. He has met Skinn, a seventeen-year-old Afrikaans girl who similarly experiences her identity in a way that resists a typical arboreal sense of self. She has opted to discard her distinctive Afrikaans name, Yvette Skinner, hiding it from Ben. They encounter Buthelezi – a sergeant of the South African Police who is an ex-MK soldier.[48] Buthelezi has grown-up during apartheid and survived it, installing in him a very rigid understanding of who he is and who others should be. Ben, according to Buthelezi, must speak in Xhosa, must prove that he has Xhosa culture in his blood by dancing pantsula.[49] Skinn is treated as the historical oppressor. Buthelezi says to her:

> But I can see you are no different to the people who raised you. You think you are automatically right. You own the truth, neh? So you can come in here to an officer and demand I do as you command.[50]

---

44   Ubuntu is a term that directly translates to human-ness. The Nguni word was popularized under Nelson Mandela's presidency and has come to stand in for an ideal of togetherness, of recognizing one another, and of being generous in spirit with each other. The phrase, "I am, because you are," is closely associated with the term.

45   On 16 August 2012 the South African Police Service (SAPS) opened fire on a group of striking mineworkers at Marikana, in the North West Province of South Africa, killing 34 people.

46   Mongiwekhaya, *I See You*, 35.

47   Born-frees are quite simply the South African generation born after the country's democratic elections in 1994.

48   MK is an abbreviation of *uMkhonto we Sizwe* which translates to "The Spear of the Nation." As a response to the Sharpville massacre on 21 March 1960, where 69 people protesting the carrying of passbooks were shot dead in the back, the African National Congress (ANC) formed this armed wing, co-founded by Nelson Mandela, to fight the then apartheid government.

49   Pantsula is a uniquely South African dance form that originated in the townships soon after apartheid began. It is embedded in a strong cultural sense of identity and integrates a socio-political commentary.

50   Mongiwekhaya, *I See You*, 45.

Through Buthelezi's intimidation and interrogation tactics, Ben cracks. He confesses that his uneasily defined identity has made him feel lost in the world.

> Do you know what happens when you lose your language? The world ceases to have shape. No shape no words no nothing nothing no thing. You are vanished. A ghost haunting a little boy's body. I was three years old when my mother took me overseas. I only spoke Xhosa then. No one else spoke that language. My mother wouldn't answer me. I couldn't remember the days. Only the nights. When everyone was asleep I'd hear voices. Are you a ghost? Are you really here?[51]

Ben is unable to find value in his liquid identity and articulates it as a failing, a weakness. In the closing lines of the play, Ben and Skinn disclose their birth names to each other. This ending reveals that rhizomatic identity under the rainbow is resisted, discarded, useless. Ultimately the play explores how two rhizomatic identities embodied in Ben and Skinn are forced into Buthelezi, and his comrades' arboreal sense of who he and they believe this born-free generation should be. So, the anti-rainbow play complicates ideas of identity, constructing them as liquid and uneasy to define and places these rhizomatic conceptions in conflict with any fixed or arboreal sense of self.

4   Conclusion

In *Do South Africans Exist?*, Ivor Chipkin explores the boundaries of the democratic imaginary, unpacking notions of Nationalism, and the Identity of "The People." He asks the question, "On what grounds (are) South Africans a single people?"[52] He isolates two failed attempts after apartheid to produce a definition of the South African people, the first being the TRC project with its appeal towards a common history and the second, via what he calls "a divine transcendental," namely Tutu's "rainbow people of God."[53] He then turns to the country's constitution:

> We, the people of South Africa,
> Recognise the injustices of our past;
> Honour those who suffered for justice and freedom in our land;

---

51   *Ibid.*, 58.
52   Ivor Chipkin, *Do South Africans Exist?*, 174.
53   *Ibid.*, 186.

Respect those who have worked to build and develop our country; and Believe that South Africa belongs to all who live in it, united in our diversity.

Chipkin observes that the clarification of who "we" are, "the people of South Africa," in the formulation, "We, the people of South Africa" appears to identify "a paradox of a people unsure of what they are, and seeking to remind themselves as they proceed."[54] Chipkin grapples with the question, "What is the common factor, the X, on which to base a South African identity?"[55] As he moves towards his conclusion, as I do with mine, he reminds his reader of the great French motto "Liberty, Equality, Fraternity." He hones in on Fraternity, speculating that it is perhaps this aspect of democratic life that is absent from our thinking and being in a young democratic state. Creating a sense of Fraternity requires action, it requires work. To create a South Africa that genuinely belongs to all who live in it, Chipkin rightly argues that there must be a pursuit of deep horizontal solidarity – regularising "such encounters so that they are part of the ordinary lived experience of people."[56] He notes that, "Historically speaking, since the great democratic revolutions of the eighteenth century, there has been a single, pre-eminent way of generating [the limit of a given democracy] (the internal measure of the people). This can be called a national principle. It is a way of simultaneously generating identity and difference that appeals to a horizontal relation between persons."[57] Through his study he reaches the point that living in South Africa is that X and ultimately, he makes a case that rejects the idea of a national identity for South Africa, asserting rather that "the boundary [of South Africa's democracy] encloses citizens who share a special solidarity produced in and through democratic encounters."[58] This vision or call to action is echoed by Ndebele who says, "The aim is to extend the range of personal and social experience as far as possible in order to contribute to bringing about a highly conscious, sensitive new person in a new society. This, it seems to me, is the function of art in, and its contribution to, the ongoing revolution in South Africa."[59]

I am reminded of Mike van Graan's *Brothers in Blood*, where, in the final moments of the play Brian, a Jewish father ponders how he should respond to the

---

54   *Ibid.*, 177.
55   *Ibid.*, 178.
56   *Ibid.*, 214.
57   *Ibid.*, 175.
58   *Ibid.*, 218.
59   Njabulo S Ndebele, *Rediscovery of the Ordinary*, 71.

explosive situation he found himself in with Abubaker, a Muslim father. Brian says,

> What did I do that was so bad in my previous life? I mean, I get born white and male...in South Africa of all places! And now with Israel being in the news everyday...I feel responsible and guilty all over again. Like there's a sign over my head saying "he's a Jew"! (*shakes his head*) What should I do, Gerald? Pack for Perth? Will it be better there? Do I just go on here like nothing's happened? (*Beat*) Should I have all of them around for dinner? That sounds so...lame. (*Beat*) You know we've never had Muslim people in our house? (*Beat*) What would you do? If you were me?[60]

The *them-us play, the restorative nostalgia play*, and *the anti-rainbow play* are all doing the work of guiding and conscientising South Africans on where they live and how they live, albeit in different ways. It is a theatre of struggle, a struggle to find nuance in all the political and historical noise. A theatre that aims to address contradiction, to encourage debate and dialogue. A theatre of provocation that draws on the dominant allusions and illusions of the country's history, and that, through its characters' construction, prompts its audience towards living in South Africa with a deep horizontal solidarity, where recognising common interests in jazz, painting, and brandy drinking is more possible than playing out the lexicon of nationalism and racialism.

Works Cited

Chipkin, Ivor. *Do South Africans Exist? Nationalism, Democracy and the Identity of "The People."* Johannesburg: Wits University Press, 2007.

Coombes, Annie. E. *History After Apartheid: Visual Culture and Public Memory in Democratic South Africa.* Johannesburg: Wits Press, 2003.

Farber, Yaël. *Mies Julie: Restitutions of Body and Soil Since the Bantu Land Act No 27 of 1913 & The Immorality Act No 5 of 1927.* London: Oberon Books, 2012.

Grootboom, Mpumelelo Paul and Aubrey Sekhabi. "Inter-racial." In *Reading the Palms of the Times,* edited by Monageng Motshabi, 77–191. Johannesburg: diartskonageng, 2017.

---

60   This extract from the playtext comes from the final production version of the play staged at Artscape in March 2012 and in all subsequent performances of the work. The dialogue therefore differs somewhat from the Junkets Press (2012) published version as well as the original production version presented at The Market Theatre in 2009.

Higginson, Craig. "Dream of the Dog." In *Three Plays*. Johannesburg: Wits Press, 2016.

Homann, Greg and Ralf Lawson. *A Voice I Cannot Silence*. Personal file, Johannesburg: 2015.

Homann, Greg and Marc Maufort (eds.). *New Territories: Theatre, Drama, and Performance in Post-apartheid South Africa*. Brussels: PIE Peter Lang, 2015.

Homann, Greg. *Oedipus @ Koö-Nú!* Personal file, Johannesburg, 2014.

Homann, Greg & Saint-Claire, Louise. *One Woman Farce*. Personal file, Johannesburg, 2012.

Homann, Greg (ed.). *At This Stage: Plays from post-apartheid South Africa*. Johannesburg: Wits Press, 2009.

Homann, Greg. *Previously Owned*. Personal file, Johannesburg, 2009.

Hook, Derek. *(Post)Apartheid Conditions: Psychoanalysis and Social Formation*. Cape Town: HSRC Press, 2014.

Jamal, Ashraf. *Predicaments of Culture in South Africa*. Pretoria: UNISA Press, 2005.

Krueger, Anton. *Experiments in Freedom. Explorations of Identity in New South African Drama*. Newcastle upon Tyne: Cambridge Scholars Publishing, 2010.

Middeke, Martin, Peter Schnierer and Greg Homann (eds.). *The Methuen Drama Guide to Contemporary South African Theatre*. London: Methuen, 2015.

Mongiwekhaya. *I See You*. London: Bloomsbury, 2016.

Ndebele, Njabulo S. *Rediscovery of the Ordinary. Essays on South African Culture*. Scottsville: UKZN Press, 2006.

Nuttall, Sarah and Cheryl Ann Michael (eds.). *Senses of Culture: South African Culture Studies*. Oxford: Oxford University Press, 2001.

Sassen, Robyn. *Review: Previously Owned*. Artslink, 17 April 2009.

Sichel, Adrienne. *Potent Post-Democratic Whiplash Play*. The Star: Tonight. 21 April 2009.

Van Graan, Mike. *When Swallows Cry*. Personal file, Johannesburg, 2017.

Van Graan, Mike. "A Response To Those Who Had Difficulty With How 'When Swallows Cry' Ends." Personal file, Johannesburg, 2017.

Van Graan, Mike. *Brothers in Blood*. Personal file, Johannesburg, 2012.

Winkler, Rafael. "Who has authority to talk about identity?," *Mail & Guardian* (Johannesburg), 7 February 2017, viewed 7 February 2017, https://mg.co.za/article/2017 -02-07-00-who-has-authority-to-talk-about-identity.

CHAPTER 3

Being in Two Places at the Same Time

Craig Higginson

Abstract

In this essay, Craig Higginson explores the enduring tendency in his writing to be in "at least two places at any one time." He looks at a possible origin of it and the way it has been working into the form, content and context of his writing. He draws on psycho-analytic concepts – including the Oedipus complex, dissociation, sublimation, displacement, Eros and Thanatos – as well as Bakhtin's conception of "the dialogic imagination" – but he also argues for the need for a tempered engagement as both a writer and a citizen.

1 An Anecdote

When I was ten years old, I drove with my mother from Johannesburg down to what was then called the province of Natal. We were driving a sky-blue Toyota Hilux bakkie and we were towing a horse box. In the horse box was a grey Welsh pony called Tessa and we were taking her to a stud farm in order to try and get her to have a foal. It turned out she didn't want to have a foal and some months later she was returned to us in Johannesburg. At the time of this journey, I was halfway through my first term at boarding school. My school was over the hill from the stud farm, which was just outside of Nottingham Road. Later, the school and the stud farm would provide a starting point for a couple of plays and novels – including the novels *The Hill* and *The Dream House* and the play *Dream of the Dog*.

We sound like a wealthy family – but in fact my mother was soon to run out of what money she had inherited. At the time we were living in the modest suburb of Blairgowrie, in Randburg. My sister kept her ponies – I think she had two by then – at the Inanda Club, where we were surrounded by children from families much wealthier than ours. I still remember the morning of loading the pony in the horsebox and leaving the stables. It was just getting light and it was as if we were off to a horse show. But my school things were in the back and I was about to return to a school that was a five-hour drive away and still frightening. I remember my mother holding the steering wheel and saying she felt shaky. I didn't pay her much attention. But we set off and everything seemed fine until my mother told me she was lost. The journey from Johannesburg to Durban was one she had taken many times before. She herself had gone to boarding school in Natal from the age of ten. We drove off the highway and entered a small town in what was then the Orange Free State – and we were driving slowly along the main road when her body seemed to lock backwards and she screamed – her voice starting off in a low moan and rapidly building to the kind of sound a person makes under torture. The car veered into an oncoming truck and I steered it away – although the truck clipped the back of the horsebox as it passed. The car then bumped up against the pavement and a man appeared alongside the car. He put his hand through the open window and pulled the handbrake. The car jerked to a stop and he opened the door and slapped my mother hard across the face. He did this three times, each time telling her to wake up, and I remember shouting, Don't hit my mother! But she was barely my mother. She had gone into a trance, there was froth pouring from her mouth, her eyes were rolled backwards. She had the face of the Medusas I'd seen in books about Greek myths – whose gaze would turn you to stone.

She was having an epileptic fit – a grand mal seizure, which is the most severe. I knew about her fits already. I lived with my mother and slightly older sister and I had experienced her fits before – sometimes as many as five in a day. But – at least in my memory – it was always at home and we were old enough to phone the neighbour – whose domestic worker Beauty would sometimes come and make us supper while my mother lay in bed.

But my mother had never had a fit in the car before, in the middle of nowhere, towing a horse. The back wheel of the horsebox had burst through contact with the trunk. Someone changed the wheel. My mother soon came around. I remember she couldn't remember her address or phone number – but I knew them and provided them. And then the strangest thing happened. My mother said she was feeling much better and could continue the journey – and so we were given directions on how to get to the road to Durban and we set off again.

But this time I knew what I had to do. If it happened again, I could stop the car with the handbrake. I believed I knew how to drive. And off we went, out of the town – and down a long thin road that seemed to go on through fields of mielies forever. I remember looking down the rows of corn, as row flicked by after row, and imagining this would go on forever. I remember very clearly the sensation of being in two places at the same time. In the car, with my mother, whose every move I watched like a hawk, and far away – my mind moving along each corridor of corn as if it might offer a chance of escape.

But of course it didn't offer any escape. I was in the car and we were soon lost again and we just had to keep on going. I remember we stopped at an intersection once and my mother peed on the side of the road – not even trying to hide herself. I remember how animal that moment was, how exposed – how vulnerable she was and how helpless that made me feel.

And then it happened again. We were driving fast along that straight road when she let out the same jolt, the same scream. I tried to control the car, but it veered off the side of the road. I pulled with the weight of my whole body against the handbrake, but it made no difference. Along with my mother screaming, the car engine was screaming too – as her foot was pressed flat against the accelerator.

I wasn't wearing a seatbelt. The car flew off the bank, hung in the air, and then rolled. The horsebox yanked and buckled. I stood inside the car, holding onto the handgrip by the window, my feet wedged against the dashboard and the seat, and I felt for a moment as if I was cartwheeling through space. I felt exactly like Spiderman. The car, now on its side, slid through the tall grass and came to a halt. It was still on its side – the passenger side against the flattened grass. My mother was hanging from the seatbelt above my head, gagging, as if the seatbelt was strangling her. Pink froth was pouring from her mouth. I climbed out of her window and behind me her seatbelt snapped. She landed with a hard clump on the other side of the car and remained quite still. I went to check up on the horse. The horsebox was standing on its roof and the pony was standing on the roof of it. She saw me and screeched and pulled her head so hard that the metal clasp of her halter snapped. Then she trotted off, veering and dazed, into the road.

Already there was another car there – perhaps two. I managed to catch and calm the pony and bring her back to the car. There was a small crowd of people now. They were saying my mother might have broken her neck and she shouldn't be moved. I remember holding the pony and burying my face in the soft grey silk of her neck, and sobbing. I was not sobbing for my mother. The person in the car was no longer my mother. I was sobbing for myself. I saw my whole life ahead of me – I would have to go and live with my father, who frightened me. His first daughter in his second marriage, my half sister, was dying in hospital in Pretoria at the time – of leukaemia. She was nearly four and she had been dying for most of her life.

There are several moments, looking back, when a person can say their childhood ended. I'm not sure it ever ends. I'm not even sure it is ever entirely there to start with. Childhood, like everything, is a fiction we create for ourselves and our children. But certainly on that day something died inside me and something was born. My relationship with my mother would never be quite the same again. She was two people – the mother I knew and the daemon medusa that lay inside her. There was no longer one of anyone. Inside each of us lay a shadow – a madness, a force so huge it could obliterate everything you thought you knew about yourself and others. Certainly, I would never trust my mother or any adult again.

It transpired that my mother had barely hurt herself. When she landed on the other side of the bakkie, her head had cracked the plastic around the door frame. But she was more or less unhurt – perhaps because her body had been as limp and lifeless as a sack of wheat. In the years that followed, I would look at that crack in the plastic. Whenever I was in a car with my mother, I would wait for the daemon to declare herself. I would wait for the daemon always – and sometimes, she would come – and I would do my best to cope with her – or was it a he?

But another part of me was far away. It had drifted off. It saw the whole scene from a great height: the car and horsebox being righted again, the procession of people walking towards a nearby farmhouse, where they spoke only Afrikaans and where we would spend the night. When my little sister died a year later, I was there when the headmaster gave me the news and I was not there.

Yet each of these disappointments – and there were others – pushed me further away, deeper into what I have later come to recognise as my imagined land – the landscape out of which a storyteller can begin to speak and make sense of the world that he or she has successfully escaped.

2   Dissociation and Sublimation

Psychologists call the escape mechanism I discovered on that day dissociation. It can range from mild detachment from one's immediate surroundings to more severe detachment from physical and emotional experience in general. The major characteristic of all dissociative phenomena involves a detachment from reality – and is the opposite, in a sense, of psychosis, which is characterised by a loss of reality. Dissociation is a coping mechanism that enables us to manage stress – which can include anything from boredom to a major traumatic event. Dissociation becomes compulsive rather than voluntary in its extreme form, which is when it can lead to multiple personality disorders – referred to these days as dissociative identity disorders.

Dissociation can lead to healthy and unhealthy behaviours – such as subli-mation and displacement. Displacement is a strategy for pushing reality away, but here you are projecting an unwanted feeling or emotion unconsciously onto someone or something else – and usually causing yourself and/or others harm in the process. Sublimation is seen as a more mature defence – in which there is an unconscious channelling of emotional energy into a constructive outlet. It becomes cathartic – and can include anything from writing a novel to walking the dog on the beach. Displacement is inter-personal and the damage is inflicted back onto another person or thing. Sublimation provides an oppor-tunity to find release in another thing that is not a living thing and is, in my view, the beginning of all art.

Without a detachment from reality and the capacity to daydream, acts of the imagination remain impossible. But at what point is this activity voluntary and at what point compulsive? I often say to aspiring writers that if they have to force themselves to sit down and write they probably aren't writers. Writers can't stop themselves from writing. Believe me – I have tried and failed.

It is perhaps no surprise that I started to write my first novel at the age of eleven – not long after the car accident and my sister's death. My "novel" – which filled about seven school exercise books – told the story of a boy who runs away from boarding school and goes to live in a cave in the Drakensberg with his pet owl. Later I would rewrite that story and call it *The Hill* – and the owl would be replaced with a talking dog.

I still recall the stillness of my pony Tessa at the side of the road. She was the only one of the three of us on that day to be injured. She had a long bleeding scratch along her forehead that would later form a scar – like that crack in the plastic upholstery. I have also just realised during the writing of this that the talking dog in *The Hill* was called Tess. The dog was my pony, reinvented. That dog would provide the one still point in the turning world of my protagonist – who was called Thomas, "he who doubts."

I had to dissociate in the car with my mother because I had to escape – even though I couldn't. I learned the distinction right away between Sartre's onto-logical and practical freedom. I was trapped in the car but could experience that entrapment in whatever way I liked. Classically, children dissociate when the parent is both frightened and frightening. Had I regressed into fantasy and been unable to return, I might have displaced rather than sublimated the expe-rience later – or developed the beginnings of a dissociative identity disorder. But as soon as the car stopped, I ceased being Spiderman. I climbed out of the open window, heard my mother fall and went to catch the horse. That night I was able to speak my meagre Afrikaans to the farmer and his wife who housed us for the night and tell my mother what had happened. All she could remember was leaving the Inanda stables – she couldn't recall a single thing from that day after that. Interestingly, however, by the time the friend of the farmer had delivered me to my boarding school the next day, I had already started to mediate the narrative about that traumatic day. I told my friends and teachers that we'd had a car accident, that the car had rolled – but I reduced it to one event and left out the epileptic fits. Already I was telling the truth and not telling the truth. I was inside the story and outside of it – like Flaubert's version of the artist, who is always somewhere outside of the narrative, empathetic but detached, always felt but never seen, quietly paring his fingernails.[1]

3   Oedipus

Freud's Oedipal Complex theory was at the heart of his thinking around infant sexuality and is one of the more controversial of his ideas amongst non-specialists. He first introduced the concept in the *Interpretation of Dreams*, the term deriving from the hero Oedipus of Greek legend, who unknowingly slew his father and married his mother. Its female analogue, the Electra Complex,[2] is named from another mythological figure who helped to slay her mother. For Freud, the child has an unconscious sexual desire for the parent of the opposite sex between the ages of three and five and these are an important stage in a child's sexual development.

It could be argued all acts of creation have an "oedipal" element – the male writer, in this instance,[3] is killing off the father (see Harold Bloom's *The Anxiety of Influence,* for instance) and burying himself in a procreative act with the mother/ motherland/ homeland/ re-imagined land. The death drive (Thanatos) is channelled towards the father/ authorised figure/ author, and the libido energy (Eros) is channelled towards a new, promised but forbidden land.[4]

But in this anecdote it is the mother the narrator is killing off – and leaving for dead. Instead, he is imagining a bleak future where he will be forced to commune again with an unwanted father. And he finds refuge in dissociation

---

1   Later famously picked up by James Joyce in *A Portrait of the Artist as a Young Man*: "The artist, like the God of creation, remains within or behind or beyond or above his handiwork, invisible, refined out of existence, indifferent, paring his fingernails." 219.

2   Introduced by Carl Jung in 1913. Freud, however, continued to use the term Oedipus Complex to refer both male and female infant sexuality.

3   I will be referring to the writer as "he" in this paper as the writer in question is male.

4   These terms were first introduced by Freud in Beyond the Pleasure Principle in 1920. "Beyond the Pleasure Principle," in *Pelican Freud, Volume ɪɪ: On Metapsychology: The Theory of Psychoanalysis,* (London: Penguin Books, 1985).

and the beginnings of the sublimation-impulse. This process is, in fact, the severing of the oedipal promise. The mother is both a mother and a medusa. She is half monster. She can no longer be relied on as a source of stability. She is now a source of danger.[5]

Perhaps all "mature" creative acts are about severing the oedipal promise and entering a new land, a promised land that is post-father, post-mother. Here the male writer can re-invent the land according to his desires. As Freud describes – the ego can indulge its fantasy unfettered by the x of parents or indeed of society.[6] Yet there is an interesting paradox here, since the writer can never quite escape the figures from the world he is attempting to displace. Like Looksmart in *Dream of the Dog* and *The Dream House*, the writer is condemned, in his new promised land, to repeat the same house he grew up in and that still haunts his dreams – "with slight variations, all across the valley."[7] Our internal wood-grain as writers is set down to us, and we find ourselves settling back into it no matter how hard we try to imagine alternatives: our thumbprints are all over each new creation like the thumbprints of the sculptor all over the wet clay.

Only recently have I realised that the plot of this anecdote is, in many essential elements, the same plot that is enacted in each of my plays in *Three Plays* as well as in the novel *The Dream House*. There is an older female figure who stands for the mother, there is a younger male figure who stands for the child.[8] There is a misguided/ idealised over-attachment in Act One (thesis), a violent and dramatic moment of disappointment/ disillusion/ revelation in Act Two (antithesis), and a new effort at conciliation towards the end, where the younger male figure has to reconcile with a compromised world and his life, in the final words of *The Dream House*, simply has to "carry on."[9]

As suggested above, all acts of creation, or certainly all acts of dramatic writing (insofar as they follow a Hegelian three-act structure), are oedipal in nature – involving a sense of home (whether in the body, the family, the home, the

---

5   Freud's essay on "The Uncanny" (Volume 14 of *The Pelican Freud Library*, entitled *Art and Literature*) would provide a highly revealing filter through which this episode could be read – as well as such characters as Patricia in *Dream of the Dog* and *The Dream House*. Here the human is reduced to the monster, the object – a mechanical doll – at least through the eyes of the boy in the anecdote and Looksmart in the play and novel.

6   See his essay "Creative Writers and Day-Dreaming," in *Pelican Freud Library, Volume 14: Art and Literature,* (London: Penguin Books, 1985).

7   Craig Higginson, *The Dream House* (Johannesburg: Picador Africa, 2015), 176.

8   The characters are closer in age in *The Girl in the Yellow Dress*, yet the matriarchal relationship of Europe to Africa, the so-called "First" World to the "Third," remains intact.

9   Craig Higginson, *The Dream House*, 242.

community), a casting out from that home and the creation of a new home that can withstand the howling winds of the encountered wolf – whether he (or indeed she) be real or imaginary. Yet the central relationship in the anecdote, the plays and the novel is between an older woman and a younger man and in each the younger man is rejecting the older woman as maternal figure. In the plays and the novel, these relationships also become racialised – so that they stand for the maternalism inherent in the liberal position or in apartheid South Africa or colonialism more generally. Here the dissociation and sublimation are simply more advanced. The writer is disguising his source material more successfully not only through sublimation but through the use of allegory.

4   Two Places at the Same Time

Being in two places at the same time. I only recently understood that this has been at the very heart of all of my writing – from the very start. It is revealed on every level I might consider: it is in the irony, the humour, the satire. It is in the tragic root and the comic surface. It exists on various levels as subtext – where one thing is never happening without some contradictory thing happening beneath it, or above it, or perhaps within it. It is also there in the many perspectives offered by the different narrators or characters – in a world where there is no narrator telling the reader or the audience member what to think and feel. It is also in the ambiguity that rests in the rendering of character itself – and the different perspectives characters have of one another. It is there regarding dramatic events – whether past or present – which are disputed, misrepresented, regarded with a healthy scepticism.

   The oedipal thread that runs through these works can only go so far in illuminating them.[10] Thanks to the complexity of consciousness, we remain unfathomable and inexhaustible. As the plays and the novel argue very directly and consistently, there is never one of anyone. It seems, as a writer, that I only start to become satisfied with a piece of my own writing when it has acquired the layeredness of a poem – or a rainbow cake. When at each moment more

---

10   One could argue that most writers write out of the family dynamics they grew up in. Absent fathers, complicated sisters and unreliable mothers dominate my plays and fiction. When we start to write, we write about what we know about and are invested in. But we also write in order to explore what we don't yet know or care about. We like to imagine what we might yet *become* as much as we like to imagine what we once were.

than one thing is going on – and the layers are always there, depending on how deep you are prepared to push the knife.

This idea of being in two places at the same time was something I was first struck by a few months ago while reading *At Last*, the final book in Edward St Aubyn's Patrick Melrose novels. He writes: "Forget heroin. Just try giving up irony, that deep-down need to mean two things at once, to be in two places at once, not to be there for the catastrophe of a fixed meaning."[11] Anyone who knows anything about St Aubyn will know that the writer was repeatedly raped as a small boy by his father, became a heroin addict – and took a long time to find release, through sublimation, in art.

St Aubyn also felt ambiguous about his upbringing. He was born into a very wealthy upper class English family that had a chateau in the south of France – and as a boy, abandoned by an absent alcoholic mother and anyone else who might have come to his aid, he learned to develop a deep ambivalence towards this rarefied section of humanity. As a boy, I lived alone with my mother and sister in a modest suburb, and yet we should remember that the accident took place in the early eighties in apartheid South Africa – and that my mother had only a few years before left what was then called Rhodesia with her children at the height of a bloody civil war. I lived in a beautiful land, but there was always a scar running through the heart of it – both in Rhodesia and South Africa. I wrote in my most recent novel *The White Room* that growing up in apartheid South Africa was like being in an abusive relationship in which you never knew whether you were the abuser or the abused.[12] Probably, at least as a young white South African, you were both.

I grew up with a strong sense of shame – and towards adolescence and as I grew more aware of my real surroundings – that shame extended itself towards the idea of being South African itself. That shame has never really left me – as my country continues to remain difficult to embrace. As a white, English-speaking, male writer, of course, I am continually questioning my own place as much as I question the place I find myself in. I am trapped in my own body and my own circumstances – just as I was trapped in my mother's car – and am both free and not free to do anything about it. What does shame do? It makes us dissociate. We step back, hide, hope we aren't exposed – and named and humiliated. We hope the gaze of those with power over us – whether it be real or perceived – will move away from us and alight on some more satisfying candidate. From a place of shame, we can also sublimate or dissociate. We can

---

11   Edward St Aubyn, *The Patrick Melrose Novels: Never Mind, Bad News, Some Hope, Mother's Milk, At Last* (London: Picador, 2014), 760.

12   At the time of writing, the novel is still being finalized so no page reference is possible.

project our shame back onto what is other and shame it, and reduce it to one fixed meaning, or we can find a way that opens up our own freedom and the freedom of all those we choose to engage with – whether these be fictional characters in a play or real people we encounter at the shops.

5   The Dialogic Imagination

At university, I was drawn to the continental philosophers – and Sartre in particular helped me to shape my own experience of the world, both in looking back and looking forward. I would also read many works of fiction and a great deal of commentary on fiction itself. One of the critics I came upon – although he is such a good critic he is more of an artist, a poet – is the Russian writer Bakhtin, whose books on Rabelais and Dostoevsky made a deep impression on me. In *The Dialogic Imagination*, Bakhtin contrasts the novel with the epic. The epic is set in a valourised past, is completed, uncontaminated by the present, unchanging and internally coherent. The novel, on the other hand, is an omnivorous mode of storytelling that draws into itself all other genres and is firmly rooted in the messiness of the contingent. It is open-ended, incomplete, formless – most importantly, it is alive, liberated and liberating in its aesthetic and ethic. It is the genre of becoming.[13] But the European novel, especially during the nineteenth century in England, started to lose its subversive folk roots and become an opportunity for the writer to express his or her own world view. We read Dickens, Tolstoy and Balzac in order to find out what Dickens, Tolstoy and Balzac thought. The remote, god-like wordsmith in Flaubert and the dialogic visionary in Dostoevsky, doing battle with forces of darkness and forces of light, were at odds with the time – and pre-empt Modernism and Post-Modernism respectively. Isaiah Berlin in *The Hedgehog and the Fox* also famously divided writers and thinkers into two categories: those who view the world through a single defining idea, those who know one big thing, and those who know lots of smaller things and shape their way in the world through the constant interplay of contradictory ideas and experiences.

For me, the Socratic notion of dialogue is as fundamental to western theatre as that of Aristotelian catharsis. Socrates only understood what he thought once he had tested his ideas out with an argument. And what is a piece of dramatic writing for the stage if not an argument – a range of conflicting perspectives placed into a heightened space and doing battle with each other until some fresh perspective or new understanding is encountered and publically

---

13   Mikhail Bakhtin, *The Dialogic Imagination* (Austin: University of Texas Press, 1981), xxxii.

asserted? Often, the playwright's perspective is located somewhere between the different voices and is not embedded in any one character. Shakespeare – perhaps our greatest dramatist – is famously hard to locate in his work – although there are threads and themes that are developed and that after some time start to feel like a personal quest, a philosophical investigation that is so relentlessly pursued that by the end it begins to feel deeply personal. Interestingly too, in Shakespeare's case, we aren't satisfied that one person who'd grown up in Stratford can ever have written all those plays. We forget that Shakespeare – like the rest of us – was never only one person. There is never one of any of us. What Shakespeare could do better than most of us is let the different parts of him fly off and develop their own perspectives – their own multiple personalities – so that out of one man's imagination we begin to find a maquette for the cosmos. Dostoevsky, at least through the lens of Bakhtin, showed me how this dialogic way of narrating a story or staging a series of dramatic events has been used in fiction as much as the theatre.

6   Engagement and Scepticism

I would like to remind us of that deeply existentialist word "engagement" – especially in the context of today, both in South Africa and more generally. Because having irony and dialogue at the heart of your creative work may seem like fence-sitting, or like hedging your bets. It may also seem like a strategy to rig the conversation – so that the white male artist, in this case, can pretend not to be there but can still surreptitiously orchestrate the whole endeavour to his own ends. Here the artist is the puppeteer, the ventriloquist, the dark magician trying to hoodwink the reader or audience into seeing the world in his or her own way. In this version of the creative act, all art is about promoting the self-interest of the artist – and the artwork can later be used as evidence of the imposition of the will of the creator onto an unsuspecting and passive audience.

But it is also true that we write in order to send a provocation out into the world. We want to shift something in the audience – and perhaps by doing so shift something in the world. Even if our first desire is simply to entertain. Much of the meaning of a literary work resides in the point of view – and how that point of view subjugates other points of view. Do contrary positions or positions that are considered in some way "other" have the illusion of agency and autonomy? Do their fictional lives give the illusion of transcending the framework of the artwork? Does our representation of what is other or even antagonistic feel like caricature or a failed attempt at a complex representation?

In a dialogic artwork, the act of representation knows it is inadequate before it even starts. In fact, it starts from this place – of insisting on its own subjectivity and on the subjectivity of all that is outside of it. It also knows that it is a metaphorical and not a literal space – that it doesn't represent the outside world but stands as an alternative to it – it is an elaborate hall of mirrors that now and again might reflect back at us snippets that we recognise from our own lives. In the dialogic artwork, it is up to the reader or the audience to draw these mirrors together in order to find a coherent image that stands for themselves.

It may be useful, in closing, to describe the process I like to go through when I write. My desk is in the small room adjoining our bedroom and I sit down, switch on my lamp and open my computer. Usually within a few moments I begin to type. Into the void. Each blank page becomes the site for a new pathway, a new experiment into the unknown. I am setting off like an arctic fox, nosing the air, seeking out a new den or a new source of nourishment. Each story world provides an opportunity to be somewhere else, somewhere I am not. Each character provides an opportunity to be someone else, someone I am not. I write in order to dissociate myself from what I am and what surrounds me and sublimate myself into something else – some new opportunity for growth. I often say that for me writing is never about writing what you know, or what you think you know. It is about setting off into the unknown – and finding a song to sing as you go there.

Yesterday, I was a talking dog. Today, I shall be a fox. Tomorrow, for all I know, I may find I was a hedgehog all along. What is most important, however, is to keep regaining the knowledge that I am free, and that I am forever in a state of becoming. The act of setting off is what establishes that I am still alive – and I set off with the happy knowledge that arrival will forever elude me.

But if our engagement is to be inclusive, and as respectful of the freedoms of others as it is of our own, we also have to retain a degree of ironic disengagement – of scepticism regarding our own positioning. This desire to be in two places at the same time can become a kind of trap, as we have seen – it can become compulsive rather than voluntary. Yet it should be voluntary – and for me in my own practice it is also mandatory. Disengagement while being engaged is essential because it provides that shard of scepticism, of provisionality, of open-endedness, that should accompany all healthy fiction-making. We are never writing the truth. We do not have access to the truth. And this is a cause for celebration, because it renders each of us equal and each of us free. We need this healthy scepticism, this capacity for being in more than one place at the same time, because we are slipping – as South Africans and as people of the world generality – into the same tired absolutes – of race, gender, religion. We are being told time and time again that our whiteness, or queerness, or femaleness, or indeed our god is more important or more defining to us as individuals than our shared humanity. We are erecting walls,[14] hunkering down, preparing ourselves for new wars. And in order to commit violence on someone else, we have to objectify them, we have to turn them into something they are not. We have to nurture myths of difference rather than what Derrida called *differance* – which is about the perpetual deferral of fixed meanings – and of nosing our way back into the unwritten, unprepared territory, where language, when returned to its inexhaustibility, and its capacity to be in more than one place at the same time, does as well at shaping us as anything else.

Works Cited

Anderson, Baxter, Cissna. *Dialogue: Theorising Difference in Communication Studies.* Iowa: University of Iowa Press, 2004.

Bakhtin, Mikhail. *The Dialogic Imagination.* Austin: University of Texas Press, 1981.

Bakhtin, Mikhail. *Rabelais and His World.* Austin: University of Texas Press, 2009.

Berlin, Isaiah. *The Hedgehog and the Fox.* Weidenfeld and Nicolson, London, 1953.

Bloom, Harold. *The Anxiety of Influence* (second edition). Oxford: Oxford University Press, 1997.

Freud, Sigmund. *The Pelican Freud Library: Volume 4, The Interpretation of Dreams.* London: Penguin Books, 1985.

Freud, Sigmund. *The Pelican Freud Library: Volume 11, On Metapsychology: The Theory of Psychoanalysis.* London: Penguin Books, 1985.

Freud, Sigmund. *The Pelican Freud Library: Volume 14, Art and Literature.* London: Penguin Books 1985.

Higginson, Craig. *The Dream House.* Johannesburg: Picador Africa, 2015.

Higginson, Craig. *The Hill.* Johannesburg: Jacana, 2005.

Higginson, Craig. *Three Plays: Dream of the Dog, The Girl in the Yellow Dress, The Imagined Land.* London: Oberon Books, 2016.

Joyce, James. *A Portrait of the Artist as a Young Man.* London: Grafton Books, 1987.

Laplanche, Jean and Jean-Bertrand Pontalis. *The Language of Psychoanalysis.* Translated by Donald Nicholson-Smith. London: Karnac Books and the Institute of Psycho-analysis, 1988.

Sartre, Jean-Paul. *Being and Nothingness.* New York: Washington Square Press, 1992.

St Aubyn, Edward. *The Patrick Melrose Novels: Never Mind, Bad News, Some Hope, Mother's Milk, At Last.* London: Picador, 2014.

---

14   The speech was written not long after Donald Trump famously stated that he would make the Mexicans pay for the wall along the border between Mexico and the United States.

CHAPTER 4

Theatre of the Native Tongue

Omphile Molusi

Abstract

As a black South African playwright, I have always thought only the best plays are written in English. I was wrong. This realization has forced me to confront my own colonized state of mind and how the English language has robbed us of our native tongues and sense of history. However, this essay focuses on capturing stories in the native tongue. It touches briefly on how our languages carry our history. But mostly how uncovering the etymology of our words brings us a bit closer to understanding who we are and where our people have been. Then it explores my own writing process of shifting from the English language to my native tongue; from the page to performance to the audience.

This essay explores Vernacular Theatre in South Africa. I prefer calling it Theatre of the native tongue. And so, by vernacular I mean native tongues spoken in South Africa. I used to write in English, but now I write mainly in Setswana, my native tongue. But also, depending on the characters of the world of the play, I turn to write in other native languages like isiZulu, isiXhosa, Sesotho, and Sepedi. I will break down why I have moved from English to my Native tongue in four categories:

One – A bit of history
Two – Writing in my language
Three – Acting in the native tongue
Four – Audience

So, first, here's a bit of history. In my Tswana culture when we greet we say *Dumela* and the response is *Age*. Dumela in simple terms means Hello. But the word *Dumela* has a lot of history embedded in it. It is a word older than *Hello*. The system of counting years such as A.D and B.C does not really apply to our culture. That was a system first used for church business, put forth by Dionysius Exiguus in 527 or 533 C.E. By then we were already saying *Dumela, Age*. So, if we want to know when we first said *Dumela*, we can't say; it was 2 AD or 5 BC.

And so, when we date back to African ancient times we say, *Lowe*. Just like AC and BC determine time before or after Christ, our starting point of calculating years is LOWE. Lowe as a person, but also Lowe as time. This applies to a Motswana person.

In this essay, I won't go deep into breaking down Lowe. I'm just merely bringing it up to point out that Lowe is as ancient as time itself and that is where *Dumela* came from. And to explain *Dumela*, we must first understand that in my culture, our people were once one with nature. They lived on and depended on all things natural. Medicine came from the plants and the trees. Our food came from the mountains, the rivers and the forests. We could freeze water without the use of the fridge, and this is still practiced today in villages. We knew how to measure time before the clock was invented. We used the sun and the shadow to tell time. We used the moon to tell what month it was before the Western world could use it. Nature was our science, it was our astronomy, our medicine, our education and the list goes on. When my people discovered this science, this astronomy, medicine and others, they said to the other Motswana *Dumela,* which means "believe," and the other could see and replied *Age,* which means I do or *yes.* So, the greeting *Dumela* is not only a greeting, but it connects our people to nature, to who they are, to their history. In isiZulu, when they greet you, they say *Sawubona,* which means "I see you." In Sesotho, *Kgotsong,* "in peace." In IsiXhosa *Tarhuni,* also "in peace." All these words have a deep history embedded in them. We used to have 13 months. Each month had a story that told of the intelligence of that society. Our year, for example, started with September; in Setswana we call it *Lwetse.* It was called like this because Lwala, means "to be sick" but can also mean "to massage." So, around this time, every year, the sky would be sick, or the sky would be massaging the clouds, and so rain would be expected anytime. I would go deeper into each month, unfortunately this is not a Setswana textbook. But just like these words, other native words too have history embedded in them. These words tell us a lot about our history and the societies that lived before us. I know that in English, words have their own etymology as well. Each word takes you back to that time when it was first used. This is what has come to fascinate me about my own language. Once we uncover our words, we get to learn a whole history about ourselves. Sometimes we don't even need to read history books... we can just decode our words and find our history and how we used to live.

This brings me to my second point: writing in my own language. I was born in a village, deep rural Bodibe. And in the villages, people still use these words to greet each other. But in the cities, which is where I live now, it's disappearing. We are using English a lot and we have stopped seeing value in our native languages. We are not aware that in speaking *less* of our native tongues we are slowly killing our own history. We have glorified the English language and we are now even measuring our intelligence by how much English we can speak. I too have always used English to write my work, because I believed that the English language is accessible to all. That the English language is the best language to tell a story.

I've always looked at the etymology of the English words, but never the etymology of the words of my own language. It was only when I started considering my own language as a language I want to tell stories in that I got hooked into my history and I even got to know a bit more about who I am and where my people come from. What I enjoyed most about this process was that it was a liberating experience. I remember the first time I started writing in Setswana, I would sit for hours thinking in English and trying to write in Setswana. This was a painful experience. I was not used to writing in my native tongue. It would take me hours to put together a paragraph. But it would take me a few minutes in English. This depressed me. It made me realise the depth of how colonized I was. I called myself a Motswana, yet I couldn't construct a simple paragraph in five minutes. I had never questioned who I was before, but this forced me to do so. I didn't know who I was anymore. I had embraced the English language for such a long time that I didn't realize that it was eating away who I was. My whole being was English. I don't mind the English language. I speak it every day. But I was just not happy that it had taken control of my mind. It had made me forget my native connection. I felt like English was like a virus in my system. I needed to get rid of this virus. I needed to free myself. I needed to tell stories of my people using their own language. It became a long painful process to find my Setswana pen. I had to write in Setswana every day, read books in Setswana. This was like training muscles in my head. The more I did it, the more I got used to it. It took me a long time, training my muscles and building my vocabulary. I think what helped me was also looking around my surroundings. But before, every time I would try to write a story I would struggle.

The biggest challenge I had was writing characters in English who would normally never speak English in their everyday setting. For example, in the townships, there are places called taverns or shebeens. These are places where you find people who would never communicate in English. Not that they don't like it, but that their default language is their native tongue. And a place like a tavern forces you to go to your default language. Now, if I'm to write two characters seating at a tavern having a beer, it would become hard for me to write these characters in English. I struggle to imagine them like that. So, I end up compromising their authenticity and I write them in English. But when the actors take those roles on, it becomes clear to me that I've written a lie. It's impossible to find those two specific characters speaking English in a tavern. Especially, characters we call *boMgozi*, gossipers. These are characters who have all the news of the township. They know everybody's business. They are like the township-news-channel. But their common attribute is that they are good storytellers. They tell a story like nobody else. Writing them in English would rob you of their authenticity. It would take away from the magic of storytelling created by the words they use. They are wordsmiths, and some of them invent new words every day. You miss the evolution of the native language if you write them in English. You cannot translate what they say into English. The minute you do, the magic is lost. The authenticity is gone.

Another character is the township thug – I struggle to write this character in English – the minute I do – I can even see it on the page that it's a lie. The first words I put down – "Hey you!" anybody can say these words. But a township thug says it like nobody else. *Hei wena!* is one way of saying it, with the action and everything. There's a specific way that a township thug would say these words. And when these words are written in English and we watch an actor saying "Hey you!" instead of *Hei wena!* on stage as a township thug, we know he's not authentic. He's lying to himself. I personally don't connect with his truth as a character. I would believe him if he was joking or trying to mock somebody. This is the same as two grannies speaking to each other. I can't imagine them speaking in English. This applies to a plethora of characters in the black world. And so, in my writing, I mostly levitate towards representing the township and village world. Thus, I have shifted from English to my native tongue. I find that as a black theatre maker of these times I have loved and embraced writing stories in English, but in doing this I realize that I have neglected representing my people truthfully. I think I enjoy the authenticity of creating characters that speak their truth on stage as they would in real life.

Currently, a lot of the stories that are told in the theatres are about decolonisation and identity. This was never a new conversation. This conversation has been going on for years. But recently, in the universities, the students demonstrated against colonisation. They wanted education decolonised in universities. The problem is much deeper than this, but these demonstrations sparked a huge debate in the country about decolonisation and African identity. From this, new plays were written, and among them was a play called *The Fall* by drama graduates from the University of Cape Town (UCT), facilitated by Clare Stopford, and directed by Ameera Conrad and Thando Mangcu, two members of the ensemble. The play shares the cast's experience during the #Rhodesmustfall and subsequent students' movements.

At this point, I was contemplating writing in Setswana. I was then very fortunate to be part of a production called *Lepatata*, which was written totally in

Setswana by an Amazing Setswana writer, Moagi Modise. This production became the first ever professional native tongue production to be staged at the Market Theatre 40 years after it opened. This production made me realise how much valuable our languages are. It also made me realize that acting in my language makes it easy for me to be authentic. And amongst everything that was happening in the country regarding decolonisation, it made me curious to learn more about my own language, not just as a writer, but also as a performer.

Which brings me to my third point, acting in the native tongue. First and foremost, English was never my first language. I was never good at English at School. I learned a lot of my English from American RnB and rap songs. At School, I learned English as a second language. In South Africa, we have two kinds of black actors – those who studied English as a first language in school, and those who learned English as a second language. It is always clear when these two actors are on stage together. You can tell whose English is more polished and whose is not. You can tell who was cast because they speak good English. And I've observed from one theatre play to another that speaking good English does not necessarily make one a good actor, but it gets you a lot of acting roles. I've seen a lot of good actors losing good roles because they can't speak good English. I've observed that actors who studied English as a second language at school struggle with being authentic in their roles. Their English makes them bad actors. They sound unnatural. They sing the language rather than speak it.

I've experimented with students on this. I was told that a certain actor couldn't act. So, I asked him to act in his own language. It was true that in English he was terrible, but the minute he switched to his mother tongue, he became confident. He understood what he was playing. He understood his motivations clearly. In a nutshell, he had fun and everyone's perspective about his acting changed. Everyone thought he was the best actor. This is because language freed him. It liberated him. He said that with English, he had to think a lot about how to speak a line rather than just speak it. If there was a question in a line, the director would keep telling him to really ask the question, but he wasn't sure of how to place it. He wondered about pitching it high or low or somewhere in the middle. He wasn't sure of the tone of it. He was also challenged by the proper English pronunciation of words. A word like *best*, he would pronounce as *burst*. *Work* would be pronounced as *wack*. The list goes on. The actor found himself making a lot of notes, because his mind would be more focused on how to say lines, rather than think about his action, his motivations. But the minute I asked him to play in his language, he started thinking about his actions instead of his lines. He didn't worry about the tone of a question anymore. He just asked a question. The notes became less overwhelming and he could play truthfully. Actors who studied English as a first language at school don't have this problem. They understand the English language. They are natural on stage.

I think in recent years we've been debating identity and decolonisation, but now we're implementing the thoughts that have been boiling in our heads for years. A lot of playwrights are now introducing their native tongues into their work, some are writing purely in it. We are starting to find value in our languages. We are beginning to find our identity. We are on the path of decolonising ourselves. For years, we've been afraid that people are not interested in watching a play in a native tongue; we were wrong. We were worried that South Africa has 11 official languages and that with a mixed audience we needed to communicate in English; we were wrong.

Which brings me to my last point. The audience. People are ready to receive stories in their native tongues. The first play I wrote entirely in my native tongue was *Mogatapele*. A play that deals with issues of decolonisation, but also a play that looks at history and flips it on its head. We experimented with this show with an audience that speaks its language. This is an audience that normally watches plays in English. I don't want to blow my own horn, but we had a lot of conversations after each show with the audience. A lot of the response was about how a show in a native tongue affirms not only the value of language but its power to affect the core of who we are. It reminds us of the power of our languages and why it's important to us. At the end of each run, there wasn't a dry eye in the audience. What confused me was that the play was not intense; it was not a sad story. But what I got from the audience was that the tears were not sad tears, they were tears of appreciation. They were tears of realisation... a realisation that we had devalued our languages. They were also tears of joy ... that finally, we are telling stories in our own languages. Somebody who is a fan of the theatre, who has been watching plays for a long time in English, said: "I'm glad that finally, we are decolonizing the arts." This was the first time I heard these words: "decolonising the arts." From then, I heard it on social media and everywhere. It caught fire and it's spreading.

In the city, the native tongue is dying, but when we did *Lepatata*, it was almost like we had awakened something in people's lives. It was almost like people had forgotten who they are and *Lepatata* reminded them of it. A lot of the audience we spoke to felt that, because Johannesburg is a cosmopolitan city, we find ourselves forced to speak English every day. So, when shows like *Lepatata* are produced, they inspire language to be spoken. But there was also an audience that didn't speak Setswana; some could understand and some couldn't. We didn't even have translation devices. What was fascinating was that this audience understood, language or not. I spoke to a white guy who thoroughly enjoyed the play, thought it was refreshing. I asked him how come he felt this way. He said to me: "I knew I was not going to understand. So, I was not listening with my ears, I was listening with my heart, and with my body. I could follow the emotional arc of the characters. Therefore, it was easy to follow the story." This made it clear to me, that language in the theatre is not a barrier at all. We can bring people to the mainstream theatre by telling stories in our native tongues. We can entertain and inspire people using our native tongues.

Lastly, the idea of using the native tongue to tell stories is not a new idea in South Africa. We come from a culture of oral tradition. Stories have always been told orally, in our native tongues from generation to generation. Some of them recorded and some of them not. Today, we have a lot of playwrights who are embracing that culture of storytelling. Mandla Mbothwe in Cape Town has always been telling beautiful stories in his native Xhosa tongue. Other plays written totally in the native tongue were *Mhla salamana* by Thando Doni, and Thabiso Rammala and MoMo Matsunyane's *TAU*. Sibulele Gclichana and Kgafela wa Magogodi also write in their native tongues. There are also many other aspiring playwrights who are coming up strong with plays in their native tongues like Kagiso Letsholonyana's *Seperekisi*. We are in the process of decolonising ourselves. I won't say what we are doing is right or wrong, but what we know and feel is that it is vitally necessary and important for our times and for generations to come. We're not only writing plays, we are capturing time and history.

CHAPTER 5

Transformation and the Post-apartheid Condition: The Collision of Policy and Imagination in South African Theatre

Mike van Graan

Abstract

Post-apartheid cultural policy was premised on Article 27 of the Universal Declaration of Human Rights "Everyone shall have the right freely to participate in the cultural life of the community and to enjoy the arts...," a fundamental departure from the previous era in which the cultural interests and artistic aspirations of a white minority formed the basis of official cultural policy. But how has this progressive policy played out in practice, particularly as regards theatre? This essay critically examines this question and ends by positing a fresh vision for theatre policy and practice.

1 Introduction

The overview and analyses in this article are based largely on my own experience as a theatre-maker as well as a cultural activist and writer about the arts in South Africa generally, and about theatre in particular.

The 2016 Fleur du Cap Theatre Awards in Cape Town[1] were laced with controversy because of the apparent absence of black nominees and winners (again[2]). The National Arts Festival is marketed as a "democratic space" in which everyone may compete on equal terms, and yet, those who do best at the box office and who win the key awards – generally – still reflect apartheid's beneficence, almost a generation later.[3] Recent anthologies of South African

---

1 The Fleur du Cap Theatre Awards recognise the best theatre produced each year in Cape Town and as determined by a panel of judges.
2 A similar controversy occurred in 2012, see Mike van Graan, "The Fleur du Cap Theatre Awards: Two Steps Forward...?" *mikevangraan*, May 2, 2013, https://mikevangraan.wordpress.com/2013/05/02/the-fleur-du-cap-theatre-awards-two-steps-forward-2/.
3 Mike van Graan, "The National Arts Festival 2014: Beyond the impressive figures and what they might mean for Fringe Theatre," *mikevangraan*, July 20, 2014, https://mikevangraan.

© KONINKLIJKE BRILL NV, LEIDEN, 2020 | DOI:10.1163/9789004414464_006

playwrights and international conferences on South African theatre affirm theatre-makers largely privileged by our history.[4]

Annually, there is much new theatre work – more than 200 productions take place at the country's festivals such as the National Arts Festival, Klein Karoo Nasionale Kunstefees, Woordfees, Zabalaza Arts Festival, etc – but major theatres still resurrect pre-1994 theatre such as *Sarafina* and *Sophiatown*, genuflecting to a "theatre of nostalgia."

Generally, those engaged in theatre-making avoid policy and the macro-conditions in which they are required to produce and distribute theatre, and yet these impact directly on the lives of plays and thus on the livelihoods of theatre-makers. Festivals, awards, anthologies and conference themes reflect the structural challenges in our theatre industry which post-1994 policy was supposed to transform.

How, then, do we address issues of policy so that it impacts on theatre constructively and in transforming our sector in real terms?

2   Pre-1994

The Arts and Culture Task Group (ACTAG) Report commissioned by the post-apartheid government to provide a basis for policy-making in arts, culture and heritage and the subsequent White Paper on Arts, Culture and Heritage adopted by the Cabinet in August 1996, provide insights into how the arts were structured and funded at the time of the democratic changes.

In brief, the pre-1994 theatre dispensation comprised the following:

1. Four provincial performing arts councils, each with its own theatre companies, with actors employed on at least year-long contracts, producing classical and contemporary work in English and Afrikaans; the companies comprised mostly white actors, were subsidised by the state and were required to tour their respective provinces, taking theatre to little towns.

2. Independent theatres such as the Space Theatre, the Baxter Theatre and the Market Theatre that were generally supported by international funding, the private sector, the university (in the case of the Baxter) and the box office, were non-racial in nature and placed a high premium on contemporary work that spoke to apartheid conditions.

---

wordpress.com/2014/07/20/the-national-arts-festival-2014-beyond-the-impressive-figures-and-what-they-might-mean-for-fringe-theatre/.

4   Peter Paul Schnierer, Martin Middeke and Greg Homann (eds), *The Methuen Drama Guide to Contemporary South African Theatre* (London: Bloomsbury Publishing, 2015).

3. Private theatres such as those of Pieter Toerien that – notwithstanding the cultural boycott[5] – mostly staged international work with the purpose of generating profit and wealth for the owners.

4. Independent theatre-makers and companies that worked outside of formal structures and mostly within the communities where their works resonated e.g. Gibson Kente's theatre and the Cape Flats Players.

5. "Struggle" theatre (as opposed to "Protest Theatre" – theatre work with anti-apartheid themes that were staged in formal spaces such as theatres and festivals and which were labelled such by the white theatre establishment) i.e. theatre that was consciously instrumentalized as part of the broader anti-apartheid struggle e.g. theatre at the Community Arts Project in Cape Town, generally supported by international funding.

Tertiary institutions – mainly those serving the white community in the context of apartheid's educational structure – fed the first three, while community-based structures – like the Funda and Fuba Centres and CAP – and raw talent served the latter two.

3 Post-1994 Policy

The 1996 White Paper on Arts, Culture and Heritage[6] adopted a human rights approach premised on Article 27 of the Universal Declaration of Human Rights declaring "everyone shall have the right freely to participate in the cultural life of the community and to enjoy the arts" and the Freedom Charter stating "The doors of learning and culture shall be open." This was in response to the apartheid era policies and public funding for the arts that overwhelmingly favoured the artistic practices and aspirations of white people.

Given the legacies of apartheid in other social spheres, arts and culture policy-makers were obliged to adopt a "five loaves and two fish" approach, essentially using the funds made available to serve white institutions in the past now to serve the arts aspirations of all citizens.

---

5 The Cultural Boycott was one of a series of international strategies (along with a sports boycott, an academic boycott, an oil embargo, disinvestment campaigns, military boycotts, etc.) that sought to isolate the apartheid government and force it towards political change. In terms of the cultural boycott, international artists would not visit South Africa nor make their works available to South Africa and those artists deemed to be supporters of the apartheid government were not allowed to perform abroad.

6 "White Paper on Arts, Culture and Heritage," *Department: Arts and Culture, Republic of South Africa*, June 4, 1996, http://www.dac.gov.za/content/white-paper-arts-culture-and-heritage-0.

The primary policies in the White Paper related to theatre envisaged the following:

a.   the downscaling and break-up of the performing arts councils with their infrastructure being turned into "receiving houses" accessible to all (rather than only for the use of their in-house companies).

b.   their arts companies would become independent entities, not attached to the infrastructure, and diversify their funding with declining national state subsidies over three years.

c.   the savings from the performing arts councils would be channelled through a new structure, the National Arts Council, that would democratise access to public resources (as would its provincial equivalents), with all practitioners invited to apply for public funding support.

d.   community arts centre infrastructure would be developed across the country to facilitate creation and distribution of local productions and provide access for local communities to national work through tours.

4   Post-1994 Practice

The following are some of what transpired in practice, sometimes because of, sometimes despite policy:

While there had been a recommendation that the performing arts councils' infrastructure be devolved to the cities and/or provinces in which they were located (since they served city rather than national populations and in order to free up resources), this did not take place as, at the time, to devolve an item to a lower tier of government, would require the relevant resources to be devolved too. Accordingly, the performing arts infrastructure has remained the responsibility – and budgetary burden – of national government.

Given its anti-apartheid role, the Department of Arts and Culture added the Market Theatre to its list of theatres to be subsidised. The 2016/17 budget for the national theatres amounted to R220m plus R92m for capital works for a total of R312 m.[7] (As a policy question, it has to be debated – again – if this is the best use of this amount of money annually for theatre and for the citizens of the country in terms of how they could access and benefit from theatre).

---

7   "2016 Budget, Estimates of National Expenditure: Arts and Culture," *Department: National Treasury, Republic of South Africa*, Feb. 24, 2016, http://www.treasury.gov.za/documents/national%20budget/2016/enebooklets/Vote%2037%20Arts%20and%20Culture.pdf.

There are three nationally-subsidised theatres in the country's wealthiest province – Gauteng (State Theatre, Market Theatre, Windybrow Theatre) – with the City of Johannesburg also subsidising the Joburg Theatre, the Roodepoort Theatre and the Soweto Theatre. On the other hand, there are no nationally-subsidised theatres in the country's poorer provinces – Limpopo, Mpumalanga, Northern Cape, North West and Eastern Cape – thereby making a mockery of the 1996 White Paper's goal of opening the doors of learning and culture to "all."

Initial support for establishing new and renovating existing art centres was gleaned from the ministry then responsible for Reconstruction and Development, but without local government support for the operational and programming costs of these, most centres ended up as white elephants. The absence of viable infrastructure at local levels has continued to deny most citizens access to theatre.

The "receiving house" policy with the nationally-subsidised theatres not being provided with subsidies to produce and buy work, meant that while the infrastructure was theoretically open to all, it was those who had resources – primarily those who had benefited from the apartheid past – who could access these theatre spaces. The "receiving houses" did little to promote or market the independent companies and theatre makers who hired their theatres.

As they are annual recipients of large public subsidies, the theatre infrastructure has not been immune to resource-contestation and battles to run such spaces and benefit from the large salaries allocated to management; "transformation" generally meant replacing a white with a black elite at the top.

Theatre companies were the first companies to be scrapped by the management of the former performing arts councils when funding was cut as a result of policy; this was done in favour of preserving the opera, ballet and orchestra companies that were believed would best continue to be able to use the infrastructure. The managements at two performing arts councils – the Cape Performing Arts Board (CAPAB) and the Performing Arts Council of Transvaal (PACT) – terminated the contracts of the theatre companies at their respective institutions while maintaining the opera, ballet and classical music companies. Actors – more so than dancers, opera singers or orchestra members – could find work in the growing television, film and commercial industries and be employed in theatre on an ad hoc basis.

The white Afrikaans community, with the loss of political power in 1994, believed that their language was under threat so that – with the aid of private capital – an Afrikaans festival circuit emerged, providing incentives and work opportunities for the Afrikaans-speaking theatre community.[8] Parallel theatre worlds emerged with the former performing arts council infrastructure now serving "black" people and theatre makers, while the Afrikaans festival circuit catered for the needs of the white Afrikaans community. "Social cohesion" and "nation-building" strategies were largely meaningless in this regard.

As opposed to the apartheid era, black theatre-makers no longer needed white intermediaries to access funding; they could now go directly to provincial arts councils and the NAC so that the non-racial theatre of the apartheid era, declined somewhat.

In line with the mantra at the time, subsidised theatres were demographically transformed in terms of their governance, management and staff so that they more fairly reflected the communities they were required to serve. However, at the time that they faced their biggest financial challenges with the cuts being made to their subsidies, they also had their most inexperienced leaders (many of whom had not attended the theatres they were now responsible for, whether for political or other reasons). This resulted in some of these theatres facing existential threats through poor investments in schemes that they thought would deliver quick and substantial financial gains, but which resulted in mass job losses.

Programming of subsidised infrastructure generally took on a "transformation by numbers" approach (presenting shows that were written, directed and performed by black people, hence, for instance, the appointment of Mbongeni Ngema at the Playhouse Company and his production of his musicals in that space) rather than being premised on a more fundamental vision rooted in strategies that would grow human capacity, aesthetic innovation and quality.

As for the National Arts Council, their initial funding approach was a "Father Christmas" one, doling out small amounts of funding to a number of theatre companies or theatre-makers rather than investing substantially in a few good productions annually.

The NAC did provide "company funding" to support companies but this was ad hoc and irregular, so that companies could not rely on this funding to be sustainable.

While they have become more adept at using their annual subsidies to stage work, "receiving houses" initially appointed artistic directors with little or no budgets to buy, commission or produce new work, so that the artistic

---

8 Temple Hauptfleisch, "In Search of The Rainbow: The Little Karoo National Arts Festival and The Search for Cultural Identity in South Africa," *Libopedia: Stellenbosch University wiki*, http://wiki.lib.sun.ac.za/images/c/c0/Hauptfleisch_Insearch_2007.pdf.

programme came to be determined by outside hirers (and income was generated through non-theatre events such as weddings, church services and conferences which sometimes received preferential treatment to theatre work that generated less income).

There is a need – and much political pressure – for "development" of new human resources (creative and technical), plays, etc, but development costs money and requires long-term investment. However, resources would often be spent on ad hoc projects to tick "development" boxes so that, for example, in the Fleur du Cap theatre awards in Cape Town, there are seldom black Africans who are nominated – let alone win – in technical categories such as lighting, costumes, set design (and even in categories such as directing).

Black theatre-makers are able to get to the National Arts Festival in Grahamstown, still the country's premier "national platform" for the performing arts, but with a market that is still overwhelmingly white on the one hand, and on the other, the lack of brand names, the lack of marketing capacity, the poor production values because of limited funding, result in many of these productions struggling to generate audiences, income and the momentum to project their work beyond the festival.

The current divides within the theatre community reflect a white elite (Afrikaans festivals, theatres with white artistic directors), a non-racial elite (Model C – formerly white schools, tertiary-trained individuals), a black elite around black artistic directors at subsidised spaces and largely black theatre-makers on the periphery, both in major centres but especially in poorer provinces.

Theatre remains largely an elite practice. Those who have access to it – geographically, financially, aesthetically – are generally part of an economic elite, although it is one that is more "multi-racial" than before. With more than 50% of the population living below the poverty line, the original White Paper's promise to make the arts accessible to all has floundered through a lack of vision and poor implementation of policy.

The absence of theatre infrastructure nationally means that citizens are denied access to theatre, but also that at best, practitioners tour a show within their home city, perhaps a festival (or two) and a second city, with the play having a limited life and income-stream.

Many actors do find lucrative work in television, movies and commercials, so that to sustain the life of a theatre piece is very challenging, given that they are more inclined to take up a job in television, and theatre is not able to remunerate them at the levels that television can.

Increasing numbers of theatre-makers are finding opportunities to tour their plays abroad and to earn income in international currencies, but then there are also gate-keepers who protect their avenues to these circuits.

5   Summary

In summary, post-apartheid policy and practice has
- placed an inappropriate "creative industries" policy burden on theatre to sustain itself largely in the market place, favouring those who have skills, reputation and resources.
- allocated huge sums of funding to infrastructure that serves an urban elite and continues to deny access to theatre to the majority of SA's citizens.
- largely failed to provide the vision, the strategies and the funding fundamentally to transform the industry and the role of the industry within SA, other than through superficial demographic institutional "transformation"
- failed to put practical "social cohesion" strategies into place so that racial divides e.g. Afrikaans/other, persist.
- while there has been much demographic change, there has been little *structural* change so that awards, festivals, etc continue to reflect historical privilege.

6   Towards an Alternate Vision

Based on the Discussion Document – *Towards a Vision and Strategies for the development of the South African theatre*[9] – the following would be ideal features of a dance and theatre practice.

1. One nationally-subsidised theatre in Polokwane, Nelspruit, Mahikeng, Kimberley, Pretoria, Johannesburg, Bloemfontein, Durban, Pietermaritzburg, East London, Port Elizabeth and Cape Town, with these comprising a national circuit of theatres, able to support national tours by theatre and dance companies, and with production budgets to purchase, commission and co-produce work.
2. Artistic directors are to serve a maximum of five years at state-subsidised theatres.
3. An independent theatre company of 10 and an independent dance company of 12, each at least 80% black and 50% women, resident at each of the nationally-subsidised theatres; such companies to be assured of 3-year core funding.

---

9   Mike van Graan, "Towards a policy and strategies for the growth of South African theatre," *mikevangraan*, Dec.16, 2014, https://mikevangraan.wordpress.com/2014/12/16/towards-a-policy-and-strategies-for-the-growth-of-south-african-theatre/.

4. A resident director and/or playwright and/or choreographer based at each of the nationally-subsidised theatres on 1 to 3-year contracts.
5. At least one education and training institution per province offering diploma, degree and certificate courses in dance, theatre, entrepreneurship, marketing, administration, policy, etc.
6. At least 50 multi-functional art centres located throughout all nine provinces, with highly skilled administrators/managers (rather than political deployees) running them.
7. A network of 10–15 festivals meeting with the managers of the national circuit of venues to plan, co-produce national tours by dance and theatre productions.
8. A touring agency with at least ten theatre and ten dance productions travelling abroad that year.
9. A national database of 10 000 people making their living in the dance and theatre sectors, each receiving a monthly newsletter about developments in their sector.
10. An online archive of all theatre and dance productions of the previous two years.
11. Nine provincial (primary and secondary) schools' dance and theatre festivals.
12. Legislated minimum wages for dance and theatre workers and approved remuneration scales used by all theatres, festivals and independent companies.
13. Social security for dancers and theatres with customized medical, pension and unemployment schemes.
14. A Code of Conduct adopted across the dance and theatre sectors, with a Labour Ombudsman and a Protector-type agency in place to take up issues on behalf of those who are abused within the sector.
15. An annual national theatre and/or dance conference, with monthly public forums and a national dance and theatre publication.
16. A politically non-partisan national theatre and dance structure that actively monitors, helps to implement and evaluates policies and strategies affecting the dance and theatre sectors.
17. Publicity and marketing entrepreneurs and companies in each of the nine provinces to build audiences and sustainable markets.
18. 150–200 theatre productions and 50–100 dance productions competing for excellence awards on an annual basis.
19. Funding structures and strategies in place that recognize the different functions of theatre and dance, and that assure the sustainability of these sectors.

20. Average audiences and theatre markets in excess of 50% consistently across the country.
21. Constructive and mutually-respectful working relationships between government and funding agencies on the one hand and civil society structures and practitioners on the other.
22. Support initiatives to use existing infrastructure (school and church halls, homes of individuals, etc) for rehearsal and performance space.
23. Artistic directors of the national circuit venues and companies to meet and plan national/regional tours by the companies.
24. Tertiary institutions to audition and host companies for one-year on graduation to learn the practicalities of running an independent company.
25. Theatres/companies to have resident designers, etc to provide work/opportunities for new lighting, costume, stage designers i.e. those in technical fields.
26. A research publication documenting development of theatre and profiling new entrants.
27. Annual playwriting competitions in all languages, indigenous languages in particular.
28. All subsidised venues to have translation/surtitle facilities.
29. Ongoing masterclasses be provided for actors to learn from local and international people who have excelled.

7   Conclusion

Theatre – like all other sectors of our society – reflects the structural legacies of the past and will continue to do so, unless structural interventions are made to change this. For our theatre to be released to achieve its potential, policy makers need to be freed and to have greater imagination. It is only then that our awards systems, our festivals, our anthologies will not only organically reflect the demographics of our country, but also its innovation and quality, without having to compromise these for politically correct purposes.

Works Cited

"2016 Budget, Estimates of National Expenditure: Arts and Culture." *Department: National Treasury, Republic of South Africa.* Feb. 24, 2016. http://www.treasury.gov.za/

documents/national%20budget/2016/enebooklets/Vote%2037%20Arts%20and%20Culture.pdf.

Hauptfleisch, Temple. "In Search of The Rainbow: The Little Karoo National Arts Festival and The Search for Cultural Identity in South Africa." *Libopedia: Stellenbosch University wiki*. http://wiki.lib.sun.ac.za/images/c/co/Hauptfleisch_Insearch_2007.pdf.

Schnierer, Peter Paul, Martin Middeke and Greg Homann (eds). *The Methuen Drama Guide to Contemporary South African Theatre*. London: Bloomsbury Publishing, 2015.

van Graan, Mike. "The Fleur du Cap Theatre Awards: Two Steps Forward...?" *mikevangraan*.May2,2013.https://mikevangraan.wordpress.com/2013/05/02/the-fleur-du-cap-theatre-awards-two-steps-forward-2/.

van Graan, Mike. "The National Arts Festival 2014: Beyond the impressive figures and what they might mean for Fringe Theatre." *mikevangraan*. July 20, 2014. https://mikevangraan.wordpress.com/2014/07/20/the-national-arts-festival-2014-beyond-the-impressive-figures-and-what-they-might-mean-for-fringe-theatre/.

van Graan, Mike. "Towards a policy and strategies for the growth of South African theatre." *mikevangraan*. Dec. 16, 2014.

"White Paper on Arts, Culture and Heritage." *Department: Arts and Culture, Republic of South Africa*. June 4, 1996. http://www.dac.gov.za/content/white-paper-arts-culture-and-heritage-0.

PART 2

Dramatic, Theatrical and Performance Reconfigurations

∵

Performing Athol Fugard's Outsider Art in *The Road to Mecca* and *The Painted Rocks at Revolver Creek*: Transformative Art Defies Percepticide

Marcia Blumberg

Abstract

Athol Fugard's two powerful plays set in South Africa focus on the transformative role of the arts by outsider artists. *The Road to Mecca* (1984) is based on the life and outsider art of Helen Martins in the Karoo village of Nieu Bethesda. Her Owl House and sculpture garden, known as the Camel Yard, represent her vision of Mecca. Fugard's most recent play, *The Painted Rocks at Revolver Creek* (2015), was inspired by the life of another outsider artist, Nukain Mabuza, an aging farm laborer, who lived in Barberton and generated his own domain by painting rocks on a nearby *koppie* in brilliant colors to enliven his bleak world. Although these painted rocks have deteriorated over the decades, they have been metaphorically materialized through the transformative art of theatre.

Outsider Art represents exclusion and marginalization in terms of well-defined categories of modern or contemporary art movements.[1] Yet at the same time the term offers a creative energy and an aesthetic that commands attention and ironically forms its own class of inclusion. Although mostly untrained, these outsider artists have created settings or visionary environments that can be found throughout the world. Some of these creators are often inspired to build highly personalized homes or living areas that frequently combine architecture, sculpture and landscaping in ways contrary to local traditions or building codes. More importantly, these places are usually threatening norms and can have socio-political ramifications.

---

1 My thanks to Marc Maufort and Jessica Maufort for organizing a stimulating conference on South African theatre in Brussels in May 2017. Special thanks to Paula Fourie and Athol Fugard for giving me the script of his newest play. It has recently been published by Samuel French in an acting edition. Fugard acknowledges Nukain Mabuza for inspiration and expresses gratitude for provocation to Paula Fourie who co-directed the play with him in New York and South Africa.

© KONINKLIJKE BRILL NV, LEIDEN, 2020 | DOI:10.1163/9789004414464_007

Athol Fugard has written two powerful plays set in South Africa about the transformative role of the arts by outsider artists, who represent the typical categories of exclusion and marginalization. In a 2015 interview, Fugard emphasized the personal resonances of this phenomenon for himself: "Strange as it may seem, I consider myself an outsider artist."[2] Indeed, his acclaimed play, *The Road to Mecca* (1984), is based on the life and outsider art of Helen Martins in the Karoo village of Nieu Bethesda. Her Owl House and sculpture garden, filled with statues made of cement, wire, paint, and broken glass, known as the Camel Yard, represent her vision of Mecca. While the latter has "its own logic,"[3] despite Martins' suicide in 1976, both the Owl House and the Camel Yard have to this day been preserved as a national treasure attracting local and overseas visitors.

Over a period of fifteen years, Helen Martins, with the aid of three different assistants, visualized, instructed, shaped, and created her world. Ann Emslie argues that "the work challenges definitions of art just as Miss Helen herself challenges conventional notions of the artist."[4] Now a museum which draws many visitors to its remote location, The Owl House and The Camel Yard offer more than a mere setting for the play. They constitute what Foucault calls a heterotopia, "a site in relation with other sites but in such a way as to neutralize or invert the set of relations they happen to designate, mirror, or reflect."[5] Thus, in Helen Martins' garden, sculptures re-presenting aspects of the Nativity scene are juxtaposed with figures of peacocks, owls, beer-bottle temples, human and hybridized forms, all of which refuse conventional linkages and realize one woman's vision challenging Western art, cultural structures, and routine assumptions. This real unreal place, therefore, forms a Foucauldian counter-site; the wonder-world with its disruption of norms proves celebratory for the artist and her admirers, while it appears extremely threatening to the conservative villagers.

Fugard's most recent play is *The Painted Rocks at Revolver Creek* (2015). It was inspired by the life of another outsider artist, Nukain Mabuza, an aging farm laborer, who lived in Barberton in the province of Mpumalanga, and generated his own domain by painting rocks on a nearby *koppie* [small hill] in brilliant colors, producing flowers and geometrical patterns to enliven his bleak world. The artist, JFC Clarke, has published articles, a catalogue and a book to

---

2   Roslyn Sulcas. "Athol Fugard Tells of a Great Outsider Artist." *New York Times* (New York, NY) April 29, 2015.
3   Athol Fugard, *The Road to Mecca* (London: Samuel French, Inc., 1985), 39.
4   Ann Emslie, *The Owl House* (London: Viking Penguin, 1991), 9.
5   Michel Foucault, "Of Other Spaces," *Diacritics* 16, no. 1 (Spring 1986): 24.

represent the splendor of Mabuza's vision and included interviews with people who knew him prior to his suicide in 1981. The site itself has been at the
mercy of the elements and has unfortunately deteriorated in the past decades
but the painted rocks at Revolver Creek have, however, been metaphorically
materialized through the transformative art of theatre. How do art and performance play a role in creating the inclusion of this outsider art from an aesthetic viewpoint? My essay explores common aspects of Fugard's two plays,
especially the transformative nature of art and the significant and inevitable
imbrication of art in the socio-politics of South Africa. Beginning with a brief
analysis of *The Road to Mecca*, it concentrates mostly on *The Painted Rocks at
Revolver Creek*, seeking to examine how Fugard's fictionalized vision of the
new political milieu of post-apartheid South Africa employs Mabuza's art to
alter the modality of expression and focuses on the aspiration for putative reconciliation and inclusion.

Fugard's first play about an outsider artist, *The Road to Mecca*, is set in a rural
village in 1974 during apartheid and centers on the devoted friendship between
the septuagenarian artist, Miss Helen, and a young Cape Town school teacher,
Elsa Barlow. Having inadvertently made a travel stop in Nieu Bethesda about
five years earlier, the latter was amazed at the sight of the Camel yard and over-
whelmed by the interior of the Owl House, especially when the artist performed the ritual of candle lighting in a room filled with colored glass and mirrors, thus offering a vision of radiance and vivacity. Elsa's appreciation of this
artistic vision provided a huge boost for Helen: "You revived my life."[6] It con-
trasted markedly with the stories of stones thrown at her house and statues by
the village children as well as the opprobrium meted out by the rural community at what they considered the monsters this "mad woman" had created: "cement monstrosities."[7] This Afrikaner community, which Elsa regards as "merciless as the religion they preach"[8] castigated Helen for abandoning the Church
as a new widow in order to create her art, referred to by the pastor, Marius
Beyleveld, as her "hobby ... a form of idolatry."[9] They also consider her "a genuine Karoo nutcase ... Mad as a hatter."[10] Elsa's vindication of her friend is
unequivocal:

---

6   Athol Fugard, *The Road to Mecca*, 39.
7   *Ibid.*, 79.
8   *Ibid.*, 22.
9   *Ibid.*, 77.
10   *Ibid.*, 33.

> Those statues out there *are* monsters ... they express Helen's freedom ...
> She has challenged me into an awareness of myself and my life and my
> responsibilities to both that I never had until I met her. There's a hell of a
> lot of talk about freedom ... But it's mostly talk ... Not with Helen. She's
> lived it.[11]

The most thrilling aspect of the staging, however, is the transformative role of
the artistic creations both for the outsider artist herself, her friend, who witnesses the process, and for the audience who engage with awe at the spectacle
being dramatized.

The Road to Mecca is a complex and powerful theatre work that examines
the trajectory of the artist and the transformative nature of her work. It also
includes the dynamics of an intense female friendship, issues of trust and betrayal, the dilemma of abortion, victimhood and agency, and the dichotomy
between rural Afrikaners and urban liberal English perspectives, all within the
context of the oppressive structures of apartheid. The play is also a more restrained exploration of South African politics through, on the one hand, Elsa's
anti-apartheid activism and her conviction that she should act subversively in
teaching her class in a Colored school: "Rebellion starts, Miss Helen, with just
one man or woman, standing up and saying: 'No. Enough!' Albert Camus.
French writer."[12] On the other hand, the play explores the effects of the Calvin-
ist vision of Afrikaners in Nieu Bethesda. However, it remains more muted in
its critique of the positioning of the offstage characters: Katrina, a Colored domestic worker, who is a friend of Miss Helen, and Patience, a young Black
woman with a baby, whom Elsa meets on the road.

Impacting on the performative journeys of Helen and Elsa are the narrativ-
ized journeys of Patience and Katrina, whose absent presence stresses a differential of marginalization. Unlike Helen's celebration of marginality as freedom to fulfil her artistic creativity, their narrativization, s/cited in the interstices
of the white characters' enactments, foregrounds double disempowerment:
Katrina and Patience are marked as racial and gendered Other. We are also
constantly visually reminded that two of them, the white women, are represented on stage. As the women of color are spoken about only when they impact on racially privileged people, this dynamic re-iterates structures of domination, processes of exploitation, and the issue of (in)visibility. The lengthy
expository first act lays the groundwork for the disclosure of Helen's present
artistic sterility. Concomitantly, Elsa's anguish at the termination of her affair

---

11   *Ibid.*, 76–77.
12   *Ibid.*, 30.

with a married man is juxtaposed with the seemingly disconnected vexation at her fortuitous meeting with Patience, on the road to New Bethesda. This brief encounter, to which she repeatedly refers, initially appears as an off-stage reported event but by the end of the play is central to Elsa's crisis. Fugard's first title, *My English Name is Patience*, highlights this encounter as the site of contestation of several discourses; that this ventriloquized voice is rendered visible and significant by the title emphasizes Patience's position of disempowerment in the play. Dennis Walder maintains that

> marginalizing Patience, Fugard endorses the status quo while obscuring this move by smothering it in liberal guilt. And the acceptance of her English name ... blocks the possibility ... of defiance, if not affirmation, by constructing the black woman as suffering object.[13]

Elsa terms Patience's plight "a good old South African story";[14] here, the death of a black farm labourer signifies the cessation of use-value and prompts the summary eviction of his destitute wife and baby. Elsa recounts this narrative, in which she seems to be inextricably linked to the woman, "about my age."[15] Although she recalls Patience's belongings, a baby and a bag filled with meagre goods, it takes the course of the play's action for her to comprehend the full implications of any comparison between herself and Patience. Although destitution dogs Patience, as is evident from the small bag of worldly possessions, she does carry her baby, whom, we learn by the end of the play, signifies for Elsa the seemingly unattainable riches of motherhood in the light of her own recent abortion. It is important to heed Chandra Talpede Mohanty's *caveat*: "Sisterhood cannot be assumed on the basis of gender; it must be forged in concrete historical and political practice and analysis."[16] Fugard's 1974 setting contains Patience and Katrina in a cycle of injustice, which is partially marked by the problematic rendering of voice. Dennis Walder cites this play in acknowledging the complicit relationship between literary texts and socio-political contexts:

---

13 Dennis Walder. "'My English name is patience': Mediating the voice of the other in South African theatre today," *Contemporary Theatre Review* 9, no. 2 (Jan. 1999): 56.

14 Athol Fugard, *The Road to Mecca*, 21.

15 *Ibid.*

16 Chandra Talpede Mohanty, "Cartographies of Struggle: Third World Women and the Politics of Feminism," in *Third World Women and the Politics of Feminism*, eds. Chandra Mohanty, Ann Russo, and Lourdes Torres (Bloomington: Indiana UP, 1991), 58.

> *The Road to Mecca registers* the voice of the black Other ... but it is a representation which echoes the failure of the dominant English-language liberal tradition, a failure fully to acknowledge the voiceless, even as it gestures towards their presence.[17]

I suggest that the play ventriloquizes rather than "registers" the voice of the women of color and that their lack of voice in the socius represents their concretization solely in the speech acts of their white sisters.

The play ends with Elsa's affirmation of Helen as an artist, when she suggests that Helen's problems may be caused by a "grave" omission of one creature amongst her myriad statues: "You've never made an angel ... I think that they would leave you alone if you did."[18] Miss Helen's mischievous retort manifests her sense of humor:

> Bethesda doesn't need more of those. The cemetery is full of them ... all wings and halos ... But if I did ... I'd have it pointing to the East. Where else? I'd misdirect all the good Christian souls around here and put them on the Road to Mecca.[19]

This outsider artist has obsessively concretized her personal vision in the creation of her world with a logic of its own, which disrupts conformist ideas and aesthetic categories to delight, restore souls, or alternatively threaten those with rigid and normative views. Helen Martins' transformative art has made its mark.

The other outsider artist, Nukain Mabuza, inspired *The Painted Rocks at Revolver Creek,* Fugard's newest play (2015), which received acclaimed productions in New York, Los Angeles, and Cape Town, at the Fugard theatre, named for the playwright. The play has a two-act structure set decades apart (1981 and 2003). The oppressive apartheid world of Mabuza is examined in Act One and sets the stage for a contrasting but related fictionalized event on the same *koppie* on the farm *Vredewater* [Free water] in Act Two in the post-apartheid era. At this stage, juridical structures have been officially eliminated but deep-rooted attitudes and perspectives still offer resentment and insensitivity. In the theatre the set incorporates the aridity of the countryside on a *koppie* covered with many small rocks that are brightly painted and transform the landscape into a magnificent work of art.

---

17   Dennis Walder. "My English name is patience," 55, my emphasis.
18   Athol Fugard, *The Road to Mecca,* 91.
19   *Ibid.,* 91–92.

In Act One, Mabuza's assistant, the eleven-year-old, Bokkie, helps his Tata haul a wagon of brightly colored paints from rock to rock each Sunday. Having painted 105 rocks so far, Mabuza regards this weekly ritual as his spiritual time, his moment of escape from the heavy labor and lack of dignity inflicted by apartheid. He ostensibly leaves that realm to bring beauty to his world that is otherwise unforgiving and dismal.

Our first encounter with them is an unusual occurrence and a momentous event. Mabuza, the exhausted artist is agitated because the last huge rock is covered in guano from a big black and white bird, which Bokkie calls the "Dominee Crow."[20] Bokkie's agonized cry, "He's been shitting on the rock again!"[21] exposes the havoc caused by the bird, conjures an image that represents their lack of control, and metaphorizes how apartheid structures have oppressed them and sullied their lives. As they chase the bird away, Bokkie utilizes a brush and water to clean the rock in preparation for Mabuza's next task: "The Big One is waiting, Tata."[22] But Mabuza has discovered that his inner creative well has run dry. He looks at the last big rock and admits his vulnerability: "I know that he is my last one ... so I am frightened. ... I am empty. I got no more flowers in me."[23] Fugard says: "there must come a point in an artist's life when you have to confront the possibility that it is all over ... I thought, this wonderful virginal rock is his last painting, and maybe this is my last play."[24] Nukain Mabuza and Miss Helen confront this tough realization about their loss of creativity, i.e. that the end of their art represents the end of their lives. Nukain tells Bokkie: "Now it is finished ... now I got nothing more to give."[25] Similarly, in *The Road to Mecca*, Miss Helen says: "If my Mecca is finished ... then so is my life."[26] In real life, they both committed suicide.

In *The Painted Rocks at Revolver Creek,* Mabuza asks for water and Bokkie offers to fetch him food. Mabuza's refusal, "I am not hungry Bokkie,"[27] is accompanied by our understanding that the old man is experiencing a state of soul hunger rather than physical starvation; this initiates a telling of multiple tales that include memories of childhood, surviving despite a constant state of poverty, walking hundreds of miles over time to look for employment, as well as his realization of having no place that he can call home. These stories are

---

20   Athol Fugard, *The Painted Rocks at Revolver Creek* (London: Samuel French, 2015), 2.
21   *Ibid.*, 1.
22   *Ibid.*, 3.
23   *Ibid.*, 5.
24   Roslyn Sulcas. "Athol Fugard Tells of a Great Outsider Artist."
25   Athol Fugard, *The Painted Rocks at Revolver Creek*, 13.
26   Athol Fugard, *The Road to Mecca*, 52.
27   Athol Fugard, *The Painted Rocks at Revolver Creek*, 6.

reminiscent of the offstage character, Patience, in *The Road to Mecca*, who wanders with her baby and a bag of possessions, after she was evicted, and must walk many miles to look for a new place to live. Mabuza asks his acolyte to help him paint the summit rock, the Big One, not with a flower but rather with a representation of his story, which is an abstract visual record of his life. The artist begins with advice to his young charge: "Tie your shoes together and hang them around your neck ... And then you must sing"; ("*He softly sings*: 'We Majola,' a traditional Zulu work song").[28]

In a revelatory conversation, Fugard establishes one of the tropes of the play, the phenomenon of blindness, not as a physical loss of sight but as what Diana Taylor termed "percepticide." Sara Brady contends that "Taylor first developed her idea of public self-blinding in the context of her research on Argentina's Dirty War, when violence in public was both seen and not seen by spectators: Spectacles of violence rendered the population silent, deaf, and blind."[29] Taylor argues that: "to see without being able to do disempowers absolutely. But seeing without the possibility of admitting that one is seeing, further turns the violence on oneself. Percepticide blinds, maims, kills through the senses."[30] This notion not only applies to Argentina's Dirty War but can also be traced through South Africa's apartheid struggles, the willful blindness through fear or denial, and the indifference to sociopolitical concerns, which would normally disrupt complacency when directly observed and awareness is gained. This phenomenon is exemplified in discussions in various moments throughout the play. The first mention of blindness refers to the big rock, where sight can be easily restored by painting eyes:

> **Nukain.** I think the Big One here was watching me ... waiting for me. **Bokkie.** No, Tata. Our Big One is blind ... He hasn't got eyes. He hasn't got ears. He doesn't hear Tata or see Tata laughing at him. He is just a big rock ... **Nukain.** (*He starts to laugh. Wagging a finger at the rock.*) *Wena* ... your time has come, Big One! ... (***Bokkie** watching the transformation in the old man's mood, cannot contain his excitement*) ... You must take the *kwas*[*brush*]. You must paint ... Give him eyes ... (***Nukain** fills in the black eyes with white paint. He outlines the eyes with yellow*). **Nukain** ... Now he can see me. Now he must know it is me ... Make me red. Tata is feeling full of blood ... (***Bokkie** draws a big red circle to represent a head*). Give me

28   *Ibid.*, 7.
29   Sara Brady, *Performance, Politics, and the War on Terror* (Basingstoke : Palgrave Macmillan, 2012), 39–40.
30   Diana Taylor, *Disappearing Acts* (Durham, NC: Duke University Press, 1997), 122–124.

> arms and legs. Make me strong Bokkie, like I was when I walked the roads
> ... (*Bokkie completes a stick figure*). White hair Bokkie.[31]

Nukain then presses his black-painted hand on the rock to leave his mark as he angrily throws down his *dompas*,[32] a hated oppressive instrument of apartheid. He addresses the big rock: "What do you see standing here? Old man? Just another old *kaffer?* [Pejorative term for a black man] ... I am MAN. My hair is white, my skin is black, but I am Man."[33]

To complete the scene, Tata paints a rainbow which is the inspiration for his initial vision. He proudly repeats his triumphant realization to Bokkie: "Nukain Mabuza has told his story and there it is. And I am Man." The stage directions are evocative: "[*Pause.- a rich silence*]."[34] This is one of many moments in the play when pauses or silence emphasize complex emotional truths. Marilyn Stasio, a New York theatre critic, describes this transformative event: "Watching the dead rock come to life is as thrilling for us as it is for Nukain, who before our eyes creates a primitive and powerful – and very proud – portrait of himself and his life."[35] His deliberate discarding of his passbook, the compulsory identification document that gives him an identity number as a black man, represents his refusal of his marginal status and instead confirms his humanity. Thereafter Tata shares his story of survival with Bokkie and inspires him to seek his own *koppie* which he explains will involve choosing his own work and future path in life.

In a response paper to Fugard's play, Kathe Gray cites Kathleen Stewart, an affect theorist, and her concept of "bloom -space,"[36] "a moment in which the capacity of bodies – human and non-human – to affect and be affected by one another is heightened. Just as Nukain Mabuza has transformed the *koppie*, so the stone garden has remade him; his words and his gesture to the countryside have also moved Bokkie."[37] Although there is no guarantee with a bloom-space

---

31 Athol Fugard, *The Painted Rocks at Revolver Creek*, 8–9.

32 *Dompas* is a passbook, an identity document used only by black South Africans to control their rights and movement. Fugard includes the word in the glossary on page 38 of the play.

33 Athol Fugard, *The Painted Rocks at Revolver Creek*, 10.

34 *Ibid.*, 12.

35 Marilyn Stasio, "Off Broadway Review: Athol Fugard's 'The Painted Rocks at Revolver Creek,'" *Variety*, May 11, 2015, https://variety.com/2015/legit/reviews/off-broadway-review-athol-fugards-the-painted-rocks-at-revolver-creek-1201492509/.

36 Kathleen Stewart, "Worlding Refrains," in *The Affect Theory Reader*, eds. Melissa Gregg and Gregory J. Seigworth (Durham, NC: Duke University Press, 2009), 340.

37 Athol Fugard, *The Painted Rocks at Revolver Creek*, 2.

implying change, that altered situation can potentially be positive or negative.

Tata's song is soon replaced by the humming of an Afrikaans hymn as Elmarie Kleynhans, the farm owner, visits the stone garden. Stage directions explicitly reveal the effects of her arrival when she brings a plate of food. "[*They*] *stand respectfully ... Bokkie watches as the pride and conviction that Nukain achieved in telling his story slowly drain away.*"[38] Puzzled by the representation on the big Rock, she angrily expresses disappointment at the absence of a big flower and asks where it is: "**Nukain** (*turning to the big rock, he speaks apologetically*) Ag ... just something Miesies."[39] Tata's evasion, a form of subtextual silence, irks Bokkie, who cannot contain himself and blurts out his explanation:

> **Bokkie:** It is his story, Miesies. Tata's story ... His story is his life! Because he's got no more flowers inside. Look, Miesies, this is Tata and all the roads he walked, and the rainbows. **Elmarie.** No more flowers? What nonsense are you talking! *Passop* [*Be Careful*] Bokkie.[40]

Mired in her own restricted political and religious perspective, Elmarie blames the riots in Soweto on black youth, whom she describes in denigratory language as *skollies*. She also resents the attitude of their parents, who should have inflicted corporal punishment on them to get them to toe the line. Her memories of first meeting Nukain include him laboring on the farm and the paternalistic gesture of buying him a few tins of paint to decorate the rocks. His gratitude to God for giving him work on their farm reminds her of that morning's Church service, where they recited Psalm 23 in Afrikaans. Thinking about the still waters and green pastures, she analyses her attachment to the farm, *Vredewater* [literally Peace-water].[41] While Elmarie feels gratitude that their world, unlike Johannesburg, is free of violent conflict, she repeats Baas Hennie's prediction that "the writing is on the wall. Have your guns ready as well as your Bible."[42]

When she departs, she asks Outa for a favor: "(*gesturing to the summit rock*) Next Sunday ... why don't you wipe all that away ... and make this one a big flower, your biggest flower ... to thank the Lord for all his blessings."[43] As Outa

---

38   Athol Fugard, *The Painted Rocks at Revolver Creek*, 13.
39   *Ibid.*, 14.
40   *Ibid.*, 14–15.
41   *Ibid.*, 39.
42   *Ibid.*, 16.
43   *Ibid.*, 17.

reverts to becoming her servile employee, in fear of her disapproval exacerbating a precarious future, Bokkie supports Outa's story that he had moments before imbibed and felt inspired by. Likewise, he asserts the importance of the narrative's artistic representation on the rock. This triangular situation forms a psychomachia, a conflict of the soul, when Nukain finds himself dragged between Elmarie and Bokkie; he is also stuck between what he knows is wrong and counterproductive and what he intuitively understands about his art and feels proud of.[44] Elmarie feels furious that this black child is, in her view, so disrespectful and disobedient; she tells Outa to take off his belt to give him a hiding: "I won't have a little *klonkie* [derogatory term for a black child; glossed by the essay's author] with a head full of nonsense telling me what to do."[45] Nukain and Bokkie are emotionally shattered and inhabit a shocked silence. Bokkie's "why" is met by Tata's explanation that he must clean the rock to make a huge flower; otherwise, Mrs Kleynhans, as his employer, would have the power to take away his job and forfeit his home. While only a small pondok [shack], it provides shelter and a roof over his head. He cannot chance this dispossession. Nukain explains the huge inequities between the situations of the Kleynhans' with their farm, animals, vegetable and fruit gardens, which he tends, compared to that of Bokkie and himself, who have nothing.

Nukain relates this scenario to his drawing on the Big rock: "they are like the Big One before we give him eyes. They got eyes but they do not see us ... Maybe one day Baas Hennie and Miesies Elmarie will open their eyes and then they will see us."[46] In the macro-context, Charles Isherwood argues, "the words refer to the culture of apartheid, and the *moral blindness* on which it was based" (my emphasis). He describes the play as "tender, ruminative ... [it] considers both the brutal injustices of apartheid and the violence that roiled South Africa after its dismantling."[47] Here Fugard develops the trope of percepticide. In an interview with Anchen Coetzee, Fugard considers that in this instance "the profound rifts of a country hurtling toward the end of apartheid are laid bare."[48] Tata and Bokkie's exit from the stage at the end of Act One is shrouded in

---

44   A psychomachia also exists in Act Two of *The Road to Mecca* when Miss Helen is pulled by Marius Byleveld's insistence that she give up her Owl House and Camel Yard for a room in the Sunshine Home for the Aged, while Elsa encourages her to retain her independence, continue to live in her home, and fulfill her artistic vision, which means the world to her.
45   Athol Fugard, *The Painted Rocks at Revolver Creek*, 18.
46   *Ibid.*, 19.
47   Charles Isherwood, "Review: 'The Painted Rocks at Revolver Creek,' an Athol Fugard Play," *New York Times* (New York, NY), May 11, 2015.
48   Anchen Coetzee, "Nukain Mabuza's life story rocks in New York theatre," *Barberton Times* (Barberton), March 12, 2015.

gloom and dejection; we hear in the following Act that Tata committed suicide three days later and a devastated Bokkie fled South Africa for Zimbabwe.

In Act Two, set in 2003, Jonathan Sejake, the adult Bokkie, is a newly appointed principal at the Barberton High School, who dreams of writing. He returns to the farm and the *koppie* to find the rocks overgrown with weeds; he carries a backpack of paints to restore Mabuza's story on the faded big rock and in this way to honor his life. Haunted by her earlier denigration and Mabuza's capitulation to her demands, Jonathan confronts the gun-toting Elmarie, who calls the police and the *commando*, as she is petrified by this stranger's intrusion on her property and the fact that he has breached the defenses by climbing through a broken fence. Jonathan assures her: "Violating your property rights is not one of my 'strange ideas,' Mrs Kleynhans. Our new constitution protects your rights ... as it now also does mine."[49] Elmarie is traumatized by recent attacks on nearby farmers, which she angrily and vividly recounts to Jonathan:

> Those four black brothers of yours ... didn't only ransack the house, they also brutalized and tortured that innocent old couple. Mr Potgieter is dead, a pitchfork through his neck, and Mrs Potgieter is lying in the intensive care unit in hospital ... her whole body covered with cigarette burns. And all because she couldn't remember the code for the safe! The doctors don't expect her to live.
> **Jonathan:** Black bastards? That's what hunger and desperation ... and anger has done to many of us black people.
> **Elmarie:** ... It makes no difference what kind of life those men came from, what they did was absolutely unforgivable.[50]

She is also angry and frustrated that even if the four are caught they will not get the death penalty, which was abolished in the new democratic South Africa in 1994. While their actions can never be justified, Jonathan's question is lost on Elmarie, who totally refuses to even entertain a conversation about culpability and the effects of apartheid.

While we are firmly situated in a post-apartheid setting, the politics of the play is strongly informed by the past as well as the present. The characters' focus on the topic of land marks Fugard's acknowledgement of his indebtedness to a book compiled by Maj. Gen. Chris van Zyl and Dr Dirk Hermann, *Land of Sorrow: Twenty years of Farm Attacks in South Africa*, which details over two

---

49   Athol Fugard, *The Painted Rocks at Revolver Creek*, 23.
50   *Ibid.*, 23–24.

and a half thousand farm murders: the dates, the places, and the specific circumstances. The frontispiece also provides a *caveat*: "The book carries an age restriction of 18 thus preventing children from reading the book without parental guidance."[51] In proceeding carefully through its pages, one participates in a memorialization of victims and a seemingly endless recounting of ruthlessness directed at farmers providing an eye-opening and heart-stopping experience. It is also an indictment of government inaction, apathy from the media and society in general, and the pervasive silence that has enveloped the practice of farm attacks, both from the ruling ANC and international bodies. This is yet another manifestation of percepticide and its complexity, in this instance applicable to the indifference, especially of the ANC, to Afrikaners. The latter are farm owners, people who are now victimized and were then "willfully blind" about the brutal injustices meted out during the decades of apartheid rule, which most Afrikaners supported.

In the book, Philda Essop cites Johannes Moller: "farm workers usually are not involved in farm murders. Usually, the perpetrators are ordinary criminals who know that people on farms, especially those in remote areas, are defenceless … Robbers want money, cell-phones and firearms."[52] Dr Dirk Hermann also raises the highly contentious issue of the song "'Kill the Boer!' [which] Julius Malema, the leader of the Economic Freedom Fighters and a member of Parliament, sings while holding his hand out in a gesture imitating a gun." In a skit on this theme, a clothing store in a shopping mall specializing in satirical T-shirts sells shirts with the words: "Don't shoot me, I'm a tourist, not a Boer."[53] At the Malema hate trial, they won the right to continue with this song, spreading racist toxicity with dire consequences especially for the farming community.

An article by William Saunderson-Meyer, "Our farm murder shame," published on October 27, 2017 presents the latest data: "a violent death on the farm [is] 4.5 times more likely than the SA norm … the violence meted out is also often disproportionately brutal, with the victims sadistically tortured." Saunderson-Meyer also informs us that the new minister of Police, Fikile Mbabula, maintains that "his ministry was interacting with farmers to develop a rural safety strategy."[54] However, at the same time the Police minister undercut his new project by blaming farmers for employing undocumented Zimbabweans

---

51   Chris van Zyl and Dirk Hermann, *Land of Sorrows: 20 years of farm attacks in South Africa* (Pretoria: Kraal Publishers, 2011), 3.
52   *Ibid.*, 13.
53   *Ibid.*, 9.
54   William Saunderson-Meyer, "Our farm murder shame," *Globe and Mail* (Toronto), October 27, 2017.

as cheap labor and exploiting them; thus, implying that the farmers have only themselves to blame.

This emphasis on the farmers and their trauma constitutes one set of perspectives. It is important to provide a context for another diametrically opposed set of viewpoints, which form a significant area of contention in Fugard's latest play. Firstly, The Bantu Land Act No. 27 of 1913 was the first major piece of segregation legislation passed by the Union Parliament, and remained a cornerstone of apartheid until the 1990s when it was replaced by the current policy of land restitution. The act decreed that only certain areas of the country could be owned by black people, specifically only 7% of the entire land mass of the Union of South Africa. The reserves or homelands constituted mostly impoverished rural land; these areas were to accommodate 83% of the population until some people left to seek employment in cities, where "locations" were created on the perimeters. From the 1960s forced removals of millions of people from multiracial, culturally vibrant suburbs were synonymous with severe dislocation and disruption of lives.[55] Therefore, land dispossession is a complex process that has been operative for a century and has caused untold trauma.

According to Jary and Jary, land has two broad meanings: "the landscape valued for its natural resources and the territory with which a particular people identify."[56] The effects of land issues are multifaceted: who holds rights, how was the land acquired, and how is it currently used? Land has political, economic, symbolic, as well as identity implications that concern the characters in The Painted Rocks at Revolver Creek. In Act One, Nukain addressed the big rock and asked questions that alluded to these problems: "My Papa and my Mama are sleeping in the ground but where is my home? I was born on this land. I walk and work on this land. One day I will die on this land, but I got no home."[57] Many black people retain strong links to their birth place, where their ancestors lived: "In Xhosa people speak of their rural home as their umnombo meaning their roots."[58]

The ethical and political struggle over land restitution continues to this moment. Soon after the December 2017 election of Cyril Ramaphosa, the new President of the ANC raised the land question: "South Africa could turn into

---

55   These included District Six in Cape Town and Sophiatown in Johannesburg, both of which have been immortalized in acclaimed theatrical productions.
56   David Jary and Julia Jary, Collins Dictionary of Sociology (Glasgow: Harper Collins, 1995), 148.
57   Athol Fugard, The Painted Rocks at Revolver Creek, 10–11.
58   Thembela Kepe, Ruth Hall, and Ben Cousins, "Land" in New South African Keywords, eds. Nick Shepherd and Steven Robins (Athens, Ohio: Ohio University Press, 2008), 148.

the ultimate paradise with the implementation of the policy of expropriation of land without compensation ... We can make this country the garden of Eden ..." King Goodwill Zwelithini, King of the Zulus responded thus: "'Only a very small proportion' of the people had had their land returned to them. 'We look to you to act ... with speed.'"[59] No one can predict the outcome of this momentous discussion at the highest levels of the South African government.

These seemingly insoluble problems are the foundational premises of the ideological and political conflict that undergirds the Second Act of *The Painted Rocks at Revolver Creek*, set during post-apartheid times. These struggles threaten to overwhelm the final act of the play, except that Fugard employs the transformative value of art and the inspiration of the artist to negotiate through the dialogue of the characters some measure of new and crucial understanding.

Near the beginning of Act Two, Jonathan introduces himself to Elmarie by his adult name and explains his mission but she, at first, does not recognize this apparent stranger. She ignores his motives, in order to foreground the problems with the land and the violence carried out on elderly isolated farm owners. In a heightened state of panic, after four farm incidents and deaths in her area in the past month, including her neighbors on the farm *Onverwacht* [unexpected], she tells Jonathan that her husband has suffered a stroke and is unable to speak.

Both characters are aggrieved by their passionate love for the land and their indignation at the way this important issue has been evaded. They focus on the past and bring their issues to the fore right up to the present. Elmarie traces the Kleynhans' history of ownership of this land for over 150 years as it was transformed from wilderness to its present productive state. However, she concomitantly emphasizes the terrible situation of farm attacks in the present. While Jonathan considers that the Afrikaners have stolen the land from the original black tillers of the soil and ignored the complex problem of repatriation even in post-apartheid times, Elmarie justifies the rationale for stewardship and ownership of the farm. In fact, she explains to Jonathan that though she and her husband are childless, they realized "that our child was the land and that we must look after it as our own blood."[60] Both perspectives are deeply felt and although Jonathan maintains his position about the problematic handling of the issue, he also empathizes with Elmarie at her fear of assault and upset about her neighbours: "Please Mrs Kleynhans don't misunderstand me. The

---

59   "Ramaphosa: Taking land will turn South Africa into the Garden of Eden," *Mail & Guardian* (Johannesburg), Jan. 7, 2018.

60   Athol Fugard, *The Painted Rocks at Revolver Creek*, 26.

Potgieters most certainly did not deserve what happened to them ... They were good people."[61]

Elmarie challenges Jonathan about Mabuza's story: "We've all got stories. What was so special about his?"[62] A favorite theatrical mode that characterizes Fugard's plays is storytelling; he once said: "the only safe place in the world is inside a story."[63] Just as Miss Helen shares her artistic trajectory and personal challenges with Elsa through stories in *The Road to Mecca*, here the rock art initiates a series of narratives. The main characters utilize this vehicle to dramatize their journeys and paint a verbal picture of the emotional and physical distances they have traversed.

Mabuza's story, remembered and narrated by Jonathan, exemplifies Pumla Dineo Gqola's description of some members of society as "throw-away people":

> These are people who do not matter, whose humanity, once successfully misrecognized, renders them safe to violate. Such people range in the South African public eye from poor people of various sorts who can be the nameless victims of violence, [to] farm workers in remote parts of the country.[64]

While the latter experience physical violence, we know from Mabuza's stories about his world and that of other black people who walked the country roads looking for work and shelter, that apartheid violence was also oppressive in psychological and economic terms, and putatively destructive of their humanity.

Jonathan patiently tries to paint a verbal picture of Mabuza's life, which lacked fulfilment: "All he had left in him, was what he painted on that rock. That rock is his – the only thing he could claim at the end of his life."[65] Nukain had neither his own land, home, nor possessions. Although the rocks he painted had aesthetic value, they did not offer a balm for his soul until he told his

---

61   *Ibid.*, 24.

62   *Ibid.*, 25.

63   Athol Fugard, epigraph to *States of Emergency*, Andre Brink (London: Faber and Faber, 1988),.

64   Pumla Dineo Gqola, "Brutal Inheritances: Echoes, Negrophobia and Masculinist Violence," in *Go Home or Die Here*, eds. Shireen Hassim, Tawana Kupe and Eric Worby (Johannesburg: Wits University Press, 2008), 211.

65   Athol Fugard, *The Painted Rocks at Revolver Creek*, 28.

story through the representation on the big rock. Ellen Kuzwayo reminds us that for black people "we have owned our stories while owning so little else."[66]

Then Elmarie tells her story: she stakes her claim as a god-fearing Bible-loving Afrikaner with a long history – the first Kleynhans family member out-spanned his ox wagon at the site of the farm in 1849. She also aligns herself with the suffering of Job, which is explored in the Bible and interrogated especially in the light of the dilemma of why good people should suffer. She explains that for Afrikaners the Book of Job:

> is the source of all wisdom, the foundation of our faith. It has guided my people for centuries. Given us hope and courage in the darkest of times ... and for us Afrikaners this is certainly one of the darkest ... How many more Afrikaners must be murdered before this country wakes up and realizes it is all part of a deliberate plan to drive us Afrikaners off our land! ... Nobody is doing anything about it.[67]

She admits that through the trauma of the farm attacks she has often lost her faith, which she regards as a shameful sin.

Their argument about the ownership of land continues with bitter accusations on both sides. Jonathan baldly states that "our constitution safeguards your right to your stolen land ... protecting the land of whites was a compromise that should never have happened." Jonathan also angrily challenges her to stop calling Nukain Tata or Outa: "He had a real name. It is on his grave in Barberton."[68] The fact of according him respect and using his real name concomitantly foregrounds his insistence on remembering his dignity as a human being. Given the opening, Elmarie tells Jonathan how kind she and her husband were to Mabuza: "Afrikaners are not the merciless 'boers' you all want to shoot ... our consciences demanded that he have a proper grave. So we handed his body and his passbook over to the police, together with money for the grave."[69] While showing her Christian sense of duty, this statement also highlights the impersonal nature of the transaction that involved a farm worker, an artist, and someone she had known for many years. Earlier in the conversation, she detailed everything they had done for him: they allowed him to use a *pondok* for shelter, passed on old clothes, and gave him some pay for his work on the farm. They even provided the paints for his Sunday ritual of painting the

---

66   Ellen Kuzwayo, *Sit Down and Listen* (Claremont, South Africa: David Phillips, 1990), ix.
67   Athol Fugard, *The Painted Rocks at Revolver Creek*, 26–27.
68   *Ibid.*, 28–29.
69   *Ibid.*, 29–30.

rocks. The list, while demonstrating a certain awareness of what Mabuza lacks, however, elucidates their paternalism and does not satisfactorily address his humanity.

Since Elmarie has not given Jonathan permission to restore the rock, he packs up his paints in a gesture of defeat after their confrontational discussion. Then he looks at her and offers another opportunity: "Come on Mrs Kleynhans, let us try again ... Try to understand each other. If we can't do that ... then one thing is certain: our future will be as big a mess as anything in our past."[70]

He engages her in a dialogue that represents a gradual but life-changing awakening. In it, he explains his mission of restoring the visual representation of Mabuza's story on the rock, her cruel devaluation of his creation, and the importance of Nukain as artist and human being: "In a final act of rebellion against the society in which he lived and the all-loving God you believe in, he claimed his dignity as a man ... He challenged me in a way that I know now will stay with me until the day I die."[71] This sentiment resonates with Elsa's admiration for and appreciation of Miss Helen in *The Road to Mecca* cited early in this essay.[72] It emphasizes the significance of the transformative role of art and, in these instances, the outsider artist.

After the fire and brimstone exuded by Elmarie about the issues of land and farm attacks and her justification of religion for her beliefs and actions, she also confesses to her vulnerability as a frightened old white woman. Having heard her perspective, Jonathan changes the conversation to explain his own: "Do you know what it feels like when the only person you love, is ordered to beat you ... and all because the white *miesies* is feeling challenged? ... I still feel the welts on my backside from the lashing I never got."[73] In answer to Elmarie's question about leaving, he reminds her that Revolver Creek was never his home but "became a place of disgrace, of humiliation ... the moment he, [Nukain], saw you he reverted – in an instant! – to being once again one of your 'boys' ... just another servile old '*kaffer.*'"[74] This betrayal deeply affected him; three days after Nukain was found dead, it triggered his decision to flee. Jonathan paints a verbal picture of his arduous journey as an eleven-year-old, his eventual escape to Harare, and the many years spent there. Like his fellow exiles in Zimbabwe, Jonathan monitored the situation in South Africa and decided to return after Nelson Mandela's historic release from prison in 1990. A fusion of homesickness and memories necessitated his return to Barberton;

---

70   *Ibid.*, 30.
71   *Ibid.*, 31.
72   Athol Fugard, *The Road to Mecca*, 76.
73   Athol Fugard, *The Painted Rocks at Revolver Creek*, 30–31.
74   *Ibid.*, 32.

it motivated him, after decades, to restore Mabuza's life-story through his painting on the Big Rock. For Elmarie it is a shocking recognition of what she had thoughtlessly but assiduously avoided – trying to understand otherness and appreciate the consequences of the vast inequality between the privileged and the have-nots, as well as to acknowledge the humanity of black people both on an emotional and intellectual level. Not only will Jonathan restore the painting and his own sense of self, but his words have ignited a spark of compassion in her: "(*Using black and white paint, **Jonathan** restores the eyes of the Big One ... when he is finished, he goes back to the spot where **Nukain** had stood*). 'Yes! Now you see me ... And I am Man.'"[75] Although this dynamic may perhaps sound tired or cliched when described, the incident and the final moments on stage are very powerful in performance. This scene initiates a *tentative* and *complex* process of reconciliation. Is this another bloom-space? It is certainly not a scenario of "forgive and forget." It suggests remembering, truth telling, honest exchange, and listening to vastly different perspectives to try to achieve a modicum of empathy, altered approaches and deeds.

Decades after his death, Mabuza's art remains categorized as outsider art but is no longer disregarded. Spectators seeing the play learn to understand the creative joys and problematic pain of outsider art. In Nieu Bethesda we can appreciate Miss Helen's fantastic artistic vision, which is rendered in powerful terms in Fugard's play, *The Road to Mecca*. We are moved by the transformative role of the arts, whether rock painting, sculpture, theatre making, or storytelling. Just as Nukain Mabuza gave the painting on the big rock eyes to see, so the audience has accompanied the characters on their journeys with wide open eyes and attentive ears. Viewers have engaged with the contradictory perspectives and moving stories. I suggest that this theatrical transformation challenges the willful blindness of percepticide, engages spectators, and attempts to sensitize them to deeply human problems as well as complex, uncertain future scenarios in South Africa or beyond.

Works Cited

Anonymous. "Ramaphosa: Taking land will turn South Africa into the Garden of Eden." *Mail & Guardian*, 7 January, 2018.

Brady, Sara. *Performance, Politics, and the War on Terror*. Basingstoke: Palgrave Macmillan, 2012.

---

75   *Ibid.*, 36.

Camus, Albert. *The Rebel.* Translated by Anthony Bower. New York: Vintage Books, 1956.

Coetzee, Anchen. "Nukain Mabuza's life story rocks in New York theatre." *Barberton Times* (Barberton), March 12, 2015.

Emslie, Ann. *The Owl House.* London: Viking Penguin, 1991.

Foucault, Michel. "Of Other Spaces." *Diacritics* 16, no. 1 (Spring 1986): 22–27.

Fugard, Athol. *The Road to Mecca.* London: Samuel French, Inc., 1985.

Fugard, Athol. Epigraph in *States of Emergency.* Andre Brink. London: Faber and Faber, epigraph. 1988.

Fugard, Athol. *The Painted Rocks at Revolver Creek.* London: Samuel French, 2015.

Gqola, Pumla Dineo. "Brutal Inheritances: Echoes, Negrophobia and Masculinist Violence." In *Go Home or Die Here*, edited by Shireen Hassim, Tawana Kupe and Eric Worby, 209–224. Johannesburg: Wits University Press, 2008.

Gray, Kathe. "Bloom-Space on the koppie." Response paper 6 for THST 6546, York University. March 2016.

Isherwood, Charles. "Review: 'The Painted Rocks at Revolver Creek,' an Athol Fugard Play." *New York Times* (New York, NY), May 11, 2015.

Kepe, Thembela, Ruth Hall, and Ben Cousins. "Land." In *New South African Keywords*, edited by Nick Shepherd and Steven Robins, 143–156. Athens, Ohio: Ohio University Press, 2008.

Jary, David and Julia Jary. *Collins Dictionary of Sociology.* Glasgow: Harper Collins, 1995.

Kuzwayo, Ellen. *Sit Down and Listen.* Claremont, South Africa: David Phillips, 1990.

Mohanty, Chandra Talpede. "Cartographies of Struggle: Third World Women and the Politics of Feminism." In *Third World Women and the Politics of Feminism*, edited by Chandra Mohanty, Ann Russo, and Lourdes Torres, 1–50. Bloomington: Indiana UP, 1991.

Saunderson-Meyer, William. "Our farm murder shame." *Globe and Mail* (Toronto), Oct. 27, 2017.

Stasio, Marilyn. "Off Broadway Review: Athol Fugard's 'The Painted Rocks at Revolver Creek.'" *Variety*, May 11, 2015. https://variety.com/2015/legit/reviews/off-broadway-review-athol-fugards-the-painted-rocks-at-revolver-creek-1201492509/.

Stewart, Kathleen. "Worlding Refrains." In *The Affect Theory Reader*, edited by Melissa Gregg and Gregory J. Seigworth, 339–353. Durham, NC: Duke University Press, 2009.

Sulcas, Roslyn. "Athol Fugard Tells of a Great Outsider Artist." *New York Times* (New York, NY), April 29, 2015.

Taylor, Diana. *Disappearing Acts.* Durham, NC: Duke University Press, 1997.

van Zyl, Chris and Dirk Hermann. *Land of Sorrows:20 years of farm attacks in South Africa.* Pretoria: Kraal Publishers, 2011.

Walder, Dennis. "'My English name is patience': Mediating the voice of the other in South African theatre today." *Contemporary Theatre Review* 9, no. 2 (Jan. 1999): 51–59.

CHAPTER 7

Alluring Voices from the Page to the Stage: Literary Characters and the Question of the "Real" in Reza de Wet's *Verleiding*

Petrus du Preez

Abstract

In Reza de Wet's unpublished play, *Verleiding*, the spirit of Eugène Marais, the famous Afrikaans author and mystic, haunts the stage. De Wet uses the dramatic monologue as a form to deliver commentary on the artistic and literary traditions in Afrikaans theatre and literary history, and she unsettles this form, creating a space where multiple voices are heard on stage. The play is a thematic culmination of de Wet's work, in which familiar themes and character types reappear. De Wet experiments with various dramatic genres, combining the academic lecture with other forms such as the eulogy, the confession, and ghost stories, devising a delicate landscape that destabilizes the audience.

Introduction and Framing

Since *Ampie*[1] and his donkey were brought to life on stage in 1930, Afrikaans theatre makers and audiences have been intrigued by literary figures and characters made flesh on stage. The technique of adapting novels and placing characters from prose in new and unexpected contexts has become a noticeable thematic trend in the recent years of Afrikaans theatre. Not only the characters, but the authors of these characters are also represented on stage. Why are these ghosts from literary times gone by haunting present-day Afrikaans stages? The self-conscious play between audience, character, stage, and literary work is nothing new in world literature. But are these voices from the canon of

---

[1] Ampie is the title character from a novel by Jochem van Bruggen. The famous actor, André Huguenet, performed this character for a tour of the country. Huguenet was preoccupied with the creation of "Folk Theatre" in Afrikaans and Ampie, as a character, was already well-known and loved before the adaptation was performed. In: "André Huguenet," *Encyclopaedia of South African Theatre, Film, Media and Performance (ESAT)*, Accessed October 10, 2017, http://esat.sun.ac.za/index.php?title=Andr%C3%A9_Huguenet.

Afrikaans cultural history still relevant today, and in what ways do the authors that resort to these techniques question the nature of theatre and comment on contemporary issues?

In this chapter, using Reza de Wet's one-woman show, *Verleiding* (*Temptation* or *Enticement*) as an example, I will trace how authors and characters are placed in a new (stage) context and how the already existing connotations attached to these figures are used as a framework to question issues of literary history and tradition. Another issue that arises is how truth and fiction are problematized in the work. In *Verleiding,* by Reza de Wet, the presence of the famed Afrikaans author, hypnotist, naturalist and ethologist, Eugène Marais, is ubiquitous on the stage. The voice of the now deceased dramatist, Reza de Wet, calls to life a mythical landscape of Academia, the world of Afrikaans literature and the Afrikaans theatre[2] in order to challenge dramatic genres and forms of representation. With reference to this play, I shall explore how various intertextual references challenge and shift genre and form in Afrikaans dramatic literature.

1   Reza de Wet: A Short Biography

Reza de Wet (1952–2012) is known for the wide range of dramatic works that she produced in both Afrikaans and English. Her work has been translated into various languages and published beyond the borders of South Africa. She received the Hertzog prize for literature twice, and she was also the first female dramatist to win this prize for drama.[3] Her father was judge-president of the Free State, and her mother, a relation of Eugène Marais, cultivated a love for the theatre and music in the young Reza. She studied Drama at the University of the Orange Free State (now the University of the Free State), completing an Honours degree in English, continuing her postgraduate studies at the University of Cape Town under Robert Mohr where her love for the work of Chekhov blossomed. She received a Masters degree in English from the University of South Africa.

De Wet started her career as an actress at the Performing Arts Council of the Transvaal (PACT) and also appeared in several productions at the Market

---

2   In addition to de Wet's, Willem Anker's work also explores the issues of writing, intertextual references to other literary sources, and literary figures that are personified on stage. Examples include *Slaghuis* (*Abattoir*) and *Samsa Masjien* (*Samsa Machine*).

3   Dorothea Van Zyl, "Reza de Wet," in *Perspektief en Profiel. Deel 1*, ed. H.P. Van Coller (Pretoria: Van Schaik Uitgewers. 2015), 644.

Theatre. Her career as an academic started at Rhodes University in Grahamstown where she lived and worked until her untimely death in 2012.[4] She published various plays and a novel (*Stil Mathilda*) and her involvement in the First Physical Theatre Company created a space where she could experiment with various theatrical forms.[5]

11 The Play

Verleiding was first performed in 2005 under the direction of Marthinus Basson, with Antoinette Kellermann in the role of Prof. Laetitia de Swart. The play was commissioned by the US Woordfees.[6] This was de Wet's first Afrikaans drama since her exploration of the sequels to Chekhov's *Three Sisters* in 1997. *Verleiding* takes the shape of a one-woman exhibition or show, as de Wet called it herself.[7] What makes this production different from a conventional one-woman show is the fact that video clips and slides were also presented as part of the narrative. De Wet appeared in these clips as a fictionalized version of herself, as did Heike Gehring as the student, Lizelle Van Breda. Another character that also plays an important part is the Afrikaans author Eugène Marais. Although his presence permeates the play, he is never seen on stage or screen.

On the surface level, *Verleiding* takes the shape of an academic lecture by Prof. de Swart in a lecture hall during an arts festival. De Swart stands behind a lectern whilst she delivers her speech, reading from Van Breda's research notes, her poetry and prose, and introducing the video clips and slides where de Wet and Van Breda feature. During this production, no attempts were made to create a theatrical space for the performance to distinguish it from the lecture space. Only a small table containing a framed photo of Van Breda and a vase with flowers is placed on the side of the lectern as décor piece. There is a small desk lamp on the lectern, which, when it is turned on, creates an eerie glow around De Swart. It is only when the video clips and photos are projected onto the screen behind De Swart that the auditorium lights are dimmed.

De Swart's star student, dear friend and colleague, Lizelle Van Breda, has disappeared. At the time of her mysterious disappearance, Van Breda was

---

4 For more biographical detail on de Wet, as well as a short overview of her work, see Stander (Reza de Wet) and Van Zyl (Reza de Wet) and the ESAT-page on the author.
5 See Danie Stander, "Reza de Wet – Haar lewe en werke," *Klein Karoo Nasionale Kunstefees*, Accessed 11 October 2017.
6 Dorothea Van Zyl, "Reza de Wet," 668.
7 Gerrit Brand, "'Verleiding' skep Onklaarheid: Bonatuurlike, Obsessie Fassineer Reza," *Die Burger* (Cape Town), March 3, 2005.

studying Eugène Marais's work and life. During the lecture, we hear how Li-zelle, as a timid young researcher, had fallen in love with the work of Marais and studied it as her PhD topic. For her research, she had tried to make contact with the dramatist Reza de Wet, but the latter did not return her calls. Follow-ing this, De Swart took Van Breda to Grahamstown where they finally met de Wet. It was during this visit that they recorded the video interview with her. In this interview, Van Breda heard that some artifacts relating to Marais were pre-served in de Wet's old family home in the Free State. According to Van Zyl[8] the town in the Free State is Boshof. In the play, the name of the town cannot be identified by De Swart, since:

> there are valuable things in the house, I had to hear, and the house is un-occupied. I can understand that to a certain degree … if only it wasn't under these circumstances. The disappearance … was sensational. And in all the papers. Her belongings were found in the house. It was … (*on the verge of tears*) where we lost her trail. I have even been threatened with the court. Invasion of privacy or something like that. That is why, when the town is named, you will hear an irritating bleep-sound.[9]

Still, in several places in the text, Boshof is explicitly mentioned. Elsewhere, it is simply referred to as x.[10]

This visit with de Wet was the key moment that escalated Van Breda's inter-est in Marais to a point of obsession. De Swart explains that the two ladies visited the house in x and gained access to it under false pretenses, without the consent of de Wet. She then continues and reads Van Breda's research notes about the visit. Its description differs from the style expected of academic re-search. It is written in a poetic fashion, with flowery depictions of the house and the atmosphere that she experienced in it. During this visit, they came across the life-sized bust of Marais.[11] This encounter, almost comical in its presentation at first (since the two thought it was a real man sitting in the darkened room, causing Van Breda to fall on her knees in front of it) is very

---

8   Dorothea Van Zyl, "Reza de Wet," 1.
9   Reza de Wet, *Verleiding*, unpublished playtext, 2005, p. 5 (my translation).
10   The reason for mentioning this seemingly insignificant detail will become clearer when I investigate the link between fact and fiction in the play. Boshof is only mentioned by name when De Swart quotes Van Breda's work. When she speaks in her own voice, she refers to it as x. This is, ostensibly, because information from a quote is the "truth" and she cannot be held accountable for the words of other people.
11   The story of the Couzyn-bust is told in Rousseau's biography of Marais. In the play, Couzyn is not mentioned by name but merely referred to as "a Belgium sculptor."

important. Indeed, it enacts the first appearance or ghostly apparition of Marais.

De Swart tells how the two ladies returned to their guest house where they were to spend the night. It is then revealed that Van Breda had stolen a key to the house in the hope of seeing the bust again and photographing it. Whilst De Swart stayed in the car, Van Breda entered the house and spent the whole night there, taking pictures. The latter are projected onto the screen shortly after the story is recounted; read out loud, they are also annotated by the research notes of Van Breda. After this visit, Van Breda became so obsessed with the house that she broke into it again. She was then arrested and De Swart had to bail her out.

After this incident, Van Breda spiraled deeper into her obsession with Marais, reaching a point where she believed that he (or his ghost) wanted something from her. She returned to the house, without De Swart's knowing, for a fourth time. After she disappeared, her few possessions were discovered there, though no other trace of her could be found. It is believed that she fell into the quicksand close to the river and suffocated. We hear how De Swart subsequently collapsed at the riverbank, hurt her head and was rushed to hospital. During her recovery, her hair turned completely grey. The play ends with a reading of a poem by Van Breda entitled "Love is stronger than Death." Simultaneously, slides first show how frightened she feels in the house in her white pyjamas. The next slides reveal how her face lights up with joy. The camera then moves out of the front door and the screen is filled with flickering darkness.

III   Eugène Marais: The Specter That Haunts the Stage

Although Marais is not physically present on the stage, the mythology surrounding him and his work plays a crucial part in our understanding of *Verleiding*. Eugène Nielen Marais is believed to have been born in 1871,[12] but even the year of his birth is disputed. It is also possible that he was born in 1872, or even in 1870.[13] The confusion surrounding his date of birth is but one of the many strange and wonderful stories about this artistic figure. He was a journalist and staunch critic of President Paul Kruger's corrupt Zar-government.

---

12   Leon Rousseau, *The Dark Stream: The Story of Eugène N Marais* (Johannesburg: Jonathan Ball, 1982), 3.

13   Van der Merwe (2015) expands on the possible reasons for the different years of birth (428–434).

Through his writings in the newspaper *Land en Volk*, he helped to shape the progressive public opinion in opposition to Kruger.[14] Swart points out that Marais is seen as both a hero of the Afrikaans language – considered by many as the father of Afrikaans poetry – but also as an Afrikaner iconoclast.[15]

Marais left South Africa to study law in London where he was admitted to Inner Temple. It was during this time in London that the South African War broke out. Placed under parole as an enemy alien during war time, he eventually left England to join an expedition to bring guns and medicine to the Boer forces via East Africa. He contracted Malaria on this trip and before the shipment could reach South Africa, the war was over.[16] It was also during his time in London that he developed an interest in Egyptology, the occult, psychoanalysis, and hypnotism. He expanded his hypnotic skill throughout his life. One story of how he cured a partially cripple, Aunt Hessie van Deventer, in the Waterberg has become legend,[17] reinforcing the sense of mystery and the supernatural surrounding his personality. Marais was a troubled soul. His wife died shortly after childbirth and he never married again, although he had various ill-fated love affairs thereafter. The play alludes to a scandalous affair, which reveals his allure to women. He became addicted to opiates (and later morphine) as a young man – an addiction that haunted him for the rest of his life. He committed suicide in 1936 with a borrowed double-barreled shotgun.

Marais created many of the lavishly embroidered stories surrounding his life, many of which involved references to the supernatural or the spiritual. Joan Couzyn, the sculptor that made the bust of Marais that is referred to in the play, claimed to have a telepathic link with Marais:

> 'There was definitely telepathic contact between us,' said Couzyn in an interview. 'I was frequently telepathically aware of his depressions. At one time, when I was living with the Van der Wants, I got food poisoning from tinned food. Eugène knew about it by telepathy. He came to see me every day and gave me a Websters as a present.'[18]

---

14   Swart Sandra, "'An irritating pebble in Kruger's shoe' – Eugène Marais and "Land en Volk" in the ZAR, 1891–1896," *Historia* 48, no. 2 (November. 2003): 66.

15   Swart Sandra, "The construction of Eugène Marais as an Afrikaner hero," *Journal of Southern African Studies* 30, no. 4 (2004): 847–867.

16   For a full account of Marais's stay in London and the various versions of the stories surrounding this time, see Van der Merwe, *Donker Stroom. Eugène Marais en die Anglo-Boereoorlog* (Kaapstad: Tafelberg Uitgewers, 2015).

17   Leon Rousseau, *The Dark Stream*, 212–213.

18   *Ibid.*, 468.

Reza de Wet apparently also had a supernatural connection to Marais, as Rousseau recollects in his chapter entitled "Synchronicity" in one of his books on Marais. He quotes de Wet (and I loosely translate from the Afrikaans):

'I was immediately incensed,' she recounts 24 years later. 'I have never been so angry in all my life. There were papers on the table. I wanted to tear them up, destroy everything. I then asked Chris: 'What is your father doing here?' and he answered 'He wrote a book about Eugène Marais.' I don't think at that stage I knew about your work on the book; I was too busy with the stories in my own head. And as I walked out of that room, I was no longer furious. It was so strange for me, I mean, usually you remain angry for a bit. My anger was cut off just like that.' That is Reza's story. It supposes apparently that she was used unawares as a medium or channel for the deceased Eugène Marais's (hypothetical) resentment over my book. How logical that might be, even in para-psychological terms, I don't know.[19]

Rousseau elaborates on de Wet and this synchronous (supernatural?) relationship with Marais, although it is not necessary to expound these aspects here. In his earlier work on Marais (1982), Rousseau already states:

They, among other, testify that in these years in Pretoria he [Marais] was again – as he had done years before in the Waterberg – conducting experiments (or playing games) which, in the minds of his spectators, left no doubt that supernatural powers were at play.[20]

That Marais could appear as a specter in *Verleiding* in order to lure Van Breda away to be united with him in death is entirely in keeping with the mythology that surrounds him. Also characteristic is his desire "to thank the unseen presences for their gracious acceptance."[21] This is the only "quote" from Marais, i.e. words spoken in one of Van Breda's dreams close to the time of her disappearance.

---

19   Leon Rousseau, *Eugène Marais and the Darwin Syndrome. Die dowwe spoor van Eugène Marais* (Cape Town: Ibis, 1998), 112–113.
20   Leon Rousseau, *The Dark Stream*, 462.
21   Reza de Wet, *Verleiding*, 20.

IV   Themes and Intertexts in *Verleiding*

Verleiding does not stand in isolation within de Wet's oeuvre, although it differs from her other work both in form and genre. Here, she combines various themes developed in her own writing with those found in Marais's. The thematic treatment is intricately interwoven with the intertexts that she activates. Odendaal explains how various works in de Wet's early career mirror or relate to each other: "*Mis* and *Drif*[22] relate in various ways with one another, such as the visit of the magician and the luring away of the young virgin."[23] We will discover that this pattern is also present in *Verleiding*, with Marais acting as the magical and mysterious male figure that entices the innocent girl. A discussion of the elements in the play requires an integrated analysis and description of its themes, characters, spaces and intertexts. Some of these aspects will also help to illustrate how de Wet has experimented with the form and structure of the monologue as a dramatic form.

IV.1   *Moving through Spaces*

Various spaces of importance operate simultaneously in this play. De Wet often switches between them in the text, blurring their borders as she does so. In order to see how these various spaces work together (and against each other), the image of a series of concentric circles placed on top of each other can be used. Each circle represents a space (physical and metaphorical) found in the play. The outer circle is the festival circuit wherein the play was presented (the Woordfees, and later Aardklop). The theatrical space is situated within this circle. This is followed by the (metaphorical) academic space, by the space of personal narratives (public and private, as well as historical/factual versus fictive), and finally, the supernatural space which also includes the dream-world. The festival, academic, and theatrical spaces are both physical and metaphorical in nature. A discussion of these spaces will provide an understanding of how the play was received, as well as how de Wet delivered commentary on the Afrikaans theatre audience and experimented with the monologue as a dramatic form.

The play is situated within the festival circuit of South Africa. *Verleiding* was commissioned by the Woordfees, a predominantly Afrikaans arts festival

---

22   *Mis, Mirakel* and *Drif* were published in the volume called *Trits* (1993). An English translation, and in some sense also a reworking of some of the plays, was published under the title *Plays One* (2000). The individual plays are called *Missing, Miracle and Crossing*. Steven Stead translated *Missing*. De Wet translated *Crossing* herself, and both she and Stead work together on the translation of *Miracle*.

23   Dorothea Van Zyl, "Reza de Wet," 160.

hosted by Stellenbosch University. The festival is known for its focus on literary discourses and highbrow theatrical productions. This festival space is also associated with the academic space because of the involvement of the university. The fact that this "academic lecture" takes place within the boundaries of an arts festival is worth mentioning. The text places itself inside both the festival circuit and academic space, as De Swart says:

> There are those that even allege that her lively interest in Marais and his work... eventually turned into obsession. I find such remarks unacceptable. Even... at this festival... somebody made these types of remarks.[24]

The academic space within the festival setup is invoked at the beginning of the play to prepare the audience for the metaphorical overtones of "academia." The interplay between the festival and academic space is fluid, compounded by the theatrical space wherefrom we as spectators view the production of the play *Verleiding*. The lecture hall that acts as the theatrical space complicates the issue of space and highlights the intricate spatial web that the audience has to navigate.[25] The various spaces function as intertexts and the texts are supposed to indicate to the audience how they must "read" the production. However, it is clear from the above that this is no easy task. I recall that in one of the performances, an audience member asked the professor to please speak up, since he had difficulty in hearing her. This type of reaction (or interaction) is "acceptable" or common within the space of the academic lecture, but not within the context of a theatrical production. The difference between the physical academic space and the metaphorical academic space thus becomes evident. Undoubtedly, the audience member was aware of the fact that he was watching a theatrical production. However, the format of the production created a space of liberty where he could address the actress directly, breaking the theatrical frame of the performance.

De Wet is known for her thorough stage directions and didaskalia. In *Verleiding* she carefully describes the stage space as follows:

> Professor De Swart stands at a cathedra. There is a small desk lamp on the lectern. She switches the lamp on when she delivers commentary on a

---

24   Reza de Wet, *Verleiding*, 1.
25   At the première of the play at the Woordfees, the production was staged in a lecture hall on campus. At the Aardklop National Arts festival in Potchefstroom, where the play was performed later that year, a lecture hall was once again the venue for the production. The same type of spatial fluidity characterized those performances.

slide. There is a short row of chairs on the stage. On a table with the lace tablecloth is a dry flower arrangement. In front of the arrangement is a photo of Lizelle that was taken at her graduation ceremony.[26]

Such presentation departs from the traditional arrangement of space in an academic venue. The table with the flowers and the photo of Van Breda remind the viewer of a funeral or wake. While the table can be seen as a traditional stage space, the cathedra evokes an academic milieu. We hear in the first paragraph of the play that Lizelle has disappeared. It is not stated that she is dead, but the peculiar presentation of the space already gives the audience a clue as to what the possible outcome of the story might be.

The academic space is also suggested in the text itself, as De Swart quotes from various sources in her speech. Besides presenting her missing student's research, she also quotes from Leon Rousseau's biography of Marais.[27] If you compare this citation with the original Rousseau publication, it is clear that de Wet was very selective in what she chose to insert in the text.[28] The full section gives much more detail as to Marais's relationship with Anna Hansen.[29] Not being necessarily familiar with Rousseau's work, the audience would not be able to tell if anything was left out. This hardly matters, as the point is to lend a pseudo-academic feel to the text; to act as evidence of truthfulness. However, as is typical of de Wet's dramaturgy, the truths are distorted or hidden. Although De Swart presents the research as the truth, when the personal, subjective emotions take over, the different (alternative?) truths blur the borders of the dramatic, the supernatural, the academic, and the fictional spaces.

Marais was also known for mixing scientific and autobiographical writing with fiction in his works. Du Randt states:

> Another technique that contributes to the 'obscurity' of the art, is the (intentional) attempts that the author uses to misguide his readers by using different believable 'introductions and scientific evidence' and 'explanations.' ... Moreover: This cat-and-mouse-game with the reader can be deemed a characteristic of almost all Marais's 'autobiographical' work. ... By, on the one hand, emphasizing that some stories are historically

---

26   Reza de Wet, *Verleiding*, 1.
27   Leon Rousseau, *Eugène Marais and the Darwin Syndrome*, 3.
28   Leon Rousseau, *The Dark Stream*, 293–295.
29   I will later expand on the importance of the nurse, Anna Hansen, who treated Marais during his stay with his brother.

true and on the other hand warning that others should not be read as 'autobiographical' writings, he conditioned his reader to such an extent that they started taking him at his word.[30]

This is precisely what de Wet does in *Verleiding*. Not only does she mix the autobiographical with the fictive in the play, but to confuse the audience, she introduces details taken from Marais's life into her own work as well. Using symbols and themes typical of Marais's work, de Wet also appropriates his literary aesthetic and approach, especially his style as an obscure (or dark) artist.[31] The borders between fiction, scientific writing, and historiography become vague. The shifting between these genres through the use of intertexts takes place without the audience realizing it. When they do become aware of it, spectators can become disorientated, not knowing for certain what type of work is presented to them.

Towards the end of the play, De Swart's reading of Van Breda's research gives way to poetic, impressionistic, and lyrical streams of consciousness. The style is not the objective, academic tone we expect. This change reveals Van Breda's mental deterioration, i.e. her growing hysteria and obsession with Marais. The objective world has been replaced by the subjective, emotional sphere. In the lecture, De Swart tries to justify the inclusion of such material: "These are just personal speculations that she would never have used in an academic context. I read it because it is the last prose that Lizelle wrote."[32] Indeed, Van Breda's last prose would hardly fit in an academic context:

> The woman that could see the future in dreams, that could predict love in the cards, imaginative, with magical eyes, a woman that could sing like a mermaid. This woman, seductive, mysterious, this woman that would sit for hours and hours in the cool rondavel[33] with the still, black bust of Eugène, with the somber figure. In this silence, in this deathly silence, did

---

30 William Stephen Humphries Du Randt, "Eugène Marais as 'n 'Duister' kunstenaar" (unpubl. PhD thesis, Universiteit van Pretoria: 1965), 289.

31 Some of these themes include ghosts, rivers, wind, and water. For more detail on themes developed in Marais's work, see Du Randt (Duister, 137). In Marais's work, death is often associated with a river. Van Breda's disappearance takes place in the quicksand next to a river. In *Crossing*, the river in flood takes the lives of those foolish enough to try and cross it. It is also suggested that Sussie would drown herself in this river to join Maestro.

32 Reza de Wet, *Verleiding*, 18.

33 A rondavel is a round hut. The bust of Marais was kept in a rondavel outside the house in x. The woman Van Breda is referring to is Freddie Marais, de Wet's grandmother.

they speak with hushed voices to one another? About that which no soul will ever know?[34]

By contrast to the excerpts from Rousseau's work used by De Swart, the quotes from Van Breda's research notes cannot serve as "proof" for a scientific argument. Thus, we have departed from the historical, factual, into a spiritual, fictive, personal space.

De Swart stays behind the cathedra for the most part of the play. It is only much later, that the pace of the story escalates to Van Breda's eventual disappearance. This happens once De Swart moves away from the cathedra to go and sit on one of the empty chairs. She feels light-headed and distressed,[35] as she is overcome with emotion, constantly drying her tears. She is no longer delivering a lecture; she has become the eulogist mourning the death of Van Breda, a process in which we participate as spectators.

This display of personal grief fits more inside the theatrical space than in a lecture hall. When the personal space and emotions of De Swart take over, she is forced into the theatrical space. Even so, her emotions are just as "truthful" as the academic facts that she delivered at the beginning of her lecture. Her realization at the end of the play of the circumstances of Van Breda's death constitutes the climactic point of these emotions. This response also blurs the line between the personal narrative and the supernatural space. The spectators experience her grief much more intensely, as they are taken off guard by witnessing it in a space where emotions seem out of place:

> Ah well, I... went to see the river... I couldn't stay away! ... Far over the railing... of the rusted bridge I leaned... the river was full after the summer rains. In the river were big black rocks... round and smooth... like terrible animals. A terrible feeling... came over me. As if... my mouth became... full of sand. Full of moist... muddy... sand... a darkness overwhelmed me and a dark haze overcame me. Yes... yes... that was when I collapsed.[36]

Even though one could question whether or not the experience that De Swart relates actually happened in this way, whether or not it is plausible, she sees it as the *truth* and as something that has deeply affected her. In de Wet's oeuvre, the mixture of the "real world" and the supernatural is not uncommon. These

---

34   Reza de Wet, *Verleiding*, 18.
35   *Ibid.*, 19.
36   *Ibid.*, 22.

two spheres operate at the same time, and the supernatural, or the magical, appears just as 'real' as the ordinary world. In *Verleiding*, the dream-world as supernatural space is also present and influences its characters, as the above example illustrates. I shall now turn to an analysis of the dream as space, since it plays an important part not only in this text, but in the work of Marais as well.

During his stay in London, Marais became interested in the work of Sigmund Freud, and especially in the symbols contained in dreams. Rousseau expands on this issue:

> A famous interpreter of dreams, tant Francina du Toit, lived near Nylstroom at the time. Marais spent several weeks in her house, apparently to study her philosophy and methods. Descendants of this woman state that Marais treated patients psychologically by questioning them about their dreams and then discussing basic themes which had appeared in them. We shall see later that Marais also conducted experiments to determine whether supernatural abilities bore any relationship to the dream state.[37]

Hauptfleisch underlines the two writers' similar interest in the dream:

> The core of Reza de Wet's dramas is the dream; the dream as nightmare and constraint, but also the dream as lyrical sigh and release: a cosmos where everything is possible, everything is interchangeable and changeable – and everything is eventually and astonishingly true.[38]

Stander (*Channeling*) has explored some of the ways in which de Wet uses the concept of the dream in her other works. Van Heerden[39] approaches de Wet's work from a psychoanalytical perspective, while also highlighting the importance of the dream in her oeuvre. In the latter, the dream-world becomes an alternative reality that influences the characters as much as the real world impacts them. This is especially true in *Verleiding*, in which Van Breda is seduced by her dream images of Marais. In her descriptions of various physical and dream spaces, de Wet also refers to the magical. Krueger comments on de Wet's work:

---

37 Leon Rousseau, *The Dark Stream*, 215–216.
38 Reza de Wet, *Trits: Mis – Mirakel – Drif* (Cape Town: Haum-literêr, 1993), 19.
39 Joni Van Heerden, *'n Psigoanalitiese perspektief op geselekteerde Afrikaanse dramatekste van Reza de Wet*, (unpublished master's thesis: University of Ford Hare, 2013).

In some way her work is about liberation from repression since she sees fantasy, a category with which she repeatedly associates her work as "a primary way of expressing repression in society."[40]

The dream also extends its usual associations to include drug-induced euphoria, hallucinations, and states of hypnosis.[41] De Wet points out that the video interview between Van Breda and Reza de Wet (as a character in the play) should be shot in very dim lighting. Both Reza de Wet and Van Breda should appear like specters in the video.[42] The image of the ghost-like figure recurs at the end of the play.

In De Swart's lecture, physical spaces reflect the metaphors of a dream world. Reza de Wet's house is described as surrounded by an overgrown garden and as having window shutters that let through slits of dim light. The fact that it once served as a hospital for the English settlers in the Eastern Cape endows the house with an aura of mystery and secrecy. It is an extraordinary place, with a chained garden gate to keep people out. At the time of their visit, the tenacious De Swart had to remove the chain herself and push the nervous Van Breda in.

After the interview, as De Swart relates, Van Breda was adamant that she had to return to the house in x:

> She said that to be in that house would be for her like ... as if she saw through Marais's eyes. As if she sees what he sees. Because the house was still exactly the same. And then also... she could walk where Eugène walked and sit where he sat. Even in the same chair. (A teary laugh.) She could be so spirited.[43]

Although Van Breda had not seen the house at all at this stage, she was sure that the space would give her more insight into the man and his work. When De Swart and Van Breda visited x for the first time, they did not know its location and asked around to find it. The townspeople referred to it as "the ghost house," thereby clearly linking it with the supernatural. This side remark

---

40   Anton Krueger, *Experiments in Freedom: Explorations of Identity in New South African Drama* (Newcastle upon Tyne: Cambridge Scholars, 2010), 181.

41   In *Crossing*, the largest part of the play is a flashback that takes place through a séance, which can also be seen as a dream-state. During this séance, we see how Maestro hypnotizes Esmerelda, which represents a dream within a dream.

42   Reza de Wet, *Verleiding*, 5.

43   *Ibid.*, 6.

by De Swart is another subtle reminder that, in this play, the combination of historical/personal information is intricately combined with fictional, even mythical aspects. While de Wet (the dramatist) gives insight into her family's history, the biographical details are sometimes fictionalized when she adds an extra magical layer to the representation.[44] This technique is amplified in the description of the house in x. De Wet spends more than a page on the description of how De Swart and Van Breda found the house and gained access to it. De Swart reads from Van Breda's research notes, and also interjects her own thoughts and recollections of the event:

> The inside of the house looks like a cave... filled with green light that falls through the creeper plant on the outside of the house. A strong and very sweet smell comes from this plant that is covered in small white flowers. A lot of bees are busy in the plant. They zoom and vibrate as if the walls are alive.[45]

In the last room, they came across the bust of Marais:

> My heart almost stopped. A figure that sat motionless while he stared out in front of him. Lizelle was petrified and clung to me, but for her sake, I controlled myself. At second glance, I realized that it is not a man, but a bust. Life-sized. With a dark, almost black patina. I wanted to tell Lizelle ... but she gasped. 'It's Eugène!' She yelled. 'It's him!' She fell to her knees in front of the desk ... extended her arms in front of her ... and stroked, with her sensitive fingers, with unending tenderness, across his whole face. [...] While she stroked the face with her fingers ... Lizelle started to cry softly. I could perfectly understand that. It was so unexpected. And then also ... the strange ... ghostlike atmosphere.[46]

The illicit visit to the house later on in the evening of the same day is also filled with eerie images:

> After a while I could see thin slits of light that shone through the shutters, curtains and leaves. I would have blown the car horn if I spotted someone.

---

44 We must also remember that, for her Master's thesis, Van Breda conducted research on Marais's life and examined how certain biographical events influenced his poetry.

45 Reza de Wet, *Verleiding*, 6.

46 *Ibid.*, 7.

... It was dead quiet. The out of tune church bell rung twice. Just a big, white owl ... as big as a cat ... sat in the road in front of me.[47]

In addition to the place and the events, the cat and the owl are both associated with death or the supernatural. All these descriptions, written by Van Breda and read by De Swart, together with De Swart's own recollection quoted above are necessary intertexts, as they pave the way for our understanding of Van Breda's obsession later on in the play and her confusion between dreams and reality. In the notes to the slides that De Swart presents us, we learn how Van Breda started to identify with the Danish nurse, Anna Hansen, who took care of Marais when he stayed in Boshof. It was speculated that Marais and Hansen had a sexual relationship. At that point, Van Breda's lyrical prose recalls that of a cheap romance novel. Van Breda clearly created a fantasy world around Marais, in which she cast herself in the role of Anna Hansen:

Had she perhaps lain and listened to the movements, the sound in the house? Had Eugène's voice, perhaps his bedroom door that opened, his footsteps down the hallway, make her heart beat faster? Make her gasp for breath. Did she sit up halfway in bed in the dark ... her hand on her heart? And perhaps, one warm summer's evening with the big full moon that hung in the window frame, had Eugène softly opened the bedroom door and watched the young woman where she lay asleep whilst a breeze, like a warm breath, moved the lace curtains?[48]

In her fantasy, Eugène watches over the sleeping woman.[49] The same image is conjured up in Van Breda's notes about how Marais had possibly hypnotized Emily Marais (Emily was married to Senator Charles Marais, Eugène's older brother). Neither Anna nor Van Breda would have known if this were the truth or just a dream. The fact that Van Breda is in a dream state is significant, since Van Breda became certain that Marais came and spoke to her. De Swart explains:

Eventually she told me ... that he wants something from her. When I asked her of whom she is speaking, she said 'Eugène.' She apparently

---

47   *Ibid.*, 8.
48   *Ibid.*, 12.
49   This image also recalls the fairytale of *Sleeping Beauty*. The fairytale genre works as an important intertext in the work of de Wet.

dreamt of him. In the dream, she woke up and saw him standing at the foot of her bed. Formally dressed in a wedding suit. He was apparently very charming, elegant and courteous. He apologized for his untimely visit. He then spoke to her, but not in words, but with one glance of his very blue eyes. That was, she said, how everything was 'revealed' to her.[50]

It is noteworthy that Van Breda woke up into this dream. This suggests that her state of mind has deteriorated to the point that dreams within dreams are not only possible, but also a source of the "truth." After her first visit to the house, she already could not distinguish between dream and reality. De Swart recollects: "What happened?" Lizelle continued to ask. "Was it a dream?."[51] As Van Breda's obsession and dream world grew more and more intense, De Swart confesses that she cannot sleep after her student's disappearance. When she does she is haunted by terrible nightmares. For Van Breda, the dream-world is an escape, whereas it is a haunted space of turmoil for De Swart.[52] Whether a pleasant fantasy or a nightmare, the dream is a manifestation of repressed emotions. Krueger points out:

> As de Wet says, 'if you repress something it will shatter you… any deep repression that is never faced will destroy you' […]. Her plays, then, can be read as ways of permitting access to unconscious material, of allowing what has been repressed back into consciousness, whether this is something out of one's past which one considers to be destructive, or whether it is a positive aspect of one's identity which has never been acknowledged.[53]

For the two women, sexual repression and frustration can be seen as the cause of their constructed dream-worlds: Van Breda identifies with the innocent virgin that must be seduced to surrender to the magical male figure, albeit through death, and De Swart with the spinster (or possibly latent lesbian) who loses a dear friend. The possibility of an escape exists for both: Van Breda is liberated from her life, while De Swart, through the confessionary style of the lecture, reaches a catharsis after Van Breda's disappearance.

---

50   Reza de Wet, *Verleiding*, 20.
51   *Ibid.*, 8.
52   *Ibid.*, 9.
53   Anton Krueger, *Experiments in Freedom*, 182.

IV.2   *A Rich Web of Intertexts*

As the previous discussion has shown, de Wet was a master storyteller who could activate various intertexts in her work. In this respect, she was influenced by earlier Afrikaans authors, including Alba Bouwer and H.A. Fagan, to name but a few. She also drew inspiration from international writers such as Chekhov, Bessie Head, and Daphne du Maurier. Eugène Marais can be added to that list of authors, as Marais's life and work, as well as de Wet's own personal history are reflected in *Verleiding*. The latter also contains slightly obscurer intertexts, to which I would now like to turn, even though they are not fully developed in the play.

IV.2.1   Fairytales

The connection between fairytales and the thematic approach of de Wet's earlier plays has been well-documented.[54] De Wet herself pointed out the presence of magical realism in her earlier work as a link between her plays:

> In fact, the thematic link between the plays (which otherwise function independently) could be seen as a desire to escape the oppressive confines of a too narrowly defined reality in order to enter a more fluid, magical realm. This intimation of a more alluring world underlying the everyday monotony that most of these characters are condemned to; the presence of the extraordinary in the midst of the ordinary, is a particular concern of mine and finds expression in both my Afrikaans and my English writing.[55]

This approach to the magical is clearly at work in the fairy-tale elements manifest in the play.

Verleiding echoes the story of Little Red Riding Hood. In the original story, the "moral" was explicitly stipulated: the innocent young girl should be careful of what has been termed in common language the Big Bad Wolf. In *Verleiding*, Marais has become the Big Bad Wolf – the seducer – while Van Breda plays the part of the innocent girl. Moreover, the entire story is told from the perspective of her mother. But why does *Verleiding* not conclude with a happy ending? This type of artistic rendition, I would contend, falls in line with other themes explored in de Wet's oeuvre.[56]

---

54   See Joni Van Heerden, *'n Psigoanalitiese perspektief.*
55   Reza de Wet, *Plays One: Missing – Crossing – Miracle* (London: Oberon, 2000), 9.
56   This can also be noted in her novel, *Stil Mathilde.*

In its original form, the fairy tale is often dark, even grotesque. It does not spare young children the unpalatable aspects of life. Ironically, in the narration of the life and death of Van Breda, the teacher learns the moral lesson, although one would expect her to teach us. By retelling the story, the narrator becomes its subject. Through the act of telling, the truth is revealed, even though it will never be completely comprehended. The apparently unhappy ending is in fact a happy one, since Van Breda has joined her lover, albeit in death.

Within the realm of the fairy tale, the magical release functions as a Deus ex Machina, creating a space where a logical climax and denouement would be unsuitable. But the god in the machine also makes it possible to interpret this magical interference. What type of god is Marais in this story? As the title of the play suggests, he is not necessarily a benevolent figure, but rather a Mephistopheles luring the virgin to the underworld. He becomes the archetype of the tempter, especially in the way that De Swart interprets the story of Van Breda's death. He morphs into the harbinger of death through his powers of persuasion, or more exactly, through the magnetic and hypnotic allure he holds for the innocent victim, the damsel in distress as personified by Van Breda. This type of male figure that casts a magical spell or hypnotic trance over an innocent young girl recurs in many of de Wet's plays, including, as stated earlier, both *Missing* and *Crossing*.[57]

IV.2.2   Egypt, Freemasons, and Spiritualism

During his time in London, Marais discovered Theosophy. In particular, the writings of Helena Blavatsky influenced his philosophy and world view. At the turn of the 19th century, esoteric and spiritual aspects were often regarded as general subjects of study. Moreover, Van der Merwe indicates that the aims of the theosophists correlated with those of the Freemasons, a congregation of which Marais was a member.[58] His interest in the work of Blavatsky might have led him to his studies of ancient Egypt. This fascination with the occult did not sit well with Van Breda or De Swart. Referring to a slide where some of Marais's freemasonry artefacts are shown, De Swart comments:

> In this black box, documents were found that indicated that Charles, Eugène and Gèrard were members of the Freemasons. These are clearly secret documents, partially written in Latin. Strange illustrations of pyramids and unknown symbols. Lizelle felt that she did not want to take

57   Reza de Wet, *Plays One*.
58   Carel Van der Merwe, *Donker Stroom: Eugène Marais en die Anglo-Boereoorlog* (Kaapstad: Tafelberg Uitgewers. 2015), 98.

photos of these documents. She said she felt repulsed. And I have to agree. Still, she did take a photo of this strange piece of clothing that was also found in the box.[59] That such refined people, high standing Afrikaners, could take part in such heathen ... foreign ... occult. Let me not continue about that.[60]

These allusions to freemasonry reveal de Wet's sense of humour. The Freemasons have been ostracized in the Afrikaans community largely because the apartheid government vilified them as members of a "secret society" standing in opposition to church and state.[61] In "Freemasonry. Its secrets and Dangers," Van Niekerk tries to illustrate how masons reject the Christian dogma.[62] The implication here is that Marais, as an important figure of Afrikaans society and literature, would surely not have followed such a heathen path. Freemasonry does not fit into the idealized picture of Marais that Afrikaans society has created. Once again, we are confronted with the dual nature of Marais's personality and the uncertainty surrounding some aspects of his life.

Actually, at the time that Marais joined the Transvaal Lodge in April 1892, it was not uncommon for men in higher society to be part of the English Constitution of Freemasonry (the South African Constitution was only formed much later). Van der Merwe indicates that Marais was later expelled from the English Constitution because he failed to pay his membership fees.[63] The Egyptian connection to freemasonry and the Egyptian hieroglyphics (or codes) in Marais's bible help to create a sense of the other-worldly and the mysterious in *Verleiding*.

As mentioned above, Van Niekerk deemed the alleged Egyptian sources of masonry to be inappropriate for Afrikaans society. In *Verleiding*, the Egyptian and masonic material shape de Wet's delightful underhanded comment about the way in which academia and the Afrikaans community, can swipe unwanted or uncomfortable facts about their "heroes" under the carpet, just as was the case with Marais. As de Wet claims:

We think we know who they were. Marais was difficult to capture: it wasn't possible to whitewash him. On the one hand he is 'our Eugène,' but

---

59   I could not establish what exactly this piece of clothing was. If connected to freemasonry, one could assume that it is a Masonic apron or related regalia.

60   Reza de Wet, *Verleiding*, 14.

61   See F.N. Van Niekerk, *Vrymesselary. Sy geheime en gevare* (Bloemfontein: Suid-Afrikaanse Calvinistiese Uitgewersmaatskappy, Bpk. 1960).

62   *Ibid.*, 294.

63   Carel Van der Merwe, *Donker Stroom*.

he was involved in Freemasonry, the occult, and so forth; he does not fit into the one-dimensional image that was created of him.[64]

By not exploring Marais's involvement in the "mysterious" freemasonry or occult in the play, de Wet undermines male dominated structures and subverts male power, since freemasonry is associated with strong, patriarchal structures. Furthermore, the side remark about these "unsavory" aspects of Marais's life creates an even stronger mystical image of the writer.

In *Verleiding*, de Wet introduces several other references associated with Egypt, all intertextually connected with Marais's life and work. She seamlessly integrates them all into the narrative of the play. Marais drew "several hieroglyphics" in the bible his mother gave him. According to de Wet, Leon Rousseau could not clarify the meaning of these strange symbols.[65] The latter were actually not hieroglyphics, but codes that were later deciphered,[66] of which de Wet must have been aware. Rousseau quoted her in the very book in which the decoded meanings were published, so we can assume that de Wet was familiar with the content of the book. Moreover, de Wet's grandmother had sent Rousseau a hand-written copy of those symbols, subsequently published in Rousseau's book. Clearly then, de Wet uses "facts" that are tainted through a fictional lens.

Some other references to Egypt are almost undiscernible to the audience. For instance, Lizelle took a photo of the run-down rondavel where Marais's bust was kept. In her notes, she referred to it as "broken down... forgotten... like a desolate sarcophagus of a Pharaoh."[67] In her final poem, Lizelle also alludes to Egypt, when she depicts the boat taking her across the river as being "fragile like a papyrus leaf."[68] In this poem, crossing a river in a thin, fragile boat, through darkness and distress, leads to a reunion with her lover in the light of the other side. In Egyptian mythology, crossing a river in a ferry serves as a metaphor for death. In addition, both the living and the dead travel together on a river. In an echo of this mythological tradition, the merging of the two worlds of life and death likewise functions as a potent metaphor in *Verleiding*.

Although the intertexts analyzed above may not be unusual in de Wet's oeuvre, the structural and dramatic ways in which she approaches them in *Verleiding* is most definitely innovative and therefore deserves consideration.

---

64   Gerrit Brand, "'Verleiding' skep Onklaarheid."
65   Reza de Wet, *Verleiding*, 13.
66   Leon Rousseau, *Eugène Marais and the Darwin Syndrome*, 67.
67   Reza de Wet, *Verleiding*, 16.
68   *Ibid.*, 22.

If *Verleiding* can be seen as a recapitulation of earlier themes, it also reveals de Wet's structural and generic experimentation.

v   Experiments with Genre and Form

De Wet has called *Verleiding* a thriller, an exhibition or a show, which evidences the difficulty of categorizing it. On the surface, it could be regarded as a one-person show, although many voices populate the stage. Not only does De Swart quote Lizelle and Rousseau extensively in the text, we also see and hear Reza de Wet as a character as well as Lizelle on the screen in the video section.

In his study, Gentile (Cast) offers a thorough description of the development of the one-person show. In this respect, Gentile underlines the prevalence of literary figures performing their work for audiences, a characteristic that has also become a regular feature of arts festivals. Indeed, at festivals such as the Woordfees, academic lectures on writers and their work is commonplace. De Wet has combined all these aspects in *Verleiding*: while activating intertexts and different contexts in this work, she also shifted genre and structure boundaries in the process.

Marais used the narrative voice in a similar way in many of his short stories, in which he only retold the stories gleaned from "other sources." A comparable device can be found in *Verleiding*, in which De Swart evokes the story of Van Breda by predominantly using her own words. *Verleiding* thus expands the genre of the one-person show to such an extent that Van Zyl called the production a dramatic monologue.[69] In contrast to the singular voice of the monologue, *Verleiding* is structured like an academic lecture relying primarily on quotes. One could argue that de Wet has crafted a polyphonic monologue. Foregrounding variations in style and genre, the play often combines lecture, narration, lament, confessional, poetry and prose reading, and multi-media exhibition. This aesthetic is relatively uncommon on the Afrikaans stage.

The generic indeterminacy of the play resulted in negative criticism. Botha (Stof, 6), one of the only reviewers, wished that the interactions between the Marais family members had been the subject of the play.[70] Moreover, *Verleiding* was de Wet's first Afrikaans play in a long time. Indeed, she had been very unhappy about the reception of her play *Drie Susters, Twee* by Afrikaans

---

69   Dorothea Van Zyl, "Nuwe Drama: Op die spoor van Eugène Marais. Reza de Wet skryf weer in Afrikaans," *Die Burger* (Cape Town), Feb. 21, 2005.

70   Danie Botha, "Hier is ryke stof, maar nog geen drama," *Die Burger* (Cape Town), March 12, 2005.

audiences. In *Verleiding*, she did not provide easily accessible theatre: her shifts in genre and form made the audience uncomfortable. The lack of a traditional dramatic arch constituted another point of criticism, since, as shown above, the buildup to the emotional climax occurs very late in the play.

VI   A Deep and Dark Stream

Verleiding has not been published, which I regard as a pity. This play offers a culmination of various themes that have recurred through de Wet's work over many years. From the perspective of an audience, it might not be one of her "easier" plays. However, as an experiment in form and genre, *Verleiding* opens up a new discourse in Afrikaans drama, in which a web of intertexts and themes can deliver a rich theatrical experience. In this work, de Wet has shown how the spaces between fact and fiction, the real and the mystical, can coexist on the stage. In the movement between these spaces, various intertexts can be activated. Since de Wet's untimely death, she has, just like Marais, become an iconic figure in Afrikaans dramatic literary history. Like Marais, she promotes herself in *Verleiding* as a mysterious figure; one that might haunt the South African stage in the future.

Works Cited

"André Huguenet." *Encyclopaedia of South African Theatre, Film, Media and Performance (ESAT)*. Accessed October 10, 2017. http://esat.sun.ac.za/index.php?title= Andr%C3%A9_Huguenet.

Botha, Danie. "Hier is ryke stof, maar nog geen drama." *Die Burger* (Cape Town), March 12, 2005.

Brand, Gerrit. "'Verleiding' skep Onklaarheid: Bonatuurlike, Obsessie Fassineer Reza." *Die Burger* (Cape Town), March 3, 2005.

de Wet, Reza. *Trits: Mis – Mirakel – Drif*. Cape Town: Haum-literêr. 1993.

de Wet, Reza. *Plays One: Missing – Crossing – Miracle*. London: Oberon. 2000.

de Wet, Reza. *Verleiding*. Unpublished playtext: 2005.

Du Randt, William Stephen Humphries. "Eugène Marais as 'n 'Duister' kunstenaar." Unpublished PhD Thesis, Universiteit van Pretoria, 1965.

Gentile, J.S. *Cast of one: one-person shows from the Chautauqua platform to the Broadway stage*. Illinois: University of Illinois Press, 1989.

Hauptfleisch, Temple. "Die Dramaturg as towenaar; 'n Inleiding tot *Mis, Mirakel* en *Drif*." In *Trits: Mis – Mirakel – Drif*. Resa de Wet, 9–19. Cape Town: Haum-literêr, 1993.

Krueger, Anton. *Experiments in Freedom: Explorations of Identity in New South African Drama*. Newcastle upon Tyne: Cambridge Scholars, 2010.

Odendaal, Louw. "Die Afrikaanse Drama sedert 1978." *Perspektief en Profiel. 'n Afrikaanse Literatuurgeskiedenis. Deel 1*. Edited by Hendrik P. Van Coller, 150–214. Pretoria: J.L. van Schaik, 1998.

"Reza de Wet." *Encyclopaedia of South African Theatre, Film, Media and Performance.* Accessed October 13, 2017. http://esat.sun.ac.za/index.php?title=Reza_de_Wet.

Rousseau, Leon. *The Dark Stream: The Story of Eugène N Marais*. Johannesburg: Jonathan Ball, 1982.

Rousseau, Leon. *Eugène Marais and the Darwin Syndrome. Die dowwe spoor van Eugène Marais*. Cape Town: Ibis, 1998.

Stander, Danie. *Reza de Wet's Channelling of the Long Nineteenth Century on Post-1994 South African Stages*. Unpublished Master's Thesis: Stellenbosch University, 2016.

Stander, Danie. "Reza de Wet – Haar lewe en werke." *Klein Karoo Nasionale Kunstefees* http://kknk.co.za/reza-de-wet-haar-lewe-en-werke/ 18 April 2017. Accessed 11 October 2017.

Swart, Sandra. "'An irritating pebble in Kruger's shoe' – Eugène Marais and *Land en Volk* in the ZAR, 1891–1896." *Historia* 48, no. 2. (Nov. 2003), 66–87.

Swart, Sandra. "The construction of Eugène Marais as an Afrikaner hero." *Journal of Southern African Studies* 30, no. 4 (2004): 847–867.

Van Coller, Hendrik Petrus, ed. *Perspektief en Profiel: 'n Afrikaanse Literatuurgeskiedenis. Deel 1*. Pretoria: J.L. van Schaik, 1998.

Van der Merwe, Carel. *Donker Stroom. Eugène Marais en die Anglo-Boereoorlog*. Kaapstad: Tafelberg Uitgewers, 2015.

Van Heerden, Joni. *'n Psigoanalitiese perspektief op geselekteerde Afrikaanse dramatekste van Reza de Wet*. Unpublished Master's Thesis: University of Ford Hare, 2013.

Van Niekerk, F.N. *Vrymesselary. Sy geheime en gevare*. Bloemfontein: Suid-Afrikaanse Calvinistiese Uitgewersmaatskappy, Bpk. 1960.

Van Zyl, D. "Nuwe Drama: Op die spoor van Eugène Marais. Reza de Wet skryf weer in Afrikaans." *Die Burger* (Cape Town), Feb. 21, 2005.

Van Zyl, D. "Reza de Wet." In *Perspektief en Profiel. Deel 1*, edited by Hendrik P. Van Coller, 644–680. Pretoria: Van Schaik Uitgewers, 2015.

CHAPTER 8

From the Stage to the Page: Trauma, Reconciliation and Remembering in Craig Higginson's *Dream of the Dog* and *The Dream House*

Mathilde Rogez

Abstract

In the wake of the demise of apartheid and the hearings of the Truth and Reconciliation Commission (TRC), a number of South African plays directly addressed the issues raised by the TRC, in particular the difficulty of achieving reconciliation and of recovering from a traumatic past. Some ten years later, Craig Higginson's play *Dream of the Dog* revisited these issues of trauma and reconciliation in a more subdued manner. This essay offers to look more closely at the workings of trauma and the possibility for reconciliation that the play's several versions and revisions foreground, as well as at the specificities of the theatrical genre they reveal. This suggests that the past may take time to be properly re-membered.

Immediately after the end of apartheid and the hearings of the Truth and Reconciliation Commission (TRC), South Africa witnessed the emergence of a spate of plays which directly tackled the issues raised by the TRC, in particular the possibility to achieve reconciliation and recover from the trauma of the past. Some especially wondered if theatre may enable a form of catharsis the country seemed to be hoping for. A decade later, Craig Higginson's play, *Dream of the Dog* (2010), continues this meditation on post-apartheid trauma and reconciliation in a more subdued, intimate manner, as the setting testifies: restricted to the dining-room of an old farm in KwaZulu-Natal about to be sold to developers, the play stages the reunion of Patricia, the elderly white lady of the house, and Looksmart, a young black man, who grew up on the farm under Patricia's close supervision and – ambiguous – care before leaving abruptly after a traumatic event. Now a successful businessman, Looksmart has come back to confront his former white masters. This essay examines the intricate workings of trauma and the possibility for reconciliation in *Dream of the Dog*. The play's multiple versions and revisions in themselves show the complex nature of such negotiations: indeed, the fact that Higginson rewrote the play

© KONINKLIJKE BRILL NV, LEIDEN, 2020 | DOI:10.1163/9789004414464_009

before turning it into a novel with further alterations a couple of years later – a fairly uncommon process, as novels are more frequently adapted into plays[1] – suggests that it may take time for the past to be properly re-membered, for the pieces of its complex and painful puzzle slowly to be put together and their meaning tentatively unravelled. This continued dialogue between works of different genres highlights the real challenge represented by the ideal of "dialogic truth," which was set as a goal for the fledgling South African democracy by the TRC report. Indeed the interplay between personal and interpersonal issues, and a more national context, staged in Higginson's plays and novel, could be analysed in the light of Pierre Rosanvallon's recent writings on "narrative democracy."[2] Moreover, this shift from the stage to the page also interrogates the alleged specificities of the theatrical genre, of its language and idiom, particularly in twenty-first century South Africa: this essay thus underlines how Higginson's theatrical practice and his insistence on dialogism could be interpreted as a gesture towards a "poetic representation"[3] through what J.M. Coetzee would call a "poetics of reciprocity."[4]

1   Figuring on Stage: Articulating the Individual and the Collective

The conditions in which the TRC was set up foretold its frustrating outcomes: inscribed in the 1993 provisional Constitution as a promise to investigate the period from the Sharpeville Massacre to December 6, 1993, its ambit was extended by more than six months, which proved difficult to implement, as the hearings of witnesses and perpetrators were not allowed to exceed an overall period of two years. These restrictions were further compounded by the constraints the Commission set itself, as it investigated "gross violations of human rights,"[5] yet limited itself to the testimonies given by individuals. Although several hearings were later extended to groups like the media, political parties or religious institutions around a few general themes and issues more specific to them, amnesty could not be granted to a collective entity. Testimonies were viewed as individual narratives of that previous "untold suffering,"[6] putting

---

1   See for instance Higginson's comments on the subject in his interview in Classic Lifestyle.
2   Pierre Rosanvallon, *Le Parlement des invisibles* (Paris: Seuil, 2014), 26.
3   *Ibid.*, 38.
4   J.M. Coetzee, *Doubling the Point: Essays and Interviews*, ed. David Attwell (Cambridge, MA: Harvard University Press, 1992), 55.
5   "Promotion of National Unity and Reconciliation Act 34," Department: Justice and Constitutional Development, Republic of South Africa, 1995, 1. www.justice.gov.za/legislation/acts/1995-034.pdf.
6   *Ibid.*, 2.

flesh on the bones of a system of oppression which had precisely too often been considered in terms of abstractions, with little regard for its daily concrete consequences on the targeted human beings. The risk, critics pointed out, was precisely to lose sight of apartheid's systematic scale and scope, and to get bogged down in repetitive stories which indeed people seemed gradually tired of hearing, unless they were from a surfeit of unimaginable and ever more gruesome horrors. Unsurprisingly, those obstacles were not all overcome by the Commission, which acknowledged its own shortcomings in its report; nevertheless, it is more striking that, in the same report, the Commissioners should insist on redefining truth and expanding its scope beyond the closure of the proceedings of the TRC, as a possible means to reconcile national and personal issues around the very questions of truth and reconciliation. The "narrative" or "personal truths" of individual testimonies were thus seen as part of a "national memory." The "social or 'dialogue' truth" they sought to generate was regarded as complementing the "factual or forensic truth" of the bulk of the TRC investigations themselves,[7] although the report devoted only one chapter to samples of such testimonies. It is hardly surprising that the Commissioners should also have called on writers to prolong what they saw as the "South African story," and to help, through their art, achieve a "healing and restorative truth." Thus, national history was viewed as some sort of story in the singular-plural, combining the intimate and the social, the individual and the collective experiences. In that configuration, the victims of apartheid – the previously "silenced and voiceless" – are akin to the people Rosanvallon deems to be "invisible" in most of today's societies and in need of having their "ordinary" lives and stories "acknowledged" and "represented," poetically and politically. They also need to be articulated within the "common" and the "collective."[8] The historian's phrases are aptly reminiscent of Njabulo Ndebele's in his seminal essay "The Rediscovery of the Ordinary," as I shall later explain.

Whether heeding this plea for a re-evaluation of the ordinary or responding to their need to find a means to channel their own reactions to the TRC's disclosures, numerous novelists and playwrights have represented the national and individual traumas of the country in particular in what has been called "reconciliation theatre." Indeed, the theatrical genre seems most favoured to deal with such traumatic themes, as testified by the tremendous amount of plays hinging around such issues. This generic preference calls to mind the belief in the cathartic potential of theatre inherited from Aristotle, as if the performance of singular plays, repeated on stages throughout the country,

---

7   TRC Report, vol. 1, Chapter 5, 110–114.
8   Pierre Rosanvallon, *Le Parlement des invisibles*, 10–27.

could be endowed with some form of symbolic, if not magical, power of re-
demption through the collective experience undergone by the audience, consisting of a different sample of the South African nation each night. Critics
have extensively commented on such type of theatre and its shortcomings, in
particular the way the political agenda of national reconciliation seems to
frame and restrict the playwrights' aesthetics, a limitation that also affected
earlier protest theatre.[9] Nevertheless, Michael Titlestad points out how a play
like Craig Higginson's *Dream of the Dog* eschews those pitfalls and illustrates a
different mode of playwriting.[10] Set in the intimate space of a modest dining-
room, this play, first performed some ten years after the proceedings of the
TRC, still examines the traumas of the past with its resurfacing images.[11] In
light of Titlestad's brief introduction to Higginson's works, which stresses "the
need [for] new modes, techniques and discourses" in post-apartheid theatre,[12]
this essay aims to show how Higginson's use of theatrical language and devices
in this play and its novelistic version helps to achieve a fuller and more satisfac-
tory form of literary dialogue – one which may consequently be more forceful
in terms of politics and ethics.

Indeed, *Dream of the Dog* already articulates, in both meanings of the word,
the imperatives that Rosanvallon underlines as necessary for a "common
society"[13] to emerge: while the character of Looksmart comes back to Patricia's
farm to settle personal matters, he constantly links them back to more general,
national issues. However, one notes a revealing evolution in the very words and
phrases he uses in the unravelling dialogue, an evolution which goes against
that generalising tendency. Early on, Looksmart opposes "most of us" to "the
rest of them,"[14] as he contrasts his and his fellow black people's fate to Patricia
and Richard's supposedly comfortable situation as white people. Thus, the "us
vs. them" rhetoric he initially resorts to pictures these two white protagonists
as notoriously afraid of whatever might happen to them and endanger their
privileges. The third person pronoun further turns such generalisations into

9   Among other possible references, see Blumberg.
10   Michael Titlestad, "Craig Higginson," in *The Methuen Guide to Contemporary South African
       Theatre*, ed. Martin Middeke, Peter Paul Schnierer and Greg Homann (London; New York:
       Bloomsbury, 2015), 232, 238.
11   See : Marc Maufort, "Negotiating the Post-apartheid Condition: Violence, Trauma and the
       Realist Aesthetic in Contemporary South African Drama," in *New Territories*, ed. Greg
       Homann and Marc Maufort (Brussels: Peter Lang, 2015), 240–260.
12   Michael Titlestad, "Craig Higginson," 237.
13   Pierre Rosanvallon, *Le Parlement des invisibles*, 27.
14   Craig Higginson, "Dream of the Dog," in *Three Plays* (London: Oberon, 2016), 34, 36.

abstractions: the "pronoun of non-person,"[15] in its plural form, doubly excludes Patricia from the conversation which it ultimately precludes. Thus, in the beginning, the dialogue between the two characters is quite halted and limited in its outcomes, but it nevertheless goes on. As it is about to draw to an end, the pronouns, although still oscillating between the individual and the collective, have somewhat shifted:

> Patricia. Anyway – I'm glad you came. It's been good to get to know you a little.
> Looksmart. You know nothing about me. A few words – that's all.
> Patricia. Sometimes a few words can be enough. To know what a person is.
> Looksmart. Ah, Madam – this is a strange land we live in. For your generation, you white people, you still want to be the mothers and fathers, and we – we must be something like your children. But that relationship can have no place in the future of this country.[16]

The interpersonal pronouns "I" and "you," the basis for dialogue, delineating the minimum ground for understanding between two people, are hardly uttered when Looksmart shifts back to the collective. Yet, in this passage, the pronoun referring to his interlocutor remains in the second person. However minimal, however tentative, this conversation is an explicit acknowledgement of the mutual understanding that cannot be ignored when voiced on stage. That understanding continues throughout the work despite the enduring disagreements between the two characters: exchanged during the play, their "few words" have, performatively, brought forth some revelations they can share with the audience. And, indeed, "a few words can be enough" to underline a meaningful change: in the first version of the play, Looksmart sounds much more assertive with respect to what would be allowed, as he resorts to the modal "must."[17] By contrast, in the definitive version of the play, this modal is replaced by the more pragmatically oriented "can." The latter still leaves room for adjustments, accounting for the presence of an interlocutor whose differing view may be taken into consideration.

Interestingly enough, these changes occur after two rewritings of the initial script and after two other memories have been evoked. As Looksmart comes to

---

15   Emile Benveniste, *Problèmes de linguistique générale* (Paris: Gallimard, 1976), 255–256. My translation.

16   Craig Higginson, "Dream of the Dog," 60.

17   Craig Higginson, *Dream of the Dog* (London: Oberon, 2010), 48.

demand an explanation from Patricia and therefore sets the tone of their discussion – the articulation between the collective and the individual hinges around the way he tosses phrases back at her. Initially, he merely repeats what she has just said and opposes her statements. In doing so, he denies they share any individual or interpersonal memory, referring instead to a larger time scale:

> Looksmart. As you can see, Madam – I am a different man.
> Patricia. Yes. You certainly look different. ...
> Patricia. Times have changed, haven't they?
> Looksmart. Have they? ...
> Patricia. Only the other day I was thinking about you.
> Looksmart. Oh yes?
> Patricia. The day you caught your first fish.
> *Silence.*
> Patricia. Do you remember that?
> *He turns away, moves off.*[18]

The revised version of the play insists more strongly than the first on how the conversation constantly runs the risk of breaking off through this lack of mutual acknowledgement and understanding. Thus, right from the start, the situation is even tenser than in the first script. Nevertheless, in both texts, Looksmart first resorts to question tags or repetitions merely to echo Patricia's words. Thus, he empties them out of any meaning after the first evocation of the fishing episode quoted above, which he denies remembering at all – yet all the while keeping the conversation going. Later on, however, he evokes that memory again and alters it by shifting the meaning of the words themselves, playing on their literal and figurative senses:

> Looksmart. Actually, I do remember the day we caught the fish. I remember the rock you gave me. To smack its head. You made me hit its head with a rock.
> Patricia. Nonsense, we let that fish go. ...
> Looksmart. But I've come round to your way of thinking. I think we do far too much of this – letting people off the hook. Ja, Madam. You'll find I'm a far more effective fisherman now.

---

18   Craig Higginson, "Dream of the Dog," 29–30.

He picks up the apple. He picks up the knife.
During the following, he peels the apple into a slow spiral, very pointedly.[19]

Higginson's revisions are here again quite enlightening: the first version explicitly stressed the shift from the literal to the figurative: Looksmart started by using a general turn of phrase, which Patricia, significantly enough, had trouble understanding. She thus asked him to clarify his meaning: "Looksmart. How easily you let yourself off the hook. Patricia. What hook?"[20] By contrast, in the definitive version, this interplay of meanings occurs slightly later in the course of the dialogue, which at the start emphasizes the potential for violence between the characters in a more implicit and figurative fashion. First, this occurs through the details Looksmart insists upon, with reference to the fish, carefully separating them in nominal sentences or using repetitions for greater relief. Secondly, it is also suggested through the stage directions, which in the revision of the play are no longer made verbally explicit. Patricia's reaction as phrased in the first version ("You make that sound almost like a threat"), which made Looksmart's handling of the knife too obvious and unambiguous, has been omitted here: the threat is still conveyed, but only implicitly, in the performance of the text on stage. This omission and change draw attention to the very nature of theatre: this genre uses words with a topical reference (the situation on stage) while figuratively endowing them with other possible meanings. Indeed, theatre *is* both figuration and representation. In this passage, therefore, the shift from a literal and topical meaning to a figurative and more collective one, is mirrored at the level of the script itself. Indeed, its definitive version relies more implicitly on what is essential to the theatrical stage, this articulation between several levels of reference being intrinsic to that medium. As Looksmart transforms the factual fishing hook of that specific occasion into the figurative phrase "let off the hook," which this time refers to the ongoing national debates around reconciliation, so the play, as a theatrical medium, transforms words into figurative allusions on stage. Similarly, Looksmart's gesture of holding the knife and peeling the apple potentially signifies another, more threatening gesture, which may also be related to the collective fear of violent tensions within the country, although this fright is not actualised directly and topically on stage but only hinted at as a possible interpretation.

---

19   Craig Higginson, "Dream of the Dog," 34–35.
20   Craig Higginson, *Dream of the Dog*, 21.

2   Re-membering the Intimate Body

This possibility of articulating the individual and the collective through theatre's linguistic representation and figuration on stage as well as the performativity of the genre's idiom are what further lies at the core of the other nodal point in the play: indeed, the first shift commented upon and the ongoing dialogue between the two characters are made possible by the fact that they have, earlier in the play, re-membered the death of a loved one. *Dream of the Dog* accumulates several versions of that traumatic event – we could even say entangled events. Likewise, Higginson's use of the specificities of the theatrical genre is in itself multi-layered: this essay shall thus focus on how this operates through the various intimate memories, representations and gradual reconstruction of the body, and incidentally of a female body by means of words uttered and exchanged on stage.

Indeed, Looksmart has come to evoke with Patricia the death of his former lover and her former servant, Grace, who was savagely killed by her employers' dog several years ago. Looksmart not only experienced Grace's demise as an intimate loss, but he also links it to the historical context of racial oppression in South Africa. The two characters' memories of that incident are, at least at the beginning, very much at variance, being framed by their individual perspective. This is evidenced in their differing account of the dog's attack: Patricia sticks to the preterit throughout, whereas Looksmart resolutely adopts the present tense, shifting at times to the continuous form to actualise the process he is reminiscing even more vividly. He also uses time markers which noticeably enhance both the tension of these past events and their current dramatization through Looksmart's storytelling.[21] The passage thus fully relies on the performativity of language on stage, through the use of hypotyposis coupled with prosopopoeia, as Looksmart simultaneously insists on the cries uttered by Grace at the time. She therefore becomes embodied again through words, first in Looksmart's recounting of the event and later thanks to similar devices in the version of another servant, Beauty: Grace is literally – or theatrically – re-membered.

However, the constant use of the present tense – even when Looksmart refutes Patricia's addition to his story – coupled with the deictic[22] also emphasise

---

21   The first version of the text slightly differs in this respect, as it further stresses the actualization on stage through more explicit shifts to the present tense in Looksmart's account, for instance in "Oh, and now." Craig Higginson, *Dream of the Dog*, 30.

22   "There was nothing like that" (Craig Higginson, "Dream of the Dog," 44) mentioned in the present tense in the first version of the play (Craig Higginson, *Dream of the Dog*, 30).

the fact that Looksmart's is only one possible version of the event. His account may also be biased and may not constitute "the" truth, as Beauty's words of caution[23] and her own slightly diverging version of the events confirm a moment later in the play. In Looksmart's own perception of what happened, "there [is] nothing" that resembles the accident suggested by Patricia, because it is, to a point, his reconstruction of the event, elaborately structured and highly rhetorically rephrased and represented. The fact that their two narratives, although dissimilar if only because of their different uses of tenses, become interlaced suggests that Looksmart may only be giving part of the picture, or a partially slanted vision of it. Another phrase uttered earlier in his first exchange with Patricia about the fishing episode already hinted at this possibility: "If I remember *myself* correctly."[24] This phrase, which sounds rather odd, draws one's attention not to what is remembered, but to the process of remembering itself as well as to the person who remembers something and therefore shapes it, represents and recasts it in a certain, personal way. There is thus an element of subjectivity in all the memories represented in Higginson's play, so that they may not fully agree with one another. Indeed, Beauty's account of Grace's death adds yet something more, which, although he does not fully get to hear it, does not completely tally with Looksmart's own version of the truth. Looksmart wants Patricia to acknowledge his version of "the facts," rather than merely to repeat Richard's words: several phrases (such as "he said") mentioned in quick succession significantly equate Patricia's and Richard's stories.[25] Looksmart would thus like to counter this narrative with his own account, which could take place if Patricia in turn echoed his own words, as if through some maieutic process. However, his reliance on prompts often pre-empts his interlocutor's answer, as does his use of question tags, which linguistically foreclose dialogue. These tags are to be found again when Beauty gives her first version of the events in Looksmart's presence. One may thus question the validity of how she relates the story, and hypothesize that she actually responds to Looksmart's cues. She seems to be merely assenting to what he says, to end on a tellingly vague and hesitating: "That – is it."[26] This sounds like an imperfect tautology that only echoes what Looksmart has asserted, when in fact the audience and Patricia later realise the complexity lurking behind this "it": "that" was *not* "it," or in other words, that was not the whole story. Maieutics

---

23   See how she answers Patricia when the latter points out that "Looksmart has his own
       story. He's very persuasive about it. Must I now believe you?": "Mesis, you must find the
       truth for yourself." Craig Higginson, "Dream of the Dog," 69.
24   Craig Higginson, "Dream of the Dog," 31. My emphasis.
25   *Ibid.*, 44–46.
26   *Ibid.*, 49.

seems at times to be verging on ventriloquism, and only later does Beauty reveal "it" all, adding a key piece of information which she omitted earlier because "Looksmart would not be able to hear *something* like *that*."[27] As the audience and Patricia are informed of these previously unheard elements, this
additional information does not mean that whatever Looksmart might say
should be dismissed: it is rather an invitation to ponder the validity of any version of "the truth" the spectators can hear in the play, and to learn how to put
each of them into perspective, like the pieces of a puzzle. It is how those pieces
relate to one another, as in a verbal mosaic actualised on the stage in this instance, which gives them their meaning. Thus, while Looksmart's strategy at
times borders on ventriloquism, dialogism forms the basis for the play's overall
structure. The characters may never fully concur, but it is actually an intrinsic
part of the conception and dynamics of the play, as it is built on the characters'
discussion of their disagreement: *Dream of the Dog* thus sets on the theatrical
stage an aesthetic form akin to the TRC's "dialogue truth." In this sense, Higginson's play goes back to what Anne Ubersfeld sees as the very essence of
theatre:

> [dialogism] is constitutive of theatrical dialogue, through an unexpected
> device, of a common or shared presupposition. If there is dialogue (and
> dialogism), it is because all consonances and dissonances, all conflicts
> and agreements occur in relation to that common core. When Bakhtine
> rejects the concept of dialogism in theatre he is right to the extent that he
> recognizes that common core. He is wrong because it is that very com-
> mon core that makes it possible for theatre to mount the confrontation,
> juxtaposition, montage and collage of different voices.[28]

Theatre not only potentially allows for "confrontation, juxtaposition, montage
and collage": it foregrounds them as essential. Higginson's play first and foremost uses this mode, thus tackling from a specific angle what might otherwise
be decoded as purely national issues. This is actually characteristic of the literary genre *Dream of the Dog* belongs to: through the plasticity and versatility of
language, Higginson makes full use of the dramatic performativity of words on
the stage.

This feature can be found in the very passages previously analysed: there
again, the text relied on the multi-layered meaning of language and on both

---

27   *Ibid.*, 69. My emphasis. See as well Patricia's remark then: "He said 'Is that all?' It wasn't,
      was it?"
28   Anne Ubersfeld, *Reading Theatre* (Toronto: University of Toronto Press, 1999), 184–185.

the topicality and the figurativeness of some phrases ("that," "it"). An analysis of the variations between the two versions of the opening of the play significantly highlights a growing precision in the language used by the characters. It also reveals therefore the importance granted to the referentiality of words, to the relation between signifier and signified. In the first version, Patricia literally does not call a spade a spade, as she refers to the tool Richard carries just as a "thing."[29] At the same time, she and Richard omit their late daughter's name, resorting instead to the third-person or non-person pronoun. This omission at the start of the play is all the more ambiguous as the audience cannot know who they are talking about. It is only later that Patricia mentions Rachel's name, incidentally when speaking to Beauty; by contrast, the end of her conversation with Richard points to hidden meanings and words merely hinting at their signified, a situation which is repeated again towards the end of the play when Patricia has to force Richard to say Rachel's name, and then Grace's, instead of a shameful, vague "it." She also urges him to acknowledge his unspeakable deed in so many words. Patricia's early antiphrasis "tell me about it"[30] has its meaning both literalised and inverted by the end of the play when Richard actually starts "tell[ing her] about it." The same result is achieved thanks to the complementary accounts given by Looksmart and Beauty, however personal and limited they may be. By then, both Patricia and the audience get to understand what "a bloody mess" everything is, and how literally "bloody" what Richard cryptically referred to at the start of the play was. Indeed, it then becomes clear that he alluded to the deaths of Rachel, Grace, and the baby she was pregnant with. In the meantime, the words and their signified have taken shape on the theatrical stage, and it is certainly no coincidence that the word "blood" should also recur throughout the dialogue in that later section of the play, both in its figurative and literal uses, once things have been called by their names and embodied through words. Thus, Higginson right away explores the issue of both the versatility and the performativity of language through the dramatic genre, which precisely relies on how language points to what it figures. By the end of the play, some of this meaning has been unveiled through this process, however painful it may be in this instance, thanks to those various layers or personal versions of the accident presented in succession: the two beloved beings thus evoked have been gradually re-membered, given back their names and a shape on stage through this performative use of language, even if only provisionally and tentatively. From the beginning, issues such as taboos, the possibility to represent and to say what cannot be said are foregrounded. The

---

29   Craig Higginson, *Dream of the Dog*, 6.
30   Craig Higginson, "Dream of the Dog," 25.

whole text thus revolves around the difficulty of acknowledging things through adequate words in order to offer the most accurate version of what happened. Thus, despite the potential unreliability of Looksmart's version of "the truth," its recounting and staging in the play itself constitute some kind of achievement. It is on stage that Looksmart spells out, quite emphatically, what he believes has happened: "Mur-der!"[31] Repeated three times in the space of a few lines, this word, with its detached syllables, is quite visible on the space of the page. It even more unquestionably reverberates when uttered on the theatre stage: the insistence on the performativity of language makes it clear that what has been uttered cannot be unsaid, and thus cannot go unheard and unheeded.

3   Literary Genres in Dialogue: "Poetic Representation" and
       "Imagined Communities"[32]

Compounded by the variations offered by the novel, further intimations in the play suggest that it is the evocation of intimate memories, particularly those involving the female body, through the loss of a lover or a child, that paves the way for a true dialogue between people. It is thus only after Patricia has shared with Looksmart some memories of her own, including her most personal ones, that they agree on a common ground for dialogue. Only then can they experience a common vision of other memories, and even share a laugh:

> Patricia. I wanted to move my roses, but, you see, you can't? They're used to the soil here. ...
> Looksmart. Ja, and if you over water them, the leaves will turn yellow and suddenly fall off. My God! (*He laughs.*) I did that to the ones in the pots. You remember?
> Patricia. I most certainly do.
> Looksmart. ... You tried your best to be nice about it. But hell, you were cross!
> *They are both laughing.*[33]

---

31   *Ibid.*, 40.
32   The former phrase derives from Rosanvallon, while the latter is obviously borrowed from Benedict Anderson.
33   Craig Higginson, *Dream of the Dog*, 48–49.

In that particular instance, the first version of the play is a little more elaborate than the last one, as those memories incidentally prompt Looksmart to acknowledge partial guilt (over-watering the roses) while playing with pronouns again. The first "you" used when he picks up Patricia's words conveys a general sense, but without any of the oppositional value as in the previous similar instances. Then, he falls back again on the singular and reciprocal "I" and "you," which are interlaced in his sentence. The definitive version of the play is more economical in its suggestion of reciprocity, as Looksmart simply asks Patricia whether she remembers the mishap, but the attentive spectator or reader will note the direct symmetry with Patricia's earlier question about the fishing episode, at the very start of their dialogue ("Patricia. Do you remember that?"[34]). The rest of the script relies on the same interplay of pronouns, and both versions end on a similar stage direction in which the subject of the verb in a plural form associates the two characters in a common action.

Prior to this moment of sharing, Looksmart has had to listen to Patricia's most intimate confession, which she was initially reluctant to share, before compelling him to listen until the end. During this confession, she also corrects Looksmart's quite revealing, albeit mistaken, assumption: that Patricia's child should have been a boy. Looksmart readily expresses a wish to have known about him, before becoming more hesitant when he hears it was a girl, who besides never lived. Although the dead body of Rachel is evoked in terms recalling the description of Looksmart's body at birth, this echo suggests that it is precisely those moments of shared intimacy around the female body that prepare the ground for the possibility of correspondences, and therefore of dialogue. Later, Beauty reveals to the characters and to the audience that violence was exerted on Grace's body. On that occasion, Beauty is visually depicted on the stage as equal to Patricia. Higginson's novel reinforces that impression through numerous allusions to Beauty's body and its barrenness, so that she and Patricia suffer from the same trauma of loss, or lack. Thus, the female body, in what is most intimate and personal about it, appears as a negotiating site around which issues of the collective and the individual may best be articulated, and which leads to some form of reciprocal understanding, if not of interpersonal reconciliation. This is achieved through the gradual recounting of painful stories in the singular-plural.[35]

What those disclosures further lead to is indeed an acknowledgement, on Patricia's part, of a more serious crime than the one Looksmart confesses to.

---

34   *Ibid.*, 30.
35   Incidentally, a similar insistence on the body can be found in Rosanvallon.

Gone is the light banter about a "hell" secularised by the set phrase of the harmless interjection in the passage previously quoted:[36]

> Patricia. The shame. The shame of it. Oh, I don't know. That dog was try-
> ing to please us, that's all. It had learned that. To be like that. From the
> country. Richard. Me. A poison we have, we grow up with. Now it's been
> passed onto you. The dream of the dog. The dream of the dog doing its
> work. Destroying everything. ... I owe you an apology. ... I am sorry. Even
> if that doesn't seem enough.[37]

The two versions of the play slightly differ in the way in which they again articulate the collective and the individual in this passage: Higginson operates a shift between the figurative and collective meaning of "grow" and its literal and personal sense in the first version,[38] while this collective/individual connection is more closely established in the rewritten version through the juxtaposition of nominal sentences: "the country. Richard. Me." Strikingly, this time, in both versions, the movement from the literal to the figurative works in reverse, even though the strong allusion to the poison in the last version[39] is couched in phrases which sound figurative. This is more particularly true as they refer to the title of the play with its marked alliterative pattern, almost halfway through the play. "The dream of the dog" conjures up the image of the ubiquitous guard dog, with which Looksmart started his exchange with Patricia ("The dog," – even though it was also a quite specific dog he had in mind).[40] The word "dog," and its literal and figurative (and often rude) variants, ceaselessly recur until the end of the play: on the one hand, it is the symbol of a widespread and commonly shared white fear;[41] on the other hand, "the dog" also takes an individual shape – again not so differently from what the play itself, because of this very

---

36   Craig Higginson, *Dream of the Dog*, 49; "Dream of the Dog," 62.

37   Craig Higginson, "Dream of the Dog," 47–51.

38   Craig Higginson, *Dream of the Dog*, 35.

39   This allusion remains more subtle in the first version and is more readily rejected by Pa-
      tricia: "Oh, Looksmart – please don't let this be passed on to you!" Craig Higginson, *Dream
      of the Dog*, 35.

40   Craig Higginson, "Dream of the Dog," 28.

41   One is reminded of a comment in J.M. Coetzee's novel *Disgrace* about guard dogs: they are
      "bred to snarl at the mere smell of a black man" (110), which incidentally recalls Romain
      Gary's *Chien blanc* – even though the latter is set in the United States. One could argue
      that in Higginson's play the "dog" is both topical to South Africa *and* universal. One could
      say that the genre of the *plaasroman* the title of Higginson's novel evokes, restricts the
      larger, more international "imagined community" of the audience addressed by the play
      to a more strictly South African one.

process, achieves as it is performed on stage, a process of putting things into uttered words which is further stressed here by the recurring use of vague pronouns ("it," "that") in Patricia's speech, as well as of halted, truncated sentences. Thus, it is no wonder that, in her confession to Looksmart, Patricia should use the word "shame" rather than "guilt," thereby referring to a shared, collective sense of responsibility, in an echo of Eric Dodds's distinction.[42] Such a linguistic choice shows that she still situates herself as part of that larger white South African "imagined community."[43] Yet it is "guilt" that Looksmart wants from her, i.e. an acknowledgement of personal responsibility stemming from interpersonal relations, as becomes explicit in the last version of the play: "Looksmart. I am saying that I wish for you guilt! ... I want you to remember that dog like I remember that dog ... Patricia. I do understand how you feel."[44]

In the meantime, Patricia has admitted refusing the wounded Beauty be transported to the hospital in her expensive car, so that her later personal apologies may ring true: the play operates not on the level of gross violations, or on a national scale either, but within the closed space of a sitting room, almost in camera, and features individuals who acknowledge not so much deeds but thoughts and private feelings, as well as reciprocity. They do so in front of spectators, who may thus also be asked to identify with them and acknowledge in turn the "little perpetrator" existing in each of them. Thus, Higginson's play, *Dream of the Dog*, avoids repeating the same mistakes as those lamented by the TRC report, namely the excessive emphasis on "what could be regarded as the exceptional – on gross violations of human rights rather than the more mundane but nonetheless traumatising dimensions of apartheid life that affected every single black South African," with "the result ... that ordinary South Africans do not see themselves as represented by those the Commission defines as perpetrators, failing to recognise the 'little perpetrator' in each one of us."[45] Patricia is not a monster, which would both theatrically and morally induce some distance from the audience, nor is what Looksmart reports "spectacular," to borrow from Njabulo Ndebele's and Guy Debord's terminologies. His is not a "singular" testimony, either referentially unique or morally exemplary, which would preclude its articulation to the "common" his account *is* "common," ordinary and individual, and shareable by a larger collective.[46] Higginson's play

---

42   Eric R. Dodds, *The Greeks and the Irrational* (Berkeley, CA: University of California Press, 2004), 29–64.

43   See for instance how Andreas Langenohl articulates Jaspers' types of guilt and Anderson's concept of "imagined community" (Langenohl 169).

44   Craig Higginson, "Dream of the Dog," 51.

45   TRC Report, volume 1, Chapter 5, 132–133.

46   Pierre Rosanvallon, *Le Parlement des invisibles*, 16–27.

thus favours what Ndebele refers to as "the ordinary," i.e. a mode of "representation" which Rosanvallon also likens to Michel De Certeau's unprecedented approach in *The Practice of Everyday Life*.[47] This mode is first and foremost based on aesthetic choices and a "poetic representation,"[48] but it is also, as Ronsavallon shows, a political or ethical gesture: it constitutes a meaningful alternative and complement to political representation – meaningful precisely because it gives precedence to the poetic, to the literary and the theatrical. Higginson's play may not purge the South African nation of all its traumas or evils through some sort of miraculous catharsis. Nevertheless, it is by going back to the essence of theatre that this work favours and enables embodied interpersonal relations, which Coetzee would call a "poetics of reciprocity."[49] The latter is detectable in the symmetrical structure of Looksmart's sentence balanced around "you," "I," and "like I": "I want you to remember that dog like I remember that dog."[50]

Dream of the Dog thus eschews what Debord would denounce as "the spectacle": this play does not consist in a mere copy of contextual issues or in weak echoes of national debates. Such simulacrum is instead found in the soulless, impersonal replicas of the house which Looksmart's company intends to reproduce identically around the original farm on the plot of land it has bought from the Wileys.[51] It is striking that this image of duplicated buildings should also be what gives its title to the novelistic version of the play, *The Dream House*: this narrative no longer focuses on dogs but on houses, and more particularly on the farm, which as a consequence situates the novel in the more specific genre of the *plaasroman*.[52] The Wileys' farm and the genre are metonymically evoked by the cover of the latest edition of the novel, which reproduces the photograph of a fence, a symbol of the stereotypical farm in *plaasromans*,[53] taken by Higginson himself. The author thus deliberately inscribes his work in that genre,[54] as is also confirmed by the novel's opening lines:

---

47   The French and South African contexts were then utterly different, but it could be noted
      that both texts date from the 1980s.
48   Pierre Rosanvallon, *Le Parlement des invisibles*, 38–49.
49   J.M. Coetzee, *Doubling the Point*, 55.
50   Craig Higginson, "Dream of the Dog," 51.
51   Michael Titlestad, "Craig Higginson," 230.
52   See: *Ibid.*, 231.
53   One cannot help thinking of van Heerden's short story: while it reads as a short anti-
      plaasroman, the story is tellingly enough entitled "Fences," or "fallen fences" in the Afri-
      kaans version ("Slapgrensdrade").
54   Craig Higginson, Interview with author, 14 May 2017.

> She draws back the curtains to reveal the mist. It has filled the whole val-
> ley and invaded every cupboard of the house. Her bedroom overlooks a
> row of kennels, silvery grey and subsiding at odd angles under a great
> green wave of brambles. The bloodwoods, solemn as totems, are barely
> visible above the old dog-run.[55]

Sight is prominent here: the novel opens with Patricia's perspective as she un-
veils a view of the farm from the house. The verb "overlook" acquires a double
meaning here: the raised location of her room echoes her (supposedly) "superior" social position. Master of all she surveys… Looksmart acts in a similar
fashion in the first chapter devoted to him:

> It is still the same sign: Dwaleni Farm. The white drawn-out letters on the
> blistered tin, tied at an odd angle against the barbed wire fence … [E]
> verything else looks exactly as he left it. The impenetrable shadow of the
> wattle and gum plantation in the mist, the rattle of the cattle grid as he
> passes over it, the air of stillness, everything suspended and impossible to
> comprehend.
> He lowers his window and inhales the smell of wet earth and rot.[56]

The second line of this passage introduces the element of the fence, duplicated
by the sign with the name of the farm, while the window is again opened and
explicitly frames the vision the reader gets of the farm as seen from Looksmart's
point of view. His perception is further translated in the syntax: for instance,
the suspension in time is directly transcribed in the absence of any verbal form
in the present tense or active mode, thus of any inscription in the flow of time,
in the nominal sentence at the end of the first paragraph. This parallel between
the opening lines of both chapters corresponds to Higginson's broader strategy
based on the concept of duplication, which manifests itself in the alternation
of points of view: Patricia's perspective is thus replaced in the second chapter
by Beauty's, who will soon enjoy the panoramic view in a house of her own:

> Beauty has lived all of her life in one of the whitewashed rondavels near
> the bottom dam. The compound and the blue gums surrounding it have
> now been levelled, and she and Bheki and a few hangers-on have since
> moved into one of the half-finished houses … Bheki put temporary win-
> dows and a door into Beauty's room as soon as she moved in.

---

55   Craig Higginson, *The Dream House* (Johannesburg: Picador Africa, 2015), 3.
56   *Ibid.*, 33.

> It has been her dream to have a house of her own. ... She wants the house
> to be on the road to Giant's Castle ... Here she will have the same view of
> the Drakensberg she knows from the farm, but it will be closer – so close
> that she will be able to see the water streaming down the rock.[57]

There may not be real windows yet in Beauty's "dream house," but there is a
view: the same as her mistress's, but from a closer perspective, her own indeed. Thus, those alternations reveal that Higginson is deliberately debunking
the image of a particular South African nation which the traditional *plaasroman* tried to convey.[58] The writer does so through the very means specific to
the novel, namely the interplay of different points of view, particularly about
the representation of space, as this genre allows for a greater expansion and
exploration of the setting than the play. Indeed, by contrast to the latter, the
novel is not limited to the Wileys' home: the other most striking element is
the narrative's insistence on the many times the characters cross the bridge
between the farm and the valley. This structure therefore does not so much
separate these two places as it connects them through a series of crisscrossing
patterns reminiscent of Jean-Pierre Vernant's reflections on "Crossing a Bridge"
["Franchir un pont"]: "To cross a bridge, a river or a border is to leave behind
the familiar, personal and comfortable and enter the unknown, a different and
strange world where, faced with another reality, we may well find ourselves
bereft of home and identity."[59] Vernant further insists on the necessary connection between the goddess of the home, Hestia, and the god of the roads,
Hermes: "For home to truly exist, however, it must be open onto the outside to
welcome and enfold it. And each human being must assume being both part
Hestia, part Hermes ... Between the two shores of the same and the other,
Man is a bridge."[60]

---

57   *Ibid.*, 24.
58   The *plaasroman* or farm novel is a genre which developed in South Africa in the first half
      of the twentieth century: once the wild populations and beasts had been tamed, tales of
      exploration were replaced by farm novels providing the vision of a domesticated land and
      landscape (Jean Sévry, "La Littérature sud-africaine et ses espaces." *Travaux de l'Institut de
      Géographie de Reims* 25, nos. 99–100 (1998): 20). The motif of the farm gradually became
      an epitome of the country and a model for a controlled, strictly enclosed space. The genre
      symbolically prolonged on the page the very real struggle on the ground over the posses-
      sion of the land in South Africa (see in particular Coetzee's *White Writing*).
59   Jean-Pierre Vernant, "Franchir un pont," in *La Traversée des frontières* (Paris: Seuil, 2004):
      179. My translation.
60   *Ibid.*, 180.

4 *Ars Poetica*: Performing Dialogism

Higginson's rewriting of his play in a novelistic form thus allows him to explore further the concepts of foldedness and entanglement,[61] which are necessary for any true form of dialogue or attempt at reconciliation, as these notions go back to the articulation between the individual and the collective. Such issues were already present in the play, but its novelistic rewriting highlights the specific means each genre enlists to deal with such material. In conclusion, this essay contends that this dialogue between genres could be read as some kind of *ars poetica* for Higginson's theatrical practice: this interplay from the page to the stage and back again precisely reveals the importance of articulation and foldedness, which are actually a key "mode" of operation of theatre, as Titlestad suggests.[62] The theatrical genre relies on the embodiment of this articulation, which is always only potential: a performativity that always requires performance, possible figurations asking to be actualized on stage.

Higginson has several times alluded to his practice of adapting works into another genre: when it comes to this more unusual adaption from the stage to the page, he insists on "the unsaid" which can indeed be explored, as has been observed, through a reflection on points of view.[63] As it happens, the unsaid also plays a major role in *Dream of the Dog*, including in the form of hardly uttered sentences. This is noticeable in the tentative and repeatedly out-of-synch declarations of filial love and surrogate relationship between Patricia and Looksmart, as silence keeps invading that part of their dialogue in the play:

> Patricia. I could never understand it. The way you went off. I had to think of you as another dead child.
> *Silence.*[64]
> Looksmart. I loved you more than my own mother.

---

61   Sarah Nuttall, *Entanglement, Literary and Cultural Reflections on Post-apartheid* (Johannesburg: Wits University Press, 2009), 1, 15–16; Mark Sanders, *Complicities: The Intellectual and Apartheid* (Durham: Duke University Press, 2002), 11, 17; Michael Titlestad, "Craig Higginson," 231.

62   Michael Titlestad, "Craig Higginson," 237.

63   Tamara LePine-Williams, "Classic Lifestyle with Craig Higginson," Radio interview, *Classic 1027: South African Classic FM*, Aug. 18, 2017; Anne Fuchs and Geoffrey Davis, "'Truth is in the detail.' Craig Higginson Talks to Anne Fuchs and Geoffrey Davis," in *New Territories*, ed. Greg Homann and Marc Maufort (Brussels: Peter Lang, 2015), 381.

64   Craig Higginson, "Dream of the Dog," 56.

Long silence.[65]
Patricia. Yet you were like my son, Looksmart. At least as close as I ever got to having one. (*Off his look*)[66]
Looksmart. *Sala kahle*, Mama. Don't worry – I'll let myself out.
Looksmart leaves.
Patricia. (*To herself*). *Hamba khale*, Phiwayinkosi.[67]
Patricia. He's gone. [...] I never thanked him properly.[68]

Moments of connection and shared intimacy are thus constantly threatened by a gnawing silence, or by the fact that one's voice may not be heard, because the declaration comes either too early and seems to fall on deaf ears (at least momentarily), or too late and is only heard by the audience – but it is expressed nevertheless. This can actually be linked to the direct allusion to the play found in its novelistic adaptation: early into the narrative, Patricia finds a ticket for the performance of a play entitled *Dream of the Dog*,[69] in London. The latter precision suggests an awareness of the concrete issues of the production of a play and of the question whether shows target South African or international audiences, "imagined communities" of a kind. Therefore, this very dialogue between genres in Higginson's practice as both playwright and novelist, in the case of this specific work, precisely sheds light on the essence of the theatre, which could also be called its intrinsic "iterability."[70] This characteristic makes theatre, essentially, both a poetic and political representation. Higginson's rewriting of his own play shows that *Dream of the Dog* and theatre at large thus call for performance, for an embodiment of the text through the voice of real actors on stage, "theatre being defined in its most essential definition as the interaction between someone who performs and someone who watches."[71] It thus further puts at its core the very site of articulation between the "I" and the "you," namely, the voice:

> [the voice is] the seat of the [subject] left empty, the seat that each of us longs to occupy: an exit out of oneself, such as it signifies and signals what is most proper to oneself, that however remains fleeting, elusive as soon as it is not written down. The ... subject is the voice of the other, the

---

65   *Ibid.*, 60.
66   *Ibid.*, 61.
67   *Ibid.*, 64–65.
68   *Ibid.*, 67.
69   Craig Higginson, *The Dream House*, 37.
70   Mark Sanders, *Complicities*, 17.
71   Greg Homann and Marc Maufort (eds.). *New Territories: Theatre, Drama and Performance in Post-apartheid South Africa* (Brussels: Peter Lang, 2015), 12.

one who speaks, it is the voice of all the others who speak inside of me, and the one I address to others.[72]

This is but another way of going back to the essence of theatre as readily dialogic and performative, leaving, as Ubersfeld points out, the last word to the spectator: "What is so unique to the theatre is the fact that, because it is no longer (as the poet said) 'one's person's voice' – since the scriptor has voluntary withdrawn – it so implicates the spectator that it ends up being the voice of us all."[73]

Works Cited

Anderson, Benedict. *Imagined Communities: Reflections on the Origin and Spread of Nationalism*. London; Verso, 1991 (1983).

Bailly, Jean-Christophe. *L'élargissement du poème*. Paris : Christian Bourgois, 2015.

Benveniste, Emile. *Problèmes de linguistique générale*. Paris: Gallimard, 1976 (1966).

Blumberg, Marcia. "Reconciling Acts: Theatre beyond the Truth and Reconciliation Commission." In *SA Lit beyond 2000*, edited by Michael Chapman and Margaret Lenta, 137–158. Scottsville: University of KwaZulu-Natal Press, 2011.

Coetzee, J.M. *Disgrace*. London: Vintage, 2000 (1999).

Coetzee, J.M. *Doubling the Point: Essays and Interviews*. Edited by David Attwell. Cambridge, MA: Harvard University Press, 1992.

Coetzee, John Maxwell. *White Writing: On the Culture of Letters in South Africa*. New Haven, CT: Yale University Press, 1988.

Debord, Guy. *La Société du Spectacle*. Paris: Gallimard, 1992 (1967).

De Certeau, Michel. *The Practice of Everyday Life*. Berkeley: U of California P, 1984.

Dodds, Eric R. *The Greeks and the Irrational*. Berkeley, CA: University of California Press, 2004.

Fuchs, Anne and Geoffrey Davis. "'Truth is in the detail.' Craig Higginson Talks to Anne Fuchs and Geoffrey Davis." In *New Territories*, edited by Greg Homann and Marc Maufort, 371–381. Brussels: Peter Lang, 2015.

Gary, Romain. *Chien blanc*. Paris: Gallimard, 1995 (1972).

---

72   Jean-Michel Maulpoix, "La quatrième personne du singulier," in *Figures du sujet lyrique*, ed. Dominique Rabaté (Paris: Presses Universitaires de France, 1996), 153. My translation. Maulpoix refers here more specifically to the lyrical subject and the lyrical voice (see also Bailly). However, one could argue that the interplay between the mode of *Dream of the Dog* and its novelistic rewriting via the subgenre of the *plaasroman* recalls the reflections on the lyrical and the epic found in another novel by Higginson, *The Landscape Painter*. An analysis of such interplay would exceed the scope of this essay.

73   Anne Ubersfeld, *Reading Theatre*, 192.

Higginson, Craig. "Dream of the Dog." In *Three Plays*. London: Oberon, 2016.

Higginson, Craig. *Dream of the Dog*. London: Oberon, 2010.

Higginson, Craig. *The Dream House*. Johannesburg: Picador Africa, 2015.

Higginson, Craig. *The Landscape Painter*. Johannesburg: Picador Africa, 2011.

Homann, Greg and Marc Maufort (eds.). *New Territories: Theatre, Drama and Performance in Post-apartheid South Africa*. Brussels: Peter Lang, 2015.

Jaspers, Karl. *The Question of German Guilt*. New York: Dial Press, 1947.

Langenohl, Andreas. "Memory in Post-Authoritarian Societies." In *A Companion to Cultural Memory Studies*, edited by Astrid Erll and Ansgar Nünning, 163–172. Berlin; New York: De Gruyter, 2010.

LePine-Williams, Tamara. "Classic Lifestyle with Craig Higginson." Radio interview, *Classic 1027: South African Classic FM*, 18 August 2017.

Maufort, Marc. "Negotiating the Post-apartheid Condition: Violence, Trauma and the Realist Aesthetic in Contemporary South African Drama." In *New Territories*, edited by Greg Homann and Marc Maufort, 240–260. Brussels: Peter Lang, 2015.

Maulpoix, Jean-Michel. "La quatrième personne du singulier." In *Figures du sujet lyrique*, edited by Dominique Rabaté, 147–160. Paris: Presses Universitaires de France, 1996.

Ndebele, Njabulo. "The Rediscovery of the Ordinary: Some New Writings in South Africa," *Journal of Southern African Studies* 12, no. 2 (1986): 143–157.

Nuttall, Sarah. *Entanglement, Literary and Cultural Reflections on Post-apartheid*. Johannesburg: Wits University Press, 2009.

"Promotion of National Unity and Reconciliation Act 34" *Department: Justice and Constitutional Development, Republic of South Africa*. 1995. www.justice.gov.za/legislation/acts/1995-034.pdf.

Rosanvallon, Pierre. *Le Parlement des invisibles*. Paris: Seuil, 2014.

Sanders, Mark. *Complicities: The Intellectual and Apartheid*. Durham: Duke University Press, 2002.

Sévry, Jean. "La Littérature sud-africaine et ses espaces." *Travaux de l'Institut de Géographie de Reims* 25, nos. 99–100 (1998): 15–26.

Titlestad, Michael. "Craig Higginson." In *The Methuen Guide to Contemporary South African Theatre*, edited by Martin Middeke, Peter Paul Schnierer and Greg Homann, 227–239. London; New York: Bloomsbury, 2015.

"Truth and Reconciliation Commission of South Africa Report." *Department: Justice and Constitutional Development, Republic of South Africa*. 1998. http://www.justice.gov.za/trc/report/.

Ubersfeld, Anne. *Reading Theatre*. Toronto: University of Toronto Press, 1999.

Van Heerden, Etienne. "Fences." In *Mad Dog and Other Stories*. Cape Town: David Philip, 1992.

Van Heerden, Etienne. "Slapgrensdrade." In *My Kubaan*. Cape Town: Tafelberg, 1983.

Vernant, Jean-Pierre. "Franchir un pont." In *La Traversée des frontières*. Paris: Seuil, 2004.

CHAPTER 9

South African Theatre and the Politics of the Improvisatory

Ralph Yarrow

Abstract

This essay explores, with reference to South African theatre practice from the 1980s to the present, ways in which the capacity to be in a state of improvisation has resonances for political, existential, psychological and social performativity, agency and responsibility. Much improvisatory practice is concerned with ways in which the body, in and as performance, remembers and/or composes meaning. The essay traces the improvisatory (a condition rather than a single outcome) across different modes: from resistance to "formal hybridity," moving towards a theatre rich in physical immediacy, and evoking a refusal to avoid trauma or pain as direct experience, engendered in and transmitted by the body in action, which operates a multi-layered presencing of history.

Over the last few decades theatre in South Africa has had to evolve to face a variety of social, political and personal challenges, ranging from the overt oppression of apartheid to disillusionment with the nostalgic mythologies of heroism and legitimacy and the dimming of the "rainbow" vision and the functioning democracy which underpinned it. "State capture" by ruling caucuses and international finance threaten to betray that vision, undermine parliamentary democracy, divert economic resource and institutionalise corruption. In face of a monolithic, moribund party structure, a politics of denial and factional and international rapacity, can the energies which impelled resistance realign themselves as critique and creativity in order to reclaim spaces for individual and collective vitality?

Jacques Lecoq suggests that improvisation and innovation in performance practice is particularly strong in response to restrictive and oppressive historical and political situations.[1] A recent conference on improvisation[2] illustrated

---

1   Anthony Frost and Ralph Yarrow, *Improvisation in Drama, Theatre and Performance* (Basingstoke: Palgrave Macmillan, 2015), 221.
2   "Impro Talks": a symposium held in 2016 (Zurich University of the Arts). Proceedings published by Zhdk – Zürcher Hochschule der Künste Darstellende Künste und Film, 2017.

© KONINKLIJKE BRILL NV, LEIDEN, 2020 | DOI:10.1163/9789004414464_010

the variety of dimensions, contexts, modalities and interfaces which improvisation and the improvisatory can take – as practice, methodology, event structure, cognitive functionality, aesthetics and politics. It identified, exemplified, and demonstrated intellectually and practically that improvisation is a process and set of behaviours located in psychophysiological, interpersonal, communal and "universal" terrains. It thus suggested that improvisation may be useful as a methodology both of human behaviour and creativity and of innovation in performance modes, in addition to or in parallel with the kinds of textual or performative content it may generate.

This essay asks what aspects of South African theatre practice over recent decades can be seen as "improvisatory," what the major effects of this are in terms of a response to the political situation, and in what ways they give evidence of potentials for "resistance" and/or renovation of a complex kind which may influence behaviours within and beyond performance. I look at work under apartheid, in the years following it and more recently, in order to explore different dimensions and views of what constitutes improvisation or improvising and examine how it relates to habit and practice. In consequence, I suggest that South African theatre practice is shot through with improvisatory characteristics which enable it to stage a politics which is both personal and public, attitudinal and activist, and to offer the possibility of reconfiguring the parameters of identity and community.

If, in post-structuralist thought, "performance" mounts a challenge to the hegemony of "text" (the spectrum of debate here ranges between Schechner and Phelan, between Deleuze and Zarrilli...), then improvised performance – and to a large extent, the use of improvisatory techniques to develop performance either individually or collaboratively, within or across genres and modes – represents the epitome of that capacity; it is a mode of unmaking and remaking languages, physical and mental processes, structures and conceptions, habits and default positions. Its process, as well as its product, is a politics; it locates the condition from which structural and attitudinal change may ensue. Much South African theatre under apartheid, though not necessarily improvised at the stage of performance, is improvisatory in this sense and functions as a reclamation of the space and sense of performance and the agency of performers. In addition, Anton Krueger notes that – perhaps largely as a result of this inheritance – "the majority of significant productions in the country are devised, or choreographed, as physical theatre and contemporary performance pieces."[3] This has benefits and drawbacks: immediacy, directness,

---

3   Anton Krueger, "A Heritage of Violence," in *Syncretic Arenas. Essays on Postcolonial African Drama and Theatre for Esiaba Irobi*, ed. Isidore Diala (Amsterdam, NY: Brill/Rodopi, 2014), 237.

topicality, appropriate generic convergence on one hand; on the other, the awareness that "[i]n many ways, South African theatre today is still largely a DIY industry – if one doesn't perform, direct, or in other ways get involved in producing one's own work, it's rare that somebody else will";[4] and relatively few productions result in a script which makes it to the stage of publication. Thus much, perhaps most, South African performance work has been and is both devised and developed through improvisatory methodologies and also retains strong imprints of those determinants of its development.

I think this is visible from the 1970s on, in the work of Magnet Theatre, Theatre for Africa, Sibikwa, Handspring Puppet Company; in the ethos and practice of South African University Drama and Performance departments like UCT, Wits and Rhodes and associated performers and companies (e.g. Fleishman/Reznek and Magnet, Andrew Buckland, Gary Gordon and First Physical Theatre Company); in the readiness to programme such work at The Space, The Market Theatre, The Baxter and other venues; and of course subsequently in the case of many other creators, performers, providers and teachers and in collaborations with other genres and other modes (dance, puppetry, site-specific work, township collaborations etc.). All these aim to work rigorously and consciously on the edge of forms, at the juncture of history and memory as well as narrative and truth. Though these kinds of shift beyond text-based and proscenium-oriented drama are of course also characteristic of developments in the nature of theatre and performance across the globe during the same period, the South African situation is particularly intensive and pervasive.

In the years since the establishment of the "new South Africa," the essentially binary or oppositional character of much "early" work came to be perceived as canonical or "monological,"[5] in need itself of revising. Homann suggests that subsequent work targeted a more complex process of engagement with the past in order to construct a more nuanced understanding of contemporary roles and responsibilities; current political realities present perhaps an even more problematic scenario, as Homann puts it later: "plays deal with issues of identity, notions of land, reconciliation, negotiation, xenophobia, generational conflict, corruption, violence, abuse and prejudice. Drama and theatre have been functioning as influential and powerful counter-discourses against a society dominated by segregation, exploitation and oppression."[6]

---

4   *Ibid.*, 238.

5   Greg Homann, "Preamble," in *At this Stage*, ed. Greg Homann (Johannesburg: Wits UP, 2009), 2.

6   Martin Middeke, Peter Paul Schnierer and Greg Homann (Eds.), *The Methuen Drama Guide to Contemporary South African Theatre* (London: Bloomsbury, 2015), 7.

So there is a legacy of performance strategy which possesses strong elements of what I call the improvisatory; and equally there are several sets of highly problematic political and social circumstances which any conscious artistic endeavour has to reflect, reflect upon and negotiate.

1   The Improvisatory: Some Definitions

Improvisation, specifically in drama, theatre and performance, but also more generally is:

– a history: lots of people have done it at different times in different contexts and in different ways which relate to, comment on, challenge or redefine those contexts and the systems and structures which frame them; examples include the repartee of the clown, the quick wit of the Fool, carnivalesque inversions, miscegenous structural alliances of the fixed and the on-the-spot like *Commedia*, Long Form and West African concert parties;[7]
– a set of practices, similarly culturally embedded and potentially transgressive: including but not limited to sets of training procedures from across the globe which hone skill in reacting verbally and physically, accessing taboo areas of the psyche, exploring emotional and embodied memory, circumventing habit, working collaboratively and creatively together and acquiring a technical resource base from which innovation becomes possible;[8]
– an underpinning set of principles or theoretical positions: avoiding blocking, "yes-saying," accessing *disponibilité*, outmanoeuvring internal or external censorship.[9]

In this respect, improvisation is both diachronic and synchronic. It both manifests itself as always different across time and signals a "universal" set of understandings or claims. A recent book by Gary Peters proposes that "improvisation isn't so much a genre, idiom, style or technique – it's a predicament we are thrown into, one we find ourselves in."[10] Hence it is not principally the particular "in-the-moment" reactions, responses or performance choices, but essentially a "mode of decision" to be available, open to and prepared for making things new at any moment. It is, in this perspective, a condition rather than an act or sequence of acts; it is that which makes the acts possible. As such, it is a

---

7   Anthony Frost and Ralph Yarrow, *Improvisation in Drama*, 3–141.
8   *Ibid.*, 145–214.
9   *Ibid.*, 215–246.
10   Gary Peters, *Improvising Improvisation: From Out of Philosophy, Music, Dance and Literature* (Chicago: University of Chicago Press, 2017), front cover.

psychophysical capacity which has to be acquired over time through repeated practice and is ultimately internalised in the body/mind as the ground of action.

Over several versions, the book I co-wrote with Anthony Frost broadly traces a historical and methodological line from the use of improvisation as a component in the rehearsal and preparation of "conventional" theatre towards becoming a form in its own right (including Chicago "improv" and its derivatives); and signals its emergence as the nub of deconstructive and reconstructive modes of performance, for individuals, groups and audiences.[11]

Improvisation can be said habitually/traditionally to operate an ethos of deconstruction of *habitus* in the sense of unfixing the fixed, opening up space for renewal and realignment. It is a claiming of agency, of the ability to insert the self (the performer in/as participant in the [re]-construction of "text" or texturing) into the making of new versions, truths, realities and compositions. Its tools are bodies, voices, the stuff or sensorially-transmitted matter of sounds, movement, shapes, words, things. Their trajectories of communication are visual, tactile, auditory; their affect modulates into effect through staging "other" possibilities of utterance, role and function.

Thus, in terms of methodology and practice, improvisation implies:

i)   utilising ad-hoc capacity/response and "poor theatre" modes to create "on the spot" resistance/response/space-claiming-performance as *mobile acts*; (space = linguistic, physical, social, political, personal);

ii)   the ability to return over and over again to the "beginning," to the point from which you think and make the new, to accept the continual disruption of received wisdom/habit/positions.

Both these require psychophysical, formal, aesthetic and intellectual agility. Mode i) opens up a big reservoir of resources but may also, like the ANC's claim to inviolability as the icon of "The Struggle," risk leading to relatively simple repetition and encrustation. Mode ii) is ongoing, continuous; carried out fully, it does not let you off the hook, it requires scrutiny and reformulation of both past and present acts and patterns. It is less about responding to an empirical challenge than about living and creating a continuous reinsertion in challenge. And in practice i) can and probably should mostly bleed into and act as a "training" methodology for the aesthetic (the making of perceptible, sensible, transactional form) of ii).

Much improvisatory practice is concerned with ways in which the body, in and as performance, remembers and/or composes meaning. Simon Murray describes the major aim of Lecoq's school as "to investigate the corporeal basis of

---

11   Anthony Frost and Ralph Yarrow, *Improvisation in Drama*, xi–xix.

creativity."[12] Fundamental principles of the exercises presented by Murray are a) movement generates emotion; and b) the body remembers. So, in targeting a "site to build on,"[13] Lecoq is interested not just in the physical flexibility of his early sports training, but more crucially in the body's potential for registering, remembering and engendering experience at subtle and profound levels. For Lecoq, the body moves and speaks as it moves. Its speaking is an act of memory and an act of creation, an invention of corporeal, imaginative and theatrical languages, an embodied poetics ("provoquant [l']imagination à produire des langues").[14]

These formulations aim to identify an attitude which is embodied, rooted in the acquisition of particular ways of functioning which predispose body and mind (the "bodythink" which Clive Barker's seminal *Theatre Games* targets for performers and which underpins many performance-training methodologies centrally using improvisation and games/exercises)[15] to function as the generative site of new formulations and out-of-the-box thinking and action. They also rest on the capacity – in many cases the necessity – to view the performance space and the properties of performance as transportable, fluid, subject to rapid dis-and re-assembly into other configurations and relationships. Evidence of both of these dimensions is also found in "early" (apartheid-era) South African theatre.

2   Interstitial Theatre: Form as Resistance to Oppression

South African resistance theatre under apartheid is a theatre of multiple voices. Voices which speak different verbal languages – many of them officially proscribed –, as well as the languages of bodies and space, of rhythm and register. Its process is a negotiation across the spaces between those languages; its theatreing is the activation of the silences between. Between languages, identities, modes and kinds of being; between that which is felt and experienced

---

12   Simon Murray, *Jacques Lecoq* (London: Routledge, 2003), 158.
13   *Ibid.*, 63.
14   Jacques Lecoq, *Brochure de l'Ecole Jacques Lecoq* (Paris: n.d.), n.p.
15   Viola Spolin, *Improvisation for the Theater* (Evanston, IL: Northwestern UP, 1963); Keith Johnstone, *Impro: Improvisation and the Theatre* (London: Methuen, 1981); Chris Johnston, *House of Games: Making Theatre from Everyday Life* (London: Nick Hern Books, 1998); Dymphna Callery, *Through the Body: A Practical Guide to Physical Theatre* (New York: Routledge, 2001); Augusto Boal, *Games for Actors and Non-Actors*, trans. Adrian Jackson (London: Routledge, 1992).

and that which is articulated. Voices from the margins which find a space which is not "permitted."

These "spaces in between" function, in terms of form, in South African theatre, from the 1960s to the late 1980s, as:

- Shifts between languages (found almost without exception). Language as a locus of statement, challenge, transgression, assertion of status and identity. Monologic State discourse is the language of singularity (usually implied to be Afrikaans, although in most of the well-known plays represented through English), which is overtly contested either by characters deliberately claiming their own tongue (e.g. by the isi-Xhosa of the women's protest song in *You Strike the Woman, You Strike the Rock*; by a kind of *sangoma*-speak in *The Native Who Caused All the Trouble*); or by characters whose multi-linguistic skill enables them to satirise the "stupid Boer" position (Styles in *Sizwe Bansi is Dead*, the intelligent insect in *The Ugly Noonoo*).
- Changes of character and role in mono-acting or two-handed sequences: in *Woza Albert!* and *Sizwe Bansi*, two performers play numerous roles, shifting from black to white, male to female etc. In *Horn of Sorrow* human actors play a large variety of birds and animals as well as people. The *Ugly Noo-Noo* is a one-person virtuoso creation comprising humans, cockroaches, a dog and a chicken.
- Switches and juxtapositions of time, place, register, tone, mode, genre or style: frequent use of song, often in indigenous languages – e.g. the recollection of the 1956 Pretoria march in *You Strike the Woman*; register as a mark of status and challenge to status; "poor" stage as mobile and transformable location signalling both the vulnerability of life and the danger associated with performance itself.
- Collaborations between writers, directors, actors, puppeteers, often including – forbidden – cross-racial work. (Fugard, Kani, Ntshona; Simon, Mtwa, Ngema; Junction 71; Taylor/Handspring; etc.).

Most of these are common to much theatre practice – and my argument also relates to some extent to that – but in South African theatre they are particularly numerous and conscious, in large measure because they represent deliberate political choice: the choice to work across boundaries which were set by apartheid and the accompanying restrictions on what kinds of performance were permitted. In a world where, as John Kani puts it, "you never knew whether by waking up you weren't breaking the law,"[16] shape-shifting characteristics were both pragmatically necessary and also an act of conscious defiance, claiming a form and place to be. They also ask questions: they act as a

---

16   "*The Island*; an historical piece?," *Open University Digital Archive*, A 319; 06; 1996.

kind of framing to each manifestation or location of person and situation, relativising it and interrogating it in ways which were for the most part neither permissible nor possible outside the theatre. The improvisatory touchstone of *play* takes on the quality of a political act. (Play as a measure of flexibility – the play of a hinge; as irreverence or quizzicality; as that which makes and follows its own rules; as the child's propensity for wonder; as fun and as the joy of creating things together; as the capacity for sense-making which is the touchstone of human capacity – *pace* Schiller, Huizinga, Caillois.)

In such work, role emerges out of performance as something which is in the making, generated from or by the negation or absence of role imposed by apartheid: black people feel that whites do not see them; often they do not address them by their name but as "boy" or as a pass or "Dombook" number (*Sizwe Bansi*), or by derogatory names like Bobbejaan (Baboon) (*Woza Albert!*). Andrew Buckland's Man in *The Ugly Noo-Noo* attempts to annihilate the "Parktown prawn" (cockroach) which incorporates white fears of the other, but as the play goes on the prawn reveals itself as articulate and reasonable, despite regularly losing bits of its anatomy; the actor likewise has to find a way to pass through a kind of limbo and discover how to be the cockroach, as well as the Man.

So performance is a remaking from and across a gap; the identities it puts together, including its own "poor" material status as "theatre on the run," are provisional, vulnerable, porous, but autonomous. This porosity is often evident as irony: the jokey *négritude* of Bobbejaan is accepted by the character and throws the whites' insulting appellation back in their faces. In the play, both he and the actor playing him are much more than that, and never the same for very long: identity is not fixity but movement and in that lies its efficacy and its power. Performance too is never, in its location and its genre, static; it is constantly posited against an abyss (censure, closure, prohibition) and in defiance of the fact that it is not officially allowed, or only at best provisionally allowed (a bit like Kafka's K in *The Trial*), to exist in this way.

3   After Apartheid

The post-apartheid situation presents new challenges. Perhaps one of its most striking characteristics, which also feeds into performance both in terms of content and of poetics, is *anxiety* about role ("given" social or individual role or identity, role as constructed in performance, and performance's sense of its own role and function).

Under apartheid, and in many forms of "traditional" cultural matrix, role is "officially" constructed and/or determined; although this of course generates contestation and resistance, as depicted in "classic" resistance work like *Sizwe Bansi is Dead* and *Woza Albert!*. But there is a clear divide, in that such contestation becomes a claiming of space and moral high ground, against oppressive or reactionary forces. There *is* a role or identity which is threatened or negated by the system, and which it is courageous and morally justified to claim or reclaim. In this situation, hybrid performance styles, practices and resources (as recalled briefly above) are embraced as a site and mark of resistance, of flouting enforced boundaries, of sorties beyond the "permitted" order. Hybridity is here a political stance, and thus a source of pride rather than anxiety.

The post-apartheid situation is much less sure about this. In part because, constitutionally and to some degree in practice, more and more complex roles are available. It is legal to speak any one of eleven languages, to identify with, to desire and to campaign for a range of political, economic, racial, sexual and ideological options. In part also because to claim an unequivocal status on the basis of role has become, recently in particular, suspect. It is no longer, as in the heady post-"victory" years, an unquestioned right; but rather an existential undertaking, something which involves a series of choices and actions which have continually to be interrogated and justified. Those who have claimed superior status as a result of their role in the struggle – and those who have joined the "party" more recently – have increasingly been subject to scrutiny on the basis precisely of the disjunction between claimed status and actual behaviour; in the national political domain, role has become a highly contested category, from that of the President down; it is more a question of a crisis of legitimacy, played out in an ongoing series of corruption scandals and legal challenges.

Identity is thus inevitably positioned much more precariously as a complex set of negotiated choices. So the inherited polymorphous poetics of South African theatre is now intensified, problematised, remixed and renegotiated. As Ashraf Jamal signals,[17] the "formal hybridity" and "liminal impurity" of theatre makes it "well placed to expose the contradictions which threaten a projected national unity."

It is significant that among the few new plays Homann picks out in the postapartheid period are two by Zakes Mda. Mda's work has always engaged with the wider issues of African negotiation of the "post-revolutionary" situation, and, for instance in *We Shall Sing for the Fatherland*, highlights precisely those

---

17   Qtd. in Greg Homann, "Preamble," 2.

dangers – of the Revolution/Tyranny cycle, or of the creaming-off of the spoils by a côterie – which have affected many African nations and now threaten South Africa.

Homann indicates that from about 1990, there is a gradual shift from the well-known protest "monologic" form – in the sense that the "poor theatre" model of highly mobile/transportable theatre performed by a small number of actors usually in multiple roles, offering a message of resistance and solidarity, had become ubiquitous and more or less *de rigueur*, for pragmatic reasons.[18] Hence part of the problem for South African theatre as for South Africa itself as a "new democracy" was to find ways of moving beyond the seductive but frozen image of noble resistance, which out of necessity worked with binary models of gender, race, ethics and political choice which now appear reductive and oversimplified. On the other hand, to equate identity with resistance is also to posit it as provisional, shifting, liminal, transgressive – everything that can outwit or outrun the hegemony of state power which would box it into set categories or refute its right to exist at all. Thus many of the dynamics and energies of that endeavour remain inscribed in the performance practice of subsequent phases: here, the problematic is to grapple with and formulate an "identity" which is now *authorised as* plural, multigeneric, multilinguistic and so on. But the territory on which that negotiation takes place has also changed, so that contemporary social and political experience, charged with delivering a "new South Africa," actually feels insecure about that kind of instability and yearns nostalgically for the simple, noble, and impossibly mythic binaries of the past. Thus once more theatre finds itself at odds with political hegemony, nowhere more perhaps than in Mike van Graan's *Green Man Flashing* (2004) or John Kani's *Nothing But the Truth* (2002). In a way then, it has regained, in another historical and political dimension, its apartheid function, in the sense that it exposes and excoriates; but it has fitted itself to new conditions by using the multiple strands of linguistic and performative skills to address complex and shifting problems which traverse the political, social and racial spectrum. The nature of performance is still contentious (a site of contestation) and evocative (of the wounds of memory, of the unresolved injustices of the present): in both dimensions it manifests improvisatory qualities in its quick-witted response to the contemporaneous, its foregrounding of "buried" material and its multigeneric dexterity.

---

18   Martin Middeke, Peter Paul Schnierer and Greg Homann (Eds.), *The Methuen Drama Guide*, 4.

Krueger also points to the ubiquity of violence in (South) African societies. In part this arises from its ultimate justification as a form of resistance to oppression, which has been remodeled as "a struggle for justice in the new dispensation."[19] Violent resistance, Krueger notes, "has been crucial to the formation of virtually all statehood in Africa."[20] However, violence also belongs to the domain of a nostalgia for certainty, for the old binaries, which forms part of many "alt-Right" ideologies and rhetorical strategies; it rests on assumptions about fixity of (largely gendered) roles, it represents a relatively "easy" acceptance of existing models which are largely illusory or incomplete. Instances of violence in many forms (rape and dispossession in Lara Foot's *Karoo Moose* and *Tshepang*, for instance) and the appeal to "tradition" invoked to justify it are both foregrounded and interrogated on stage, so that here too difficult and complex journeys are mooted rather than simplistic "solutions." Indeed, the function of many performances is, as Adrian Jackson says of Boal's "forum" model, to "difficultate" rather than facilitate.[21] Whereas "holding on to heritage" and "sustaining traditions of patriarchy"[22] signal a paralysis, the key processes in the work discussed above have to do with unseating, unsettling, looking and thinking again. For Krueger, they tend to produce "new" kinds of structural features in terms of plot, character and context. The plays "unsettle expectations and needle out sometimes uncomfortable nuances of emergent identities" and lead to "new modes of being, new definitions of selves attempting to negotiate the contexts in which they have located themselves."[23]

In the period he designates as "early post-apartheid" (1996–2000) – roughly contemporary with the start of the TRC – Homann particularly singles out *Ubu and the Truth Commission*[24] and *Ipi Zombi?*[25] *Ubu and the Truth Commission* is concerned with "the intricacy of truth-telling,"[26] juxtaposing accounts from Truth Commission witnesses against attempts to wriggle off the hook by the duplicitous reincarnations of Ma and Pa Ubu as defendants and manipulators of the truth, and framing its many versions through different media (projected superscript and image, puppets, characters behind a transparent screen which

---

19   Anton Krueger, "A Heritage of Violence," 243.
20   *Ibid.*, 245.
21   Augusto Boal, *The Rainbow of Desire*, trans. Adrian Jackson (London: Routledge, 1995), xix.
22   Anton Krueger, "A Heritage of Violence," 246.
23   *Ibid.*, 242.
24   William Kentridge, Jane Taylor and the Handspring Puppet Co, *Ubu and the Truth Commission* (Johannesburg: Wits UP, 1998).
25   Brett Bailey, "Ipi Zombi?" in *Plays for a New South Africa*, ed. David Graver (Bloomington & Indianapolis: Indiana UP, 1998), 200–219.
26   Greg Homann, "Preamble," 7.

is both protective witness box and oppressive custodial location, actors, visible puppeteers who sometimes speak). The play juxtaposes and interweaves many channels of semiosis and requires audiences to bring them together by inter-pretative action. So, continuous cross-checking and relativising is stimulated: truth-making and validating is directly experienced as a complex process of negotiation. Here it is primarily the audience which is asked to engage in im-provisatory activity, constantly refocusing their receptive and interpretative antennae.

Bailey's work explores "the boundless chaotic domain underlying the skin of order upon which we build the flimsy structures of our existence" – incorporating ritual, trance, rural performance practices including chant and dance – and often quizzically and sceptically, not simply "reproducing" but interrogating ritual behaviours as forms of coercive or oppressive pressure; the play also focuses on "patterns of cultural collision."[27]

Jamal claims that both plays utilise the "mechanics of staging the enigma that dogs received truth...challenges its hegemony."[28] Homann says they "shift-ed the paradigm in South African theatre";[29] they lead towards new collabora-tions and forms of liminality as well as crossing the stage/audience divide. In the case of *Ubu and the Truth Commission*, the barrier crossed is between pup-peteers, puppets and "real" characters. They show a "fascination with address-ing the nuances and complexities of *representing* truth";[30] more materially, they actually *instigate and embody* the process of representing it, so that it is directly experienced by the audience. The structural mechanics of the play and the interpretative work of the audience combine to locate the "action" repeat-edly at this junction point of different strata of lived experience, degrees of authenticity and modes of representation. Both "theatre" and being in theatre are here recalibrated as forms of activity requiring continuous readjustment and reassessment. Similar to the refusal of narrative closure which Patrice Pa-vis calls "displacement," this operates across junctions which Jane Turner terms "connectors," "secators" and "shifters," in discussing reception processes in Eu-genio Barba's multicultural and multi-generic work.[31]

In the "post-apartheid" period as described by Homann (2002–8), John Kani's *Nothing But the Truth* (2002) is a key play. It adopts a realist mode to in-voke critical interrogation of the past in terms of previously unacknowledged

---

27   Qtd. in Greg Homann, "Preamble," 8.
28   Ashraf Jamal, *Predicaments of Culture in South Africa* (Pretoria: Unisa Press, 2005), 137.
29   Greg Homann, "Preamble," 7.
30   *Ibid.*, 9.
31   Jane Turner, *Eugenio Barba* (London: Routledge, 2004), 86ff.

tensions within the ANC/black/resistance community which, unresolved, may fester. *Nothing But the Truth* is a deliberately "well-made" play which charts a kind of Freudian psychopolitical journey from suppression of uncomfortable aspects of the past through admission and encounter to articulation, revealing the "hidden stories"[32] underlying family history, in this case an iconic family with deep roots in the Struggle.

The challenges posed by *Nothing But the Truth* include a "polemic in opposition to the aura of heroism that surrounds certain leaders of the struggle," and the overt questioning of "a limited set of historical roles."[33] This deconstructive move ironically takes place on a deliberately prescribed (by a diagram in the published text) box set which identifies location, race and social class. The frame signals a classic "naturalist" endeavour (though one which is conscious of the force of releasing "ghosts") in order to underline the sharpness of the attack on accepted versions. The play is also highly significant because Kani, an iconic theatre figure of the struggle years, delivers – as author and as lead actor – this public scrutiny. These several dimensions of metatheatricality intensify the force with which the play incites a sense of unease and attempts to function as a historical and political question-mark. Its interrogation of the "natural" is both historically astute and theatrically ironic: it declares itself to be an entirely "proper" piece of scripted theatre, but precisely in doing so shifts the ground that this mode appears to substantiate.

Nothing But the Truth signals a confrontation with the insufficiency of memory and the familiar post-revolutionary practice of rewriting and/or editing history to create a weighted narrative, and a concomitant desire to open up spaces of memory to alternative versions of truth. In many ways plays, of memory, accountability, justice etc. are paramount and parallel or extend the functioning of the TRC during this period. *Reach!* (Lara Foot, 2007), *Dream of the Dog* (Craig Higginson, 2007) and *Shwele Bawo!* (Motshabi Tyelele, 2004) also engage with this territory in light of the contemporary South African situation (Black Economic Empowerment, corruption, crime and factors underlying it, ANC splits, AIDS etc.); their settings reflect this, emblematically, representing a space which holds a past revealed as fissured and problematic, in process of deconstruction.

In *Reach!* and *Dream of the Dog*, the past is unraveled and reconfigured, different versions collide as stories which are deliberately or inadvertently gappy and defective, physicalised in characters (young, old, black and white) whose different versions are censored or constructed for different and contending,

---

32   Greg Homann, "Preamble," 12.

33   *Ibid.*

but equally comprehensible, reasons. There is no single truth or right here, the past is manifested as difficulty, a difficulty which in each of these plays leads to painful, possibly traumatic confrontation. However, the imaginary of theatre uses bodies, feelings and the insights they stimulate to engage more directly with this territory than does the rhetorical horn-locking of many of the contenders for power and influence in the political spectrum.

Nadia Davids, in her Author's Notes to *Cissie* (2008), a play about a key woman politician in District Six, writes, in words which could equally apply to *Nothing But the Truth*, "we are still in a process of reparative history-making, of restoring truths and treating wounds ... we are only just approaching the moment when we can critically engage with liberation leaders of the past."[34] She also echoes Mark Fleishman and Jennie Reznek, whom she assisted in their work on *Önnest'Bo*, in saying: "theatre makers can find porous moments in the archive and create an emotional landscape around them."[35] Such moments begin to occur in the opening monologue, which senses "histories covered by grass and brick and dirt": those of District Six, and of her protagonist, Cissie Gool, a "woman of colour" shunted out of most records in spite of being a Councillor for over twenty years and the first non-white to achieve an MA at the University of Cape Town. The work of imagination may enable these people to "begin to lose the transparency of the forgotten"[36] and emerge as a weft of fact and fiction, of intercut time-zones, of different formats (interviews, monologues, montage, invented scenes) which offer a collage of sometimes contradictory perspectives on a single life. What I am suggesting is that all the work referred in the last couple of pages is dramaturgically improvisatory, in the sense in which I am using this term, by virtue of seeking and exploiting "porosity" in the representational mode and in the relationship of theatre to its social world and audience.

Mike van Graan's *Green Man Flashing* (2004) was described as "a new brand of politically active theatre" with "its finger firmly on the pulse of the precariousness of our democracy";[37] the play was commended for courageously tackling contentious themes, and theatres were initially unwilling to produce it. Although it predates the former South African President (then ANC Deputy President) Zuma's trial on a charge of rape, it is remarkably prescient in this and other aspects of contemporary politics, probing "corruption and evasion

---

34   Nadia Davids, *Cissie* (Cape Town: Junkets, 2008), viii.

35   *Ibid.*, ix.

36   *Ibid.*, 11.

37   Qtd. in Mike van Graan, *Green Man Flashing* (Cape Town: Junkets, 2010), inside front cover.

in 'the party'":[38] the plot hinges on an attempt by her former lover, a (black) ANC negotiator, to put pressure on white administrator Gabby to drop a charge of rape against her boss, a current high-profile ANC Minister with an impeccable anti-apartheid record. By locating the dirty linen of the political elite in a personal setting, it achieves an intensity which matches that of *Reach!*, *Dream of the Dog* or van Graan's own disturbing and finely-balanced two-hander, *Some Mothers' Sons* (2005), the story of two lawyers, one black, one white, representing each other in arrests at different historical junctures which bring into relief major questions about justice and civil society.

So, this theatre is rich in physical immediacy, signalling and evoking a refusal to avoid trauma or pain as direct experience, engendered in and transmitted by the body in action. A mix of Stanislavskian and Grotowskian intentions to engage with the body as a site of experience and availability, perhaps. If so, it employs those trajectories which both would have thought of as improvisatory: the attempt to get the performer (and if possible the audience) to encounter and traverse the rawness and the complexity, the difficulty and the danger, of the "situation" (personal, political, historical, communal). For this is something which theatre can take on, and is in many ways more prepared to do so than most public behaviours; yet it can also signal that the methods it uses are not just a form of recovering history, of engaging its porosity and siphoning up through the apertures and fissures a multitude of material which some might prefer to leave buried, but many recognise that they need desperately to confront in order to live. These theatrical strategies also contain a recipe for negotiation, hints and tactics about how to engage another gear, to develop an internal dialogue, to live a kind of plurality, to open up the body and the emotions to experience and to be able to frame it, to engage with it and thus to understand and function, however uneasily, within it.

This is an ecology of theatre – a template of its process – which on the one hand is aware of and engages with the dis-ease and discomfort of recognizing that we are co-responsible for the messes we make (socially, politically, environmentally); and on the other hand which unashamedly aims, in an Artaudian fashion, to "directly affect the organism," to produce a visceral internalization of that unease. It does not apportion blame or identify "others" as scapegoats. The centrality of bodily practice to many forms of South African performance produces a set of habits which can work with, rather than run away from, intensities of insecurity, trauma and absence of a recognizable track to follow. It keeps performers and audiences in contact with the raw places from which reformulation can start.

---

38   Greg Homann, "Preamble," 13.

Like these plays, *Shwele Bawo!* also contains the mix of languages, registers and discourses of many apartheid-era plays. *Shwele Bawo!* is a one-woman multi-role play, containing many voices, rhythms, attitudes (cf. also Yael Farber's *A Woman in Waiting*). The submerged past emerges volcanically as a complex plurality of memories, forms of conditioning, influences; it not merely shapes an embodied and internalised legacy but in so doing reveals itself as the challenge of the present: to confront, engage, maybe reconcile, but ultimately acknowledge and negotiate, as much as possible. The improvisatory in theatre is here a set of practices which engages the full scope of humanity and signals a lack in the body politic.

This reconstitution of (collective) memory, a kind of theatrical version of the TRC, operates a multi-layered presencing of history as constitutive act, performed by both producers and receivers: a theatre which remembers and engenders as it reconstructs, a magnet which locates and repositions the fragments. It engenders the "potency of memory" and underlines the fact that "theatre's relationship with truth is constitutively restless and provisional."[39] Can the improvisatory and the fragmentary (re)constitute "history"? Whereas "history" implies coherence of narrative, perhaps even the monologic voice and/or the appearance, at least, of "objectivity," the improvisatory is inevitably fractured and incomplete, partial and perhaps only half-remembered. Yet at the same time it poses an explicit challenge to the conventional understanding of history, a re-telling of its incomplete stories. Partial or marginalised, alternative or other voices and modes collide and reframe the composing and the composed. However, we are not just talking about a different *writing* but about a reworking and reliving.

4   History, Gaps and Spaces: "The Possibility of Lived Experience"[40]

This (re)-encounter with history is carried further by Magnet Theatre.[41] In the programme note to *Önnest'Bo* ("Upside Down"), Mark Fleishman and Jennie Reznek claim that their work with Magnet Theatre in Cape Town frequently "explores the terrain between performance and historiography" to create "moments and experiences that they transform and interpret through theatre." *Önnest'Bo* uses a combination of movement, the spoken word in several

---

39   Greg Homann (Ed.), *At this Stage* (Johannesburg: Wits UP, 2009), 17.

40   Programme note to *Önnest'Bo* (2002).

41   See: Megan Lewis and Anton Krueger (Eds.), *Magnet Theatre: Three Decades of Making Space* (Pretoria: Intellect, 2015).

languages (some of it improvised in performance), music and set (a collection of boxes) to present experiences of forced removal, of which the most notable under apartheid occurred in Johannesburg's Sophiatown (1955) and Cape Town's District Six (1985). This is theatre on the borders of history, fiction and memory – recreated by the original directorial and performance team in collaboration, together with input from researchers attached to the District Six museum – which "address[es] the gaps and spaces between facts" and may "stumble across a moment in history that is porous, fragmented, a hole in the archive," in order to "imagine, fictionalise and represent the *possibility* of the lived experience at that time." These "moments" represent a crossover point between the diachronic narrative of history and the synchronic in-depth illumination of a multidimensional performance event.[42]

Önnest'Bo, along with other work by Magnet like *Cargo* (2007), reenacts South African history, as lived experience rather than discursive narrative. Shards of documentary evidence appear as objects, things held and used and resisted; as snatches of experienced time; as images of people and places, transformed by structure, design, illumination, costume. These phenomena, which in performance are present, tactile, intrusive, resistant, may in official written histories be neutralized, archived, "put away," filed, boxed. Re-engendering them requires composing a process of experience in which component elements are located not as words on a page, but as moments and sensations in time and space, separated by lacunae. In much improvisatory practice, as Lecoq identifies, forgetting is the most essential thing to learn.[43] Fleishman describes his project as one of "interpretation to bridge the gap between the past event and the present memory"; necessary here and now because much, both in history and in performance knowledge in South Africa, requires "disinterring and reconstituting" (an endeavour which recalls the ethos of the Truth and Reconciliation Committee, as is especially manifest in the Gladstone bag stuffed with incriminating papers in Jane Taylor/Handspring Puppet Co.'s *Ubu and the Truth Commission* [1997]).

Magnet's productions may include fragmented texts of all kinds, even a trunk full of unidentified documents, but the completeness of a narrative, a "his-story" is constantly denied; because the fragments of sound and sense evoke a multi-layered response, they do not tell but point towards. Some of my

---

42   See also Jennie Reznek's analysis of the many dimensions in which Magnet's work with the moving body rests on "a political understanding of the notion of constant change" in Megan Lewis and Anton Krueger (Eds.), *Magnet Theatre: Three Decades of Making Space* (Pretoria: Intellect, 2015), 146.

43   Anthony Frost and Ralph Yarrow, *Improvisation in Drama*, 72.

memories of Magnet productions are: an old VW on a darkened stage; freezing cold in a disused industrial space and a woman in a swimming costume; strange sounds in the dark; wet performers; sets which de-and re-construct, produce people and things from inside them; flaming torches, shadows, choral voices, darkness; sand spraying; people who drown, are covered in earth or sand, are huddled together or crushed into confining spaces, who suddenly burst out with a movement of flight...

These sudden and separate moments call up memories of frightening places, in-between-ness, no-man's lands – where I am lost; edges and elements; echoes of violence and harmony, restriction and freedom; puzzlement; discomfort; sudden recognition and uplift. These images, sensations, fluid perceptions take me to places and experiences which I do not quite recognise; or cannot quite stitch together. They draw me back before sense has quite been made, so that I have to work myself and them out from there. This attempt to engage with a history not made but in the making, difficult or painful of access and uncertain of outcome, is also a touchstone of other recent South African theatre and performance work. Thus, the process of performance signals that the difficult task of *living* history, rather than accepting it as a completed story, is vital to really engaging with the full resonance of the present. It also confirms that experiencing the "gaps" is common to the improvisatory and to the needs of the present.

Practices of this kind are not "holding on" to an imagined past, but (re)memorising and (re)materializing it: "disinterring" proceeds by discovering (each time) the equivalents in the body and the things it holds and interacts with. The latter compose a sensorium through which that past can, in as much of its complexity as possible, be (re)encountered. Improvisation often "repeats" the same stimuli, the same riffs, the same notes or words or gestures; but that is not it. These components are also *not* "the same": the "new" thing has to be remade each time, but it is haunted by as-precise-as-possible an imagination of its precursor. What frames and releases this is a feeling, an intuited pattern, a sense of a shape. Desire, decision and activation underlie and impel the (re)creation, which is itself enabled by technique and focus.

A woman inhabits several roles from different periods, languages, ethnic and social divisions, with dance and text, accompanied by an androgynous vocalist whose interventions and extensions are perhaps always slightly different, maybe operating in partnership with the moves and words like a conversation between tabla and sitar in a raga. A collage of music, dance, puppets, fragile machines and projected text asks the audience to reimagine what a bird of fire might be. Both pieces, *Womb of Fire* and *The Firebird*, which I saw at the Grahamstown Festival in 2017 and 2016, explore identity, history, restriction and desire, through an interplay of genre – and both, like Magnet's *Cargo* and *Önnest'Bo*, pull the audience into an encounter with the energies of transformation by working with bodies, movement, text, music and materials.

These are not "improvisations" in the most common sense. They are highly crafted. But they work in the zone of the improvisatory, they take us to places where we cannot quite put a name to what we experience. There is in much South African performance practice the recognition of the ineluctable necessity to inhabit this zone, to keep focusing on the process of making. Improvisation in this sense is political because its business is the pragmatics of creating new acts and taking new responsibilities, and never letting it just happen.

The hallmark of such work is this very precise encounter of the physical body with the business of creating new performance modes and forms. It is as though many of the performers had emerged from a combination of Lecoq, Mnouchkine, Grotowski and Barba's work. To this, they seem to have integrated the rhythmic and musical sensibilities which hear and move with the sounds of Africa, as well as a wide spectrum of dance and movement work, together with a sense of the ritual openings of *sangoma* and indigenous integration with the natural world. All this produces a kind of South African body in performance which is deeply imbued with the capacity and intentionality to improvise. This is an ecology of performance – and space/set/materials also partake of this – which has imbibed and embodied a habit of operating at the very point of loss and reformulation, of inhabiting loss and recovery, of living a praxis of both entropy and negentropy: perhaps too of being in what, as Peters notes, Heidegger terms "the zone of truth."[44] Whether that then manifests as rehearsal and development process and/or as product and formal structure is not as important as the fact that it exists and underpins the moves into form and into the crafting of response to the experience of being in South Africa now.

Works Cited

Bailey, Brett. "Ipi Zombi?" In *Plays for a New South Africa*, edited by David Graver, 200–219. Bloomington & Indianapolis: Indiana UP, 1998.

Boal, Augusto. *Games for Actors and Non-Actors*. Translated by Adrian Jackson. London: Routledge, 1992.

Boal, Augusto. *The Rainbow of Desire*. Translated by Adrian Jackson, London: Routledge, 1995.

---

44   Gary Peters, *Improvising Improvisation*, 46.

Buckland, Andrew. *The Ugly Noo Noo*. Johannesburg: Unpublished script 1989.

Callery, Dymphna. *Through the Body: A Practical Guide to Physical Theatre*. New York: Routledge, 2001.

Davids, Nadia. *At Her Feet*. Paarl: Qshun, 2006.

Davids, Nadia. *Cissie*. Cape Town: Junkets, 2008.

Farber, Yael. *Theatre as Witness*. London: Oberon, 2008.

Fleishman, Mark and Jenny Reznek. Programme note to *Önnest'Bo*. 2002.

Foot, Lara. *Tshepang*. Performance: Grahamstown, Cape Town, London, 2003.

Foot, Lara. *Tsehpang*. Johannesburg: Wits UP, 2005.

Foot, Lara. "Reach." In *At this Stage*, edited by Greg Homann, 31–67. Johannesburg: Wits UP, 2009.

Foot, Lara. *Karoo Moose*. London: Oberon Books, 2009.

Frost, Anthony and Ralph Yarrow. *Improvisation in Drama, Theatre and Performance*. Basingstoke: Palgrave Macmillan, 2015.

Fugard, Athol, John Kani and Winston Ntshona. "Sizwe Bansi is Dead." In *The Township Plays*, Athol Fugard, 147–192. Cape Town: Oxford UP, 1993.

Fugard, Athol, John Kani and Winston Ntshona. "The Island." In *The Township Plays*, Athol Fugard, 193–227. Cape Town: Oxford UP, 1993.

Gilbert, Helen (Ed.). *Postcolonial Plays*. London and New York: Routledge, 2001.

Handspring Puppet Company with Jay Pather (choreography). *The Firebird*. Unpublished performance piece. Grahamstown National Arts Festival, 2016.

Higginson, Craig (2009) *Dream of the Dog*. In *At this Stage*, edited by Greg Homann, 141–177. Johannesburg: Wits UP, 2009.

Homann, Greg (Ed.). *At this Stage*. Johannesburg: Wits UP, 2009.

Homann, Greg. "Preamble." In *At this Stage*, edited by Greg Homann, 1–16. Johannesburg: Wits UP, 2009.

"Impro Talks": A symposium held in 2016 (Zurich University of the Arts). Proceedings published by Zhdk – Zürcher Hochschule der Künste Darstellende Künste und Film, 2017.

Jamal, Ashraf. *Predicaments of Culture in South Africa*. Pretoria: Pretoria UP, 2005.

Johnston, Chris. *House of Games: Making Theatre from Everyday Life*. London: Nick Hern Books, 1998.

Johnstone, Keith. *Impro: Improvisation and the Theatre*, London: Methuen, 1981.

Junction 71. *Sophiatown*. Johannesburg: Wits UP, 1988.

Kani, John. *Nothing But the Truth*. Johannesburg: Wits UP, 2002.

Kani, John (Ed.). *More Market Plays*. Johannesburg: Ad Donker, 1994.

Kentridge, William, Jane Taylor and the Handspring Puppet Co. *Ubu and the Truth Commission*. Johannesburg: Wits UP, 1998.

Klotz, Phyllis, Maqhutyana, Thobeka, Qosha, Nomvula, September, Xolani, Tsira, Poppy and wa Lelulehre, Itumeleng. *You Strike the Woman, You Strike the Rock*, video and unpublished script, Benoni: Sibikwa, 1986; also in Kani (Ed.) *More Market Plays,* 163–204.

Krueger, Anton. "A Heritage of Violence." In *Syncretic Arenas. Essays on Postcolonial African Drama and Theatre for Esiaba Irobi,* edited by Isidore Diala, 237–249. Amsterdam, NY: Brill/Rodopi, 2014.

Lecoq, Jacques. *The Moving Body.* Translated by David Bradby. London: Methuen, 2000.

Lecoq, Jacques. *Brochure de l'Ecole Jacques Lecoq.* Paris: n.d.

Lewis, Megan and Anton Krueger (Eds.). *Magnet Theatre: Three Decades of Making Space.* Pretoria: Intellect, 2015.

Magnet Theatre. *Önnest'Bo.* Performance: District Six Museum, Cape Town, 2002.

Magnet Theatre. *Cargo.* Performance: Grahamstown, Cape Town, Johannesburg, 2007.

Mda, Zakes. *We Shall Sing for the Fatherland.* Johannesburg: Ravan Press, 1993.

Mda, Zakes. *Fools, Bells and The Habit of Eating.* Johannesburg: Wits UP, 2002.

Middeke, Martin, Peter Paul Schnierer and Greg Homann (Eds.). *The Methuen Drama Guide to Contemporary South African Theatre.* London: Bloomsbury, 2015.

Murray, Simon. *Jacques Lecoq.* London: Routledge, 2003.

Peters, Gary. *Improvising Improvisation: From Out of Philosophy, Music, Dance and Literature.* Chicago: University of Chicago Press, 2017.

Reznek, Jennie "Magnet Theatre and the Moving Body." in *Magnet Theatre: Three Decades of Making Space,* edited by Megan Lewis and Anton Krueger, 143–162. Pretoria/SA: Intellect, 2015.

Simon, Barney, Mbongemi Ngema and Percy Mtwa. *Woza Albert!.* London: Bloomsbury Academic, 1983.

Spolin, Viola. *Improvisation for the Theater.* Evanston, IL: Northwestern UP, 1963.

The Mothertongue Project: Sara Matchett and Rehane Abrahams. *Womb of Fire.* Unpublished performance piece. Grahamstown National Arts Festival, 2017.

"*The Island*; an historical piece?," *Open University Digital Archive,* A 319; 06; 1996.

Turner, Jane. *Eugenio Barba.* London: Routledge, 2004.

Tyelele, Motshabi. *Shwele Bawo!.* In *At this Stage,* edited by Greg Homann, 113–139. Johannesburg: Wits UP, 2009.

van Graan, Mike. *Green Man Flashing.* Cape Town: Junkets, 2010.

van Graan, Mike. *Some Mothers' Sons.* In *At this Stage,* edited by Greg Homann, 69–110. Johannesburg: Wits UP, 2009.

CHAPTER 10

The Fault-Lines of Idiom: New Thematic and Stylistic Trends in the Plays of Allan Kolski Horwitz

Vicki Briault Manus

Abstract

Horwitz's plays explore the truths and complexities of the transition from a closed, authoritarian society to a pluralistic, supposedly egalitarian one, but also deal with the sense of betrayal felt by so many South Africans twenty years into the democratic era. A feature of his writing has been to take characters from different classes/cultures and put them in situations which combine elements of the past (apartheid) and the present (post liberation period), examining the contradictions between their personal drives and the political context and laying bare their overarching commonality as human beings with remarkably similar responses to the ironies and paradoxes of life. Particular emphasis will be laid on the "creolized" linguistic features of *The Pump Room* (2009), *Comrade Babble* (2012), *Boykie and Girlie* (2014) and *Book Marks* (2016).

1   Introduction

Allan Kolski Horwitz is a veteran performance poet, writer, activist and publisher. Born in 1952, he is a mature writer but a young playwright, having only been writing and producing plays since 2009. His plays are about contemporary South African reality, yet they have relevance for many other societies which, after a long period of violence and oppression, must face the challenges of coming to terms with the past and turning to the new battles ahead. This essay will present the themes of the plays and examine the use of dialogue, language, style and some other stagecraft idioms in recent performances, with a view to placing them in the context of emerging trends in South African theatre and discourse.

The plays examined are: *The Pump Room* (2009), *Comrade Babble* (2012), *Boykie and Girlie* (2014), *Jerico* (2015) and *Book Marks* (2016). The second part of the essay will focus on Horwitz's notable use of varieties of English inflected with other languages and speech-styles. Having previously focused on the stylistics of English in black South African fiction and linguistic issues in African

literature,[1] examining new linguistic trends in South African theatre in English
is of particular interest to me. Horwitz's purpose requires him to break away
from the Standard English or Afrikaans dialogue generally expected by middle-class audiences. Language or speech-style is undoubtedly the most con-
spicuous distinguishing characteristic in South African society left over from
the days of separate communities. Much has been written about the
importance of multilingualism in terms of South Africa's eleven official
languages – widely recognized as a source of difficulty in the quest to become
a united nation[2] – and perhaps rather less about the varieties within those
languages[3] and the township lingoes.[4] We shall return to this matter in the
Conclusion.

2   The Literary Climate of the Second Decade of
       South African Democracy

The tensions and repressions of apartheid which reached boiling-point in the
late 1970s and the 1980s gave rise to the most prolific creativity right across the
arts and especially in the theatre of indictment by playwrights such as Athol
Fugard, John Kani, Gibson Kente and Winston Ntshona. Then in the 1990s, during a honeymoon period celebrating hard-won freedom of expression, there
was an upsurge of innovative fiction from talented young writers such as Sello
Duiker and Phaswane Mpe, to name but two, whose work delved into the complexity of personal lives during those oppressive times... the difficulties faced
by homosexuals and other lovers across the racial groups assigned by the Ré-
gime, rural youths encountering the sex, drugs and violence of the city, the

1 See, for example, my monograph *Emerging Traditions: Toward a Postcolonial Stylistics of Black
   South African Fiction in English* (Lanham MD: Lexington, 2011). or my chapter, "Future Linguistic Approaches to African Literature" in *The Future of Postcolonial Studies*, ed. Chantal
   Zabus (Oxford/ New York: Routledge, 2015), 48–66.
2 Neville Alexander, *An Ordinary Country: Issues in the Transition from Apartheid to Democracy
   in South Africa* (Pietermaritzburg: University of Natal Press, 2002); Neville Alexander, "Mainstreaming by Confluence: The Multilingual Context of Literature in South Africa," *World Literature Today* 70, no. 1 (Winter 1996): 9–11 ; Neville Alexander, "Racial Identity, Citizenship
   and Nation-Building in Post-Apartheid South Africa" Lecture given at the East London campus of the University of Fort Hare 25 March 2006.
3 Kwesi Kwaa Prah (ed.), *Mainstreaming Afrikaans Regional Varieties* (CapeTown: The Centre
   for Advanced Studies of African Society, 2012).
4 Rajend Mesthrie ed., *Language in South Africa* (Cambridge: Cambridge University Press,
   2002).

terror of gang-controlled street-life, women raped or forced into prostitution, the taboo of AIDS, the side-effects of the perverted ideology on street-children. Novelists such as Zoe Wicomb or Achmat Dangor crafted intricate excursions into the lost histories of groups or communities left out of the official narratives, or threw light on commonplace tragedies resulting from the cruel laws of apartheid. It seemed that there were no taboos, everything could be aired. Artistic freedom came as part of the "new dispensation."

However, by the mid-Noughties, as the second decade of democracy slipped into gear, it became obvious that despite some changes, the beautiful promises of the Freedom Charter, the hopes of a better life for all, would not be fulfilled. Black Economic Empowerment seems only to concern a tiny black elite, sandwiched between the white masters of international finance and the black working classes whose lot had barely changed beyond the colour of their bosses' skin.

Allan Kolski Horwitz feels that, though the theatre of indictment and protest of the 1970s and 80s clearly belongs to the past, there still needs to be a political theatre of radical critique that reflects the lives and denounces the errors of the present for the newly emergent social groups, no longer race-defined in theory, but living on the fault-lines of socio-economic inequalities which so often coincide with ethnic allegiance and geographical location.[5] Often more complex than those of the apartheid era, today's issues require a subtler, or more poetic, approach, notwithstanding the humour that characterizes so much of South African popular culture. This is where language and style come into their own.

There was, and no doubt still is, a distinctive socio-linguistic signature associated with each of the pseudo-ethnic "racial" groups and sub-groups designated and then, through the enforcement of closed communities, cultivated by the nefarious apartheid laws of the 1950s, each of which had its own language or language variety. Robert Mshengu Kavanagh (1985) effectively describes how political and cultural distortions could occur in a play's language when white English-speaking writers wished to put words in the mouths of black characters. Due to their total ignorance of either the relevant African language or the way speakers of the language speak English, coupled with unquestioning belief in the superiority of English, some playwrights made clumsy attempts to represent the Native using broken English or Afro-American slang. Kavanagh wrote: "Thus the attitude of the play to the thematic problem

---

5   Allan Kolski Horwitz, Private correspondence with author, Spring 2017.

of language is shaped by a cultural concept which is both inauthentic, i.e. not true to life, and 'colonial.'"[6]

The English language should not remain the preserve of "the static maintenance syndrome," as Neville Alexander called the colonized mind, making speakers of other languages believe that their languages or varieties of English are "useless" and reinforcing their "voicelessness."[7] Thus the sticky yet highly sensitive issue of language cannot reasonably be neglected in any area of cultural life in post-liberation multilingual South Africa and is now, more than ever, especially crucial in the dialogue of a play.

So the case of Horwitz as a self-professed monolingual English-speaking South African on the one hand and a fervent supporter of authentic multilingualism in the form of multilingual poetry on the other,[8] is bound to be interesting. How authentically, in plays in English embedded in South African reality, does Horwitz handle the other languages and varieties that are such an inevitable part of the personae of his characters?

In this essay, after a brief presentation of Horwitz's five plays to date, I shall take a closer look at the stylistics of two of them, *The Pump Room* and *Comrade Babble*, which incorporates both language variety, in the sense intimated, and poetics in the more usual sense of literary devices and word-play, such as metaphor and puns. Furthermore, we shall see that just as the themes of each play are different, so are the stylistics.

3   The Playwright and His Art

Allan Kolski Horwitz's five works here discussed dramatize the new issues confronting South African society in the aftermath of 46 years under the apartheid regime, characterized by racial segregation and totalitarian oligarchy. Horwitz's "political theatre" plays out power relations between individuals as a reflection of those prevailing in society, treading a fine line between rhetoric and dialectics. In the former, characters lack imagination, are predictable and one-dimensional; in the latter, the shifts, changes and complexities of characters must unfold and, notwithstanding, any fantastical elements must hold true as a representation of reality.

---

6   Robert Mshengu Kavanagh, *Theatre and Cultural Struggle in South Africa* (London: Zed Books, 1985), 78–83.
7   Neville Alexander, "Racial Identity, Citizenship and Nation-Building in Post-Apartheid South Africa."
8   Botsotso, the publishing house Horwitz directs, publishes avant-garde multilingual poetry among other things.

There is little doubt now that the new, free and fair society that so many fought, died or longed for, has not come about.[9] While poverty, unemployment and crime escalate, only a small self-serving elite reap the benefits of hard-won power, too many of whom are embroiled in nepotism and corruption scandals.

Horwitz's plays explore the truths and complexities of the transition from a closed, authoritarian society to a pluralistic, supposedly egalitarian one. The plays comprise: *The Pump Room* (2009) where victims of apartheid confront their aggressors, the political satire *Comrade Babble* (2012), *Boykie and Girlie* (2014), *Jerico* (2015) and *Book Marks* (2016, first staged in January 2017).[10] *The Pump Room* and *Book Marks* share a dual viewpoint linking past apartheid horrors to post-apartheid confusion, while *Comrade Babble* and *Boykie and Girlie* are more anchored in the present, their characters driven by ambition and riven by contradictions, though the latter is a Pinteresque duologue, less obviously political. *Jerico* (2015) deals with betrayal using the Biblical story as an allegory for both present-day Israel and South Africa where political issues of trust, bad faith and duplicity poison social relations.

No doubt characterization is one of Horwitz's great distinguishing features, as he tries to deal with the inevitable relics of half a century of institutionalized racism in various subtle ways, never by merely confining himself to characters from only one or two of the apartheid "categories,"[11] yet never openly mentioning ethnicity except insofar as it emerges from the dialogue and context, rather as social class does in British drama. In South Africa, even more than in Britain, the way a character speaks reveals a plethora of information – socio-economic, cultural, ethnic and geographical – about his or her background.

Language is thus of exceptional importance in Horwitz's work, not only because of word-play and stylistic/ literary devices used to great effect throughout, but also as a crucial element of characterization. He writes, "In a society as divided [...]as South Africa, being able to listen to and engage with people of different backgrounds and classes and to do so on the basis of an equal humanity is a worthwhile challenge."[12] This essay will outline briefly the themes of the

9   Statistics of crime, poverty, educational failure, unemployment, racism and inequality make it quite clear that policies are failing the people of South Africa, see for example, the South African government's Statistics website:http://www.statssa.gov.za/?p=10334.

10   Allan Kolski Horwitz, *Collected Plays 2009–2017* (Braamfontein: Paardeberg Arts Trust and Botsotso, 2017).

11   See: Emile Boonzaier and John Sharpe (eds.), *South African Keywords: The Uses and Abuses of Political Concepts* (Cape Town & Johannesburg: David Philips, 1988).

12   Allan Kolski Horwitz, e-mail correspondence with author, May 2017.

plays before delving into aspects of the linguistic material deployed in two of them, the main focus being stylistic analysis rather than theatre criticism.

4   Brief Description of the Five Plays

The Pump Room (2009) is set in the pump room of a whites-only public baths in Sea Point, Cape Town (a metaphor for sanitizing the filth from privileged White South Africa) on the sea-front. Though taking place soon after Liberation in the late 1990s, its back-story is steeped in the dark days of apartheid. The protagonist, Peter, a mixed race ("Coloured") man in his 50s, had been an actor and underground political activist in the bad old days and had spent some time in police detention without trial, at the mercy of agents like Mike and Lombard – both white. Of the six characters that come together in the pump room where Peter is the attendant, Lewis and Elsie are clearly younger than the other four and less connected to the recent past. Mike and Lombard had tortured Peter, then an activist, and his white girlfriend, Sandra, who subsequently left the country to pursue her acting career abroad. Mumsie, an older friend of Elsie's, has connections of an intimate nature with Lombard and Peter. Though not present in the flesh, Sandra, visible in a giant poster at the back of the stage, is a seventh character in the play. It becomes apparent as the play unfurls that all the characters except Elsie are involved in using drugs and drug-dealing, so that the drug underworld comes to echo the power-relations and inequalities of apartheid, and to symbolize the post-apartheid malaise.

Horwitz's second play, *Comrade Babble* (2012), is a provocative satirical drama of contemporary South African issues of corruption and betrayal. It is based on the case of corporate fraudster Brett Kebble, who had a brief but dazzling career as a mining magnate with high-ranking connections in government, the ANC and the Youth League, making them and himself very rich in the name of Black Empowerment. He lived a life of flamboyant wealth, owning jets, mansions, cars and art works. Finally his fraud was uncovered. He refused to negotiate a "deal" and supposedly arranged his own "suicide." The play opens with Babble's return from the dead in order to give his own version of the facts and win public sympathy – the audience is constantly appealed to as the "public." His character is revealed through his dealings with five other characters – caricatures of people (or composites of people) who were actually involved with Kebble. The play unfolds through a parade of the various forms of corruption which marked Kebble/Babble's rise and fall, showing how he had manipulated key individuals and interest groups. It is a story with a moral, in one sense, but as he interacts with the different characters, we also see the human side of the tycoon.

Peter Butler, who acted in *Comrade Babble*, wrote, "The play ran for 90 minutes without intermission. As a two-hander with six characters, we switched between characters (off stage) several times during the show. Full costume changes, but the stage was never empty. Lebohang Motaung, the other actor, was excellent with accents, and drawing people in. "It's Italian farce," Allan kept saying ... The quick changes were the biggest challenge on *Comrade Babble*. But Allan's dialogue and terminologies are spot on."[13] Lebohang Motaung speaks all the South African languages except Venda, as well as two street lingoes, Tsotsitaal and Isiscamtho. He happened to have a Jamaican accent up his sleeve too, having frequented the Rastafarian community in Yeoville and mastered Italk, "a spin-off from Jamaican patwah."[14]

In the third play, *Boykie and Girlie* (2014),[15] Boykie is an unsuccessful playwright and Girlie is a lawyer. The play opens as Girlie comes home to their Johannesburg flat to find Boykie in a foul mood as usual. Set in their kitchen with a toilet where Boykie struggles with his constipation, the talk swivels from mood to mood, subject to subject, and we learn about their life together, their values, ambitions, needs and disappointments, while Girlie prepares the supper Boykie refuses to eat. The couple spar and cajole in language that is both poetic and coarse, testing each other and their relationship which is overshadowed by Boykie's despondency.

Boykie's "hunger strike" or anorexia, his sexual nostalgia for an Ethiopian woman he once knew, his punctured ego and subsequent sense of self-loathing– all place an enormous strain on Girlie as she has to bear not only the responsibilities of her job as a lawyer but the pressure of living with a partner who, despite moments of euphoria, is mired in depression.

However, by the end of the play, they "retire to their bedroom" rather than throw themselves into the abyss of separation. In this way there is no apocalyptic *dénouement*, no neat conclusion.

The situation is something of a cliché – though it dips into the absurd, it is always engaging, realistic yet almost melodramatic. On stage, the actors generate a convincing gamut of emotions which flow very naturally even when the gears collide, as they shift subjects and moods.

---

13   Peter Butler, e-mail exchange with author, May 8, 2017.
14   Lebohang Motaung, e-mail exchange with author, September 23 and October 3, 2017.
15   I saw *Boykie and Girlie* on CD with Craig Morris and Khutjo Bakunzi-Green produced by Allan Kolski Horwitz with a grant from the National Arts Council of South Africa on 14 January 2015 at the Alexander Theatre, Strand St, Cape Town, filmed by Peter Butler.

As a piece of political theatre, the fourth play, *Jerico* (2015), straddles the genres of morality play and historical drama. It takes place in Palestine rather than South Africa, a setting which resonates allegorically with the similarities between Israel/Palestine and apartheid South Africa. The question posed by *Jerico* is how to break the cycle of violence created by human communities competing for land, water and other essential resources. Using the Biblical account of the conquest and destruction of the ancient Canaanite city of Jerico (sic), the play examines how the Israelite tribe arrogated itself the right to destroy the city and its inhabitants in the name of their god; and why the people of Jerico failed to try and reach some compromise with the Israelites. Lastly it bleakly evokes how the Israelites themselves, many generations down the line, fell victim to a modern programme of extermination and, in response, are again dispossessing the latter-day inhabitants of Palestine of their land and culture.

Four of the Israelite characters are inspired by the biblical Book of Joshua, portrayed as the imperfect agents of a wandering and impoverished tribe. They are the whore, the two Israelite spies and Joshua. The interactions of extra Canaanite figures created by the playwright provide an interesting counterpoint to the Israelite dynamics.

The fast-paced play is structured into four acts, divided into twenty-nine short scenes, and shifts between the Israelite camp and Jerico itself. Sub-plots and monologues allow each character to reveal more about his/her inner life and motivation. The play's climax, which links the destruction of Jerico with the Nazi holocaust, shows the continuum of human inhumanity and the paradox whereby today's victim becomes tomorrow's villain.

Book Marks (2017), the most recent of Horwitz's plays to have been staged, is set in the contemporary period of growing unrest over the widening inequality gap between whites and the great majority of blacks, and the failure of the ANC government to follow through with the aspirations of the people.

Stanton de Villiers, a gay white Afrikaner of cultivated tastes, invites two middle-aged comrades from the Struggle days for the launch of his book club. First Vish Naidoo arrives, a sex-pest and heavy drinker and now a successful businessman. Later, Cornelia, a young Coloured schoolteacher, daughter of their old comrade Nettie, turns up. The conversations are prickly despite Stanton's attempts to create a cosy atmosphere, exposing issues that had not been dealt with in the 1980s. Vish's crude innuendo implies that Cornelia's mother, Nettie, was more of a groupie than a bona fide comrade, and he pesters Cornelia until she threatens to leave. Just then the third comrade, Julius/Mncedisi Matanzima, who has become radicalized by Black Consciousness, rushes in covered in blood. Interactions among the four continue raggedly, at times bitterly, turning on racism, misogyny and violence. Old race-based resentments from the past resurface. They have forgotten the ideals they shared and fought for together. Only Cornelia's clear voice and good sense signal hope for the future, showing up how rotten and futile the three former revolutionaries' lives have become, a faint reflection of the corruption and mismanagement of the ANC regime.

It is a two-act play, the first being a series of monologues by which the characters present themselves and their lives. The action plays out against a backdrop of load-shedding, with the now-familiar black-outs, red-outs and candle-lit scenes that underscore the government's failures.

While this play was being written, the removal of the Rhodes statue at the University of Cape Town in 2015 in response to student protest signalled the advent of a new non racial generation who will no longer tolerate racial bias and the huge disparities of wealth, education and land distribution that persist in the wake of apartheid. Cornelia belongs to this generation.

5   Language and Speech-Styles

Before writing plays, Allan Kolski Horwitz was a founder member of Botsotso, begun in 1994, a group of performance poets, writers and artists producing and publishing work that gives expression to the varied cultures and life experiences of people in South Africa, in all the country's many languages and speech varieties. In his plays, Horwitz continues in the Botsotso spirit to juggle language styles and a variety of themes and characters.

Kavanagh[16] discusses the issue of authentic representation of language varieties at length, supporting his arguments with excerpts from Modikwe Dikobe's *The Marabi Dance*[17] where there is Tsotsitaal[18] or Zulu dialogue, made accessible to the monolingual English reader with literal, correct translations from Zulu – far more graceful and true than broken English, as he points

---

16   Robert Mshengu Kavanagh, *Theatre and Cultural Struggle in South Africa*, 78–83.

17   The play *Marabi*, staged as musical theatre in 1981–82, was based on Modikwe Dikobe's novel *The Marabi Dance* (1974). Marabi is a South African jazz and dance style popular in the townships of Johannesburg in the 1940s.

18   "Tsotsitaal is a South African township argot used mainly [...] by black males in various urban centres. It is a mixed code [with] Afrikaans for structure and a variety of languages for its lexis [and] robust Bantu language texture." K.D.P.Makhudu, "An Introduction to Flaaitaal (or Tsotsitaal)," in *Language in South Africa*, ed. Rajend Mesthrie (Cambridge: Cambridge University Press, 2002), 398–406.

out – and various methods cushioning or contextualizing[19] the phrases of Tsotsitaal.

Kavanagh's remarks led me to wonder how authentic Horwitz's representation of South African speech-styles, albeit English-based, might be. Of the five plays mentioned, *The Pump Room*, set in Cape Town, and *Comrade Babble,* in Gauteng, provide the widest range of varieties from those two areas, respectively.

6   Language Variety in *The Pump Room*

The language used by the Capetonian characters of *The Pump Room* appears on the page to be standard English laced with Cape slang, the latter identified by the liberal use of coarse English slang words like "fucking," "bloody" and "whore" and plenty of Kaaps[20] and Afrikaans words which, though unintelligible to European audiences, are familiar to English-speaking South Africans, there naturally being a slight mingling of the speech patterns across language boundaries. Horwitz, who grew up in Cape Town, has been familiar with the speech varieties of mixed-race Capetonians since childhood though he does not practise Cape Flats English or Kaaps. He claims that in *The Pump Room* "the Coloured characters are all speaking English but with the patterns and cadences of Kaaps – which is how working-class Coloured people speak in the Cape. It is an English which is liberally peppered with Afrikaans terms."[21] It is also typical for people to code-switch, from a standard or acrolectal form of English to a more basal, slang-ridden variety, according to their interlocutor and to the context, as exemplified in the play.

---

19   For an explanation of the linguistic terms "cushioning" and "contextualizing," see Chantal Zabus, *The African Palimpsest: Indigenization of Language in the West African Europhone Novel*, Cross/Cultures 4 (New York & Amsterdam: Rodopi, 1991).

20   Kaaps is a language of the Western Cape, a variety of Afrikaans spoken mainly by the Coloured community who account for the majority of Afrikaans-speakers in the Western Cape (see South African Census 2011). The eminent poet Adam Small (1936–2016) named the language and there is a movement to have it granted official status. For a discussion of the need for Standard Afrikaans to embrace regional and ethnic varieties of Afrikaans, see Hein Willemse, "Considering a more multi-faceted Afrikaans," in *Mainstreaming Afrikaans Regional Varieties*, ed. Kwesi Kwaa Prah (CapeTown: The Centre for Advanced Studies of African Society, 2012), 63–88.

21   Allan Kolski Horwitz, Telephone conversation with author, May 2017.

Two of the six characters belong to the multi-ethnic, multi-cultural Cape community who were grouped together as "Coloureds"[22] under apartheid. The community thus has a particularly rich and varied cultural and linguistic heritage going back to the earliest colonial times and even before. Vernon February's (February 1981) is the fullest account to date of how the various ethnic groups came together. Studies show that Coloureds tend to be bilingual, using Afrikaans and English, the main two official languages of the province, and that the spoken language is one of two creoles, Cape Flats English – an English-based creole with Afrikaans or Kaaps influence – and Kaaps, a variety of Afrikaans that has been pejoratively considered as an Afrikaans-based creole, though many deem it to be a language *per se* that should be given official status. Indeed, when a film in Kaaps was shown in Johannesburg in early 2017, *Noem my Skollie*,[23] it was billed as being in a "foreign language" and subtitled in Afrikaans.[24] Without going too deeply into its fascinating history, Kaaps contains elements of several Khoesan languages spoken by the first peoples of South Africa and of all the languages and creoles which could be found in the Cape in the 17th century: Dutch, French, German, Portuguese, Xhosa, Malay and other languages from the Far East and from East and West Africa, along the Dutch East India Company's trade-routes. Add to this fertile mix the extraordinary vitality and creativity of all living, non-standardized language varieties that adapt to and flourish in all social situations, especially those of a richly diverse sea-port city like Cape Town and its suburbs, and you have a language that inspires passionate emotions of attachment or rejection, hilarious laughter and intolerant rage.

Horwitz said, "in *The Pump Room* I was trying to capture the speech rhythms, inflections and word usage of Coloured people in Cape Town in the 1980's and early 90's."[25] As I was curious to know whether he had succeeded or not, he put me in touch with Peter Butler, an internationally known Capetonian film and television actor who has played in two of Horwitz's theatre productions. Butler

---

22   I use this word as it is the one most commonly used in the literature on South African linguistics, with my sincere apologies to those Capetonians who understandably dislike the term.

23   *Noem my Skollie/ Call me Thief*, Dir. Daryne Joshua, Screenplay John W. Fredericks, initial release August 2016. This crime film based on the true life story of a young thief ("skollie") who earns protection in jail by becoming a story-teller was a huge box-office success in South Africa.

24   Vera Mihailovitch-Dickman, Correspondence with author, April 2017.

25   Allan Kolski Horwitz, e-mail correspondence with author, May 2017.

told me in correspondence that although Mike is an English-speaking white paramedic – a "soutpiel,"[26] and Lombard an Afrikaner detective with Special Branch, their speech patterns and vocabulary, while similar enough on the page, are distinctly different on the ear. For the three minor characters (Lewis, Elsie and Mumsie), also mixed-race, Butler writes:

> Each character speaks a slightly different patois informed by their very different backgrounds – though on the page that may not always be evident. A play is meant to be acted, to have life breathed into it – and when actors take ownership of the characters, lift them off the page and invest themselves, only then are the characters defined. [I]n rehearsals, I might shuffle Allan's words and grammar around to better suit the accent my character speaks with, which immediately makes my character identifiable to the audience.[27]

An early review demolished *The Pump Room* with a series of damning comments, couched in a style far from academic, none backed up in any way scientifically. I am only really concerned with the claims made by the reviewer about linguistic anachronisms: the only three words cited as anachronisms (the discourse marker "ek sê" (I say), the noun "lahnies" (bosses, rich people) and the second person plural pronoun "youse") are not only all in current usage, but very banal. "Youse" especially is used across quite a wide spectrum of varieties of English, from uneducated Afrikaner through various township and rural speech styles, and indeed, in Great Britain, Ireland, the southern states of the USA, and elsewhere.[28] The reviewer writes, "the [...] problem with all of the characters [is] that their tone and manner of speaking is often hard to distinguish from each other (sic), and most of the time they end up sounding like a hip English white guy of Horwitz's generation."[29] This I find very hard to credit. The quotes I provide from the actors (both originating from popular

---

26   Soutpiel is "a very rude, boorish and boerish, Afrikaans word for people who divide their time between South Africa and Britain. Sout means salt and piel means penis, because such people are said to have one foot in South Africa, one foot in Britain, and their penis dangling in the Atlantic Ocean." See http://blog.inkyfool.com/2012/09/soutpiel.html, accessed 7.5.2017. This description was corroborated by Peter Butler, email exchange, 8 May 2017.

27   Peter Butler, e-mail exchange with author, May 8, 2017.

28   https://www.collinsdictionary.com/dictionary/english/youse; https://www.dictionary .com/browse/youse; https://en.oxforddictionaries.com/definition/youse.

29   Anton Krueger, "*The Pump Room*," *South African Theatre Journal*, 26, no.1 (2012): 101.

backgrounds in Johannesburg and Cape Town respectively, and speakers of the lingoes referred to in the plays and my essay) make it clear that Horwitz manages quite well to create the linguistic patchwork he is aiming for.

Of the six characters, Peter is clearly the best-educated, a former actor who occasionally quotes from Shakespeare and indulges in philosophical musings. Thus his speech is at the "Standard English" end of the continuum, free of slang during the first four acts until the *dénouement*, when a less savoury aspect of his hitherto innocuous character is revealed. Until then, his cultivated middle-class speech endows him with the authority of the protagonist and wins him the audience's trust. His shiftless young helper, Lewis, makes extra money through drug-dealing which puts him in contact with undesirable customers. As a low-lifer, he uses a basal variety of English and slang, switching to a coarser register when interacting with Lombard and Mumsie, themselves given to extremely foul language. Code-switching thus operates within and between the specific speech-styles. Mumsie adds to her earnings as a domestic worker through prostitution, which means that she frequents the gangster underworld and speaks accordingly. In her capacity as Peter's girlfriend, on the other hand, she is less coarse. Mike, Lombard's pal, comes across as the better-educated of the two, with Standard English, and a calmer, more thoughtful personality. There are suggestions that he was a doctor or health worker. It also transpires that he and Lombard were involved in torturing Peter and Sandra under the previous dispensation, but that Lombard was the dangerous brute while he, Mike, restrained him. Like Peter's, this image is set to swivel right round in the *dénouement* at the end. Finally the youngest character, Elsie, Lewis's girlfriend and Mumsie's fellow domestic worker, whose main contribution to the action is that she incites Lewis to give up his life of crime, speaks Cape slang with a minimum of swear words. She aspires to a better life with Lewis and their baby but has a secret sexual relationship with Lewis's gentler brother, George, whom we never see and whom Lewis finally admits to killing. This, like Elsie and Lewis's discussion about the grim fates of their babies so far, is a shocking demonstration of the ignorance and heartlessness that grinding poverty can engender.

7   **Language and Other Idioms in *Comrade Babble***

Comrade Babble is set in Johannesburg. Here again there are six characters, but never more than two on the stage at the same time, so they can be played by only two actors, both male, one white and one black, who divide the roles between them.[30] The white characters are the eponymous bankrupt tycoon Mephistopheles Medici Babble; Butch Deratti – a Mafioso-style gangster; and Umshini de Boom, the "murderer." The black ones are public prosecutor, Buti Bhunga; Youth League leader, Professor Ndlovu; and the vivacious transsexual *artiste*, Wilhelmina Randridge. As well as the human characters, there are life-sized puppets made of wire and plastic,[31] wearing various items of headwear: a safari helmet, a woman's straw hat, a jester's hat, a Zionist Church (ZCC) peaked hat, a kaffiyeh and a skull cap, at hand to be used by characters during the performance.

Horwitz has a field-day with language-play in this piece. The names are full of puns and allusions: not only is the eloquent but diabolical Babble called Mephistopheles, but his middle name is Medici, as he was a patron of the arts. The name of his protégée, Wilhelmina Randridge, is a play on an internationally renowned artist's name.[32] Non South African audiences would not know that in Zulu, "bhunga-bhunga" is the buzzing of a bee; or that "umshini" means "machine-gun," evoking Jacob Zuma's signature song, "Mshini wami" (bring me my machine-gun); or that "ndlovu" means "elephant." The name Butch Deratti speaks for itself!

With only two actors playing six roles, speech-style is as important as costume and headgear in distinguishing characters. The play takes the form of a series of dialogues, with one or two crucial monologues. Babble and Bhunga, the most educated, speak standard English with, respectively, a white South African and a black South African accent, though Babble slips into a much coarser register when taunted by Professor Ndlovu who had double-crossed the double-crosser. Umshini the thug speaks slang English laced with Tsotsi-taal and Afrikaans. Ndlovu, a slippery customer much given to posturing, puts

---

30   Ironically, until what Anne Fuchs calls "the mixed cast syndrome" in 1980, there was little opportunity for non white actors. In: Anne Fuchs, *Playing the Market: The Market Theatre* (Johannesburg. Amsterdam & New York: Rodopi, 2002), 157. Nowadays, usually for economic reasons, a "mixed cast" of six can be played by two actors, regardless of their ethnic origin, though Lebo Motaung writes that it can be insulting to an audience to let a black actor play a black character with a black accent. (Email exchange with author, September 23, 2017.)

31   "Puppets have long made their mark in South African theatre; the idea of using wire figures came from Albie Michaels who directed the second production of *Comrade Babble*. The life-size figures were created by Zimbabwean wire artists who sell their wares by the roadside. They did a beautiful job and the figures have a special presence both as symbols and as participants." Allan Horwitz in email correspondence, early May 2017.

32   The award-winning South African artist William Kentridge, born in 1955, is well-known in the fields of Contemporary and Performance Art.

on different accents. He uses an American accent in his dialogue with Babble, then later switches to Jamaican, then American again, then working-class African for his "life-story" monologue at the end of the scene. The monologue begins and ends with him singing a well-known struggle song, "My father was a garden boy" which gets laughs from a South African audience. We cannot be sure whether any of the accents are his normal way of speech. He says rather defensively he is Shangaan, a pejorative name[33] for the Tsonga people of the Eastern provinces. The gangster Deratti uses a phony Italian accent. Horwitz commented, "the imitation of accents is a staple of stand-up comics; in theatre it is rarer."[34] In the South African context, there is clearly plenty of scope for accents; but with the addition of American, Jamaican and Italian varieties, the play shrewdly extends beyond that compass, with its specific baggage.

As actors change roles, characters switch speech-styles, and hats pass from one to another, there is constant instability among the identities translating a general lack of integrity. Man-sized wire-and-plastic puppets around the stage do nothing to brighten the bleak image of humanity. The only characters whose identities seem reliable are Prosecutor Bhunga, representing truth and justice, and Wilhelmina whose authenticity as an *artiste* ironically encompasses her trans-sexuality. In satirizing the precariousness of power and ambition and the corruption of those in positions of influence or power, the play makes use of changing speech-styles to denote inconstancy and to underscore the double-dealings of the characters. The quickness of dialogue, light-footed changes of costume and scene and the humorous banter keep the play amusing despite the grim reality it portrays, but after the performance it is a searing critique of corruption and cronyism that the audience takes home to ponder on.

Peter Butler played three of the roles in *Comrade Babble*, involving fast costume changes and switching speech-styles. I asked him whether it posed a problem of credibility for a mixed-race actor to play white men. He replied:

> During the Apartheid era it was commonplace for white actors to 'darken up' to play non-white characters on stage, but that is no longer the case. In *Comrade Babble* I played Babble, who was a relatively sophisticated white man, a tycoon – as well as Deratti, who was a South African Italian and sometimes spoke with a quasi Italian accent – and Umshini de Boom, a lower echelon Jo'burg Coloured thug with a mouth like a toilet. [...]

---

33   To learn why Shangaan has pejorative connotations, see: https://www.vivmag.co.za/
      archives/10388.
34   Allan Kolski Horwitz, e-mail correspondence with author, May 2017.

To some degree we have transcended "colour" on the South African stage, but we still have a way to go. In my own experience, audiences are willing to make the leap, they love to see actors portraying different co-lours of our rainbow. All the characters [in *Comrade Babble*] are very well drawn. We all know those types. They're recognizable to audiences. And people respond to them across the colour line.[35]

8   Conclusion

The Pump Room and *Book Marks* share a dual viewpoint linking past apart-heid horrors to the post-apartheid confusion, while *Comrade Babble* and *Boykie and Girlie* are more anchored in the present with its own specific con-cerns. *The Pump Room* is still quite close to apartheid; the ghosts are very tangible, "casualties" on both sides drifted into the late 1990s just as things started to really go wrong with the liberation movement – the corruption and waste of the arms deal, depriving people of anti-retroviral drugs and so on. *Book Marks*, on the other hand, is very current, set in a period when all the unfinished business of 1994 continues to fester; this is expressed as continued white oligarchic economic domination as well as the rampant corruption of a black neo-colonial government. However, what happened during the Struggle years is a key element in the play – it is the reference point for the subsequent degeneration, the foundation of the dynamics that are being played out in the present.

Comrade Babble and *Boykie and Girlie* have passing reference to the apart-heid period; when they refer to the past it is more likely to be their personal histories than anything overtly political. It is their individual psychology which is the dramatic focus, though the figure of Babble was a key political manipula-tor at the highest levels of South African politics. In a review of *Jerico* we read that Horwitz's work "plays an important role in opening this country's theatre industry to new work and new perspectives."[36] It is political theatre, yet char-acterization and dialogue, making use of the full range of South African speech-styles and more besides, bring it right to the audience in a very inti-mate, contemporary way.

We do not have space here to discuss all the social, political and cultural is-sues raised by the depiction of different social and ethnic types through the

---

35   Peter Butler, Email exchange with author, May 8, 2017.
36   Robyn Sassen, "Allan Kolski Horwitz," *My View by Robyn Sassen*, accessed May 3, 2017, https://robynsassenmyview.wordpress.com/tag/allan-kolski-horwitz/.

use of socio-linguistic and paralinguistic material in the two plays focused on. Nor to address critical reviews on other aspects of the plays and stage-craft generally. However, language variety is clearly an integral and salient aspect of the societal complexity of post-apartheid South Africa. To many playwrights, from Shakespeare's day and no doubt before, the palette of socio-linguistically marked speech-styles is a precious signifying tool enabling the aesthetic, touching, humorous or simply realistic portrayal of character types.

The particularly rich diversity of languages and varieties found in South Africa is the result of the decades of segregation and oppression, forging highly specific speech-communities and leaving a unique "linguistic-genetic" landscape that functions as a laboratory for language scientists and could do so for playwrights too. There is a great deal to be done. For example Lebo Motaung, who was not alive in 1957 when the vibrant multicultural Johannesburg suburb of Sophiatown/ Kofifi was destroyed, mentions that he picked up its particular 1950s Tsotsitaal or "Ringas" lingo from other actors and people who lived in that era.[37] The imbrications of language and speech styles with social history provide precious relics that perhaps only theatre (and actors' gift of mimicry) can showcase.

Although the 1996 South African Constitution recognizes eleven official languages and guarantees mother-tongue education for every citizen, over 20 years later the picture for many languages in education is fairly bleak. Professor Hein Willemse cites articles from 2011 including a diagram entitled "Moedertaalsprekers in Suid-Afrika" (Mother-tongue speakers in South Africa) that illustrates how linguistic ethnocentrism thrives in the 21st century: "Not only is language linked to so-called national stereotypes, but excepting speakers of Afrikaans and English, speakers of other languages are also depicted in premodern dress. These speakers and the languages they represent are unambiguously construed as culturally static, which by definition precludes them from 21st century modernity."[38] English, though the mother tongue of only 8% of the population, maintains its prestige and hegemony to the detriment of other languages. At the same time Neville Alexander warns that reifying the ethnic, cultural and language differences engineered by apartheid would impede the "transformation of consciousness" needed to overcome those very divisions.[39] Could new theatre trends help here?

---

37   Lebohang Motaung, email exchange, 23 September and 3 October 2017.
38   Hein Willemse, "Considering a more multi-faceted Afrikaans," in *Mainstreaming Afri-kaans Regional Varieties*, ed. Kwesi Kwaa Prah (CapeTown: The Centre for Advanced Studies of African Society, 2012.), 67.
39   Neville Alexander, *An Ordinary Country*, 97.

Lebo Motaung writes, "I cannot say when this practice [of using other speech-codes and languages in theatre] began, but things have been changing. We, especially artists, are finding our voice and taking back our identity, liberating ourselves from colonial psychosis. As we speak, I know writers who are making a concerted effort to write plays in our South African languages. In 2015 *Lepatata* was the first completely Setswana play to be staged at the Market Theatre and won an award at the Naledis."[40]

Let it be clear that the English-based linguistic variety in Horwitz's work, discussed in this essay, is but a sub-category of the education-led multilingualism that would enable South African citizens fully to communicate across society. However, the fact that South Africa's multilingual diversity is increasingly manifest in theatre is a progressive sign, both reflecting and encouraging greater naturalness and lack of constraint between citizens once kept apart and now urgently needing to come together and understand one another. The linguistic variety alongside the social parody or observation that we are seeing in such plays as Horwitz's is surely a step towards that greater naturalness and ease.

Let Peter Butler have the last word: "[Horwitz has] mastery with language; he's also great at locking in on characters from across the spectrum of South Africans. He is a voice for the people. Whether at arts festivals or in sub-economic townships, his writing resonates."[41]

Works Cited

Alexander, Neville. *An Ordinary Country: Issues in the Transition from Apartheid to Democracy in South Africa*. Pietermaritzburg: University of Natal Press, 2002.

Alexander, Neville. "Mainstreaming by Confluence: The Multilingual Context of Literature in South Africa." *World Literature Today* 70, no. 1 (Winter 1996): 9–11.

Alexander, Neville. "Racial Identity, Citizenship and Nation-Building in Post-Apartheid South Africa." Lecture given at the East London campus of the University of Fort Hare 25 March 2006.

Botsotso (ed.). *Against the Tide: Three Plays, an Opera Libretto and an Essay*. Braamfontein: Botsotso Publishing, 2013.

---

40   Lebohang Motaung, email exchange, 23 September and 3 October 2017. *Lepatata* was written by Moagi Modise, directed by Makhaola Ndebele, produced by the Market Theatre & the Windybrow Theatre and won the Naledi Award for Best Ensemble in 2015.

41   Peter Butler, email exchange, 8 May 2017.

Boonzaier, Emile and John Sharpe (eds.). *South African Keywords: The Uses and Abuses of Political Concepts.* Cape Town & Johannesburg: David Philips, 1988.

Briault Manus, Vicki. *Emerging Traditions: Toward a Postcolonial Stylistics of Black South African Fiction in English.* Lanham MD: Lexington, 2011.

Briault Manus, Vicki. "Future Linguistic Approaches to African Literature." In *The Future of Postcolonial Studies*, edited by Chantal Zabus 48–66. Oxford/New York: Routledge, 2015.

Dikobe, Modikwe. *The Marabi Dance.* Oxford: Heinemann, 1973.

February, Vernon A. *Mind Your Colour: The Coloured Stereotype in South African Literature.* London & Boston: Kegan Paul, 1981.

Fuchs, Anne. *Playing the Market: The Market Theatre, Johannesburg.* Amsterdam & New York: Rodopi, 2002.

Horwitz, Allan Kolski. *Collected Plays 2009–2017.* Braamfontein: Paardeberg ArtsTrust and Botsotso, 2017.

Horwitz, Allan Kolski. "Comrade Babble." In *Against the Tide: The Coloured Stereotype in South African Literature*, edited by Botsotso, 51–88. Braamfontein: Botsotso Publishing, 2013.

Horwitz, Allan Kolski. Email correspondence with Vicky Briault Manus, May 2017.

Horwitz, Allan Kolski. *The Pump Room.* Braamfontein: Botsotso Publishing, 2009.

Kavanagh, Robert Mshengu. *Theatre and Cultural Struggle in South Africa.* London: Zed Books, 1985.

Krueger, Anton. "*The Pump Room.*" *South African Theatre Journal*, 26, no.1 (2012): 100–102.

Makhudu, K.D.P. "An Introduction to Flaaitaal (or Tsotsitaal)." *In Language in South Africa*, edited by Rajend Mesthrie, 398–406. Cambridge: Cambridge University Press, 2002.

Mesthrie, Rajend, ed. *Language in South Africa.* Cambridge: Cambridge University Press, 2002.

Prah, Kwesi Kwaa (ed.). *Mainstreaming Afrikaans Regional Varieties.* CapeTown: The Centre for Advanced Studies of African Society, 2012.

Sassen, Robyn. "Allan Kolski Horwitz." *My View by Robyn Sassen.* Accessed May 3, 2017. https://robynsassenmyview.wordpress.com/tag/allan-kolski-horwitz/.

Willemse, Hein. "Considering a more multi-faceted Afrikaans." In *Mainstreaming Afrikaans Regional Varieties*, edited by Kwesi Kwaa Prah, 63–88. Cape Town: The Centre for Advanced Studies of African Society, 2012.

Zabus, Chantal. *The African Palimpsest: Indigenization of Language in the West African Europhone Novel.* New York & Amsterdam: Rodopi, 1991.

CHAPTER 11

Revisiting the Past, Imagining the Future: Aesthetic of Creolization in Post-apartheid South African Drama

Marc Maufort

Abstract

In the years that followed the advent of democracy in the new South Africa, initial dreams of harmony gave way to corruption, violence, and poverty instead of completely transcending the painful legacy of apartheid. However, there emerged an attempt to move beyond homogenization in the arts and to stage the full spectrum of colours of the South African nation potentially suggested by the rainbow metaphor. Four significant 21st century plays are placed in conversation in this essay in order to illustrate the creation of what could be called, in an echo of Edouard Glissant's famous concept, an aesthetic of creolization: Omphile Molusi's *Itsotseng* (2006), Greg Homann's *Oedipus@ Koö-nú.* (2014), Craig Higginson's *The Imagined Land* (2015), and Mike van Graan's *When Swallows Cry* (2017).

The dominant dream of the early years of post-apartheid South Africa was certainly encapsulated in Desmond Tutu's and Nelson Mandela's metaphor of the rainbow as a symbol of a united, yet diverse, new democratic nation. It is generally accepted that the first years of the post-apartheid era saw the apex of "Rainbow Nation(ism)."[1] Not only did this concept project a highly optimistic view of the nation. Ironically, it also implied a homogenizing perspective, as if the different colours of Mandela's rainbow did not get enough visibility. In the years that followed the advent of democracy, the dreams of the new era gave way to corruption, violence, and poverty instead of completely transcending the painful legacy of apartheid. And yet, the South African stage remained as inventive as it had been in the apartheid era, when playwrights boldly

---

1 Greg Homann, "Claiming Western Texts for Contemporary South African Theatre. Issues of Relevance and the Dead-end Pursuit of National Identity," in *New Territories: Theatre, Drama, and Performance in Post-apartheid South Africa*, ed. Greg Homann and Marc Maufort (Brussels: Peter Lang, 2015), 123.

challenged the oppression of apartheid. Not only was the failure of the rainbow dream to materialize criticized by new artists, there also emerged an attempt to move beyond homogenization and to stage the full spectrum of colours of the South African nation potentially suggested by the rainbow metaphor.[2] This occurred through innovative works articulating a vast range of thematic issues and displaying a rich array of new stage idioms. It is naturally beyond the scope of this essay to give an exhaustive account of this new aesthetic. However, four significant 21st century plays will be placed in conversation in these pages in order to illustrate the creation of what could be called, in an echo of Édouard Glissant's famous concept, an aesthetic of creolization: Omphile Molusi's *Itsotseng* (2006), Greg Homann's *Oedipus@Koö-nú.* (2014), Craig Higginson's *The Imagined Land* (2015), and Mike van Graan's *When Swallows Cry* (2017). My understanding of creolization draws on the theories of Édouard Glissant, who first explored this phenomenon in the Caribbean region but later conferred it a global reach.[3] In contrast to Negritude, *Antillanité*, *Créolité*, Glissant argued, creolization resists homogenization while favouring a continual process of relations. In other words, it differs from the mere juxtaposition of hybrid binaries, favouring instead genuine interactions between opposed identities. In his *Poétique de la relation* [*Poetics of Relation*], he foregrounds the endless possibilities of creolization: "... creolization seems to be a limitless *métissage*, its elements diffracted and its consequences unforeseeable. Creolization diffracts, whereas certain forms of *métissage* can concentrate one more time."[4] In *Traité du Tout-Monde*, Glissant further argues that the world at large is characterized by creolization,[5] which counters the homogenizing tendencies of globalization. Viewed through the grid of Glissant's theory, it becomes clear that South African drama allows the various entities of Mandela's rainbow to be clearly identified, even while undergoing continuous change: "Creolization is not a fusion, it requires that each of its components

---

2   For a survey of the major playwriting trends characterizing the post-apartheid period, see Greg Homann ("Preamble" as well as "New Territories: Exploring the Post-apartheid Stage"). Studies of the apartheid theatre can be found in Temple Hauptfleisch's *Theatre & Society in South Africa. Reflections in a Fractured Mirror* as well in Loren Kruger's *The Drama of South Africa. Plays, Pageants and Publics since 1910*.

3   I acknowledge the fact that the concept of "creolization" does have its detractors. I nevertheless find it an appropriate heuristic tool within the context of South African dramaturgies. I have discussed these issues in detail with my co-editor in the introduction to this volume.

4   Édouard Glissant, *Poetics of Relation*, trans. Betsy Wing (Ann Arbor: University of Michigan Press, 1997), 34.

5   Édouard Glissant, *Traité du Tout-Monde. Poétique IV* (Paris: Gallimard, 1997), 194.

continue to exist, even as it is already in the process of changing."[6] I contend that in the four plays under scrutiny here, the wealth of thematic issues and aesthetic devices used by the authors lend the rainbow metaphor its full creolization potential, even in a context of globalization, as my analysis of Mike van Graan's play will suggest. The aesthetic creolization of these works "diffracts" notions of the South African nation, inviting readers and spectators to reassess the country's past and to imagine its future potentialities from a non-essentialist perspective.

∙ ∙ ∙

In *Itsotseng*, young Setswana playwright Omphile Molusi deals with the traumatic past of the apartheid period from both public and private perspectives, while also addressing the failure of Mandela's rainbow dream to bring about healing. *Itsotseng* was first performed in Johannesburg and the National Arts Festival in Grahamstown in 2006; it was subsequently produced at Stratford-upon-Avon by the Royal Shakespeare Company in 2007. In 2008, it was presented at the Baxter Theatre Centre in Cape Town and the Edinburgh Festival. In this playlet, all roles are meant to be performed by a single actor, a solo performance which has become a staple feature of postcolonial drama on a global level.[7] Through its emphasis on the unfixed notion of self, *Itsotseng* could be construed as a postmodern adaptation of African storytelling, a work in which the creolization of contemporary Africa is foregrounded through the multiple identities embodied by the single actor (Molusi himself) as well as the through the various linguistic code shifts manifest throughout the text. Moreover, as my analysis will show, it could be regarded as a theatrical ritual of mourning for the shattered hopes of a better democracy and of a happy married life. The central character, Mawilla, eventually attends the funeral of his

---

6   *Ibid.*, 210. My translation. An English-language overview and critique of Glissant's notion of creolization is provided in: Dominique Chancé, "Creolization. Definition and Critique," trans. Julin Everett, in *The Creolization of Theory*, eds. Françoise Lionnet and Shu-mei Shih (Durham & London: Duke University Press, 2011), 262–267.

7   Helen Gilbert, "Introduction to Guillermo Verdecchia's *Fronteras Americanas (American Borders)*," in *Postcolonial Plays. An Anthology*, ed. Helen Gilbert (London & New York: Routledge, 2001), 421. Helen Gilbert states, in relation to Guillermo Verdecchia's iconic *Fronteras Americanas (American Borders)*: "In Canada, as elsewhere, the one-person, semi-autobiographical play has become a powerful mode of expression for the postcolonial subject" (*Ibid.*).

lover, Dolly, feeling engulfed in a sense of despair that does not augur well for the future.

Itsotseng immediately introduces us to the life of destitute protagonists in small townships. As Molusi indicates in his introduction to the play:

> Itsotseng was part of the Bophuthatswana homeland, led by Lucas Man-gope and set up by the apartheid government. During the 1980s, Itsotseng township enjoyed the fruits of Mangope's regime, never knowing how these fruits had been harvested. During the 1990s, people became aware of Mangope's tyrannical antics of leadership. His government was run by his family, important posts were occupied by his trusted friends, Bophu-thatswana became a military state.[8]

Eventually, after the end of the apartheid era, Molusi continues, the "Bophu-thatswana regime was overthrown."[9] People even destroyed the shopping cen-tre that Mangope had built. While the township residents hoped that with the new rule economic prosperity would be restored, they are left struggling with poverty and poor delivery service as the play opens. As Molusi emphasizes, life in Itsotseng has become synonymous with "survival." Ironically, Itsotseng means "wake yourselves up," suggesting a note of hope contradicted by the events unfolding in the play.[10]

The play's characters include male and female parts, all performed by Mawilla: Buda Six, a man who incites the young residents to revolt, Dolly, Mawilla's lover, Tsholofelo, Dolly's female friend, a prostitute and a pimp, Fora, a township bum, Tosi, an alcoholic, as well as a female SABC reporter. The ac-tion takes place in the burnt down shopping centre, a symbol of the homeless-ness in which the characters are trapped.[11] The prison metaphor thus implic-itly resonates throughout the play. The multiple township identities enacted by Mawilla suggest a first level of creolization, resulting from a lack of fixity, which is further underlined by the playwright's special use of props. All of those props are located inside a prominent trunk owned by Mawilla – the sym-bol of the wealth and innocence of the past: "*Crawls to the trunk and flips it open, sticks his head inside and shouts "DOLLY!," then throws out his childhood toys from the trunk all over the stage, some he got from Dolly.*"[12] Mawilla further

---

8   Omphile Molusi, *Itsotseng* (Mowbray: Junkets Publishers, 2008), 18.

9   *Ibid.*, 19.

10   *Ibid.*

11   *Ibid.*, 20.

12   *Ibid.*, 30.

uses a doll to mimic Dolly's unwanted pregnancy: "*He sees a doll made of a blue cloth on the floor. It's one of the things he threw out of the trunk. ... He picks up the doll and throws it on his back, as if it is a child. ... He takes the doll from his back and puts it under his shirt to create a big belly.*"[13] A blanket he finds in the trunk and wraps around himself helps effect transitions between different imaginary characters: the SABC female reporter[14] and a younger incarnation of Dolly. As Dolly confesses her love for him, Mawilla "*hugs the blanket.*"[15] In the final moments of the play, we see him engaging in an imaginary dance with the deceased Dolly: "*He picks up the blanket and dances with it as if he's dancing with Dolly as he sings a soft tune.*"[16] Props do not only serve to convey moments of deep emotional involvement: they can also introduce funny touches, especially when Mawilla imitates the police intervening during a riot: "*Picks up an old blue rusty bowl, just a piece of junk lying around, puts it on his head as a police cap and a toy duck that looks somewhat like a loudspeaker phone.*"[17] Props thus complexify Molusi's creolization aesthetic.

Naturally, creolization is also manifest in the constant oscillation between linguistic registers Molusi uses to hybridize the English language of the play. This could be viewed as an early attempt to reproduce what the playwright describes as the African vernacular in his essay collected elsewhere in this volume, i.e. township spoken language – inspired by the African Setswana language and Afrikaans. Instances of this code switching abound. Let it suffice to provide a few examples: "Daar is nex hierso [There is nothing here]";[18] Tsholofelo exclaims: "He wena Mawilla, ha o a chelate, ha o na koloi, o dula ko galona mare ona le ditedu. [Hey! You, Mawilla, you don't have money, you don't have a car, you've got a beard but you still stay with your mother]."[19] Fora's lines are equally bilingual, as he switches from English to township lingo: "Ha! Grootman...Eintlik...Itstseng e kwala motho ncondo ngwana wa mtswala. That is why he tsuba dikata, co keng...dimpula ncondo ngawan wa mtswala ... [No, Bro. Itsotseng sucks out a person's thinking capacity. That is why I smoke zol. Coz why? It opens my mind]."[20] Further linguistic creolization is achieved through the reproduction of specific accents. The smooth and formal English of the SABC reporter contrasts with the standard township English: "Angry

---

13   *Ibid.*, 35–36.
14   *Ibid.*, 44.
15   *Ibid.*, 50.
16   *Ibid.*, 53.
17   *Ibid.*, 43.
18   *Ibid.*, 23.
19   *Ibid.*, 33.
20   *Ibid.*, 46.

residents of Itsotseng next to Lichtenburg in the North West province block-
aded roads with tanks, stones and burning tyres, with the intention of rendering the township ungovernable because of poor service delivery."[21] A similar
effect is produced by the accent of an old woman, who says: "It is only our
township and our poor shopping complexe that was never reconstructete."[22]
This aesthetic of creolization forms the background against which the storytelling of tragic human experiences takes place.

Mawilla first revisits his own painful past when he mentions he lacked a father: "We don't know him. Some rich man, with some rich family, living in
some rich suburb, somewhere in the land of the rich."[23] Mawilla also tells us
the story of the protest riots against economic discrimination, which led to
police repression in the township: "The police didn't hesitate to answer with
shots. ... All of a sudden tyres were burning on the tar roads. It was like the re-
birth of the Soweto uprising."[24] However, the most tragic event in the play is
the progressive deterioration of the love relationship between Mawilla and
Dolly. Under the negative influence of Tsholofelo, Dolly is forced to become a
prostitute. When prompted by Mawilla on this topic, she answers: "Mawilla,
I'm trying to survive."[25] The worst irony occurs when an elated Mawilla, who
has finally found a job, hopes to be able to marry Dolly. Unfortunately, when he
reaches her house, disaster strikes: "The first thing I saw was people crowded in
front of the gate, then the ambulance. I stood there, trying to figure out what
was going on. The next minute, they brought out her body in a black body
bag."[26] This leads Mawilla to completely reject the rainbow myth of prosperity:
"Sometimes I wish all the townships would be burned to the ground ... We are
still living in a curse."[27] It transpires that Dolly died of exhaustion after giving
birth to two babies and having three abortions. The role of props is foregrounded again in the climactic moments of the play, as Mawilla performs a private
ritual of burial of "her soul."[28] To that end, he places three bottles on top of a
small wooden box in a "triangle shape," adds a white cross to it and scatters
flowers around.[29] The play concludes on a dream vision, as he imagines he is

---

21   *Ibid.*, 44.
22   *Ibid.*, 42.
23   *Ibid.*, 37.
24   *Ibid.*, 44.
25   *Ibid.*, 34.
26   *Ibid.*, 51.
27   *Ibid.*, 52.
28   *Ibid.*
29   *Ibid.*, 52–53.

dancing with Dolly: "Sometimes I wish me and Dolly were born a hundred years from now. ... I would be putting on my blue suit and black shoes for our wedding, not the funeral. I would ask her to dance with me, the whole day."[30] This searing vision lends a strong emotional impact to the play's coda. The future remains at best uncertain, while the present continues to entrap the characters. The promise of a South Africa becoming fully creolized from a racial and social point of view, as Glissant envisions this process of change, remains unfulfilled. Greg Homann's *Oedipus@Koö-nú* voices similar concerns about the future of the new democracy.

• • •

This play was developed for production at the National Arts Festival with the support of the Standard Bank Young Artist Award the playwright received in 2014. As the author stated, it was meant as a tribute for the twentieth anniversary of the advent of democracy in South Africa. It enacts an allegory of the potentialities of the new South Africa through a localized rewriting of Sophocles' *Oedipus at Colonus*, in which the protagonist can be decoded as an equivalent of President Mandela. As Greg Homann himself claims, his ageing and ambivalent Oedipus can be likened to Mandela. He represents

> A victim, perpetrator, and hero. So here is a character that encapsulates the three post-TRC [Truth and Reconciliation Commission][31] identities that have become engrained in the South African psyche. His secret grave holds in him the power to protect a nation, as does Mandela's in that his legacy, if continued, would remedy perceived notions of how South African society is being corrupted. He is also a symbol of a generation that has been cursed with a burden that is almost too unbearable to carry. Then he is a father struggling to say goodbye, struggling to reconcile, and shameful of his past.[32]

This is confirmed in the play when the Chorus describes Oedipus as an allegory of the contradictions inherent in South African society: "He is like us all. The refugee. The once-famed leader. The hero. The Liberator. The perpetrator. The

---

30   *Ibid.*, 53.

31   For more information about the Truth and Reconciliation Commission, see: Greg Homann, "Preamble," in *At This Stage. Plays from Post-apartheid South Africa*, ed. Greg Homann (Johannesburg: Wits University Press, 2009), 9.

32   Greg Homann, "Claiming Western Texts," 120–121.

victim. He is us all."[33] The multiple facets of this Oedipus/Mandela-like character thus prevent any homogenisation of South African identities, rather
suggesting a process of creolization, of constant evolution resulting in multiplicity. As my analysis will indicate, Oedipus/Mandela is considered as a character at a symbolic crossroads, a liminal positioning between past and future:
he personifies the lack of fixity, the in-betweenness of the present state of the
nation, which could revert to chaos or move on to becoming a better place. In
this respect, Thebes is construed as symbolizing the "damaged past," presumably that of apartheid, whereas Athens signals hope, arguably that of the new
democracy were it to develop in a productive manner.[34] The danger is for these
binaries to result in an attitude of simplistic one-ness, over-confidence and
excessive optimism.[35] As such, *Oedipus@Koö-nú* constitutes a postmodern reworking of Sophocles' iconic play. This postmodernity manifests itself in the
play's metatheatrical framework: in an echo of Beckett's *Waiting for Godot*, the
crossroad can be interpreted as the apathy, the threat of stagnation that awaits
any person faced with multiple choices.[36] The two black and white prisoners
echo Sophocles' citizens, Beckett's Vladimir and Estragon, as well as the well-
known South African play, *The Island*, co-authored by Winston Ntshona, Athol
Fugard, and John Kani. Indeed, in *The Island* two Robben Island prisoners
"plan to stage Antigone."[37] While linking Western and South African classics,
these prisoners also underline the metatheatrical dimension of Homann's
work, when they say: "We are a dramatic device to signify the long-standing
conflict in this place."[38] This metatheatrical aspect urges theatergoers to meditate on the different political options embodied by Oedipus, Theseus and Creon, rather than merely empathizing with either one or the other stance.

    This ties in with the process of creolization that is already evident in the ti-
tle of the play, which, Homann points out, is reminiscent of the birth and burial place of Mandela.[39] Being situated "in-between" Athens and Thebes,[40] it
evokes a myriad of possibilities. It further suggests diversity as the crucible of
South African identity:

---

33   Greg Homann, *Oedipus@Koö-nú* (Johannesburg: Unpublished script, 2014), 34.
34   Greg Homann, "Claiming Western Texts," 122.
35   *Ibid.*, 124.
36   *Ibid.*, 122–123.
37   *Ibid.*, 122.
38   Greg Homann, *Oedipus@Koö-nú*, 5.
39   Greg Homann, "Claiming Western Texts," 121.
40   Greg Homann, *Oedipus@Koö-nú*, 23.

... one way to pronounce Koö-Nú! ... is to say it the same way you would pronounce the Xhosa word Kowenu, which translates to "your home." My original intention though was to create a new word that embodied multi-lingual reference points – the "K" and "ö" being prominently used in Afri-kaans, the exclamation mark referencing Xhosa, Zulu and other Nguni based languages, and "Nu" being the thirteenth letter in Greek, but also alluding to German and Yiddish usages. The addition of the ampersand was intended to counterpoint the ancient story of Oedipus with a con-temporary orientation.[41]

This aesthetic of creolization is also perceptible in the numerous different the-atrical techniques used in the work. First, one should not fail to mention the blurring of boundaries between comedy and tragedy. Theseus, meant to be performed by a female actor in this play, first appears on the stage on a bicycle: *"Enter THESEUS on a bicycle with flashing blue lights."*[42] Further, the strange presence of open-air toilets and boxes of textbooks,[43] an allusion to poor deliv-ery services,[44] adds a surreal touch to the setting. This reintroduces comic overtones, when the blind Oedipus inadvertently *"sits on a toilet."*[45] Moreover, Homann appropriates the elevated tone typical of a Greek tragedy in a highly personal way: the use of a chorus recalls the ancient dramatic form, but in this instance, the female chorus is interchangeable with Theseus who has morphed into a woman. One of the early entrances of the chorus adds a sense of parody to the Greek role of the chorus: *"CHORUS enters. She has a loudhailer with her and communicates with her superior via some kind of ear-piece or walky-talky. She is dressed in the official uniform of Athens"*[46] The shifts between stylistic registers are further enacted in the ritual of appeasement staged by Antigone and Ismene. It is meant to exorcise Oedipus' woes through the process of dance and recollection:

> *They continue with the ritual preparation. ANTIGONE prepares the bowls. ISMENE helps ANTIGONE. OEDIPUS dances, a tired man now but lost in some trance. The thunder and the lightning continue to build. CHORUS, as a figment of OEDIPUS'S mind, appears and joins his prayer. She takes over the chanting as OEDIPUS begins to remember his story in a dance. The*

41   Greg Homann, "Claiming Western Texts," 121.
42   Greg Homann, *Oedipus@Koö-nú*, 21.
43   *Ibid.*, 5.
44   Greg Homann, "Claiming Western Texts," 122.
45   Greg Homann, *Oedipus@Koö-nú*, 10.
46   *Ibid.*, 9.

> PRISONERS *appear as a figment of his imagination and enact a dumb-*
> *show. How he murdered his father and married his mother. How he solved*
> *the riddle of the Sphinx. How he discovered his sins. The thunder is now*
> *close and the lightning is more regular. A great spectacle of dance, sound,*
> *and singing.*[47]

During this scene, extra-verbal means of expression are foregrounded. A comparable instance of aesthetic creolization is found when parodic theatre language is enlisted to satirize the shortcomings of the rainbow nation dream. As Homann himself comments, a dance number is inserted "using the theme to the Rugby World Cup of 1995," a symbol of the closest the new South Africa ever got to a sense of national unity.[48] Theseus poorly sings, while a rainbow appears and a rain of rugby balls falls from the sky:

> *It's a special dance of optimism and hope. ...*
> THESEUS: Gathering together. One mind, one heart. Every creed, every
> colour, once joined never apart.
> *A rainbow appears.*
> THESEUS: It's the world in union. The world as one. As we climb to reach
> our destiny, a new age has begun.
> *It is theatre magic with rugby balls raining from the sky.*
> THESEUS: We must face high mountains. We must cross rough seas.
> Every creed, every colour once joined, never apart. It's the world in union
> ... The world as one, as we climb to reach our destiny. A new age has
> begun.[49]

This aesthetic creolization thus serves the playwright to articulate a critique of excessive faith in the benefits of the "new age." In order for the future of South Africa to improve, it will eventually become necessary to overcome, i.e. to creolize, the simplistic binaries of the brute power of the past (represented by the male characters of Creon and Oedipus' sons) and the over-confidence of a female Theseus, even if the latter embodies the potentialities of the future. As she claims: "My government and I are building a future for everyone based on the principles of human dignity, equality, and freedom for all."[50] This optimism alone, the playwright seems to suggest, does not guarantee that the sins of

---

47   *Ibid.,* 20.
48   Greg Homann, "Claiming Western Texts," 123.
49   Greg Homann, *Oedipus@Koö-nú,* 25.
50   *Ibid.,* 24.

patriarchy will not be repeated. The solution lies somewhere in-between, as the symbolic location of the action at a crossroad indicates.

Achieving such a balance is far from easy, especially as Oedipus is now crippled with apathy (an indirect allusion to the political stagnation characterizing the new South Africa). In this instance, apathy recalls the prison metaphor so pervasive in Molusi's *Itsotseng*. Antigone exclaims:

> What is destiny and fate? It is apathy dear sister. It is sitting on a rock, and waiting. The time for waiting and watching and moaning and doing nothing, is over. [...] Hope and fate. Two words that done us in. Why? Because neither allow us to act. That is our plague. In a democracy we are empowered to act, and look at us. Look at our father. The protagonist sitting there, doing nothing.[51]

Oedipus finally decides to act, however. He courageously rejects the violence embodied by Creon and Polynices as they try to make him return to Thebes.[52] Further, because Theseus agreed to have him buried in Koö Nú, Oedipus makes her a gift of wisdom as he feels his is about to die:

> OEDIPUS: You must never reveal the exact spot where I die. It must be hidden.
>
> ...
>
> OEDIPUS: Keep my memory and what I fought for alive, and my secret burial place will always be a defence for you. Stronger than native shields and the spears of your comrades.
>
> ...
>
> OEDIPUS: Theseus, on my death I will share more mysteries, which you must pass down to your successor. From leader to leader. Then, and only then, will you keep this land forever safe. Ten million men and more have committed violence on one another, but you are a woman and can end this cycle of violence. Never let your leadership become like that of men who have gone before.[53]

Avoiding apathy and violence as well as remembering the energy of early ideals thus seem to constitute the key to achieving the dream of the South African rainbow without over-idealizing and homogenizing it. As the chorus and the

---

51   *Ibid.*, 16.

52   *Ibid.*, 34, 37.

53   *Ibid.*, 40.

two prisoners indicate at the very end of the play, the process of creolization is an arduous journey, one that depends on the strong will of the people: "CHORUS: This is a play about today. Today does not look different from yesterday. Tomorrow might look like today/PRISONER 1: It's all up to us now./PRISONER 2: I suppose it is."[54] Thus, the conclusion of *Oedipus@Koö-nú* offers only a glimmer of hope for the new South Africa.

● ● ●

Craig Higginson's *The Imagined Land* prolongs the metatheatrical, postmodern allegories about the new democracy devised by Omphile Molusi and Greg Homann. It particularly echoes *Itsotseng* in its emphasis on storytelling, albeit in the form of Western-style narratives. It was premiered at the National Arts Festival in July 2015. Like Higginson's earlier play, *Dream of the Dog*, it deals with personal and national traumas inherited from the apartheid era. While in *Dream of the Dog* the full horror of the trauma is revealed, this play articulates the impossibility of voicing traumas, or at least the impossibility of assuming the existence of standard forms of trauma for black and white people. Like Molusi and Homann, Higginson insists on the difficulty of homogenising national identities. In his introduction to the play, Titlestad claims: "Existence, it transpires, cannot be reduced to singular determining moments, rather it is a filigree, a composite, intricate pattern of linked representations."[55] Through his attempt to anatomize trauma, Higginson thus suggests that clear-cut patterns of relationships between black and white people cannot adequately reflect reality. Rather, as the title of the play intimates, one must consider the human mind as an "imagined land," which can only be apprehended through the nuanced discourse of differentiation, the fluid process of creolization. Also related to the vagaries of representation of trauma is the difficulty of remembering, which already affected Richard, the husband protagonist of *Dream of the Dog*. As Greg Homann argued, in *Dream of the Dog*, Higginson articulated a critique of the amnesia that characterized post-apartheid South Africa regarding the evils perpetrated during that period of oppression.[56] In *The Imagined Land*, Bronwyn, an ageing white liberal writer, is confused from the start, and after

---

54   *Ibid.*, 41.

55   Michael Titlestad, introduction to *Three Plays*, ed. Craig Higginson (London: Oberon Books, 2016), 14.

56   Greg Homann, Introduction to *At This Stage. Plays from Post-apartheid South Africa*, ed. Greg Homann (Johannesburg: Wits University Press, 2009), 22–24.

undergoing brain surgery, she withdraws in the ivory tower of her mind. This issue of remembering is linked with the difficulty of correctly perceiving the other's trauma: Edward completely misunderstands the role Bronwyn played as a mother to Emily. The process of creolization eventually emerges between Edward and Emily, as they are willing to listen to each other's nuanced rendition of their traumatic experiences. This conjures up the heterogeneous and unfixed nature of reality. Ironically, the moment when such a conversation starts takes place in the spring, a symbol of regeneration and hope.

In Part One, the metatheatrical/metafictional aspect of *The Imagined Land* is readily underlined, as we discover the sitting room of Bronwyn's Johannesburg house. Prominent in the set are *"an old wooden chest – but most of all many books, mainly novels."*[57] This allusion refers to Bronwyn's artistic career, which is Edward's chief concern as a young black academic. Indeed, he seeks Bronwyn's permission to write her authorized biography. Bronwyn immediately states her belief that narrative can hardly represent life, when she describes her early childhood:

> BRONWYN: I was actually born in East London. The tenth child in a Catholic family. My father was in the merchant navy. As I was born, a German U-boat bombed my father's ship and killed everyone on board. My mother didn't know what to do, so I was handed over to the nuns. I was about to be adopted by a tobacco farmer in Southern Rhodesia, but the nuns didn't want to hand me over to a family that wasn't Catholic ... It's a narrative I like to trot out at interviews. Not that I believe a narrative can ever represent a life. Imagined lands – that is all we are, all we have access to. ... Imagined lands are not the same as imaginary lands, Dr. Smith. I never tried to represent alternative realities. The one around me always sufficed. And even that became increasingly impossible to represent.[58]

This postmodern vision of the constructedness of narratives ushers in the main theme of the play, which interrogates the very notion of mimesis. In a subsequent conversation between Edward and Emily, the latter claims that her mother only gave him access to her papers because he was black. Emily admits she left to New York where she became an academic in order to avoid her mother, which evokes a conflict Edward later completely misconstrues. The other sister, we are told, left to Australia for the same reason: "Why do you think my sister and me chose to live abroad? We didn't run away from South

---

57   Craig Higginson, "The Imagined Land," in *Three Plays* (London: Oberon Books, 2016): 153.
58   *Ibid.*, 157.

Africa. We ran away from her."[59] Through this notation, Higginson suggests the globalization process in which South Africa is now involved. As Part One closes, Edward and Emily kiss each other. The female protagonist confesses: "… I have my mother eyes. I have a blind spot when it comes to back men."[60] Like her mother, she underlines the postmodern concern with the limitations of representation: "I've always liked that word 're-search.' The idea of searching for something again and again without the prospect of ever finding it."[61] Will Edward, Emily and Bronwyn ever understand each other's inner selves?

In Part Two, Bronwyn is further confused, having undergone brain surgery. Edward, who has started reading her notebooks, feels interested in a particular passage: "There was something about the scene in the lounge that struck me as odd. Emily was standing in front of 'X,' who was sitting on the couch, his hand on her shoulder, leaning towards her as if he had just whispered something in her ear … I had a terrible feeling suddenly – that I had handed Emily over to something monstrous. Felt what the parents of sacrificed children must have felt."[62] When prompted to identify this "X" person, Bronwyn says: "He was a poet. A black consciousness poet who was staying for a few weeks in our house."[63] She further denies any validity to this event: "There are literally hundreds of such notebooks around the place. How do you know that the incident I described even took place in the outside world?"[64] Edward persists in wrongly suspecting Bronwyn of covering up some form of rape, a view that bespeaks his prejudiced view about black/white relationships in South Africa:

> EDWARD: What if something unspeakable really was taking place in your sitting-room, while you were up there in your ivory tower, Lost in your own imaginings? …
>
> You know what your preoccupation is. Guilt. The anatomy of guilt. I used to think it was the collective guilt of all your people. You were like a surgeon, cutting through the hypocrisy of the times with a carefully honed sentence. But it was your own guilt that you were trying to comprehend, wasn't it? All the rest – the politics of the time, any social injustices – those were just the trappings, the excuse, a way of making what you were doing seem more respectable.[65]

---

59   *Ibid.*, 163.
60   *Ibid.*, 164.
61   *Ibid.*
62   *Ibid.*, 169–170.
63   *Ibid.*, 170.
64   *Ibid.*, 171.
65   *Ibid.*, 172–173.

To Edward, then, Bronwyn embodies the predicament of white South African liberals, who are only interested in avoiding blame for apartheid woes, not in truly remedying them. As many of the characters in Molusi's and Homann's plays, Edward is condemned to remain in the metaphoric prison of his prejudiced perception of the white/black other. Although he boldly tells Bronwyn: "I've opened your wooden chest,"[66] this only reveals his naïve, homogenized rather than creolized, perception of reality. As the section concludes, he confesses to Bronwyn he wants to marry her daughter, suggesting a difficult racial reconciliation in a South African context.

In Part Three, as they are making love, Emily tells Edward stories about the accidental death of her father, in an attempt to complicate Edward's simplistic notions about her life:

> My father was a pilot ... I remember having lunch one day at Victoria Falls Hotel with a pilot friend of his ... I wanted to be in my father's friend's plane because it had curtains in the windows. A week later as he was flying out of Kariba, he and his plane were shot down by a group of guerillas. The survivors – some of them babies and children – were bayonetted and shot. Unspeakable things were done to their bodies ... Apparently, he [her father] became delusional, paranoid. My mother told me he injected himself with morphine not long after that Viscount was shot down. But she never talks about it.[67]

However, she quickly denies the certainty of this truth: "But even that I might have dreamed. Who knows what happened and didn't, right?"[68] We later learn that Edward got the academic job Emily had been applying for, because he was "simply the darker candidate."[69] At this juncture, Edward alludes again to his conviction that Emily was raped. He reiterates she did not receive any help from her mother, who was living in a world of her own. He even suggests Emily covered up the incident and erased the name of the perpetrator from her mother's notebooks. He makes the mistake of over-interpreting her traumatic experience: "Is that why you were drawn to me? Was I another black man without a face? Is that what you want – to re-enact your experience of abuse?"[70] As he declares he intends to write a novel about it all, she blames him for misinterpreting her: "It's becoming clearer and clearer to me that you wouldn't

---

66   *Ibid.*, 174.
67   *Ibid.*, 175–176.
68   *Ibid.*, 177.
69   *Ibid.*, 179.
70   *Ibid.*, 186.

recognize love or truth if they were staring you in the face."[71] This Third Part ends with a declaration of war between the two of them, a sign that they have failed to engage in a truly mutual process of understanding and creolization, continuing as they do to homogenize expressions of trauma.

Part Four further complicates the difficulty of coming to terms with the real nature of trauma. Emily seeks to get to the bottom of her mother's relationship with her husband's friend, Henry, who was, according to Bronwyn: "Like a bird on fire. He fell from the sky ... And I loved him."[72] In doing so, she attempts to offer a narrative about her mother countering Edward's simplistic views about her. Like Edward, Emily has read her mother's notebooks, but she refuses to distort their meaning. She discovered a passage in which Bronwyn describes how the father sought to kill his family on the eve of the war: "He had the syringes and enough morphine for each of us. He came and told me that. He said we would lose the war. That it was just a matter of time before we'd all be slaughtered in our beds. He said it would be easier if we went to sleep now. While still together, as a family."[73] Bronwyn then reveals she fled to Johannesburg with the children. When Emily confesses to her mother she is pregnant with Edward's child, Bronwyn shows herself under a more favorable light: "It's about time I had another son. This time, you'll see – I'll do a better job of it. I want him to smile more easily, love more fiercely."[74] She subsequently claims: "I have hundreds of children. Far too many heads to count,"[75] which seems to indicate she has lost awareness of who she is. Emily concludes by articulating the evanescence of the self: "There are so many versions of a person. How do we know which one to hold on to and which one to relinquish?"[76] Through such an assertion, she rejects Edward's flawed notion of fixed identities in favour of Glissant's fluid process of creolization.

This process reaches a climactic point in the final Part Five, which takes place in the spring, thus suggesting some measure of hope. However, Bronwyn seems even more lost in her world of fiction, which adds a final metatheatrical touch to the play. As Emily says: "I sometimes think she can understand me, at other times she seems completely blank. Like a page without any writing on it."[77] When Emily meets Edward again, we learn that the publication of his flawed book about Bronwyn cost him his job. Comments Emily: "Perhaps the

---

71   *Ibid.*, 184.
72   *Ibid.*, 188.
73   *Ibid.*, 190.
74   *Ibid.*, 192.
75   *Ibid.*, 193.
76   *Ibid.*
77   *Ibid.*, 197.

problem with your book is the problem with most criticism. This source material never quite manages to fit into the argument."[78] She clearly indicts Edward's insensitivity:

> EMILY: All you said was that something terrible had been done to me as a child because of my mother's neglect. You mention a prominent poet – and withhold his name as if you know it but out of some ethical compunction have decided not to disclose it. Your argument is that my mother was cold, hard, a narcissist – yet you ignore those hundreds of journals that are about little more than her children, and her friends and all the things in the world she loved.[79]

However, even Emily fails to perceive the exact nature of Edward's trauma: "We've had sex, Edward. I know you can only get aroused when you're drunk. I have felt parts of you that perhaps no one else has experienced, and I have glimpsed them time and again, like hideous phantoms, peering from behind every paragraph of your book."[80] Edward counters violently, suggesting that, through him, Emily homogenizes the trauma of all black people:

> EDWARD: You want me to tell you I was raped, is that it? While my father was lying drunk in his garden hut, I was up in the house, with the big white boss, being abused? Is that the sordid little story you want me to trot out? ... Naturally that's why I hate white people. I'm walking around with that big ungovernable wound. And that is why I'm incapable of governing myself ... I'm not ready to spill my guts all over this floor for your entertainment. My people have given enough. And I'm not going to make myself acceptable, digestible, comprehensible to you![81]

Upon hearing this, Emily tells Edward she miscarried his son, who "was almost ours."[82] This revelation radically alters the final mood of the play, as the characters come to a better understanding of each other. Interestingly, Bronwyn starts writing a new fairytale-like story of hope that involves Edward:

---

78   *Ibid.*, 199.
79   *Ibid.*, 201.
80   *Ibid.*
81   *Ibid.*, 202.
82   *Ibid.*, 204.

One upon a time, there was an old woman who sat in the top of a tall house that overlooked a difficult city. She told stories to herself, but she intended them for other people … One of these books landed in the lap of a young man called Edward … The young man read her stories and decided to change his life. He continued to travel the world with the old woman's words flying around inside him, creating little pathways in his head that soon became his own.[83]

This last metatheatrical twist prompts both Edward and Emily to stop homogenizing and to really listen to each other's trauma, thus introducing a spark of hope. As Bronwyn continues to write: "One day, the young man met a woman. She was holding a glass of water. The young man stepped forward and took the glass, and he started to drink."[84] The protagonists' last words initiate the arduous path towards the genuine differentiation of creolization as a process of continual exchange between the different ethnic groups of South Africa. Interestingly, in keeping with Craig Higginson's postmodern belief in the multiplicity of truth and the difficulty of articulating it, the story is supposed to be told after the curtain has dropped and spectators are left to imagine what it could be: "EDWARD: I'd like to tell it to you – my story. If you're still interested/EMILY: of course I am [...]/EDWARD: It isn't easy/ EMILY: who said it had to be."[85] All in all, then, by the end of the play, Emily and Edward seem to transcend their prejudices, an allegorical equivalent of a transition into a creolized rainbow nation. In Mike van Graan's *When Swallows Cry*, no such frankly optimistic outcome is perceptible. As he examines the potential for creolization in an age of globalization, van Graan offers little hope for radical change. However, the last moments of his work suggest a possible escape from the prison of contemporary woes.

• • •

First produced at the Johannesburg Market Theatre in January 2017, *When Swallows Cry* amplifies the postmodern perspective of the works analyzed above to encompass a transnational outlook. Indeed, *When Swallows Cry* broadens the South African background of the plays studied so far to examine a diffraction, indeed creolization of (South) African identities at a global level,

---

83   *Ibid.*
84   *Ibid.*, 205.
85   *Ibid.*

at a time when painful immigration issues are increasingly foregrounded internationally. As the introduction suggests, the work's three playlets *are inter-
spliced with each other, all of them commenting on the theme of migration, from
different perspectives.*[86] In Playlet One, a Canadian teacher named Charles Stevenson, "travels to an African country 'to make a difference' as a teacher."[87] This
country is not clearly defined, but is described as "a failed state, with high unemployment, great inequality between a politically-connected elite and the
poor masses."[88] As a result, Charles is kidnapped by bandits, who hope to get a
good ransom in exchange for his life. The other two actors are the black commandant and an African soldier.

Aesthetic creolization is manifest from the start in Playlet One, as the Commandant speaks in an unidentified African language, the translation of which
is projected onto a screen: *"The language is made up of words of different languages and names of languages not peculiar to any country, but could be somewhere on the border between Cameroon and Nigeria."*[89] A metatheatrical/inter-
textual allusion is introduced when we discover that Charles Stevenson is a
Shakespeare teacher. He hopes to make Africans discover the so-called universal values of *Hamlet*.[90] We soon realize that, like Hamlet in the prison-like
kingdom of Denmark, the characters remain the prisoners of a binary mode of
thought separating African from Western people, as the process of colonization is still going on, hampering creolization. Western education, van Graan
implies, does not provide solutions to African needs. In his transition to Scene
2/Playlet Two, Mike van Graan broadens his spectrum to include Somalia and
South Africa: *"Slides are projected, with images of an African map. Somalia high-
lighted [...] and finally South Africa."*[91] This transnational and transcultural perspective reverberates in Playlet Two, where a black and a white US immigration officers are reticent to allow a Muslim Somalian to enter America.
Although the Somalian fled his country in order to escape a certain death, the
homeland security officers suspect him of being a potential terrorist.[92] When
the Somalian visitor shows the visa he got in South Africa, they finally for-
bid him to enter the US. Mike van Graan then establishes the binary division
between the black US officer and the Somalian.[93] The latter, in a moment of

---

86   Mike van Graan, *When Swallows Cry* (Cape Town: Unpublished script, 2017), 2.
87   *Ibid.*
88   *Ibid.*
89   *Ibid.*, 4.
90   *Ibid.*, 10.
91   *Ibid.*, 12.
92   *Ibid.*, 13.
93   *Ibid.*, 16.

despair, hoping to reach across racial barriers, ironically tells the black officer he wanted to "keep America great."[94] Nonetheless, the Somalian is left outside the metaphorical prison of the United States, eventually killing himself with one of the officers' gun rather than facing deportation.[95] Scene 3/Playlet Three shifts the focus to an Australian detention centre, reintroducing the prison metaphor derived from *Hamlet*. In this confined space, "two Zimbabweans are held ... having arrived there illegally on a boat transporting Africans to Vanuatu. They overpower the white officer in the detention centre, and debate plans to escape in order to make new lives for themselves in Australia."[96] All of their dreams are quickly shattered, however. One of the detainees tries to make the white officer understand how harsh life has been for them in Africa, where they lost their jobs: "Riaison: ... as human beings to another human being ... you must understand how traumatic this has been for us."[97] The other detainee, Josh, blames his mate's optimism on his admiration for Nelson Mandela, which inserts a reference to the flawed rainbow metaphor: "You're so naïve, Riaison ... Mandela has always been your hero ..."[98] Although the white officer in charge has an Australian accent which "belies traces of Southern Africa,"[99] he feels no sympathy for the two Africans. He voices his anger at what he had to face when he lived in Rhodesia:

> Clark: ... You see, my family had a farm in the bread basket of Southern Africa... Rhodesia...before you mints turned it into the basket case of (*exaggerated African accent*) Zimbabwe. ... I lost an uncle in the Rhodesian war...trying to keep you barbarians at bay. From fucking up the country that we built. We tried to civilize you. Christianize you. Teach you our values. But we lost the war. ... So we lost our farms. But we're here now in paradise. And I'll be damned if we let in the barbarians this time![100]

Unable to escape his binary thinking, the white officer precludes any form of global creolization process: he violently kills Riaison and Josh.[101] While Playlet Two and Three are thoroughly pessimistic, the more developed Playlet One,

---

94   *Ibid.*, 18.
95   *Ibid.*, 55.
96   *Ibid.*, 3.
97   *Ibid.*, 27.
98   *Ibid.*
99   *Ibid.*, 21.
100 *Ibid.*, 56.
101 *Ibid.*, 57.

which concludes the play, nevertheless offers a measure of hope. In the course of this Playlet, we learn from the Soldier that the Commandant suffered the trauma of jail after refusing to kill miners who had gone on strike:

> Soldier: ... The miners went on strike. For a long time. The mine owners were foreign ... So government sent in the army to break the strike. Twenty-two miners were shot dead. Commandant was in the army at that time. He refused to shoot...He knew many of the miners, including his cousin. They jailed him for five years.[102]

Such a passage echoes the failure of the rainbow dream of harmony manifest in the plays analyzed earlier, particularly in *Itsotseng*. When learning that Charles Stevenson's father owned the Makudari mine, where these painful events took place, the Commandant decides to kill the Canadian teacher by pouring petrol on him. Clearly, he cannot overcome fixed and homogenizing cultural binaries. Stevenson is not burned alive, however, as he and the Soldier manage to overpower the Commandant. The Soldier, in the naive belief that Stevenson is really going to help his village, once he has been released, drives him to the city and thus to freedom. Naturally, the irate commandant blames the Soldier for having done this and wants to shoot him: "*Commandant is still pointing gun at Soldier's head. There is a tense silence for a few beats.*"[103] In a gesture of hope that suggests one could escape a new cycle of violence, Commandant decides that the Soldier will simply have to leave the village if the Canadian does not send in money within three months. Instead of killing the Soldier, he shakes his hand and concludes in his Indigenous African language: "*You're a good man, Soldier. A bad soldier, but a good man.*"[104] While Playlet Two and Three focus on the woes that the excessive reliance on cultural binaries inevitably produces, Playlet One opens up an avenue for the differentiation possibilities of creolization in a global and African context, as the three characters have managed to come closer to a mutual understanding of their differences.[105] Like Glissant's "creolization," van Graan's vision of globalization is one that ultimately diffracts homogenization, albeit hesitantly. Despite its

---

102   *Ibid.*, 31–32.
103   *Ibid.*, 59.
104   *Ibid.*, 60.
105   I am aware that my understanding of van Graan's play differs from Homann's highly pessimistic account of it earlier in this volume. This difference of perspective could be attributed, I would argue, to van Graan's ability to invite a variety of political interpretations of his plays, without privileging a single one.

bleak overtones, this play suggests there is still some hope for the South African rainbow to shed its full spectrum of colors on the world at large.

∙∙∙

The four plays examined in this essay, commenting on the thematic and aesthetic possibilities of creolization, re-examine in various ways the legacy of Nelson's Mandela dream of a rainbow nation. While Omphile Molusi's *Itsotseng* may be the play that is most oriented towards a reassessment of the past (it may be significant in this respect that it is the less recent play dealt with here), all of the other playwrights considered imagine the future potentialities of South African democracy with only glimmers of hope. Whether dealing with township life, recontextualization of Western classics, racial tensions in the rising new middle class or the woes of migrancy in our transcultural global age, these plays gesture towards a possible solution in the full creolization of the rainbow metaphor, as Édouard Glissant perceived it, i.e. as a way of avoiding homogenized binaries in favour of the multiplicity an ongoing process of interrelations can provide. Only at that price could harmony eventually be achieved, but to paraphrase the concluding words of Prisoner 1 in Greg Homann's play ("It's all up to us now"), this immense challenge will clearly affect the lives of South Africans for generations to come.

Works Cited

Chancé, Dominique. "Creolization. Definition and Critique." Translated by Julin Everett. In *The Creolization of Theory*, edited by Françoise Lionnet and Shu-mei Shih, 262–267. Durham & London: Duke University Press, 2011.

Gilbert, Helen. "Introduction to Guillermo Verdecchia's *Fronteras Americanas (American Borders)*." In *Postcolonial Plays. An Anthology*, edited by Helen Gilbert, 419–422. London & New York: Routledge, 2001.

Glissant, Édouard. *Poetics of Relation*. Translated by Betsy Wing. Ann Arbor: University of Michigan Press, 1997.

Glissant, Édouard. *Traité du Tout-Monde. Poétique* IV. Paris: Gallimard, 1997.

Hauptfleisch, Temple. *Theatre & Society in South Africa. Reflections in a Fractured Mirror*. Pretoria: J.L. van Schaik, 1997.

Higginson, Craig. "The Imagined Land." In *Three Plays*. London: Oberon Books, 2016.

Homann, Greg. "Claiming Western Texts for Contemporary South African Theatre. Issues of Relevance and the Dead-end Pursuit of National Identity." In *New Territories:*

Theatre, Drama, and Performance in Post-apartheid South Africa, edited by Greg Homann and Marc Maufort, 105–127. Brussels: Peter Lang, 2015.

Homann, Greg. Introduction to *At This Stage. Plays from Post-apartheid South Africa*, 17–29. Edited by Greg Homann. Johannesburg: Wits University Press, 2009.

Homann, Greg. *Oedipus@Koö-nú*. Johannesburg: Unpublished script, 2014.

Homann, Greg. "Preamble." In *At This Stage. Plays from Post-apartheid South Africa*, edited by Greg Homann, 1–16. Johannesburg: Wits University Press, 2009.

Homann, Greg and Marc Maufort. "New Territories: Exploring the Post-apartheid Stage." In *New Territories: Theatre, Drama, and Performance in Post-apartheid South Africa*, edited by Greg Homann and Marc Maufort, 11–21. Brussels: Peter Lang, 2015.

Kruger, Loren. *The Drama of South Africa. Plays, Pageants and Publics since 1910*. London & New York: Routledge, 1999.

Molusi, Omphile. *Itsotseng*. Mowbray: Junkets Publishers, 2008.

Titlestad, Michael. Introduction to *Three Plays*, 11–15. Craig Higginson. London: Oberon Books, 2016.

van Graan, Mike. *When Swallows Cry*. Cape Town: Unpublished script, 2017.

PART 3

Female Playwriting

∵

CHAPTER 12

Intimate Exposure: Solo Women Performing in Post-apartheid South Africa

Veronica Baxter

Abstract

This essay explores the work by South African solo women performers in monopolylogues or monodramas through the lens of Bystrom and Nuttall's "intimate exposure." In addition, the essay considers these works from the point of view of post-apartheid testimony and memory, and the evolving aesthetic choices made by theatre practitioners. The solo women's performances studied here comprise *What the Water Gave Me*, *At Her Feet*, *Shwele Bawo!*, *Mother to Mother*, and *I Turned Away and She Was Gone*.

This essay expands on my previous discussion of solo theatre-making and performances by South African men published in Middeke, Schnierer and Homann.[1] That chapter investigated the style of the monodrama where one actor performs one character throughout, and the monopolylogue,[2] a single performer playing many roles, or what Elspeth Tilley calls a polycharacter monodrama.[3] I investigated the monodrama or monopolylogues of Ronnie Govender, Rajesh Gopie, Greig Coetzee, Andrew Buckland, Bheki Mkhwane, Omphile Molusi and Philip Dikotla. My research speculated that male writer-performers' use of narrative structures often required multiple characters, particularly in using the "body as mask" under the influence of Jacques Lecoq's

---

1 Veronica Baxter, "The Theatre Makers in One-Person Drama," in *The Methuen Guide to Contemporary South African Theatre*, eds. Martin Middeke, Peter Paul Schnierer and Greg Homann (London: Methuen. 2015), 109–121.

2 Michael Peterson, *Straight White Male: Performance Art Monologues* (Jackson, MS: U of Mississippi P, 1997). See also: Jill Dolan, "'Finding Our Feet in the Shoes of (One An) Other': Multiple Character Solo Performers and Utopian Performatives," Modern *Drama* 45, no. 4 (Winter 2002), 495–518.

3 Elspeth Tilley, "Staging a 'Plurality of Vision': Diasporic Performance in Polycharacter Monodrama," *Modern Drama* 55, no. 3 (Fall 2012): 304–328.

© KONINKLIJKE BRILL NV, LEIDEN, 2020 | DOI:10.1163/9789004414464_013

training.[4] I also examined the disillusionment expressed with the lack of South African social transformation in some of the performances.

This essay explores the work by South African solo women performers in monopolylogue or polycharacter monodramas through the lens of Bystrom and Nuttall's "intimate exposure"[5] and Jill Dolan's discussion of the monopolylogue's potential for intercultural exchange.[6] In addition, the essay considers these works from the point of view of post-apartheid testimony and memory, and the evolving aesthetic choices made by theatre practitioners. The solo women's performances studied here comprise *What the Water Gave Me*,[7] *At her Feet*,[8] *Shwele Bawo!*,[9] *Mother to Mother*,[10] and *I Turned Away and She Was Gone.*[11]

The apartheid era had a few profound effects on theatre-making that are salient to considering women and solo performance. One of these effects was the rejection of individual narratives in favour of the presentation of collective voices against apartheid. Indeed, the private narrative was sometimes labelled bourgeois, and was rejected by the cultural commissars in the revolutionary struggle.[12] The Post-1994 Truth and Reconciliation Commission (TRC) reopened these private and individual narratives to the public, simultaneously resulting in theatre makers crafting many private narratives as a public theatre of testimony. The argument for such work has often revolved around the purported healing value of testimony for the performer and the audience who have witnessed trauma. Through the theatre (or public gatherings), they experience catharsis.

The new space for testimony countered the apartheid-era's secrecy, censorship, scrutiny, ways and reasons to hide. South African society had been closed

---

4   Simon Murray, *Jacques Lecoq* (London: Routledge, 2003).

5   Kerry Bystrom and Sarah Nuttall, "Private lives and public cultures in South Africa," *Cultural Studies* 27, no. 3 (2013): 307–332.

6   Jill Dolan, "'Finding Our Feet in the Shoes of (One An) Other': Multiple Character Solo Performers and Utopian Performatives," Modern *Drama* 45, no. 4 (Winter 2002), 495–518.

7   Rehane Abrahams, "What the Water Gave Me," in *New South African Plays*, ed. Charles J. Fourie (London: Aurora Metro Press, 2006), 16–32.

8   Nadia Davids, *At Her Feet* (Cape Town: Oshun Press, 2006).

9   Motshobi Tyelele, "Shwele Bawo!," in *At this Stage: Plays from Post-apartheid South Africa*, ed. Greg Homann (Johannesburg: Wits University Press, 2009), 113–139.

10   Sindiwe Magona, Janice Honeyman and Thembi Mtshali-Jones, *Mother to Mother* (Unpublished script, 2012).

11   Jennie Reznek, *I Turned Away and She Was Gone* (Unpublished script, 2016).

12   The Culture Desk of the Mass Democratic Movement in the late 1980s determined whose work had struggle credentials, and whose was counter-revolutionary. Breyten Breytenbach referred to the Culture Desk as "Stalinist jackasses" who claimed to ensure the value of people's art. In: Breyten Breytenbach, "From the night of the possible to the grand game of reality," *Weekly Mail* 1, no. 3 (1990): 4.

off to itself: gates, burglar guards, closed doors, windows, net curtains and whispering were commonplace. Under the moral watchdogs of the Censorship Board and the Information Act, strict bans were placed on anything considered pornographic, including magazines that exposed people's privates and anything deemed to endanger state security. Even celebrities' public lives were kept relatively private. Rumour mills and farm telephone lines slowly gave news of marches, attacks, and massacres. News always followed the event, heard on the radio or later in sanitised versions of television news.

The advent of democracy changed all that – as if the dam wall broke, and a great pouring out began. Live broadcasts of something other than sport became commonplace, South Africa was in love with the freedom to speak, to tell stories – the Truth and Reconciliation Commission (TRC) began before it started. Not only was South Africa an international celebrity country, but all the colours of the rainbow had a story to tell. But what to tell, what not to tell? How to tell?

The TRC battled with those questions, eventually shoe-horning the act of telling into a controlled, highly curated event, where a nation and the world could hear testimony that was "true," in a form that emphasised our maturity and dignity.[13] Suffice it to say that the TRC could not contain the flow – either in or out of the hearings. Stories took on lives of their own, media covered the minutiae of individual stories, productive mis-readings of testimony and performative acts disrupted the organised event.

At the same time as the TRC, Oprah, Dr Phil, *Khumbul'ekhaya* (a television programme that researches missing relatives and reunites them), newspapers and popular magazines endorsed the idea that you could somehow heal through telling your story, that your story would make a difference to someone, if not you.

In that biographical act of exposure, the speaker/performer could come to terms with, transcend or change an aspect of their past life, move forward into a new life. That was posited as the whole point of having a TRC, so that South Africans could deal with the past, and move forward into the future. This compulsion to tell, testify, witness, reveal, cracked open the boundaries between the public and the private, and in keeping with the celebrification of Western society, South Africans became quite obsessed with personal disclosures.

One of the legacies of the (apartheid) past are perceptions that revealing "inner lives is said to degrade the integrity of private life," and "erode[s] dignity

---

13   See: Catherine Cole, *Performing South Africa's Truth Commission: Stages in Transition* (Bloomington: Indiana University Press, 2009).

of exposed subjects."[14] Njabulo Ndebele counters these perceptions in his analysis of anti-apartheid literature that is (citing Barthes[15]) "a spectacle of excess" or spectacular.[16] Ndebele argues that:

> [the] spectacular documents; it indicts implicitly; it is demonstrative, preferring exteriority to interiority; it keeps the larger issues of society in our minds, obliterating the details; it provokes identification through recognition and feeling rather than through observation and analytical thought; it calls for emotion rather than conviction; it establishes a vast sense of presence without offering intimate knowledge; it confirms without necessarily offering a challenge.[17]

Ndebele is arguing for a "rediscovery of the ordinary" in South African writing and culture to counter the spectacle, and in part this is a call to find ways to express the strength, dignity and human-ness of the ordinary citizen. It is also a call for complexity and ambiguity in the expression of people's stories, a point made by Albie Sachs in his essay, "Preparing ourselves for Freedom."[18] Initially delivered in an ANC in-house seminar in 1989, Sachs's essay suggested that in anti-apartheid or struggle arts "our rulers stalk every page and haunt every picture" of South African writing. He also argued (in theatre as elsewhere) that the heroes of the struggle were identified by being able to "recite sections of the Freedom Charter...at the drop of a beret."[19] Sachs' arguments resonate with Ndebele's descriptions of anti-apartheid literature as "demonstrative" and sharing "exteriority."

Theatre-making has since the early 1990s increasingly embraced individual interiority, engaged with affect and looked at the minutiae of everyday, "ordinary" life. Contemporary scholars often characterise this as being a move from "effect" to "affect."[20] This has reshaped and diversified the styles available to

---

14   Kerry Bystrom and Sarah Nuttall, "Private lives and public cultures in South Africa," 318.

15   Roland Barthes, *Mythologies*, trans. Annette Lavers (London: Jonathan Cape, 1972), 15–25.

16   Njabulo Ndebele, "Rediscovery of the Ordinary: Some new writings in South Africa." in *Rediscovery of the Ordinary: Essays on South African Literature and Culture*, (Pietermaritzburg: University of KwaZulu-Natal Press, 2006), 31–54.

17   *Ibid.*, 41.

18   Albie Sachs, "Preparing ourselves for Freedom," in *Spring is Rebellious*, eds. Ingrid De Kok and Karen Press (Cape Town: Buchu books, 1990), 19–29.

19   Carol Steinberg, "Albie Sachs: Our Shakespearian Fool," *TDR: The Drama Review* 35, no. 1 (Spring 1991): 194–199.

20   This is often referred to as the "affective turn," and can be seen in the writings of Sara Ahmed, Laurent Berlant, Michael Hardt, amongst others. See Melissa Gregg and Gregory J. Seigworth, *The Affect Theory Reader*, 2010.

South African theatre-makers, and is relevant to the solo performances discussed in this essay, starting with an examination of Sindiwe Magona, Janice Honeyman, and Thembi Mtshali-Jones's monodrama, *Mother to Mother*.

First performed in 2012, *Mother to Mother* is an adaptation of the eponymous book written by Sindiwe Magona, based on the real events of the murder of foreign student, Amy Biehl, by four youths in Gugulethu, South Africa.[21] The script takes the shape of an imaginary letter written by Mandisa, mother of one of the youths, to Amy Biehl's mother in the USA. Her story (a monodrama) tells of the ordinary day of waking her children for breakfast and travelling into Cape Town to work as a domestic worker. She hurries home like hundreds of others when she hears that violence has occurred in Gugulethu, finally discovering that her son, Mxolisi, is one of the mob who have killed "a white woman." The play is a testimony of her grief and pain at her son's actions, as well as her anger towards the brutal apartheid conditions that have corrupted her son's humanity.

Mandisa regrets what she was unable to do for her son, suggesting that this at least, is not part of her "Sister-Mother's" (Biehl's) pain: "But let this console you – you never have to ask yourself; 'What did I not do for this child?'"[22] She notes her inability to provide a secure life for Mxolisi. This is underscored when she suggests this is due to the cumulative legacy of apartheid in South Africa. She alludes to her son's involvement with the anti-apartheid struggle when mentioning "the spear," a reference to Umkhonto weSizwe (1961–1990).[23]

She regrets that Amy Biehl "had absolutely no sense of danger... That was your daughter's weakness."[24] Mandisa concludes her letter connecting the two mothers through their sorrow – "You, as I, did not choose this coat that we wear. It is heavy on our shoulders." She finishes her testimony:

> Mandisa: Only a slow, simmering, rage that burst and spilled her tender blood on the green late winter grass of a far-away land.
> One boy lost, hopelessly lost. One girl, far away from home!
> The resentment of 300 hundred years made him deaf to all her pleas.
> My son, the deaf, the spear of the wrath of his race, and your daughter, blindly chosen, the sacrifice of hers.[25]

---

21   Sindiwe Magona, *Mother to Mother* (London: Penguin Random House, 2000).
22   Sindiwe Magona, Janice Honeyman and Thembi Mtshali-Jones, *Mother to Mother*, 26.
23   Umkhonto weSizwe (spear of the nation) was the armed wing of the African National Congress.
24   Sindiwe Magona, Janice Honeyman and Thembi Mtshali-Jones, *Mother to Mother*, 25.
25   *Ibid.*, 27.

The performance is simply presented and comprises only a candle and a few props to suggest Mandisa is cleaning as well as cooking. A large suspended screen projects images of Amy Biehl and scenes that she and her friends would have seen on their way to Gugulethu. Projected images contextualise the brutality of the apartheid state including forced removals, the bleak poverty of Gugulethu, and of Mandisa's day. A soundtrack provides an additional layer of mood. The style of performance creates intimacy with the audience, as the events of that fateful day are revealed. Mandisa speaks directly to her audience, as if they are the recipient of her letter (Linda Biehl) but the prevailing feeling is one of interiority, as she tries to make sense of her feelings. She is reliving the day: her last words to her son that morning, the fraught bus ride back to Gugulethu, her neighbour telling her the news of the murder, preparing supper, the police's late-night search for Mxolisi, and eventually his reluctant confession to her. Mandisa's narrative refutes the idea that individual testimony "undercuts the classical functioning of public sphere,"[26] but rather that it validates "interiority," "intimate knowledge" and "detail."[27] *Mother to Mother* focuses on the affect for the real and imaginary characters of this tragedy, although it is grounded in an analysis of the socio-political conditions from the personal perspective of an ordinary woman. This performance space emphasises the domestic, private and affective realms of people's lives. It is theatre of testimony, Mandisa's intimate story echoing the experiences of many mothers in the apartheid era.

The shift away from the spectacular narratives of apartheid towards the intimate is carried forward into *What the Water Gave Me* by Rehane Abrahams. The play "carries stories of where we came from," drawing on "girl child" archetypes all too familiar to the South African environment.[28] Premiered in 2000 by Abrahams, directed by Sara Matchett, the performance is structured around the four elements, Air, Earth, Fire and Water. A circular staging (although not necessarily in the round) has four stations. Each represents an element and a female character or storyteller.

The framing device of the play is a Malay-sourced tale of the three sisters, Bowa Mera, Bowa Puti and Taki Taki. Narrated by Air, the fate of these three sisters relate to all the other elements' stories. Styled with elements of *Bharatha Natyam*,[29] in particular *mudras* (stylised hand gestures), the narrator tells the

26   Kerry Bystrom and Sarah Nuttall, "Private lives and public cultures in South Africa," 318.
27   Njabulo Ndebele, "Rediscovery of the Ordinary," 41.
28   Rehane Abrahams, "What the Water Gave Me," 16.
29   Bharatha Natyam (Bharatanatyam) is a form of classical Indian dance, said to be the oldest. See for example, Barba and Savarese's *A Dictionary of Theatre Anthropology: The Secret Art of the Performer*, 2005.

story of how the three sisters are turned into fish by a monstrous man. They are pushed into a pool where the man can ogle them. The two older sisters lose their lustre in captivity, as the monster man feeds off their beauty, songs and laughter. Insightful Taki Taki, the more phlegmatic sister, eats insects – seemingly making the most of whatever comes her way. Their loving parents search for the sisters, invoking the Sea and the Moon for help. Eventually, they are rescued by the Moon and the Sea, and reunited with their parents. The monster man is drowned, and half eaten by a school of fish. The sisters were each altered by their experience. Arguably, Taki Taki had not expected much from her world. As a result, she is plumper and still cute. Although the story has a happy ending, in that the sisters are rescued by the power of love and the spiritual world, their experiences will shape their futures.

Fire is a time traveller, who remembers coming "here" in a pirate ship, abducted. She is stalking and being stalked, she has been raped, and she sees dead people and aborted foetuses. She is constantly in fear of the walls crumbling, of the tunnels and of falling into the pit.[30] Falling (or was she pushed?) into perhaps the same pool/pit as the three sisters have fallen into – a place where, as Fire states, "violation is my historic condition being as I am five generations out of slavery and a woman. They are looking for a hole. A hole to put their violence in."[31]

This theme is picked up by Water, a child narrating her exposure to porn magazines and rape by an adult teacher. She is forced by her teacher to draw fishes while on his lap, as he "does his business in her." When she speaks of this to a female teacher, she is blamed for telling stories and told that "whosoever digs a pit shall fall into it."[32] She is connected to Fire in this moment, to the fear of the pit, and to the three sister-fishes pushed into the pool to be ogled by a man.

Water's story is directly linked with the predatory world of girl-children discovering for the first-time pornographic magazines with friends from her neighbourhood – where they learn that children and adults do "play together."[33] Water professes to "like it with Sharief better" because "at least he's my same age." Her world weariness with being a plaything, like the doll she bathes in the water, is revealed through a reference to her having "to ignore dead feeling." She thus concludes that "Nothing is wrong. Just you're not allowed to tell."[34]

---

30   Rehane Abrahams, "What the Water Gave Me," 26.
31   *Ibid.*, 21.
32   *Ibid.*, 30.
33   *Ibid.*, 24.
34   *Ibid.*, 24.

Earth has journeyed her way through to resilience, despite feeling "the knife changing shape. I feel the rapist and the rape."[35] Drawing on her ancestors for strength, she has reclaimed her pride, and her resilience. The language (and accent Abrahams used in the original performances) hints at a Cape Coloured vernacular. Moreover, the character is presented as somewhat streetwise with an edge of a hippie. The character of Earth seems to be autobiographical, testifying to Abrahams' belief in using theatre as healing.[36] In Air's story, the sister, Taki-Taki, keeps up her strength, not fighting against the things she cannot change. She relies on her own stoicism, the love of her parents and the universe to pull her through. Similarly, Earth survives through reconnecting with what Abrahams calls "cellular memory and ancestral line,"[37] embracing shamanic rituals in which her spiritual energy keeps her safe.

All in all, *What the Water Gave Me* exposes the tragedy of sexual violence on children, and the question of identity, particularly through the Earth character. It merges the personal quest to explore and come to terms with the trauma carried in violated bodies. Furthermore, it seeks to reveal the abjection of women and girls through the characters of Fire (who is consumed) and Water (who is trapped in a cycle of sexual molestation). Earth and Air show possibilities of transformation and release from abjection, through a spiritual path (Earth) and interdependence of a caring community (Air).

The audiences of *What the Water Gave Me* are asked to participate in a ritual ending to the performance. Jill Dolan argues that this is a part of the utopian performative, by citing D'Erasmo: "[I]t seemed to her that there should be a parting ceremony for leaving the theatre. Some sort of solemn, deferential gesture. That the audience was the one that should bow."[38] The ritual at the end of *What the Water Gave Me* acknowledges the "ancestral line" that is potentially healing. This ritual allows each participant to examine their interior world and personal connection with the world of the performance.

Bystrom and Nuttall suggest that arguments against the use of personal testimony are that "it de-politicises structural violence by transforming underlying social issues into questions of individual pathology and psychology."[39] The four vignettes in *What the Water Gave Me*, through their differences, do not pathologise the four characters, but rather the social context and painful heritage. In contrast to many struggle-era South African works, the self is brought

---

35   *Ibid.*, 30.
36   *Ibid.*, 16.
37   *Ibid.*, 16.
38   Qtd. in Jill Dolan, "Finding Our Feet in the Shoes of (One An) Other," 495.
39   Kerry Bystrom and Sarah Nuttall, "Private lives and public cultures in South Africa," 318.

into play, raising questions around identity and the impact of personal trauma. The four stories are facets of the same person – the multiple identities that people carry simultaneously.

What the Water Gave Me is also reflective of the social pathology characterising South Africa, which includes far too many child abductions, rapes and murders.[40] While the play does not reflect directly on the apartheid era, or the specifics of violence in the struggle years (as *Mother to Mother* does), the four vignettes clearly articulate a dystopian society where dysfunction is experienced simultaneously at public, political, and deeply intimate levels.

> Lauren Berlant argues that researching the "intimate public sphere" is an attempt to make the hegemonic national icon/stereotypes and the narratives that maintain the political culture that they operate in look unfamiliar and uninevitable, while also shifting the ways mass politics, critical practice, identity, embodiment, and intimate political feelings can be imagined and mobilised.[41]

Most salient to this argument at a public level is the question of how the notion of birthright citizenship leaves out the subaltern, in this case, children and women of colour. Berlant argues that a democratic citizenship makes a promise "to people caught in history."[42] *What the Water Gave Me*, first conceived in the much vaunted "rainbow nation" time of post-apartheid, precisely addresses these questions – what does it mean to be a (newly) democratic citizen when the violence carried out against children and women is an open wound?[43] How does the advent of democracy allow people to renegotiate their identities? While Berlant argues that the emphasis on affective testimonial by subalterns is often "juxtapolitical," Bystrom and Nuttall (using Raymond Williams' term, "structures of feeling") ask whether the "intimate public sphere in the context of a divided democratic South Africa [can] create structures of feelings

---

40   2018 government crime statistics show that 23 488 sexual offences against children were committed in the previous year, https://www.thesouthafrican.com/crime-stats-women -children-victims-murder/.

41   Lauren Berlant, "Introduction: The Intimate Public Sphere," in *The Queen of America Goes to Washington City: Essays on Sex and Citizenship*, (Durham: Duke University Press, 1997), qtd. in Kerry Bystrom and Sarah Nuttall, "Private lives and public cultures in South Africa," 14.

42   *Ibid.*, 19.

43   While Berlant is writing about the United States of America, her critique is still relevant to South Africa.

that bind groups of people together in socially generative ways."[44] The experience of the theatre performance binds the audience together as intimate strangers, who re-consider their birthright citizenship in relation to the performance, to the characters, to each other and to the world.

Carolyn Hamilton argues that the focus on self and the importance of subjectivity in the public sphere constitutes a reaction to the past in South Africa. Moreover, Ndebele contends that "personal thinking" is an antidote to "dramatic and huge brushstrokes."[45] All these writers suggest that the turn to the personal reveals the potential for theatre to provide a forum for mutual understanding in audiences, which hints at the transformation of the social pathology in South African society.

Jill Dolan, in discussing the monopolylogue, suggests that this form has the potential to reveal glimpses of utopia, in particular due to the intersubjectivity between characters played by one actor. She suggests that a space opens up for modelling social change, as we (the audience) see the embodiment of several characters in one actor. We realise that we are comprised of multiple identities and subjectivities simultaneously and acknowledge our inter-connectedness with others, even when we disagree.[46] Certainly, this is true if the performance text of *At Her Feet* is considered.[47]

Nadia Davids wrote *At Her Feet* in response to an honour killing of a young woman in Jordan and the Islamaphobia in the aftermath of the 2001 attacks on the World Trade Centre. Her concern was to show how Muslim women in Cape Town may respond to this event and to Islamaphobia.[48] The result offers a spectrum of six women that Davids suggests are all resonant with her experiences. She argues that when she writes, "the story almost dictates the form – it will insist on how it wants to be told."[49] In the case of this play, the form is that of a monopolylogue, multivalent voices of women expressing their pain, grief

44   Kerry Bystrom and Sarah Nuttall, "Private lives and public cultures in South Africa," 321.
45   In *Ibid.*, 324.
46   Jill Dolan, "Finding Our Feet in the Shoes of (One An) Other," 496.
47   I will not go into detail about Nadia Davids' text, although it clearly fits into the stylistic characteristics of a monopolylogue. Indeed, it has been extensively analysed in other publications. For example, see Carol M. Kaplan, "Voices Rising: An Essay on Gender, Justice, and Theater in South Africa," *Seattle Journal for Social Justice* 3, no. 2 (2004): 711–748; Marcia Blumberg, "South African theatre beyond 2000: Theatricalising the unspeakable," *Current Writing: Text and Reception in Southern Africa* 21, no. 1–2 (2009): 238–260; Nicola Cloete, "Gendering performance in *At Her Feet*," *South African Theatre Journal* 25, no. 1 (2011): 45–53.
48   Nadia Davids, *At Her Feet*, 16.
49   "Nadia Davids," *Free Spirit on SABC3*, May 8, 2014. https://www.youtube.com/watch?v=6UNOQ8EOs9s.

and uncertainties. The embodiment of many characters allows, as Jill Dolan argues, moments "to offer even more multivocal, competing perspectives on the same socially scarring event."[50]

The remarkable sight of one woman performing multiple roles and perspectives creates possibilities in the minds of the audience, or as Anna Deavere Smith says:

> The spirit of acting is the travel from the self to the other... If we were to inhabit the speech pattern of another, and walk in the speech of another, we could find the individuality of the other and experience that individuality viscerally. Learning about the other by being the other requires the use of all aspects of memory, the memory of the body, mind and heart, as well as the words.[51]

If *Mother to Mother* is monodramatic in form, *What the Water Gave Me, At Her Feet* and *Shwele Bawo!* move towards the monopolylogue in the sense that Deavere Smith suggests above. The distinguishing features of the monopolylogue are that it is polyvocal and multivalent, as the interpretation of the text resists a singular meaning. The writer/actor often appears from behind a character's "mask," breaking the fourth wall illusion, and opens up the possibility of dialogue between the characters themselves and the audience. Another South African trait is the athleticism in performance,[52] i.e. the use of vocal and physical muscularity to move from character to character through a change of voice, a shift in weight or spine, eye focus and gesture, and a symbolic costume or prop. Motshabi Tylele's *Shwele Bawo! [A Grave Injustice]* is a good example of this rapid transition between characters.

Written and performed by Motshabi Tyelele in 2004, this performance text is technically a two hander, with the protagonist (Dikeledi) taking on multiple roles. She is imprisoned, constantly under the surveillance of a warder. In the published text, the latter is cast as one who "represents the other voiceless women."[53] *Shwele Bawo!* further develops the theme foregrounded in *What the Water gave me*, specifically locating the testimony of the main narrator, Dikeledi Nkabinde, within a cycle of patriarchal and traditional values, abuse and

---

50   Jill Dolan, "Finding Our Feet in the Shoes of (One An) Other," 512.
51   Qtd. in Jill Dolan, "Finding Our Feet in the Shoes of (One An) Other," 495.
52   David Alcock, "Somatic Emphasis in South African Theatre: Intervention in the body politic," in *South African Theatre and/as Intervention*, eds. Marcia Blumberg and Dennis Walder (Amsterdam: Rodopi Press1999), 49–58.
53   Motshobi Tyelele, "Shwele Bawo!," 113.

violence. The action takes place after the murder of her husband, for which she has been sentenced and imprisoned for life.

Her justification for his murder (and her blamelessness) is based on the violence he perpetrated on her and other girl children. She recounts how she was sexually groomed by Solly Nkabinde at the age of sixteen, when he was in his forties. He was a sugar daddy, or what is known on social media in South Africa as a "blesser." Dikeledi was pregnant by eighteen years of age, and married to him by nineteen, moving from her one-room home to a seven-room palace, and the life of a nouveau riche. She claims to have been "sentenced to life imprisonment long before coming to jail,"[54] trapped into acceptance of her husband's many infidelities with "girls," his violence against her for supposedly flirting, walking provocatively or just disagreeing with him. She is abused by his family members, who refer to her as an uncultured "boesman."[55] It is her great aunt who gives the most chilling advice to Dikeledi – that her responsibility as a wife is to accept that her husband is "an axe and should be lent and borrowed."[56] In other words, she is expected to be complicit in his seduction of other women and girls, and be compliant when "his axe" falls on her.

In the denouement of the story, it is revealed that her daughter Bontle, whom Solly had sent away to the USA supposedly for her education, had been repeatedly raped by him. Dikeledi repeats the phrase "the mother of the child holds the sharp end of the knife,"[57] and this is in part her bitter-sweet rationale for killing her husband, i.e. the axe. This sentence also articulates Dikeledi's exhortation for other mothers to protect their children, even at the cost of their own lives and freedom. Her solution is to plan Solly's death, as she feels plagued by guilt for being unable to protect her child. Mandisa in *Mother to Mother* also felt grief for failing to provide Mxolisi with hope, a reason not to hate. Both women hold "the sharp end of the knife," suggesting that to have a child is committing to pain.

Motshabi Tyelele talks about theatre satisfying our need to witness, to hold a mirror up to our society and to teach.[58] But I would argue that the polycharacter monodrama does more than reflect how things are. Through its multiple voices and points of view, it provides a space for the reconsideration of society and its shaping. Foucault argues that

---

54   *Ibid.*, 118.
55   Pejorative term meaning bush man or Bushman, as when referring to the San people.
56   Motshobi Tyelele, "Shwele Bawo!," 119.
57   *Ibid.*, 135–136.
58   "Meet Matatiele's Great Beauty," *ETV Channel on Youtube*, last modified April 9, 2015. https://www.youtube.com/watch?v=XHc-3YaeUto.

> In the mirror (*theatre*), I see myself there where I am not, in an unreal, virtual space that opens up behind the surface; I am over there, there where I am not, a sort of shadow that gives my own visibility to myself, that enables me to see myself there where I am absent: such is the utopia of the mirror.[59]

Indeed, in the monopolylogue, the characters are "me" and "not me." This theatrical form provides an intercultural dialogue through the multiple characters – as is most manifest in *What the Water Gave Me, At Her Feet* and *Shwele Bawo!*. The monopolylogue serves the purpose of reminding audiences that we are multivalent as people. While there are differences, there is a common humanity. Dolan argues that, in the processes of theatre, one finds social interaction and cultural exchange, which creates spaces for new interpretations of the world and of interpersonal relations.[60]
   Along the same lines, Helen Gilbert and Jacqueline Lo argue that

> In post-colonial monodrama, the distinction between actor and role is often foregrounded as the performer enacts multiple subjectivities which resonate against – and dialogise – others in the course of the performance. This enables the colonised Other, on the one hand, to draw attention to the dominant tropes of representation to which she is subject, and on the other hand, to subvert the monologic tendency by emphasising her hybrid identity which enables multiple subject positions to be played out – and played with.[61]

In theatre we anticipate an audience who is the "other" to the performers, whereas in a monopolylogue the characters are "other" to each other. They are juxtaposed, which enables them to comment on and mediate each other and the psycho-social realm. They are also performed with greater exteriority than in the monodrama, *Mother to Mother*. In *Shwele Bawo!*, the caricatures of Black Bitch, White Bitch, Great Aunt and Granny are devised to emphasise the protagonist's serious story. They also reveal, in Gilbert and Lo's words, "the dominant tropes of representation to which she [Dikeledi] is subject."[62]

---

59   Michel Foucault, "Of Other Spaces: Utopias and Heterotopias," trans. Jay Miskowiec, in *Diacritics* 16, no. 1 (Spring 1986): 22–27.
60   Jill Dolan, "Finding Our Feet in the Shoes of (One An) Other," 496.
61   Helen Gilbert and Jacqueline Lo, "Performing Hybridity in Post-colonial Monodrama," *Journal of Commonwealth Literature* 31, no.1 (1997): 1–19.
62   *Ibid.*, 5.

At the very end, Dikeledi tells us (rather than showing through action) that we as audiences have responsibilities to the children:

> Tell me, ladies and gentlemen,
> If we protect the Sollys of this world,
> What kind of mothers are the Bontles going to be?
> What kind of fathers are the Lesegos and Kgotsos going to be?
> Tell me... just tell me![63]

Her invocation for us to take action, as she did, moves towards the imagining of a utopian dream in the words of Daisy Zamora's "Song of Hope":[64]

> One day the fields will be forever green
> And the earth will be black, sweet and moist.
> Our children will grow tall on her,
> And the children of our children.
> And they will be free as the trees
> And the birds of the wilderness.

The images of the freedom of the wilderness – nature unchecked – and of "our children" are echoed in the last performance text under consideration, *I Turned Away and She Was Gone*, written and performed by Jennie Reznek.[65] The text is loosely based on the Demeter/ Persephone story from Greek mythology. Demeter, also known as the Earth goddess, presided over fertility and harvest. As such, she was much beloved by women and farmers. Her virgin daughter, Kore, was abducted by the god of the underworld, Hades. Demeter searched for her, preoccupied, and neglected the land and harvests. When everything began to die, Zeus commanded Hades to free Kore, now renamed Persephone. Hades agreed to release her, on the condition she did not eat anything whilst in the underworld. However, Persephone had tasted some pomegranate fruit, which bound her to return to the underworld for a part of each year. In Greek mythology, this incident caused the cycle of the seasons.

Demeter is also said to be a collective name for three phases of grain germination. Likewise, as a goddess, she embodies three forms of development. Kore

---

63   Motshobi Tyelele, "Shwele Bawo!," 137.
64   Daisy Zamora, "Song of Hope," in *For our comrades inside: New Year's Book 1988* (Berkley California: The Real Dragon Project, Political Books for Political Prisoners, 1988).
65   First performed in 2015. Directed by Mark Fleishman.

is the young maiden, the green grain waiting to be planted; Persephone is the nymph, the grain ready to be harvested; and, Hecate is the crone, the harvested grain.[66] Reznek has constructed a text around this division. However, in her story, Demeter is initially the mother figure, the daughter is Kore-who-becomes Persephone, and Hecate the old crone could be regarded as a grandmother.

With the help of a gardener, Demeter created a fecund garden world as a playground for her daughter. However, Kore is not allowed to go to the bottom of the garden – "the wild" – where dangers lurk. Mother and daughter are entwined in each other's lives, as they repeat the reasons why they love each other. To emphasize this, Reznek uses physical ideograms[67] and repeated lines of text to create an imprint on the audience's memory, for example;

> Her sudden laughter when she reads something funny
> The sound of her keys around her neck
> The blood colour of her lips
> Her Raphaelite hair.[68]

I Turned Away and She Was Gone opens with a sequence of Demeter's dream, in which she tells of plunging into a volcano, falling into a dark hole – or was she pushed? When she woke up, the memory had gone. Kore ventures into the forbidden garden, falls in love with her own image in the dark pool of water, sensually dances into self-discovery and then slips away while her mother's back is turned. In the sequence in which she is floating in dark muddied water (literally in a tin bath of water), she starts to forget herself, her name, and the previous version of herself. The actor breaks out of role at the end of this sequence, and becomes herself, towelling off the water and changing into a dry dress, while she speaks directly to the audience and even the technical crew, suggesting that:

> there needs to be a series of rivers... a river of woe, a river of fire – the river Styx. The river of unbreakable oaths and the river of forgetfulness.

---

66 "Chapter four Persephone/Demeter/Hecate," *The Ravings of a Complete Lunatic*, last modified March 3, 2010, https://etheria888.wordpress.com/2010/03/03/chapter-four-perse phonedemeterhecate/ and "Triple Goddess (Neopaganism)," *Wikipedia, The Free Encyclopedia*, last modified oct 31, 2018, argue that the interpretation of the Persephone/Demeter/ Hecate story is a neo-Paganism construct.

67 Also known as finger "tutting," these are stylized movements that distil the essence of an image.

68 Jennie Reznek, *I Turned Away and She Was Gone*, 6.

That memory flush that happens at adolescence that washes away early childhood memories...[69]

Demeter frantically searches for her daughter, introducing the phrase "I turned away and she was gone," repeating the ideograms of caring for a child, as a mother does. She suggests that Kore was taken, and in this moment the audience becomes aware of the resonances with many other contemporary abductions – the 200 Nigerian girls abducted by Boko Haram, the daily disappearances of children in the Western Cape, in South Africa and abroad.

The sequence does not simply evoke literal abductions: it also focuses on the adolescent process of separating from the mother figure, of moving into adulthood. Demeter reveals her fear – that her daughter will forget her and what they were to each other. This morphs into a press conference, in which Demeter appeals to the abductor to return Kore, without penalty. Demeter externalises the disappearance of Kore, not allowing herself to think about the possibility that Kore left of her own will.

In a poignantly funny sequence, Demeter then becomes Hecate in the bath and seems to be losing her mind. Hecate cannot remember the right name for soap: "Not because I forget but because it doesn't matter anymore."[70] She saw Kore being abducted by a man, but no one listens to her because they think she is senile. The sting Hecate introduces is that Kore left willingly to escape the prison that Demeter had devised. Hecate's cruelty derives from feeling discarded and parcelled off between relatives, as well as her own loss of self, memory and place as maternal figure. It is at this point that the cycle of life and death takes over the performance, as Kore buries Kore to become Persephone and Demeter mourns that Kore left her to become another person. When Persephone returns to Demeter, she endures only the bitterness of a mother who feels rejected: "Good luck to you when time clutches at your heart so you can no longer breathe/ Or say their names for the pain they have caused you."[71] At this point, all three women merge into the old crone, Hecate. The latter dies while surrounded by a woman who calls her mother, by her husband and by her children (who have green eyes and Raphaelite hair). Hecate remembers the name Kore carved into the bark of a tree, although she is not sure if this is her name. The final moment of the performance focuses on the death of

---

69   *Ibid.*, 13.
70   *Ibid.*, 17.
71   *Ibid.*, 27.

Hecate/Demeter/Kore, as she says: "Did I go without me noticing? Did I slip away while I was thinking of something else? Was I pushed?"[72]

The merging of the three characters is indicative of the crisis of identity that women face in each of the three ages, and of the contradictions and ambiguities that seem universal, while still being intimate and specific. The instant of loss, falling into a pit, drowning in a pool, being sucked into the water, exulting in the wild, the unknown and the dangerous – these fears are felt for themselves and for their children. This instant is also a performance about leaving or being left behind, being unloved and forgotten.

The narrative of this play shifts between these characters, at first distinguishing between them quite strongly, and then gently erasing the particulars, blurring what makes the characters specific. In this process, the narrative reveals the relationships between mothers and daughters, the erasure of memory, and their gradual estrangement. Reznek's play foregrounds both the way in which we turn away from each other through literal physical loss and the way in which memory fades. In short, we live, like theatre, "on the boundary between [our] own context and another, alien, context."[73]

Reznek has also confounded the boundaries between the monodrama and the monopolylogue in this performance. At one level, the text plays out as a linear monodrama set anywhere in the world; that is, Demeter losing her child, getting back a stranger with a new name, and then descending into old age, senility and death. The performance also reveals, in Gilbert and Lo's words, the figures of mother/daughter/crone, as a "hybrid identity which enables multiple subject positions to be played out" in keeping with postcolonial intersubjectivity.[74] Viewing the performance as a monopolylogue shows us the characters of the protective mother, the rebellious child, the crazy grandparent, and then the slippage of these identities into the possibly universal experience of fear and loss. While the monopolylogue can be understood as a personal story, it is also a cautionary tale about South Africa's post-apartheid pathology – abduction, abuse, neglect, sexual predators, sexual grooming, public testimony and grief, fear, and the dangers of "the wild" for girls and women.

A "structure of feeling" emerges for South African post-apartheid theatre in the *Mother to Mother, What the Water Gave Me, At Her Feet, Shwele Bawo!* and *I Turned Away and She Was Gone*. Raymond Williams argues it is "a kind of feeling and thinking which is indeed social and material, but each in an embryonic

---

72   *Ibid.*, 29.
73   Mikhail Bakhtin, *The Dialogical Imagination* (Austin: University of Texas Press, 1992), 284.
74   Helen Gilbert and Jacqueline Lo, "Performing Hybridity," 5.

phase before it can become fully articulate and defined exchange."[75] South African theatre makers have been constructing a "structure of feeling" about the dystopian realities for children and women. The works discussed here play out in the affective realm, as the women characters protect their children from loss and erasure by making gardens, listing things they love about each other, finding spiritual growth, calling them in from play, sending them to school, and giving them warnings. Real life is unpredictable, and as too often seen in the newspapers, people fail to protect their children.

The structure of feeling is also evident in the way in which these solo performances are crafted, each theatre maker working with "intimate exposure" through their chosen style. Each one is a form of testimony that exposes a raw nerve of South African society. The performers reveal their characters' interior worlds, drawing us, as audience, into an intimacy that is enhanced by the solo performance. Bystrom and Nuttall suggest that "it may be in such acts of exposure that new ways of living together are being invented and inhabited."[76] Dolan speaks of "utopian performatives" which she describes as a moment in the theatre when:

> I feel myself reconstituting my own subjectivity and my own sense that time and space can be fluid and malleable. Something inexpressible flits before my eyes, resonates in my soul, a feeling of pleasure, a strong but inarticulate feeling of literally "imagined community."[77]

In other words, what is important is the pleasure of belonging to a public-private group that experiences the self, interiority and belonging. In South Africa, there is an urgency to address "the challenges of the unfinished democratic transition."[78] Carolyn Hamilton suggests that "rebuilding the self, the internal, subjective life of individuals and their emotional dimensions, is a crucial aspect of democracy," and argues that a great deal of public-private deliberation already takes place through performances, art exhibitions, film and speeches.[79]

Gilbert and Lo contend that theatre is uniquely placed because "multiple signifying systems of theatre – particularly as they are utilised in post-colonial monodrama – provide a Third Space which enables writers and performers to

75   Raymond Williams, *Marxism and Literature* (Oxford UP, 1977), 131. Qtd in Jill Dolan, "Finding Our Feet in the Shoes of (One An) Other," 497.

76   Kerry Bystrom and Sarah Nuttall, "Private lives and public cultures in South Africa," 310.

77   Jill Dolan, "Finding Our Feet in the Shoes of (One An) Other," 497.

78   Kerry Bystrom and Sarah Nuttall, "Private lives and public cultures in South Africa," 311.

79   *Ibid.*, 323.

dramatise cultural hybridity and the resignification of cultural difference."[80] Across the performances discussed here, and within each, one can find the elements constituting this "Third Space" where South African identities can be reconstituted, memories and trauma revealed, and citizenship re-negotiated. It is in the act of witnessing these intimate exposures that glimpses of Dolan's "utopian performatives," our shared humanity, are made possible.[81]

Works Cited

Abrahams, Rehane. *What the Water Gave Me*. In *New South African Plays*, edited by Charles J. Fourie, 16–32. London: Aurora Metro Press, 2006.

Alcock, David. "Somatic Emphasis in South African Theatre: Intervention in the body politic." In *South African Theatre and/as Intervention*, edited by Marcia Blumberg and Dennis Walder, 49–58. Amsterdam: Rodopi Press, 1999.

Bakhtin, Mikhail. *The Dialogical Imagination: Four Essays*. Austin: University of Texas Press, 1992.

Barba, Eugenio and Nicola Savarese. *A Dictionary of Theatre Anthropology: The Secret Art of the Performer*, 2nd Edition. London: Routledge, 2005.

Barthes, Roland. *Mythologies*. Translated by Annette Lavers. London: Jonathan Cape, 1972.

Baxter, Veronica. "The Theatre Makers in One-Person Drama." In *The Methuen Guide to Contemporary South African Theatre*, edited by Martin Middeke, Peter Paul Schnierer and Greg Homann, 109–121. London: Methuen, 2015.

Berlant, L. "Introduction: The Intimate Public Sphere." In *The Queen of America Goes to Washington City: Essays on Sex and Citizenship*. Durham: Duke University Press, 1997.

Breytenbach, Breyten. "From the night of the possible to the grand game of reality." *Weekly Mail* 1, no. 3 (1990): 4.

Bystrom, Kerry and Sarah Nuttall. "Private Lives and Public Cultures." *Cultural Studies* 27, no 3 (2013): 307–332.

Cole, Catherine. *Performing South Africa's Truth Commission: Stages in Transition*. Bloomington: Indiana University Press, 2009.

Davids, Nadia. *At Her Feet*. Cape Town: Oshun Books, 2006.

Dolan, Jill. "'Finding Our Feet in the Shoes of (One An) Other': Multiple Character Solo Performers and Utopian Performatives." *Modern Drama* 45, no. 4 (Winter 2002): 495–518.

---

80   Helen Gilbert and Jacqueline Lo, "Performing Hybridity," 4.
81   Jill Dolan, "Finding Our Feet in the Shoes of (One An) Other," 501.

Foucault, Michel. "Of Other Spaces: Utopias and Heterotopias." Translated by Jay Miskowiec, in *Diacritics* 16, no. 1 (Spring 1986): 22–27.

Gilbert, Helen and Jacqueline Lo. "Performing Hybridity in Post-colonial Monodrama."
Journal of Commonwealth Literature 31, no.1 (1997): 5–19.

Gregg, Melissa and Gregory J. Seigworth. *The Affect Theory Reader*. Durham US: Duke
University Press, 2010.

Magona, Sindiwe, Janice Honeyman and Thembi Mtshali-Jones. *Mother to Mother*. Unpublished script, 2012.

Magona, Sindiwe. *Mother to Mother*. London: Penguin Random House, 2000.

"Meet Matatiele's Great Beauty." *ETV Channel on Youtube*. Last modified April 9, 2015.
https://www.youtube.com/watch?v=XHc-3YaeUto.

Murray, Simon. *Jacques Lecoq*. London: Routledge, 2003.

"Nadia Davids." *Free Spirit on SABC3*. May 8, 2014. https://www.youtube.com/
watch?v=6UNOQ8EOs9s.

Ndebele, Njabulo. "Rediscovery of the Ordinary: Some new writings in South Africa." In
Rediscovery of the Ordinary: Essays on South African Literature and Culture. Pietermaritzburg: University of KwaZulu-Natal Press, 2006.

Peterson, Michael. *Straight White Male: Performance Art Monologues*. Jackson, MS: U of
Mississippi P, 1997.

Reznek, Jennie. *I Turned Away and She Was Gone*. Unpublished script, 2015.

Sachs, Albie. "Preparing ourselves for Freedom." In *Spring is Rebellious*, edited by Ingrid
De Kok and Karen Press, 19–29. Cape Town: Buchu books, 1990.

Steinberg, Carol. "Albie Sachs: Our Shakespearian Fool." *TDR: The Drama Review* 35, no.
1 (Spring 1991): 194–199.

Tilley, Elspeth. "Staging a 'Plurality of Vision': Diasporic Performance in Polycharacter
Monodrama." *Modern Drama* 55, no. 3 (Fall 2012): 304–328.

Tyelele, Motshobi. "Shwele Bawo!." In *At this Stage: Plays from Post-apartheid South Africa*, edited by Greg Homann, 113–139. Johannesburg: Wits University Press, 2009.

Williams, Raymond. *Marxism and Literature*. Oxford UP, 1977.

Zamora, Daisy. "Song of Hope." In *For our comrades inside: New Year's Book 1988*. Berkley
California: The Real Dragon Project, Political Books for Political Prisoners, 1988.
http://freedomarchives.org/Documents/Finder/DOC28_scans/28.real.dragon.proj
ect.1988.pdf.

CHAPTER 13

Recuperating Historical Narratives of Violence and Dislocation in Rehane Abrahams' *What the Water Gave Me*

Jill Planche

Abstract

Situated in unidentified places clearly localized in South Africa's rural and urban communities, *What the Water Gave Me* is Rehane Abrahams' recuperation of the buried
histories of a Malaysian slave past that weights South Africa's contemporary world.
Fusing classical Indian dance, storytelling and physical theatre, she conflates the stories her ancestors carried by the Indian Ocean to the Cape in a singular narrator compressed onto a theatrical stage evocative of Doreen Massey's space "intertwined with
time" to provide an assemblage of multiple characters categorized under the rubrics of
air, fire, earth and water. This essay implicates Deleuze's conceptualization of immanent theatre in my description of the narrator's – and Abrahams' – historical psychogeographical journey moving through inherited localities of violence and dislocation
in remaking imaginary spaces of possibility in South Africa.

> At every turn the Indian Ocean complicates binaries ... toward a histori-
> cally deep archive of competing universalisms.
>
> ISABEL HOFMEYR, "Universalizing the Indian Ocean."

> FIRE (Taxi Time-Traveller): I came back to this place in a pirate ship... .
> I'm going to find out what it is that keeps me here, then I'm going to cut it
> out, then I'm going to eat it. I'm looking for a hole. A hole in my flesh. So
> I can spy on my blood. See where it's been. Where it's coming from. Sail in
> its currents.[1]

What the Water Gave Me is Rehane Abrahams' recuperation of the buried histories of a Malaysian slave past that weights South Africa's contemporary

---

1   Rehane Abrahams, *What the Water Gave Me*, in *New South African Plays*, ed. Charles J. Fourie
    (London: Aurora Metro Press, 2006), 20.

© KONINKLIJKE BRILL NV, LEIDEN, 2020 | DOI:10.1163/9789004414464_014

world. Comingling storytelling, classical Indian dance and physical theatre, Abrahams conflates the stories her ancestors carried by the Indian Ocean to the Cape in a singular narrator compressed onto a theatrical stage to provide an assemblage of multiple characters categorized under the rubrics of air, fire, earth and water. Condensed in the performer's body, the voices spill out in a corporeal telling and retelling of the individual, multiple and complex narratives of an elided group in the Cape's record; an "infinite rehearsal" – Wilson Harris's phrase for his view of the writing process as a repeated "revision of reality from different angles and with growing consciousness"[2] – allowing articulations and subjectivities to emerge by advancing the poetics and fluidity of storytelling evocative of Doreen Massey's space "intertwined with time."[3] The metaphorical water, the flow of river and sea, releases Abrahams' violated bodies into the "healing, sexuality, fecundity, release and purification" she pursues.[4]

I advance *What the Water Gave Me* is invested in one such spatial narrative of ambiguities and fractured memories. Abrahams imbricates the "geopolitical imaginary" as a refrain to reveal her narrator's – and her own – historical psychogeographical journey in remaking imaginary spaces of possibility in South Africa's evolving social, spatial, political and cultural landscapes. Abrahams is a theatre maker, actor and director from Cape Town, whose background growing up in a Cape Malay Muslim community informs her work. A graduate of the University of Cape Town Drama School, she has performed with diverse theatre companies in South Africa, the United States, England and Indonesia. With theatre maker Sara Matchett, she is co-founder of the Mothertongue Project, which premiered *What the Water Gave Me* in Cape Town in 2000. The Project is a collective of performing and visual artists, writers and arts educators "who explore keys to the empowerment of women and practical processes of healing and transformation through the arts." An example of their concentration is demonstrated in Matchett's play *Uhambo: pieces of a dream*, which is viewed through the eyes of women taxi commuters in South Africa and "explores and challenges the continued marginalisation and silencing of women in post-apartheid South Africa."[5]

---

2   Hena Maes-Jelinek, "Wilson Harris: A Life of Writing. Dream, Psyche, Genesis: The Works of Wilson Harris," *The Wilson Harris Bibliography*, last updated May 2004. www.cerep.ulg.ac.be/harris/whintro.html.

3   Doreen Massey, *For Space* (London: Sage Publishing, 2005), 9.

4   Rehane Abrahams, "What the Water Gave Me," 16.

5   Sara Matchett and Awino Okech, "*Uhambo: piece of a dream* – Waiting in the Ambiguity of Liminality," in *Performing Migrancy and Mobility in Africa: Cape of Flows*, ed. Mark Fleishman (London: Palgrave Macmillan, 2015), 111.

Abrahams was born after her father's family was forcefully removed, as a result of The Group Areas Act (1950), from the home they had lived in since the 1700s. As a child she always sensed "an unspoken sadness around [the idea of] 'home' in the family," causing a sense of homelessness and rootlessness, "as though my roots were in shifting water, not soil." This dislocation, she says, "seemed to reach back in time to Indian Ocean places that were as vague, shifting and impossible to grasp as the ocean itself. 'Where are we from?' was a recurrent bedtime question in my grandmother Gawa Abrahams' bed."[6] Gabeba Baderoon regards the seas "as a protean theme that observes neither national nor temporal boundaries"[7] the middle passage as a site of "cosmology, memory and desire, traced in the movement, language and culture of enslaved and dominated people."[8] For the Muslim people, the ocean is a site of arrival of slaves from Indonesia and the locus of pilgrimage in the *hajj* to Mecca. Journeys become a powerful trope of literary history and memories of home and passage. In these writings, she contends, "the sea is a metaphor for experiences that transcend conventional categories, the juxtaposition of multiple histories, the transformation of the self, and memories of slavery. They map the ocean through memory and ritual."[9] The Indian Ocean's relationship to the Cape, the locus of the intersection of the Atlantic and the Indian Oceans, Abrahams says in her Playwright's Note, is particularly meaningful "because it carried stories of where we came from."[10]

Her roots in the Javanese slave history and her performance works situate Abrahams amongst such writers as Baderoon, Pumla Dineo Gqola, Zoe Wicomb, Yvette Christiansë, and Nadia Davids, who are exploring how South Africa interprets itself at a time of transition and how slavery is evoked. Faced with what Wicomb laments as "the absence of slave memory among ordinary people,"[11] and Baderoon refers to as "the silences and complexities of South African history" resulting from erasures of the historical archive she calls "charged silence" and "coded trauma,"[12] these writers are seeking new beginnings, ways to imagine anew, and to bring together complex and always moving

---

6   Rehane Abrahams, "Making Waves: What the Water Gave Me," *Box Office* 2 (2004): 5. www .aisleb.co.za/clients/UJ/Box_Office_July_2014.pdf. Accessed 25 Oct. 2017.
7   Gabeba Baderoon, *Regarding Muslims: from Slavery to Post-apartheid* (Johannesburg: Wits UP, 2001), 66.
8   *Ibid.*, 67.
9   *Ibid.*
10   Rehane Abrahams, "What the Water Gave Me," 16.
11   Pumla Dineo Gqola, *What is Slavery to Me? Postcolonial/Slave Memory in Post-apartheid South Africa* (Johannesburg: Wits UP, 2010), 5.
12   Gabeba Baderoon, *Regarding Muslims*, 50.

layers of meaning. Gqola says she views "slavery, colonialism and apartheid ... as moments along a continuum, and not as separate, completely distinct and mutually exclusive periods."[13] In *What is Slavery to me?* she asks "how a sense of self is shaped from dealing with abstraction and remnants in the psyche which ensure that yesterday lives in tomorrow, while the fantasy of the future shapes what is possible today."[14] Her project of self definition is not oppositional, but a political material engagement with "the textures of an imaginative project of claiming slave ancestry in an era long after slavery's end"[15] to overturn the constructed histories of slavery. To "reimagine ourselves anew,"[16] she says, requires "a multilayered approach to the fragments that survive"[17] by tracing the inheritances that remain in our societies from theirs, "even if such traces reside in 'modes that do not easily give up the story.'"[18] Gqola's conceptualization shares Gilles Deleuze's temporal and spatial notion of the unfolding of past and future in the present in an immanent vision of potentiality, a multilayered approach to trace the "layers and moving targets" of a condition that Carol Boyce Davies refers to as "'migratory subjectivities.'"[19]

The lines above that opened this article, quoted from Abrahams' play, are evocative of her powerful struggle to identify and tell the stories of her ancestors who, as Charles Fourie puts it, were "brought to these shores in chains by the colonial masters"[20] that is the focus for this article, which arises from my study of the way in which contemporary theatre in South Africa is implicated in the country's complex post-apartheid cultural, economic and social realities. Fully aware of the risk of entering such a fraught discourse as a white, Western academic, I propose bringing a transdisciplinary horizontal approach, privileging the transversality of the different methods of thought. I find in Deleuze's philosophy of thought, with "its constant political, social and aesthetic concerns," an immanent and creative practice for this engagement, particularly by embracing his conceptualization of being, space and time. I draw on

---

13   Pumla Dineo Gqola, *What is Slavery to Me*, 6.
14   *Ibid.*, 2.
15   *Ibid.*, 6.
16   *Ibid.*, 2.
17   *Ibid.*, 4.
18   Nkiru Nzegwa, "Creating Memory: A Conversation with Carole Harris, a Detroit-based Quilt Artist." *Ijele: eArt Journal of the African World* 1, no. 1 (2000) n.p., as quoted in Gqola 4.
19   Qtd in: Pumla Dineo Gqola, *What is Slavery to Me*, 2.
20   Charles Fourie (ed.), introduction to *New South African Plays* (London: Aurora Metro Press, 2006), 9.

the notion of "transversality" as a "materialist concept" that is "non-categorical and non-judgemental" with the potentiality to cut through imposed disciplinary boundaries.[21] In the case of apartheid, laws and boundaries not only stripped away physical freedom, but also imposed a legislation of exclusions that created a daily negation of existence resulting in a psychological condition that erased the most basic humanistic expectations and aspirations. Almost thirty years after the end of apartheid, the socio-political-cultural discourse in South Africa is changing. The initial euphoria with its attendant concept of the "rainbow nation" is being seen as a means of political amnesia; now, a new generation of South Africans is becoming engaged in the country's political debate and examination of its past, seeking their own stories and identities in face of the lack of real progress in dealing with critical issues of cultural hegemony, economic organization, and land ownership.

Performance played a strong oppositional role during apartheid as theatre of protest, songs of resistance and theatre for development practiced in formal theatre and informal, street and community venues. Now, the search is for a theatre practice that playwright and novelist Zakes Mda describes as theatre-making that heightens the community's critical social and political reflections.[22] Author and director Greg Homann points out that it was not until the turn of the millennium that "theatre-makers were finally confronting issues rather than rehashing past preoccupations."[23] The current political discourse that is examining South Africa's past and recognizing the present conditions of financial inequity and corruption are also themes emerging in various forms of theatre performance, and there is an urge for theatre-making of all kinds. Former CEO of the Arts and Culture Trust, playwright Pieter Jacobs says people are seeking their stories and identities and discovering their rich indigenous knowledge of Africa in the ritual of theatre.[24] Much has been written since the dying days of apartheid about how to develop new forms of cultural expression while acknowledging the past. A prevailing problematic these writers pose is

---

21   Helen Palmer and Stanimir Panoyotov, "New Materialism: How Matter comes to Matter," *Transversality*, Sept. 13, 2016. www.newmaterialism.eu/almanac/t/transversality.

22   Zakes Mda, *The Role of Culture in the Process of Reconciliation in South Africa*. Paper presented at the Centre for the Study of Violence and Reconciliation, Seminar No. 9, Nov. 30, 1994. www.csvr.org.za/index.php/publications/1751-the-role-of-culture-in-the-process-of-reconciliation-in-south-africa.html. Accessed 30 June 2014.

23   Greg Homann (ed.), *At This Stage: Plays from Post-apartheid South Africa* (Johannesburg: Wits UP, 2009), 10–11.

24   Pieter Jacobs, Interview with author, July 2016.

the complexity of, and the need for, finding anew a voice or a consciousness that is not oppositional but rather, as Njabulo Ndebele argues for, tells the stories of ordinary memories and histories of individuals and societies.[25]

I suggest that the post-apartheid era is not caught in a specific time, but is a period of untold, unresolved, lost memories and histories overlaid with capitalism, globalization and what is called "rainbowism." Drawing on the work of such thinkers as Gilles Deleuze and Félix Guattari, I ask: can we anticipate what we might describe as a "minor" theatre to tell the stories that have been hidden by centuries of colonization and apartheid? The term "minor" refers to the Deleuzian concept of affirmative and dynamic processes creating new political subjects; processes of "becoming" that break from the fixed, prescribed "being," that in the context of South Africa has been molded by colonial and state-imposed racial construction. How do you remake the social space? Is there potential for performance and performance spaces to be part of the discourse of destabilizing and reshaping the physical, social and psychological spaces inscribed by these legacies?[26]

The concept of the minor embraces subjectivity, space, politics and language in the process of negating or challenging the framework of what Deleuze variously refers to as the State apparatus, or capitalism, which can now be extended to globalization and neoliberalism and, for this project, the South African State. For Deleuze, "the subject is not an 'entity' or a thing, or a relation between mind (interior) and body (exterior)."[27] Rather, he conceptualizes a process of intensity and multiplicity; a continual production of differentiation working from within, in which "[p]rocesses of becoming – schematized as the intensive – are what allow one being to affect another and, through such affecting, to bring about a transformation," in which "new beings come into being." In other words, becoming minor.[28] Stephen Zepke describes such an ontology of "'minority' as a mode of being that does not obey the dominant conditions, and is insurgent," an affirmative view of continual, dynamic

25   Njabulo S. Ndebele, *Rediscovery of the Ordinary: Essays on South African Literature and Culture* (Durban: U of KwaZulu-Natal P, 2006), 42.

26   The various uses of minor that Deleuze employs – "minor," "minority" and "minoritarian" – need to be differentiated from the notion of minority as "lesser than" in quantitative terms, or the more strictly constrained denotation of "minority" when applied in an identitarian context, such as discussions of "identity politics" for example.

27   Elizabeth Grosz, "A Thousand Tiny Sexes," in *Gilles Deleuze and the Theatre of Philosophy*, ed. Constantin V. Boundas and Dorothea Olkowski (Routledge, 1994), 197.

28   Mielle Chandler and Astrida Neimanis, "Water and Gestationality: What Flows beneath Ethics," in *Thinking with Water*, ed. Cecilia Chen, Janine MacLeod and Astrida Neimanis (Montreal: McGill-Queen's University Press 2013), Kindle edition, location 1501.

processes that are always political, always in relationship to the community and to the State.[29]

Thus, Deleuze brings a series of philosophical concepts to explore theatre and performance in a milieu where geographical and social spaces are marked by race, class and gender, and wrought with historical tension. A guiding notion is his insistence on an immanent process of creative and responsive thinking that suggests Antonin Artaud's conviction that "we must believe in a sense of life renewed by theatre."[30] Artaud's preoccupation with affective theatrical production of language, body and space refers not to the known surface, but to what he calls "that fragile, fluctuating center which forms never reach."[31] Along the same lines, Deleuze rejects mimesis or representational theatre that, he insists, perpetuates systems and divests the spectator of power. Instead, influenced by the Spinozan affirmative ethico-aesthetic approach that "requires as a principle the equality of being ... equally present in all things,"[32] he advances that immanence over transcendence requires processes of thinking through intersecting, contesting and operating on all levels of differences. In other words, Laura Cull suggests, a "philosophically minded performance theorist" must use philosophy to bring *thinking* to a study of a given play or performance and allow new ideas to be created; "ideas that the thinkers have not already developed on the basis of some other encounter."[33]

These discussions offer a conduit to approaching a study and practice of theatre and performance not by overlaying or applying preconceived philosophical frameworks, but by engaging in an immanent process of thinking. An example of such a process is the performance practice of Magnet Theatre, which, co-artistic director Mark Fleishman writes, "might be understood as quite consciously making a space for ideas or generating a particular way of thinking, both about itself as performance and about aspects of the world beyond the theatre." In his reflection, he refers to Cull's call to bring processes of thinking to performance, and says, what is going on in Magnet's works is "a multitude of individual moments and flow of our processes ... a way of thinking

29   Stephen Zepke, "Schizo-Revolutionary Art: Deleuze, Guattari and Communization Theory," in *Deleuze and the Schizoanalysis of Visual Art*, ed. Ian Buchanan and Lorna Collins (London: Bloomsbury, 2014), 37.

30   Antonin Artaud, *The Theatre and its Double*, trans. Mary Caroline Richards (New York: Grove Press, 1958), 13.

31   *Ibid.*

32   Gilles Deleuze, *Expressionism in Philosophy: Spinoza*, trans. Martin Joughin (Cambridge: Zone Books, 1990), 173.

33   Laura Cull, "Performance as Philosophy: Responding to the Application," *Theatre Research International* 37, no.1 (2012): 20–27.

the world and the work." In other words, he describes an immanent theatre practice that enacts, "bringing something into being" through "a process of concepts, ideas and speculative projection that might change attitudes and beliefs" that he sees as a "project of active and creative citizenship in a transitional social context."[34] Fleishman writes that he and co-director Jennie Reznek have "always produced theatre work that begins with bodies in space rather than pre-written texts and ... engages with South African realities."[35] A demonstration of Magnet's thinking work and immersion in the world of South Africa's spatial realities is their prevailing concentration on migration – both internal and external displacements – observable, for instance, in their productions Önnest'bo (2000), dealing with forced removals from District Six, and Cargo (2007), dealing with the "archive of slaves" at the Cape. Magnet Theatre's work powerfully reveals the entanglement of the body and space – the landscape, and their philosophy of performance and their body of performance work over thirty years has been examined extensively as a source of performance research, most recently in Megan Lewis and Anton Krueger's Magnet Theatre: Three Decades of Making Theatre.

Such complex manifold narratives embedded in South African history, I suggest, can be read through the lens of what Jennifer Hyndman calls the "feminist geopolitical imaginary" to provide a critical response to violation and exploitation and "to generate a more accountable and embodied political vision,"[36] by conjuring up new interventions and new ways of "seeing, theorizing and practicing the connections between space and politics."[37] Feminist geographers invest in a complex way of thinking about human encounter that argues for convergence of spatiality and temporality, allowing voices and subjectivities to emerge by advancing the poetics and fluidity of storytelling. In what can be read as a clarion call for becoming minor, Gillian Rose maintains "unfixity must become the condition of every social identity and theory if the struggle for emancipation is to go on,"[38] which is a notion echoed in Massey's

---

34   Mark Fleishman (ed.), Performing Migrancy and Mobility in Africa: Cape of Flows (Basingstoke: Palgrave Macmillan, 2015), 55–56.

35   Ibid., 2.

36   Jennifer Hyndman, "Towards a feminist geopolitics." The inaugural Suzanne Mackenzie Memorial Lecture, June 2, 2000. The Canadian Geographer 45, no. 2 (2001): 210–222.

37   Jennifer Hyndman, "Feminist Geopolitics and September 11," in A Companion to Feminist Geography, ed. Lise Nelson and Joni Seager (Oxford: Blackwell, 2015), 569.

38   Gillian Rose, "The struggle for political democracy: emancipation, gender, and geography," Environment and Planning D: Society and Space 8 (1990): 406.

view of landscape and place as events, where space and time are not opposi-tional, but "intertwined simultaneities of ongoing, unfinished, stories."[39]

Post-apartheid theatre's ontology is complicated by its spaces of inherited and current physical and imaginary boundaries, for space in South Africa is not just geographical space, but a space of meaning, memories and histories over-laid by the colonial project. Hence, it is political, calling for a practice of inter-pretation of space that will capture the fragile landscape of ambiguities where fractured memories are revealed yet remain concealed, perhaps space imag-ined "as a simultaneity of stories-so-far."[40] For to exist in space, Massey con-tends, is to exist in social space, in existence with others in spaces of power and spaces of exclusion. As she puts it, "space is the dimension of things being, ... the dimension that presents us with the existence of the other; ... the dimen-sion of multiplicity."[41]

Similarly, Deleuze's conceptualization of space is a way of "articulating the space humans make for themselves."[42] The feminist geographers' realignment and Deleuze's ethico-aesthetic-political philosophy of thought implicating immanence and affectivity are dynamic and emancipating strategies through which to escape what he describes as the closed in, regulated spatiality of the State space of overcoding, a notion that will be particularly recognized in the South African condition of apartheid geography. The spatial concerns so insis-tent throughout Deleuze's philosophical writing, Claire Colebrook says, create a way of thinking our experience with the world, a potentiality of thought emerging from "both the movement of bodies and the images these bodies produce of each other." Thus, "the thinking brain is the site where the poten-tial of space – the intuition of the inhuman folding of space – can be actual-ized and counter actualized."[43] Central to such an immanent approach is Deleuze's belief that in our relations with space and the way it works in rela-tion to others, "space is not above and beyond nor is it inside or outside but rather self-referential in its time as an event." He breaks from the traditional notion of territory as a place of inside and outside, as a defined, bounded area

39   Doreen Massey, "Landscape and Provocation: Reflections on Moving Mountains," *Journal of Material Culture* 11, nos. 1/2 (1995): 46.
40   Doreen Massey, *For Space*, 9.
41   Doreen Massey. "Doreen Massey on Space," Interview with Neil Warburton, Feb. 1, 2013, *Social Science Bites*. SAGE Publications. www.socialsciencespace.com/author/socialsci encebites/. Accessed 28 Mar 2014.
42   Paul Patton, *Deleuze and the Political* (London: Routledge, 2000), 5.
43   Claire Colebrook, "The Space of Man: On the Specificity of Affect in Deleuze and Guat-tari," in *Deleuze and Space*, ed. Ian Buchanan and Gregg Lambert (Edinburgh: Edinburgh UP, 2005), 193.

of shared knowledge and subjectivities.[44] Rather, he envisions "a non-territorial subjectivity," based on the concepts of difference and transformation.[45] Elizabeth Grosz describes the dynamic of the Deleuzian concept of space as the "coupling of a milieu and a rhythm" that come together in his schema of the refrain as a dynamic process of conceiving being, time and space. She says, "A refrain is the movement by which the qualities of a specific territory or habitat resonate and return to form it as a delimited space, a space contained or bounded but nonetheless always open to the chaos from which it draws its force."[46]

In approaching Abrahams' play as an act of such recuperation, it is useful to consider this search for sense of self and future. In a telling that is poetic, edgy and violent, her allegorical narrative is a series of disjointed stories, set in fragmented temporal spaces, told through four characters who are interrogating the deep connections between Indonesian and Cape Malay culture, the buried histories of South Africa's Malaysian slave past and their contemporary milieu. The storyteller weaves together the stories of the hip-hop head from Heideveld who is living on the Cape Flats, an urban taxi time traveler "whose body is the city she lives in," and a child who is entrapped by the monster paedophile.[47] Abrahams situates *What the Water Gave Me* in an ambiguous, individual, multiple and complex historical narrative of transnational and translocal dislocation, situated in unidentified places clearly localized in the historicized Cape Flats. The latter, Fleishman tells us, are settled on "reclaimed land," which had earlier existed "under the sea," and continues to be "intermittently steeped in flood water or scourged by the notorious winds of the Cape of Storms."[48] The play's themes are the Indian Ocean, Abrahams' grandmother, oral storytelling, Cape Town and slavery; with global power at the centre. The Cape Malay people are described by Sarah Nuttall as "creolized bodies" who are known by the South African term "Coloured" as a "biological and social construct,"[49] a term that playwright Amy Jephta sees as "implicated in racial politics." The Cape Coloured culture has "a long rich history of artistic performances representing

44   *Ibid.*, 195.

45   Simone Aurora, "Territory and Subjectivity: The Philosophical Nomadism of Deleuze and Canetti," *Minerva – An Open Access Journal of Philosophy* 18 (2014): 10. Academia. edu.www.academia.edu/9543039/Territory_and_Subjectivity_The_Philosophical_Nomad ism_of_Deleuze_And_Canetti

46   Elizabeth Grosz, *Chaos, Territory, Art: Deleuze and the Framing of the Earth* (New York: Columbia UP, 2008), 19.

47   Ashraf Johaardien, "The Big Four-Oh," *Box Office*, 2 (2014): 1. www.aisleb.co.za/clients/UJ/Box_Office_July_2014.pdf.

48   Mark Fleishman (ed.), *Performing Migrancy*, 38.

49   Sarah Nuttall, "City Forms and Writing the 'Now,'" *South African Journal of Southern African Studies* 30, no. 4 (2004): 733.

and speaking to the Cape Coloured experience,"[50] she says, an experience that can be described as "a fluid melding and remelding of cultural elements"[51] in an "ongoing narrative pattern of displacement and migration ... shaped by the history of the country."[52]

Abrahams adopts water as the "fluid melding and remelding" that flows throughout her Malay history with its heritage of slavery, rape and violence, and evokes spaces of wide open land and the flow of river and sea to release her environment's violated bodies, emblematic, perhaps, of Deleuze's assemblages of potentiality. Her theatre space speaks to the Deleuzian smooth space of multiplicity, immanence and deterritorialisation – in other words, the unconstructed spaces that challenge the striated spaces of the State and power. For Deleuze and Guattari, water is smooth space, and the sea, they say, is "a smooth space par excellence, [which] was the first to encounter the demands of [the] increasingly strict striation" of the colonial project.[53] Abrahams' embodied narrative is suggestive of the Deleuzian refrain. Her enunciations and subjectivities emerge in the refrain of water – the flow of river and sea – evocative of the notion of water as a matter of relation and connection. In their study on the gestational character of water, Chandler and Neimanis suggest "the substance and the semiotics of water are deeply entangled,"[54] and they propose that "thinking along with Deleuze allows us to conceptualize material sociality as a mode of relation and response in both the human and more-than-human realms." We are all comprised of water, they say, "and [w]e, like all other entities, leak into and siphon from one another in response to our environment – that is, in response to all the other bodies that affect us."[55] I am drawn to their argument for water as a gestational milieu; where water provides the creative and connective capacity to create the visceral experience of transformation placed or "embodied in specific materialities and space times."[56]

50   Amy Jephta, "On Familiar Roads: The Fluidity of Cape Coloured Experiences and Expressions of Migration and Reclamation in the Performances of the Kaapse Klopse in Cape Town," in *Performing Migrancy and Mobility in Africa*, ed. Mark Fleishman (Basingstoke: Palgrave Macmillan, 2015), 166.

51   *Ibid.*, 171.

52   *Ibid.*, 165.

53   Gilles Deleuze and Félix Guattari, *A Thousand Plateaus: Capitalism and Schizophrenia*, trans. Brian Massumi (Minneapolis, MN: University of Minnesota Press, 1987), 480.

54   Mielle Chandler and Astrida Neimanis, "Water and Gestationality," location 371.

55   *Ibid.*, location 1559.

56   *Ibid,*, location 371.

It is a notion of morphology that Abrahams implicates in her geographical staging of locations north, south, east and west as a remapping or placing for characters that are evoked as the elements of air, fire, earth and water. In her director's notes, she says, "[t]he action moves in all directions simultaneously interwoven. This is theatre with emphasis on transformation and the corporeal. It is speaking the body/the body speaking,"[57] and she uses the performer's body as the connection "outward to the audience and community and inward to cellular memory and ancestral line,"[58] reflective of the racialized African, Indian, Coloured community of forced removals that fractured her traditional extended family. She says: "The geography inhabited was one of fissures, fractures, cracks like my grandmother's body, scarred with the many keloids of open-heart surgery." It was her grandmother, Gawa Arend, who held the stories of Cape Town and about her people who "had come from the East, non-specific, mythic Java, Indian Ocean and ships."[59] And, it was her grandmother who told her the story of Bawa Mera and Bawa Puti, based on an old Javanese story that she threads into her play, where the four interspersed, fractured, interrupted stories thread the fairy tale with the nightmares, and the magical with the material.

Abrahams says she believes "that theatre can be used for healing" and she uses the experience of ritual for "the creation of common space," working with her grandmother's stories and South African Shamanic techniques. "Faced with the gruesome realities of sexual violence and abuse, especially against girl children, and the constant awareness of violence in South Africa, this seemed the most potent means at my disposal," she says.[60] Her concern echoes that of Yvette Christiansë whose poem "Sunday School" condenses the notion of storytelling and the realities that we see in Abrahams' play:

> Tell me that old story, the one about
> The girl in the schoolyard. The Coloured
> Girl who was surrounded by boys ...
> ... Do you
> Remember that story? It has been
> Running between my legs like blood
> For years[61]

---

57   Rehane Abrahams, "What the Water Gave Me," 17.
58   *Ibid.*, 16.
59   *Ibid.*
60   *Ibid.*
61   Qtd. in: Gabeba Baderoon, *Regarding Muslims*, 83.

Baderoon's analysis of Christiansë's poem observes that "black women's bodies have been made the bearer of the marks of sexual violence during slavery, making them responsible for their own violation and rendering invisible the *systemic sexual violence* and miscegenation of slavery," leading to "intense internalized shame" and "a powerful form of forgetting among the descendants of enslaved people in South Africa."[62] She looks to words, particularly to poetic language, to represent erased histories in a way that avoids replicating exoticization or domestication, what she calls the "hyper-visibility of earlier representations,"[63] allowing for "regenerative ways of configuring the resilience, authority and even pleasure of those usually seen as violated bodies."[64] "Sunday School," Baderoon says, "subverts the 'old story' which turns the 'coloured' girl into a 'hunted' object and creates a counter-history," as a form of protective education for other women.[65] Images of the girl in the poem as a hunted, surrounded, sexual object weave through the "old story" in Abrahams' play. The scenes in *What the Water Gave Me* resonate with the refrain of violence and sexual abuse imbued with the history of slavery, whilst also recognizing the violence of the Cape Flats today. Violence and power is reflected in the hovering creature that incorporates the play's demons – the monster or giant centipede as metonym for an overarching dominance that is unnamed but that infuses the play in different guises as it moves in parallel with imagery of war, slavery, violence and containment into the darkening narratives of the sexual abuse of the young girl.

The *mise-en-scène* is an entanglement of space and time that can be read through the lens of Massey's envisioned stories-so-far, as well as Fleishman's contention that "the memory of the past comes to us in fragments."[66] The set is a fusion of the material in the form of the directional space of the stage and the elements that identify the characters, interwoven with the mystical in the symbols of the medicine wheel, each combining to create a station with its own character and its own props – such as a toy doll, woolen hat, incense stick, candles, or tape-recorder. In a similar interweaving, at different points throughout the play, the *"props are interchanged between characters, thus creating a*

---

62   *Ibid.*, 88.
63   *Ibid.*, 106.
64   *Ibid.*, 90.
65   *Ibid.*, 89.
66   Megan Lewis, "The Performance Labours of Magnet and Jazzart's Cargo," in *Magnet Theatre: Three Decades of Making Theatre*, ed. Megan Lewis and Anton Krueger (Pretoria: UNISA Press, 2017), 208.

sense that the characters embody aspects of one another."[67] The morphing, or entangling, of the scenic elements is a device that continues throughout the dialogue in the refrain of such words as, "walls," "flesh," "rape" and "devil" or "monster," "the pit" and "the tunnel" and "the taxi," and in the repetition of "Long ago. Yesterday. Round the corner. Far away." Abrahams' direction for entanglement of the characters, most notably reflected in the convergence of the characters in the single narrator, speaks to Deleuze's notion of the body not as "a discrete entity defined by stable boundaries and a set of fixed characteristics," but rather as an "assemblage of components bound into coherent form" that is ever temporary and always shifting.[68] His "assemblage of components," Simone Bignall says, is a process of the body constantly changing in its encounters and interactions with "other parts" and with "its existential milieu."[69] Chandler and Neimanis argue that it is a process that "does not separate the human from the more-than-human world," but rather, its "capacity to affect and be affected" extends to "all bodies."[70] "Multiplicity" is a concept central to Deleuze's minoritarian ontology, not as "a pluralized notion of identity," Grosz argues, but rather as "an ever-changing, non-totalizable collectivity, an assemblage defined ... through its capacity to undergo permutations and transformations."[71]

In *What the Water Gave Me*, Abrahams enfolds the play's assemblage of components with the elements.

> AIR [is the storyteller] – (East) is represented by a yellow circle (approx 1 meter in diameter)
> WATER [the Little Girl] – (West) by a blue circle with an empty enamel bowl
> EARTH [the Hip-Hop Head from Heideveld] – (North) by a white circle
> FIRE [the Taxi Timetraveller] – (South) by a red circle[72]

Each character encounters the fragments of her histories, the monster of her memory, in various guises. For AIR, "The stranger" becomes "the man with a dazzling smile" until he is reflected in the water when he becomes a monster

---

67   Rehane Abrahams, "What the Water Gave Me," 18.
68   Simone Bignall and Paul Patton, *Deleuze and the Postcolonial* (Edinburgh: Edinburgh UP, 2010), 83.
69   *Ibid.*
70   Mielle Chandler and Astrida Neimanis, "Water and Gestationality," location 1504.
71   Elizabeth Grosz, "A Thousand Tiny Sexes," 192.
72   Rehane Abrahams, "What the Water Gave Me," 18.

with "A face like wormy leather, huge red eyes rolling in hollow sockets. Sharp pointy teeth and a long black tongue. A hideous monster face."[73] For EARTH it is "a man-made mad Mars mission in crafts of dire purpose. In a mechnanised electrosised phallus" raping the purity of the night sky she calls "her Egyptian Goddess mother."[74] For FIRE, the figure is the centipede, "Flaming ... It's massive. Segmented. Transparent. Made of heat. It eats people and purifies them in its digestive juices."[75] WATER's monster is her teacher who molests her, "the only Christian Teacher in the school."[76] The play's action is transformative and corporeal, which Abrahams describes as moving in all "directions simultaneously interwoven,"[77] evocative of Artaud's "fragile, fluctuating centre."[78] In the production I attended at the University of Johannesburg's Con Cowan Theatre in April 2014, directed by Jade Bowers and accompanied by musician Bongile Gorata Lecoge-Zulu, Cheraé Halley embodied the characters. She reaches out to the audience with gracious gestures as the welcoming storyteller, retreating into the memories and nightmare journeys that take her to the four quadrants of the stage and hold her poignantly, and literally, crouching in a galvanized bath of water as a potential gestational place of cleansing, yet also a place of retreat and withdrawal. She is variously the small girl, the savvy rapper, and the explorer through time.

AIR (Story Teller) begins with deceptively innocent fairy tale lightness: "Once there was and once there wasn't. Long ago and yesterday. Round the corner far away."[79] She tells the story of Bowa Mera, "the prettiest," Bowa Puti, "the cleverest," and Taki Taki, "the baby and so cute;"[80] three little girls who are playing by a pool and are pushed into the water by a mysterious, monstrous figure who changes them into fishes.

> Trapped in their watery world. Each day and each night the monster came and watched them. Disappearing as suddenly as he appeared. And he drank from them. Taking in large gulps of their laughter, their songs, even their little squabbles.[81]

---

73   *Ibid.*, 22.
74   *Ibid.*, 22.
75   *Ibid.*, 26.
76   *Ibid.*, 30
77   *Ibid.*, 17.
78   Antonin Artaud, *The Theatre and its Double*, 13.
79   Rehane Abrahams, "What the Water Gave Me," 18.
80   *Ibid.*, 19.
81   *Ibid.*, 29.

Slowly, their identities slip away in the sphere of his control, clearly symbolic of what Deleuze calls the overcoding of "the state-form as an abstract machine of capture."[82] "Mera's shimmering tail began to wilt. Her shining scales grew dull. Puti's lightning mind became sluggish and turgid and Taki Taki – she ate insects." The monster "got drunk on their sweet young flesh and soft skin and sucked the light from their dreams."[83]

In her role as Taxi time-traveller, FIRE keeps running, always hailing the ubiquitous taxi, and yet she seems static – seems to be captured in the nightmare of historical memory, bound in by the repeating imagery of walls that take on the persona of the monster.

> FIRE: The walls are here. They are pulsating and wet. Singing like drunk men dreaming of running away. It is dark. The walls threaten me. They say violation is my historical condition being as I am five generations out of slavery and a woman.... . They are looking for a hole. A hole to put their violence in. Force entry into soft flesh with a word, blow, knife, cock, bullet. It is dark. I am not afraid. Porous, I am already full of holes.[84]

Abrahams' use of "taxi," in the name of FIRE's character and in the word's refrain throughout the play, reflects Matchett's description of the taxi as an "actual container" for sections in *Uhambo*. In both plays, "taxi" is used as a device to "heighten and reinforce the true nature of the dislocation" of this "ambiguous landscape of liminality"[85] and embed the dream-like stories in the consciousness of a country where taxis connote the real-life, in-between experience of waiting and departure. The sense of speed and stasis, or in Deleuzian terms "speed and slowness," of FIRE's journey amidst encounters with the fragmented stories of AIR, EARTH and WATER, manifests Deleuze's processes of becoming, discussed above. The speed and slowness with which bodies "form and transform," with which they "are affected and affect," Bignall claims, is a discursive process of "awakening to the capacity of the body towards awareness of oneself and others to form compatible relations;"[86] a process that Brian Massumi insists "renders form dynamic."[87]

---

82   Paul Patton, *Deleuze and the Political*, 102.
83   Rehane Abrahams, "What the Water Gave Me," 29.
84   *Ibid.*, 20–21.
85   Sara Matchett and Awino Okech, "*Uhambo: piece of a dream*," 123.
86   Simone Bignall and Paul Patton, *Deleuze and the Postcolonial*, 84.
87   Brian Massumi, *Parables for the Virtual: Movement, Affect, Sensation* (Durham, NC: Duke UP, 2002), 17.

Interweaving the darkness of FIRE's nightmare journey through history, is the corporeal defiance of EARTH, the Hip-Hop Head from Heideveld – an area in the Cape Flats – who is the most overtly political of the four characters, her body an immanent site of potentiality, her voice a way of thinking and "divine intent."[88] The enunciation switches from the elegiac to the rebellion of rap that echoes the interrogative of Christiansë's poem.

> EARTH: In my heart there is a flower of sedition. I am cool electrical be-ing. Uncorruptable. My flesh is sensational. Retrieving the power to feel. Retrieving the power to heal. My body displaces the priest. My body re-places the Imam. My femininity becoming its own divinity. I carry my pride inside. And outside I won't hide. The beast of shame, don't know my name, or even where to find me. In the positive-connectivity of my life I still feel the knife changing shape. I feel the rapist and the rape. One birth, one earth, one breath, one death. And still I flower with divine intent. To the full extent. Petals soft. Open. And resilient. It's cool nè? I did that. Do you want to hear it again?[89]

Her provocation of the privileging of State power, symbolized by the coloniz-ing Mars space-craft in search of "dire purpose," is entwined with the mystical "Egyptian Goddess mother" and "Gaia, Earth, my mother," as she addresses NASA which is raping the "purity of space," taunting, "You won't even get there on the Starship Enterprise."[90]

There is nothing fairy tale-like or mystical, or even defiant, about WATER's description of power and abuse. Of the four narratives in Abrahams' play, the most prosaic, yet perhaps the most touching and the most universal is her sto-ry of a small girl who is abused by the sanctimonious school teacher, Mr. Wa-ters, who chases her, and catches her. Baderoon says "[e]tymology reveals the hidden geography of sexual subjection in the Cape,"[91] where there is a "'long history'"[92] of marking the bodies of female slaves for violence and abuse "with impunity."[93] The subjection of WATER's body to sexual abuse by Mr. Waters, whom she describes as "the only Christian teacher in the school," and who se-cretly preys on her when the older girls are away at the mosque, is a refrain of

---

88   Rehane Abrahams, "What the Water Gave Me," 30.

89   *Ibid.*, 29–30.

90   *Ibid.*, 22.

91   Gabeba Baderoon, *Regarding Muslims*, 84.

92   *Ibid.*, 90.

93   *Ibid.*, 84.

this long history that runs through the play in the different dreams and memo-ries. Her friend "Celeste says adults and children don't mix," but WATER *remembers that story*, she knows that "sometimes adults and children do mix."[94]

AIR closes the play when the narrative returns to the three fishes, which are saved by the sea and restored as children in an event that reflects Chandler and Neimanis' notion of leaking and siphoning of entities. "That night when not a soul on earth or sea, not even the monster, was stirring, the moon looked down and called to the sea,"[95] moved by the sorrow of the girls' mother and father.

> The sea knew exactly what had happened to the girls, having witnessed the entire affair from the start. So the moon, using all her strength, tugged at the sea and together they made huge crashing waves that washed the fish girls right out of the rock pools into the open ocean. They were terri-fied, but the sea made little currents that kept them together all through the night.[96]

Returned home restored, well nearly so, their slightly faded prettiness, smart-ness and cuteness are now enfolded in the layers of their enslavement. And, the monster man? He is found "drowned, half-eaten by a school of little fishes and everything was as before."[97]

The play ends as the narrator/actress engages in the interactive ritual of cleansing with water at each of the quadrants of the stage. While the ambigu-ous narrative fails to provide a complete or a fairy tale ending, it embraces stories of renewed empowerment and the will to remember and to tell the sto-ries again and again in Abrahams' performance space of embarkation and de-territorialization – the Cape Flats. In what Matchett and Okech describe as the Cape's "ambiguous liminality" and "internal psycho-emotional landscapes," it is a site of "personal stories/embodied memories, communities, home, domes-tic spaces, waiting, dreams, hopes, disappointment, and disillusionment."[98] In such a space, I contend, Abrahams places her play within the potentiality of Deleuze's minor theatre, which Cull says he conceives as "one that subjects the different elements of theatre – its language, gestures, costumes and props – to the greatest degree of variation, rather than fixing them into the conventional

---

94   Rehane Abrahams, "What the Water Gave Me," 30.
95   *Ibid.*, 30.
96   *Ibid.*, 30–31
97   *Ibid.*, 31.
98   Sara Matchett and Awino Okech, "*Uhambo: piece of a dream*," 113.

organizational forms."[99] In its revolutionary nature, Deleuze suggests, such a minoritarian theatre's "antirepresentational function would be to trace, to construct in some way, a figure of the minority consciousness as each one's potential."[100] His conceptualization for theatre and performance anticipates Fleishman's description of Magnet Theatre as "a machine for thinking the future, even when ... it works with material from a past that will not easily pass."[101]

Rosi Braidotti argues that "Deleuze's thought is precisely his effort to imagine the activity of thinking differently."[102] Such a process of creative and responsive thinking, I suggest, speaks to the South African milieu, offering the "complexity, creative inflection, play and newness" Gqola envisions,[103] and the nuanced approach to a "history of complexity and connections" that Baderoon seeks.[104] At the same time, his conceptualization of the overlapping of "physical, symbolic and material," Braidotti suggests, roots the subject in the "spatial frame of the body," where the "first and foremost of locations in reality is one's own embodiment."[105] The notion recalls Jephta's consideration of an "agency of identity creation" that doesn't negate the "sense of self from the people who have claimed the description and absorbed it as part of a distinct community."[106]

Pierre Nora speaks of the responsibility of the individual to "remember and to protect the trappings of identity" in a time when "history can no longer be assumed as continuity, a visible past, but rather history as a discontinuous and invisible one."[107] In her strategies of psychogeography in tracing domination and exploitation – a concern of many feminist geographers such as Hyndman and others[108] – Abrahams moves towards discerning a mode of affirmative

99   Laura Cull, *Theatres of Immanence: Deleuze and the Ethics of Performance* (Basingstoke: Palgrave Macmillan, 2012), 20.

100   Gilles Deleuze, "One Less Manifesto: Theatre and its Critique," in *Mimesis, Masochism, and Mime: The Politics of Theatricality in Contemporary French Thought*, ed. Timothy Murray (Ann Arbor, MI: U of Michigan P, 1997), 253–254.

101   Mark Fleishman, "Making Space for Ideas: The Knowledge Work of Magnet Theatre," in *Magnet Theatre: Three Decades of Making Theatre*, ed. Megan Lewis and Anton Krueger (Pretoria: UNISA Press, 2017), 72.

102   Rosi Braidotti, "Toward a New Nomadism," in *Gilles Deleuze and the Theatre of Philosophy*, ed. Constantin V. Boundas and Dorothea Olkowski (London: Routledge, 1994), 163.

103   Pumla Dineo Gqola, *What is Slavery to Me*, 2.

104   Gabeba Baderoon, *Regarding Muslims*, 50.

105   Rosi Braidotti, "Toward a New Nomadism," 161.

106   Amy Jephta, "On Familiar Roads," 169.

107   Pierre Nora, "Between Memory and History," *Representations*, 26, Special Issue: Memory and Counter-Memory (Spring 1989): 16.

108   Lise Nelson and Joni Seager (eds.), *A Companion to Feminist Geography* (Oxford: Blackwell, 2015).

sociality as "a partial dissolution of this boundedness,"[109] eschewing slavery or servitude in favour of generative generosity. It is her answer to Nora's notion that the "psychologization of memory" gives "every individual the sense that his or her salvation depends on the repayment of an impossible debt."[110]

Works Cited

Abrahams, Rehane. "Making Waves: What the Water Gave Me." Box Office, Issue 2, UJ Arts and Culture. University of Johannesburg, July 2014, p. 5. http://www.aisleb .co.za/clients/UJ/Box_Office_July_2014.pdf Accessed 25 Oct. 2017.

Abrahams, Rehane. *What the Water Gave Me*. In *New South African Plays*, edited by Charles J. Fourie. London: Aurora Metro Press, 2006.

Artaud, Antonin. *The Theatre and its Double*. Translated by Mary Caroline Richards. New York, NY: Grove Press, 1958.

Aurora, Simone. "Territory and Subjectivity: The Philosophical Nomadism of Deleuze and Canetti." *Minerva – An Open Access Journal of Philosophy* 18 (2014): 1–26. www .academia.edu/9543039/Territory_and_Subjectivity_The_Philosophical_Nomad ism_of_Deleuze_And_Canetti.

Baderoon, Gabeba. *Regarding Muslims: from Slavery to Post-apartheid*. Johannesburg: Wits UP, 2001.

Bignall, Simone and Paul Patton. *Deleuze and the Postcolonial*. Edinburgh: Edinburgh UP, 2010.

Boundas, Constantin V. and Dorothea Olkowski, editors. *Gilles Deleuze and the Theatre of Philosophy*. London: Routledge, 1994.

Braidotti, Rosi. "Toward a New Nomadism." In *Gilles Deleuze and the Theatre of Philosophy*, edited by Constantin V. Boundas and Dorothea Olkowski, 157–186. London: Routledge, 1994.

Buchanan, Ian and Lorna Collins. *Deleuze and the Schizoanalysis of Visual Art*. London: Bloomsbury Academic, 2014.

Buchanan, Ian and Gregg Lambert, editors. *Deleuze and Space*. Edinburgh: Edinburgh UP, 2005.

Chandler, Mielle and Astrida Neimanis. "Water and Gestationality: What Flows beneath Ethics." In *Thinking with Water*, edited by Cecilia Chen, Janine MacLeod and Astrida Neimanis, location 1272–1818. Montreal: McGill-Queen's University Press, 2013. Kindle edition.

---

109   Mielle Chandler and Astrida Neimanis, "Water and Gestationality," location 1536.
110   Pierre Nora, "Between Memory and History," 16.

Chen, Cecilia, Janine MacLeod and Astrida Neimanis, editors. *Thinking with Water*. Montreal: McGill-Queen's University Press, 2013. Kindle edition.

Christiansë, Yvette. "Sunday School." In *Castaway*. Durham, NC: Duke UP, 1999.

Colebrook, Claire. "The Space of Man: On the Specificity of Affect in Deleuze and Guattari." In *Deleuze and Space*, edited by Ian Buchanan and Gregg Lambert, 189–206. Edinburgh: Edinburgh UP, 2005.

Cull, Laura. *Theatres of Immanence: Deleuze and the Ethics of Performance*. Basingstoke: Palgrave Macmillan, 2012.

Cull, Laura. "Performance as Philosophy: Responding to the Application." *Theatre Research International* 37, no.1 (2012): 20–27.

Deleuze, Gilles. "One Less Manifesto: Theatre and its Critique." In *Mimesis, Masochism, and Mime: The Politics of Theatricality in Contemporary French Thought*, edited by Timothy Murray, 239–258. Ann Arbor, MI: U of Michigan P, 1997.

Deleuze, Gilles. *Expressionism in Philosophy: Spinoza*. Translated by Martin Joughin. Cambridge: Zone Books, 1990.

Deleuze, Gilles and Félix Guattari. *A Thousand Plateaus: Capitalism and Schizophrenia*. Translated by Brian Massumi. Minneapolis, MN: University of Minnesota Press, 1987

Fancy, David. "Geoperformativity: Immanence, performance and the earth." *Performance Research: A Journal of the Performing Arts* 16, no. 4 (2011): 62–72.

Fleishman, Mark. "Making Space for Ideas: The Knowledge Work of Magnet Theatre." In *Magnet Theatre: Three Decades of Making Theatre*, edited by Megan Lewis and Anton Krueger, 53–75. Pretoria: UNISA Press, 2017.

Fleishman, Mark, editor. *Performing Migrancy and Mobility in Africa: Cape of Flows*. Basingstoke: Palgrave Macmillan, 2015.

Fourie, Charles, editor. *New South African Plays*. London: Aurora Metro Press, 2006.

Fourie, Charles. Introduction to *New South African Plays*. Edited by Charles Fourie. London: Aurora Metro Press, 2006.

Gqola, Pumla Dineo. *What is Slavery to Me? Postcolonial/Slave Memory in Post-apartheid South Africa*. Johannesburg: Wits UP, 2010.

Grosz, Elizabeth. *Chaos, Territory, Art: Deleuze and the Framing of the Earth*. New York, NY: Columbia UP, 2008.

Grosz, Elizabeth. "A Thousand Tiny Sexes." In *Gilles Deleuze and the Theatre of Philosophy*, edited by Constantin V. Boundas and Dorothea Olkowski, 187–210. New York, NY: Routledge, 1994.

Hofmeyr, Isabel. "Universalizing the Indian Ocean." *Publications of the Modern Language Association of America*, 125, no. 3 (2010): 721–729. www.jstor.org/stable/25704470.

Homann, Greg, editor. *At This Stage: Plays from Post-apartheid South Africa*. Johannesburg: Wits UP, 2009.

Hyndman, Jennifer. "Feminist Geopolitics and September 11." In *A Companion to Feminist Geography*, edited by Lise Nelson and Joni Seager, 565–577. Oxford: Blackwell, 2015.

Hyndman, Jennifer. "Towards a feminist geopolitics." The inaugural Suzanne Mackenzie Memorial Lecture, June 2, 2000. *The Canadian Geographer* 45, no. 2 (2001): 210–222. www.proxy.library.brocku.ca/login?url=https://search-proquest-com.proxy .library.brocku.ca/docview/228349682?accountid=9744.

Jephta, Amy. "On Familiar Roads: The Fluidity of Cape Coloured Experiences and Expressions of Migration and Reclamation in the Performances of the Kaapse Klopse in Cape Town." In *Performing Migrancy and Mobility in Africa*, edited by Mark Fleishman, 164–179. Basingstoke: Palgrave Macmillan, 2015.

Johaardien, Ashraf. "The Big Four-Oh." *Box Office* 2 (July 2014): 1. http://www.aisleb .co.za/clients/UJ/Box_Office_July_2014.pdf.

Lewis, Megan and Anton Krueger, editors. *Magnet Theatre: Three Decades of Making Theatre*. Pretoria: UNISA Press, 2017.

Lewis, Megan. "The Performance Labours of Magnet and Jazzart's *Cargo*." *Magnet Theatre: Three Decades of Making Theatre*, edited by Megan Lewis and Anton Krueger, 203–220. Pretoria: UNISA Press, 2017.

Maes-Jelinek, Hena. *Wilson Harris: A Life of Writing. Dream, Psyche, Genesis: The Works of Wilson Harris*. The Wilson Harris Bibliography. 2004. www.cerep.ulg.ac.be/harris/ whintro.html. Accessed 15 Jan. 2015.

Massey, Doreen. "Doreen Massey on Space." Interview with Neil Warburton, Feb. 1, 2013, *Social Science Bites*. SAGE Publications. https://www.socialsciencespace .com/2013/02/podcastdoreen-massey-on-space/ Accessed 28 Mar 2014.

Massey, Doreen. *For Space*. London: Sage Publishing, 2005.

Massey, Doreen. "Landscape and Provocation: Reflections on Moving Mountains." *Journal of Material Culture* 11, nos.1/2 (1995): 33–48.

Massumi, Brian. *Parables for the Virtual: Movement, Affect, Sensation*. Durham, NC: Duke UP, 2002.

Matchett, Sara. "Collaborative Conversations: The Mothertongue Project in Profile," Interview with Malika Ndlova, Cape Town, Oct. 2004. open.uct.ac.za/bitstream/ handle/11427/26792/Matchett_Article_2005.pdf?sequence=1.

Matchett, Sara and Awino Okech. "*Uhambo: piece of a dream* – Waiting in the Ambiguity of Liminality." In *Performing Migrancy and Mobility in Africa: Cape of Flows*, edited by Mark Fleishman, 110–124. Basingstoke: Palgrave Macmillan, 2015.

Mbembe, Achille. "The Value of African Aesthetics." *Mail and Guardian* (Johannesburg), May 15, 2015.

Mda, Zakes. *The Role of Culture in the Process of Reconciliation in South Africa*. Paper presented at the Centre for the Study of Violence and Reconciliation. Seminar No. 9. 30 November, 1994. Centre for the Study of Violence and Reconciliation Website,

20 February 1995. www.csvr.org.za/index.php/publications/1751-the-role-of-culture -in-the-process-of-reconciliation-in-south-africa.html. Accessed 30 June 2014.

Ndebele, Njabulo S. *Rediscovery of the Ordinary: Essays on South African Literature and Culture*. Durban: U of KwaZulu-Natal P, 2006.

Nelson, Lise and Joni Seager, editors. *A Companion to Feminist Geography*. Oxford: Blackwell, 2015.

Nora, Pierre. "Between Memory and History." *Representations* 26, Special Issue: Memory and Counter-Memory (Spring 1989): 7–24. https://www.jstor.org/stable/2928520.

Nuttall, Sarah. "City Forms and Writing the 'Now.'" *South African Journal of Southern African Studies* 30, no. 4 (Dec. 2004): 731–748. www.scribd.com/document/235814520/ City-Forms-and-Writing-the-Now-in-South-Africa.

Nzegwa, Nkiru. "Creating Memory: A Conversation with Carole Harris, a Detroit-based Quilt Artist." *Ijele: eArt Journal of the African World* 1, no. 1 (2000). N.p.

Palmer, Helen and Stanimir Panoyotov. "New Materialism: How Matter comes to Matter." *Transversality*. Sept. 13, 2016. https://newmaterialism.eu/almanac/t/transver sality.html Accessed 15 Sept. 2018.

Patton, Paul. *Deleuze and the Political*. London: Routledge, 2000.

Rose, Gillian. "The struggle for political democracy: emancipation, gender, and geography." *Environment and Planning D: Society and Space* 8 (1990): 395–408. journals-sagepub-com.proxy.library.brocku.ca/.

Zepke, Stephen. "Schizo-Revolutionary Art: Deleuze, Guattari and Communization Theory." In *Deleuze and the Schizoanalysis of Visual Art,* edited by Ian Buchanan and Lorna Collins, 31–56. London: Bloomsbury, 2014.

CHAPTER 14

Female Interventions in Contemporary South African Drama and Performance: An Analysis of Selected Work by Women Artists

Jessica Murray

Jessica Murray

Abstract

In *Feminist Futures?: Theatre, Performance, Theory,* Elaine Aston and Geraldine Harris credit feminist interventions in theatre and performance art with "exploring the potential of the body as a scene of, and screen for, 'writing' histories of gender oppressions and for the possibilities of 'speaking' the feminine [...]." Feminist and queer artists have turned to drama, performance and visual activism to express their concerns about violence against citizens who are marginalised because of their gender and sexuality. Such violence has, alarmingly, become part of the contemporary South African sociopolitical reality. This article offers an analysis of selected examples of dramatic interventions by South African women artists through the theoretical rubric of Feminist Studies, including works by Zanele Mohuli and Lara Foot.

In *Feminist Futures?: Theatre, Performance, Theory,* Elaine Aston and Geraldine Harris credit feminist interventions in theatre and performance art with "exploring the potential of the body as a scene of, and screen for, 'writing' histories of gender oppressions and for the possibilities of 'speaking' the feminine: marking present tense (lived) oppressions with the desires, the longings for lives lived differently" and, in particular, for lives lived "beyond the unequal social realities conditioning women's lives."[1] Feminist and queer artists have turned to drama, performance and visual activism to express their concerns about violence against citizens who are marginalised because of their gender and sexuality. Such violence has, alarmingly, become part of the contemporary South African sociopolitical reality. In some startlingly innovative work, emerging playwrights and visual activists are using performance to explore issues

---

1   Elaine Aston and Geraldine Harris, "Feminist Futures and the Possibilities of 'We'?" in *Feminist Futures? Theatre, Performance, Theory*, ed. Elaine Aston and Geraldine Harris (New York: Palgrave Macmillan. 2006), 5.

©   KONINKLIJKE BRILL NV, LEIDEN, 2020 | DOI:10.1163/9789004414464_015

that defy easy articulation. In one such example, a collective comprised of Zanele Muholi, Maureen Velile Majola and Jelena Kuljic combine stage protests, music and poetry to highlight hate crimes against lesbians in South Africa. The performance is called "Sifela i Ayikho" (this Zulu expression can loosely be translated as "We are Being Killed for Nothing") to explore "parts of South African social landscapes in which the lives of black lesbian and trans women in South Africa, including our own, are always exposed to danger."[2] This article will offer an analysis of selected examples of dramatic interventions by South African women artists through the theoretical rubric of Feminist Studies. By analysing how South African women artists are engaging with representations of violence, gender and sexuality, this article will consider how selected examples of contemporary South African performance fare in terms of refusing "to be the 'other' in some (male) body else's story."[3]

According to Elin Diamond, "[f]eminist performance can light up dark corners of the social matrix."[4] In order to explore the capacity of women's performance to illuminate and claim space for the articulation of women's stories of violence, I will consider the work of Zanele Muholi, who identifies herself as a "visual activist."[5] Although she is perhaps best known as a photographer, her prolific artistic output includes performance art, documentary films and other more difficult to define activist interventions. Pumla Dineo Gqola reminds us that, "[a]lthough critics of creative forms often assume that the clear labelling of the work under analysis is a necessary step to uncover meaning, some artistic production presents that challenge of resisting tidy categorisation."[6] She recognises Muholi's work as "an instance of such resistant border-living ... which challenge the critical tools of our literary/ filmic/ visual arts and art historical training" and she argues that it is partly the fact that the work "resists precisely such endeavors to name, tame and classify," that makes it all the more "compelling and powerful."[7] The other artist whose work will be the focus of

---

2 Aluta Humbane, "Black South African Visual Artist Lesbian, Zanele Muholi, in a Transparent Coffin of Love and Loss" accessed June 19, 2017. https://inkanyiso.org/2014/02/24/2014-feb-14-black-south-african-visual-activist-lesbian-zanele-muholi-in-a-transparent-coffin-of-love-and-loss/.

3 Elaine Aston and Geraldine Harris, "Feminist Futures and the Possibilities of 'We'?," 5.

4 Elin Diamond, "We Keep Living," *Theatre Journal* 62, no. 4 (2010): 522.

5 Zanele Muholi, "I Have Truly Lost a Woman I Loved," in *Reclaiming the L-Word: Sappho's Daughters Out in Africa*, ed. Alleyn Diesel (Athlone: Modjaji, 2011), 19.

6 Pumla Dineo Gqola, "Through Zanele Muholi's Eyes: Re/Imagining Ways of Seeing Black Lesbians," in *African Sexualities: A Reader*, ed. Sylvia Tamale (Cape Town: Pambazuka Press, 2011), 622.

7 *Ibid.*

this analysis may be more easily categorized as a playwright. However, Lara Foot is no less daring and innovative in the subject matter and dramatic techniques she develops in *Karoo Moose* (2009) and *Tshepang: The Third Testament* (2005).

Muholi's work extends beyond the powerfully arresting photographs of black lesbian life in Africa and her photographic exhibitions are often rendered all the more striking because of her inclusion of other performative elements into her shows. Neelike Jayawardane describes her experience of attending one of Muholi's exhibitions at the Elizabeth A. Sackler Center for Feminist Art. Her explanation of the various features comprising the exhibition gives one an idea of just how impossible it is to neatly slot Muholi into the category of a photographer. Jayawardene recounts how, when one enters the exhibition space, one is confronted with a

> larger than life portrait of Ayanda Magoloza, of Kwanele South, Katlehong, Johannesburg (76.5 × 50.5cm, taken in 2012). Ayanda's hair is a crown of curls arranged above her head; she is the regal queen, welcoming visitors into this gallery. Positioned directly behind her is a black chalkboard with haikus of loss and rejection. The chalk inscriptions on the board are handwritten odes, minimalist narratives of loss and rejection, threats of sexual assault and bodily harm, and records of violent deaths carried out.[8]

This image of Ayanda is juxtaposed with narratives of the epidemic of so-called "corrective" or "curative" rapes of lesbians in South African townships that constitutes the most violent subscription to the heteronormative assumption that sex without a penis is not real sex and that, lesbian desire can be "cured" by exposure to sex with a penis. Jayawardene describes how

> One [narrative in the gallery] reads, "How are you getting satisfied with a finger and tongue? You need a penis." In case you imagine that to be a playful bit of crassness, the next reads, "ONE TIME A GUY TOOK OUT HIS PRIVATE PARTS, AND SAID, 'this is what you need.'" Then, that threat is made real: "THE COACH SAID HE DOESN'T LIKE ME AS A LESBIAN AND HE WANTS ME AS HIS WIFE SO THAT I CAN STOP BEING A LESBIAN. WHEN I SAID 'NO' AND TRIED TO LEAVE, HE

---

8 Neelike Jayawardane, "Zanele Muholi's Visual Activism 'Isibonelo/Evidence' at the Brooklyn Museum" accessed June 10, 2017. http://africasacountry.com/2015/10/zanele-muholis-visual -activism-isiboneloevidence-at-the-brooklyn-museum/.

BEAT ME WITH A STRAIGHTENED CLOTHES HANGER. THEN HE RAPED ME MANY TIMES, ALL NIGHT." And another: "There are 28 stab wounds on her face, chest and legs. She even has cuts on the soles of her feet."[9]

Muholi's project has never been simply about exposing the victimisation of black lesbianism, though this is certainly part of it. Gqola explains that "Muholi's work shows up the lies that heteropatriarchy sustains about who Black South African lesbians are. Her lens [and her work beyond the camera lens] ensures that this space's jagged edges are seen."[10] Resistance is as much a part of the larger picture as the horrific violence described above, as Muholi's broad artistic gaze makes sure this fact is never cut out of the frame. In her description of the exhibition, Jayawardene notes that,

> [i]n between these stark lines, inscriptions of possibility, evidence of the ability to fight back – if we are gathered in numbers. Written in some of the smallest, most decorative writing on this board is this narrative: "They were outside the bar, a crowd of people calling them Tomboys. But she said, 'No. We are not tomboys we are lesbians.' And they left and we never saw them again."[11]

In addition to the exhibition of photographs and the screening of film clips and documentaries, Muholi inserts her own body into the exhibition as part of the performance. Jayawardene recalls that, "[o]n the day of the opening, Muholi performed a funeral, laying her body down in the Perspex casket whilst a crouching mother mourned next to the coffin."[12] At a 2014 opening of an exhibition titled *Love and Loss* at the Stevenson Gallery in Braamfontein, Johannesburg, Muholi again incorporated her own body in a Perspex coffin as part of the exhibition. After receiving an award in the presence of the Ambassador of the Kingdom of the Netherlands, H.E. Mr André Haspels, at the Wits Art Museum to honour "Zanele Muholi's contribution to culture and development,"[13] the proceedings moved to the opening of *Love and Loss*. As attendees moved into the Goodman Gallery, they were met with the site of Muholi's naked body in a transparent, coffin-like structure.

---

9   *Ibid.*
10   Pumla Dineo Gqola, "Through Zanele Muholi's Eyes," 64.
11   Neelike Jayawardane, "Zanele Muholi's Visual Activism."
12   *Ibid.*
13   Aluta Humbane, "Black South African Visual Artist Lesbian."

Humbane describes the experience as follows:

> Upon entering the gallery, all your senses went into over drive as Zanele
> Muholi's live performance art installation, threw everyone for a loop and
> left them momentarily shocked.
> Muholi was inside a custom made glass coffin, which was strewn with
> rose petals and shreds of flowers on top of it, as she laid there naked, an
> allusion of death!! The celebratory mood quickly changed to a sad and a
> somewhat sombre mood. There were expressions of awe, sadness, and
> shock.
> Some people were streaming tears at the sight of Muholi's *"corpse."* The
> feelings of pain, anger, and fear resurfaced as they were forced to con-
> front everyone's worst fears – those of losing a child, aunt, sister, friend to
> hate crimes. Suddenly death was staring us in the face. The reality of los-
> ing a friend or lover, a sister or brother registered fully![14]

The inclusion of the queer, naked, black female body of the artist into a space
where gallery visitors expected an exhibition of Muholi's photographs undoubtedly changed the dynamics as well as the rules of the interpretative
game, as Muholi had now inserted performance art in a way that radically altered the ways visitors would engage with the photographs in the rest of the
gallery rooms.

These provocative attempts to engage the audience in the reality of black
lesbians' gendered experiences of violence raise difficult questions which Antje Schuhmann identifies in her excellent chapter "Shooting Violence and
Trauma: Traversing Visual and Social Topographies in Zanele Muholi's Work."[15]
These questions include:

> How to present, to *re*present, those at the margins for the sake of docu-
> menting and celebrating their/ one's own joy, while at the same time risk-
> ing feeding the regimes of imperial gazes, hungry for the "new:" the black
> homosexual or transsexual female beaten and raped? How to tell a
> counter-story without referencing the very normative politics of Other-
> ness one aims to counter?[16]

---

14   *Ibid.*
15   Antje Schuhmann, "Shooting Violence and Trauma: Traversing Visual and Social Topogra-
     phies in Zanele Muholi's Work," in *Gaze Regimes: Film and Feminisms in Africa*, ed. Jyoti
     Mistry and Antje Schuhmann (Johannesburg: Wits University Press, 2015), 55–80.
16   *Ibid.*, 61.

Muholi herself has written on how she addresses these challenges in her work and her "attempt to develop what bell hooks calls the 'critical gaze' by returning the colonial gaze, and responding actively to the heteronormative and patriarchal constructions of black queer bodies, our genders and sexualities."[17] She notes that her work, specifically the project *Portraits of the Self*, "mirrors an ongoing reflection on [her] position as a visual activist." She continues to explain: "The self-reflexivity that photography allows, the possibility for interrogating the gaze, enables me to position myself in my work as both subject and object, as seeing and being seen in an active way. I look at the gaze as not simply a passive act, but as productive."[18] Schuhmann articulates these questions and the potential implications of productive engagement with difficult interrogations as follows:

> How to visualise, to write, or to speak about violence in the context of multi-layered signification processes? How to exile one's perspective from the conflation of hegemonic, white, middle class, feminist, of imperial, of racist, and of hetero- normative gaze regimes surrounding us? Subverting and disturbing normative signification processes can impact on the imaginary and, as such, produce social change...[19]

In the last sentence of the above quotation, one realises just how high the stakes are here. This issue also stands at the heart of much feminist research, namely the desire to bring about social change. The urgent need for the latter cannot be denied when one considers the gendered violence in contemporary South African society. Subversion, disturbance and disruption are strategies that women artists can have recourse to. Indeed, as Jeanie Forte argues, "[w]omen's performance art has particular disruptive potential" by offering alternative possibilities and "opposing the traditional conception of the single, unified (male) subject."[20] Multiple speaking positions and previously silenced voices are brought into focus in the work of artists such as Muholi and Foot.

In her article entitled "South African Theatre beyond 2000: Theatricalising the Unspeakable," Marcia Blumberg indicates that she uses the term "unspeakable" in two senses: In the first place, she is referring to the voices of previously marginalised and silenced sectors of South African society, which are now

---

17   Zanele Muholi, "I Have Truly Lost a Woman I Loved," 45.

18   *Ibid.*, 47.

19   Antje Schuhmann, "Shooting Violence and Trauma," 16.

20   Jeanie K Forte, "Women's Performance Art: Feminism and Postmodernism," in *The Routledge Reader in Gender and Performance*, ed. Lizbeth Goodman and Jane de Gay (Abington, Oxon: Routledge, 1998), 237.

"encouraged to give voice to their experiences" and, in the second place, she is referring to dramatic artists' confrontations with issues "replete with brutality and previously unspeakable horror, such as rape, torture, abuse, and political violence."[21] If the phenomenon of the so-called corrective rape of black lesbians is an issue that seems unspeakable in its horror and tendency to defy human imaginative frameworks, the rape of babies is another. The necessity of challenging imaginative patterns and reticent discourses in the face of such contemporary South African realities cannot be overstated for, as Adrienne Rich explains:

> Whatever is unnamed, undepicted in images, whatever is omitted from biography, censored in collections of letters, whatever in misnamed as something else, made difficult-to-come-by, whatever is buried in memory by the collapse of meaning under an inadequate or lying language – this will become, not merely unspoken, but *unspeakable* [emphasis in original].[22]

Although Rich is, in this now classic queer feminist text, writing specifically about lesbian representation, it remains applicable today in a range of areas and, in terms of this article, it reminds us the unspeakable must imperatively be articulated. Furthermore, it must be done in ethical ways that do not perpetuate deeply embedded and problematic patriarchal and heteronormative discursive structures. For Marcia Blumberg, theatre provides an opportunity to accomplish just this and her article partly focuses on Lara Foot's 2005 play, *Tshepang: The Third Testament*. Miki Flockemann counts Foot amongst the contemporary South African playwrights who "have developed a strong reputation for producing textured work using physical images, and generating multiple meanings through innovative stage metaphors which challenge common assumptions."[23]

Allow me first to provide some context. Foot was moved to write this play by an incident that received widespread local and international press coverage, namely the rape of a nine-month old baby in 2001 in the small Northern Cape

---

21   Marcia Blumberg, "South African Theatre Beyond 2000: Theatricalising the Unspeakable," *Current Writing: Text and Reception in Southern Africa* 21, no. 1–2 (2009): 239.

22   Adrienne Rich, *On lies, secrets and silence: selected prose 1966–1978* (New York: W.W. Norton, 1979), 199.

23   Miki Flockemann, "Facing the Stranger in the Mirror: Staged Complicities in Recent South African Performances," *South African Theatre Journal* 25, no.2 (2011): 129.

village of Louisvaleweg. The infant was renamed Baby Tshepang by the nursing staff in whose care she was placed after the discovery of her mutilated body. Tshepang means "have hope" in the Tswana language and, for legal reasons, the child's real name could not be revealed. If the rape of an infant was not unspeakable enough, the international revulsion, and much of the press coverage, focussed on the fact that this incident was initially regarded as a gang rape (another all too common South African reality with the specifically local terminology of "jack rolling") and six men were arrested for the rape. It took a few months of rife speculation before the charges against five of the accused men were dropped. Eventually, only the child's seventeen-year old mother's former boyfriend, David Potse, was convicted of the crime. Significantly, the mother had apparently ended her relationship with Potse before the attack on her baby and she "testified in court that he had abused and harassed her during and after their relationship."[24] This is particularly relevant for my following analysis of the play, as research has repeatedly confirmed that, in cases of domestic violence, women and their children are at their most vulnerable just after they have left the abusive partner.[25] Anne Ganley argues that the "primary reason given by victims of domestic violence for staying or returning to the perpetrator ... is fear of violence."[26] She asserts that this "fear of the violence is realistic," as is borne out by the research that "shows that the lethality of the perpetrator's violence often increases when the perpetrator believes that the victim has left or is about to leave." This gendered reality is, however, glossed over by the community members who are eager to shift the blame to the mother.

The cover of Wits University Press' edition of the play features an illustration by Gerard Marx, who was also the set designer, showing a young black woman with a small bed strapped to her back in a way that is reminiscent of the way African women often carry their babies. In his "Designer's Note" that prefaces the text of the play, Marx notes that the "bed is a central image in the production."[27] In the play, we are presented with two central characters: Ruth,

---

24   "South Africa Convicts Man in Baby Rape Case," VOA – Voice of America. July 26, 2002.
      https://www.voanews.com/a/a-13-a-2002-07-26-9-south-67572562/388612.html.
25   Jessica Murray, "Stitching a Female Corporeal Archive: Representations of Gender, Violence and Resistance in To the Black Women We All Knew," *Current Writing* 29, no. 1 (2017): 16–25.
26   Anne L. Ganley, "Understanding Domestic Violence," in *Improving the Health Care Response to Domestic Violence: A Resource Manual for Health Care Providers*, ed. C Warshaw and Anne L Ganley (San Francisco: The Family Violence Prevention Fund, 1995), 32.
27   Gerhard Marx, "Designer's Note," in *Tshepang: The Third Testament*, Lara Foot (Johannesburg: Wits University Press, 2005), x.

the mother of the raped baby, and the man who loves her, Simon. Ruth remains silent throughout the play (except for a quiet, single utterance right at the end) while Simon is the narrator. As the plot of the play unfolds, we learn that the "rusty single bed in front of which we find Simon, is the bed on which the rape of the baby occurred."[28] Although the complex ways in which gender, poverty and violence intersect fall beyond the scope of this article, the dire socio-economic circumstances of this couple, as well as the village in which the crime takes place, is mentioned at various stages. As Marx reminds us, "[t]he fact that this 'burdened' object is not disposable is emblematic of the couple's poverty-stricken and desperate situation."[29] At the beginning of the play, Ruth is described as a "woman, with a small bed tied to her back with a blanket [who] sits on a heap of rock-like salt, which covers a pile of animal skins. She rubs the salt into the skins."[30] While the pile of salt and the rubbing of the animal skins are also central and recurring motifs throughout the play, my focus lies mainly on the small bed tied to Ruth's back and the larger context of gender violence running like a leitmotif throughout the play.

The body of a baby is never actually present in the play, as we are told that a "loaf of bread represents the baby, and the broom represents Alfred Sorrows [the character who rapes the child]."[31] The body of Ruth, however, is always visible and references to other female bodies abound in Simon's narrative. In her analysis of women's performance art, Forte notes that the "female body as subject clashes in dissonance with its patriarchal text, challenging the very fabric of representation by refusing that text and posing new, multiple texts grounded in real women's experience and sexuality."[32] Although most of the press coverage of the incident that inspired the play, as well as the academic scrutiny of the actual play, have dealt with the horror of an infant's rape, the poverty and dysfunction of a society that produces a perpetrator of such an act,[33] and the innovative theatrical dynamics employed by Foot to bring to the stage realities resisting representation and threatening to remain unspeakable,[34] this article will concentrate on the bodies of the community

---

28 *Ibid.*
29 *Ibid.*
30 Lara Foot, *Tshepang: The Third Testament* (Johannesburg: Wits University Press, 2005), 19.
31 *Ibid.*
32 Jeanie K Forte, "Women's Performance Art," 237.
33 Marcia Blumberg, "South African Theatre Beyond 2000;" Greg Homann, "Landscape and Body," *South African Theatre Journal* 23, no. 1 (2009): 149–176.
34 Connie Rapoo, "Theatre, Place and Privation: Staging Silence and Precarious Existence in Lara Foot Newton's Tshepang," *Theatre and Performance Studies* 25, no. 2 (2015): 66–79; Greg Homann, "Landscape and Body;" Jane Bennett, "Treating One Another Like Human

women who remain after the infant is removed to hospital and then taken into foster care. Connie Rapoo argues that, in the play's representation of various female characters, "Newton dramatizes the cultural demonizing and devaluing of the female subject."[35] First and foremost, there is the body of Ruth which, despite her silence, speaks volumes to readers from the moment we encounter her on the cover with the bed strapped to her back. Although Ruth remains silent throughout the play and only utters the muffled word "Tshepang" at the end of the play, her corporeal presence is foregrounded throughout the work. According to Rapoo, Ruth's "body is actually a noisy landscape, overpopulated with inscriptions of traumatic events, including the agonizing screams of her raped baby."[36] As a contemporary feminist scholar whose educational background is steeped in Western feminist thought and activism, my first reaction to the cover was the familiar horror at the reality of baby rape immediately conjured up by the presence of the name "Tshepang" in the title. My second reaction consisted in a closer scrutiny of the woman represented on the cover. I was struck by the directness of her gaze. This suggested to me that the reader would remain immersed in the story in which this woman plays a central role. As I contemplated the female protagonist on the cover, my thoughts turned to a more recent, and contextually far removed, instance of a woman carrying a mattress on her back to represent and protest against sexual assault. I am referring to the case of Emma Sulkowicz, a student from Columbia University in the United States who carried her mattress from her dormitory room on her back after being allegedly raped in 2012. She wanted to question the university's refusal to expel the fellow student whom she accused of the rape. After majoring in Visual Arts, Sulkowicz turned her act of protest into her "senior thesis piece *Mattress Performance or Carry that Weight*". She termed this an "endurance performance art piece" and this "thesis performance entailed her carrying a mattress wherever she went on campus."[37] Sulkowicz's piece inspired a First National Day of Action across American university campuses on 29 October 2014 meant to condemn sexual assault in higher education spaces. In her astute analysis of Sulkowicz's performance piece and its effects, Mitra notes that she is

Beings: South African Engendering Within the Semantics of Current Feminist Discourse," *Southern African Linguistics and Applied Language Studies* 24, no. 4 (2006): 425–435.

35 Connie Rapoo, "Theatre, Place and Privation," 70.

36 *Ibid.*, 71.

37 Shayoni Mitra, "'It Takes Six People to Make a Mattress Feel Light…': Materializing Pain in Carry that Weight and Sexual Assault Activism." *Contemporary Theatre Review* 25, no. 3 (2015): 386.

interested in the ways in which this halting speech finds new vocabulary and circulation as a lexicon of things (a gathering of mattresses, for example), with its materiality drawing attention to the extraordinarily difficult, weighty task of articulating an adequate response to the original violation. Ultimately what enables the circulation of discourse here is the series of gestures that activate the object; the mattress must be carried. Such physical expenditure points to another way of knowing and navigating pain, as displaced and collective embodiment: one where assault is transformed into something else, a labor of protest and performance.[38]

My reference to Sulkowicz is not intended to imply any easy similarity to the experiences of Ruth's character. Their circumstances, especially in terms of socio-economic resources, are, of course, too many worlds apart to allow for such a comparative move. For the purposes of this article, I suggest that Mitra's words above resonate with the character of Ruth's unspoken yet articulate ways of "knowing and navigating pain" in *Tshepang* and that this pain can be regarded as a "collective embodiment" when one reads Ruth's story along with those of the other female characters described by Simon. Such a reading suggests that Ruth is carrying the bed on her back to signify not just baby Siesie's (as the infant is named in the play) sexual assault, but also the larger context of structural gender oppression in a community characterized by the sexual abuse of women and girl children. The epigraph of Foot's play, "Based on the twenty thousand true stories," refers to the thousands of documented cases of babies being raped in South Africa. I would argue, however, that a comprehensive understanding of the script is only possible if one recognizes that millions of women are concerned here. Moreover, one needs to bear in mind that the character of Ruth is probably traumatised and keeping silent as much because of her own experiences of gender violence and oppression as because of what happened to her baby. I argue that we cannot properly read the violation of the infant without paying proper attention to the ways in which the script represents Ruth and other women as well as the constructions of masculinity permeating this story. In this respect, it is significant that Simon, the narrator represented as a sympathetic character who loves and stands by Ruth when the rest of the community shuns her, describes the other women in the community in a highly problematic manner. With the horror of a baby found in a veld "raped, sodomised, disembowelled" who has been so violated that "in between her thighs... lay a mass... like a cauliflower; red, gooey... her derms... all bloody,

---

38   *Ibid.*, 387.

her tiny, tiny little... split open,"[39] it becomes difficult to focus on other, less visceral descriptions of discursive gender violence. It would, however, do a disservice to the woman on the front cover if we were to avert our own gazes and consider only the rape of the baby, which could easily be described as an aberration in this shocked community.

The way in which Simon portrays Sarah, the other female character featuring in the play, gives one an idea of the utilitarian view of women in this community. He points out how Sarah's brother Petrus pimps her body out to the local boys who "get on top of her and ... finish [their] business"[40] while she reads a comic book. When the boys take too long, Petrus has them "continue inside a half-loaf of white bread". Simon notes that he "always preferred the half-loaf" because "the turning of the pages just put [him] off". The only sign of Sarah's presence in these "transactions" is the sound of her turning the pages of the comic books. This distracts Simon to such an extent that he prefers an inanimate object. Significantly, Sarah's attitude involves reading a book, albeit a comic, which hints at her existence as a thinking, cognisant subject clashing with her assigned gendered role as a sex object at a very fundamental level. As Simon relates this, the stage directions indicate that Ruth "becomes restless and digs into the salt." Simon recalls that Ruth's brother, Pieter, allowed him, along with other neighbourhood boys, to "spy on her when she was washing."[41] He offers this invasion of Ruth's privacy as an example of his longstanding devotion to a woman who has been scorned by the village after the rape of her baby. For Simon, however, it seems that Ruth is interchangeable with the maligned Sarah and the symbolically laden white bread. He remembers that, "[o]ften when [he] was pomping away at Sarah ... or at the white loaf, [he'd] think of Ruth, and her softness."[42] When it emerges that the perpetrator of Tshepang's rape was Alfred Sorrows, Ruth's partner, the swiftness and misogynist bent with which judgement is heaped on her are quite startling. It appears that she "had known all along" but she was "too scared to tell them because she was his houvrou."[43] Given the gendered disempowerment of women in this community, Ruth's fear becomes understandable. One can only imagine the toll it must have taken on her to keep quiet about the knowledge that her partner raped her child. The townspeople, however, display no sympathy and answer

---

39   Lara Foot, *Tshepang: The Third Testament*, 36.
40   *Ibid.*, 26.
41   *Ibid.*, 31.
42   *Ibid.*, 32.
43   *Ibid.*, 42. "Houvrou" is a derogatory Afrikaans term that can most directly be translated as "common-law wife."

their own questions as follows: "Why had she kept it a secret? Why had she not said anything? The bitch! The whore!"[44]

After Alfred was sentenced, the "whole town was gossiping about her." Simon then looks for Ruth to offer comfort and he finds her in the bed where her daughter was raped. She had used the jagged edge of a food can to "cut out her one breast, and tried to do the same to the other." As Simon looks "at her mangled body, pieces of breast and nipple lying on the floor...," he "loved her more than before." Simon alludes to the acute vulnerability and dismembered body parts of a woman in obviously stultifying pain in a problematic, almost idealised manner, with "the sun shining through the window."[45] The passivity and silence seem to inspire care and affection while active female characters are scorned and denigrated sexually. One such character who makes a fleeting appearance in the play is "old Anna, the priest's wife, the one who had three miscarriages and bakes the best milktart."[46] This brief description reveals how the character's presence in the community is delineated along very conventional gendered lines. She is depicted as a wife who has failed in her womanly duties by miscarrying three foetuses, although she appears to redeem herself somewhat by excelling in the kitchen. The man she rescued from attempted suicide reacts as follows: "... he opened his eyes and screamed in Anna's face: 'Jou hoer! Jou hoer [you whore]!.'"[47] Independent female action is still condemned in this community: when Ruth remains silent after her child's rape, her passivity is rejected in a similarly sexualised manner. The woman as whore trope seems to be assigned to the female characters regardless of what they do or fail to do.

In her 2009 play, *Karoo Moose,* Foot creates another female character forced to confront structural gender oppression and treated as a commodity by a man in her community who is her putative protector. The play centres on Thozama and her experiences in the Eastern Cape village of Noxton. As Thozama's story unfolds, the play intermittently cuts to the white Afrikaans family, the Van Wyks. There is a simmering sense of foreboding and, as the stories of the female characters develop, their vulnerability becomes increasingly apparent. Early in the play, the narrator describes how Thozama's grandmother, Grace, "stands in the yard and looks out into the night. She is filled with a feeling of trepidation."[48] On the other side of town, Mrs Van Wyk "stands outside her house. She looks out into the night. Suddenly she is taken by a feeling of

44   *Ibid.*
45   *Ibid.,* 43.
46   *Ibid.,* 22.
47   *Ibid.*
48   Lara Foot, *Karoo Moose* (London: Oberon Books, 2009), 15.

dread..."[49] The reader of the play is encouraged to heed these women's silent anxiety by the narrator who notes that the "funny thing about older women is that they always know. They know everything."[50] Sadly, the gendered deck is stacked so significantly against them, that they can do little to protect the younger women with their knowledge. Mrs van Wyk and Grace are both far removed from one another by the racial and classed dynamics that structure this society. In contrast, they are connected by their inability to change the violation awaiting their daughter and granddaughter respectively. Grace works as a domestic servant for the Van Wyks and we learn that Thozama is fifteen, "one year younger than [Mrs Van Wyk's] daughter, Sandra."[51]

Thozama's father, Jonas, spends the day drinking and gambling with his friends David and Khola. When it transpires that Jonas is unable to pay his debts, they remind him that Thozama is "worth at least two hundred and forty." When Jonas protests, the men tell him that they would be doing him a favour since "[s]omeone has to teach her to be a woman."[52] As the men close in on Thozama, described as "defenceless" and "terrified," the girl "calls for her dad" in vain. The gang rape is represented as a soccer game with the men "taking shots at Thozama's body with the ball, as if aiming for the goal posts."[53] After they are done, Khola and David "leave the house laughing and jeering" with the greeting "See you tomorrow Boet Jonas!"[54] Thozama's predicament reveals how normalised sexual assault has become in this community as well as the impunity with which the rapists act. When he learns of Thozema's pregnancy, Khola implies that a boy child will also be schooled to perpetuate gender violence: "I see you are going to have our baby. I hope he knows how to play soccer." He also threatens Thozama with repeated sexual assault by suggesting that he is "coming back for more sweeties."[55] The rape of the young girl is represented as so thoroughly mundane that, when the rapists run into her grandmother on their way out, "[t]hey greet her and chat politely." Fully aware of what happened, Grace tells the crying child: "Thozama, You are a woman now."[56] According to the stage directions, Thozama "takes off her little dress" and washes herself. Even as they recount her rape, "as she washes all the male storytellers turn away." At this point, the narrator says that "[t]his story now

---

49   *Ibid.*, 18.
50   *Ibid.*
51   *Ibid.*, 23.
52   *Ibid.*, 27.
53   *Ibid.*, 28.
54   *Ibid.*, 29.
55   *Ibid.*, 44.
56   *Ibid.*, 30.

reflects upon itself, ashamed that it chose this particular course. It is stagnant, paralyzed, like a stick animal it rests, licks its wounds and quietly contemplates its possible outcome."[57] When Thozama tries to confront her father about his complicity in the rape, he resorts to deeply embedded gendered stereotypes about women's sexuality and culpability in his attempt to exonerate himself and shift blame to the victim. He tells his daughter: "You were asking for it, it was your fault, walking around here like a slut. God has forgiven me! He has granted his forgiveness, but he doesn't forgive whores."[58]

In a conversation with Brian van Wyk, it becomes clear that Thozama found Brian's sister, Sandra, hanging from a tree. She tells Brian that she looked "broken." They both know that she killed herself because of her father who, in Thozama's words, "used her like a goat."[59] When Thozama asks Grace whether Mrs Van Wyk ever talks about her daughter, Grace responds that they "pretend it didn't happen." However, Thozama insists that "[w]e shouldn't be quiet about these things."[60]

After Thozama gives birth to the child conceived during the rape, she suspects that her rapists have started targeting her little sister, Quinnie. Quinnie's youth is emphasised by the description of her playing hop scotch and innocently sharing the sweets she received from Khola. Thomaza confronts Khola, who then decides to take her baby away. When the baby girl is returned to Thozama, the narrator offers the following description: "Thozama carefully places the baby on the table, and unwraps the blanket. Apprehensively, she checks to see if the baby is unharmed. (*Thozama lets out a silent gasp*). Tucked inside the blanket is a roll of humbugs."[61] These are the same sweets Khola gave Thozama before he orchestrated her gang rape. As Thozama then attacks Khola, Jonas comes to her aid and kills him. The play ends with Thozama bearing her baby on her back. She is surrounded by village children whom she has picked up in a truck in which she sets off in search of "Somewhere else! Somewhere better!"[62] Thozama deliberately envisioned this possibility of escape even after being told that "[t]hat's not possible. There is nowhere else to go."[63]

Foot uses the incongruous figure of a moose in the Karoo to foster engagement with the horror of Thozama's experiences. According to Lieketso Mohoto,

---

57   *Ibid.*
58   *Ibid.*, 34.
59   *Ibid.*, 39.
60   *Ibid.*, 41.
61   *Ibid.*, 57.
62   *Ibid.*, 62.
63   *Ibid.*, 45.

the "strategy of inserting this strange 'foreigner,' the moose, creates a realm of non-reality that is distant and arguably provides a sensitive distance for the audience to experience the events as a possibility of a myth, but not necessarily as fact."[64] She goes on to argue that the play "positions the audience with enough distance from Thozama's painful and liberating experience to be critical of the society in which this sequence of events could feasibly happen."[65] After the rape, the play moves to a scene in which Thozama reclaims some power and agency during a brutal attack on the moose: "*Thozama viciously attacks the moose. We hear a terrible scream, we are not sure if it is the voice of Thozama or the moose.*"[66] Foot deftly accomplishes a number of things in this short description of the attack. The animal-like scream of Thozama offers a moment of catharsis, even though the real depth of her experiences remains unspeakable. Thozama also claims some agency, as she manages to kill the moose after an older boy in the group fails to do so. After the acute vulnerability her body suffered during the rape, she becomes a figure inspiring fear and awe as "[t]he boys stare at Thozama, the blood, the knife. There is a moment's silence as they ponder the death."[67] The scene ends with Thozama breaking off the dead animal's horns, which can be read as her final emasculation of a threatening figure. Thozama's defiance of the rules of a society that failed to protect her continues when she eats the moose meat despite the fact that such an act presumably triggers the wrath of the ancestors. She dismisses this caveat by asserting: "Aga! The ancestors are already angry!" When her grandmother warns her that the "devil might have sent it," she responds as follows: "*Thozama, with newly found courage, gestures to Jonas.* There's the devil."[68] She articulates her father's complicity in her rape, thereby breaking the silence that tends to surround rape in general and the involvement of family members in sexual violence in particular. Thozama again invokes the power of the moose when she confronts Khola after the abduction of her baby. The scene is introduced as follows:

> At the riverbank, Thozama, naked, sits on her haunches and digs furiously with a sharp knife at some wet clay. She takes a handful of clay and

---

64   Lieketso Mohoto, "Theatrical Strategies of Storytelling, Bearing Witness and Testimony for Another: An Examination of Two South African Plays," *South African Theatre Journal*, 28, no. 1 (2015): 82.

65   *Ibid.*, 85.

66   Lara Foot, *Karoo Moose*, 32.

67   *Ibid.*

68   *Ibid.*, 34.

smears it on her face. Next to her, lies the Moose's head ... She ritualisti-
cally calls on the Moose by smearing her body with wet earth ... Thozama
and the Moose become one being. Thozama now takes on the power of
the beast.[69]

In his analysis of the play, Marc Maufort contends that, while the "moose sym-
bolizes the evil of patriarchal violence" early in the play, it later functions to
assist Thozama in dealing with the trauma of the rape.[70] Maufort describes
Foot's accomplishment in this play as the creation of "a hybrid aesthetic blending storytelling, metadrama, with grotesque and ritualistic realism."[71] He further argues that "[t]hrough this type of dramaturgy, she depicts characters who
are able to escape traumatic haunting in post-apartheid South Africa." Given
the brutality of the violence that Thozama experiences, at both a discursive
and a physical level, this is no small feat.

In Foot's plays discussed above, characters such as Thozama, Quinnie, Ruth,
Sarah and the violated baby negotiate gendered violence and threats from men
in their communities and families. These works insist on articulating the violence in ways that force the readers to engage rather than to turn away and
contribute to the cloaking in silence often characterising women's experiences
of gender violence. Given the difficulty to utter and to hear these truths, the
remarkable talent of a playwright such as Foot is required to foster engagement between the raped female characters and the readers. In the case of
Muholi's work, the artist uses strategies such as the insertion of her own body
into the performance and the melding of testimonial vignettes and photographs in order to arrest the viewers' gazes. In his insightful article on the landscape and bodies in post-apartheid South African theatre, Greg Homann argues that "the South African public has been educated in a complicated and
extremely sophisticated discourse of violence, allowing a viewing of theatrical
constructions of violence that are unique to a South African society."[72] As with
the violence itself, the constructions thereof are fundamentally gendered and,
in the work of Foot and Muholi, this dimension is central to the understanding
of representations of violence. This article has demonstrated that these artists
place the experiences of female victims of gendered violence at the centre of

---

69   *Ibid.*, 59–60.
70   Marc Maufort, "Negotiating the Post-apartheid Condition: Violence, Trauma and the Re-
      alist Aesthetic in Contemporary South African Drama," in *New Territories: Theatre, Drama,
      and Performance in Post-apartheid South Africa*, ed. Greg Homann and Marc Maufort
      (Brussels: P.I.E. Peter Lang, 2015), 250.
71   *Ibid.*, 253.
72   Greg Homann, "Landscape and Body," 152.

their work. Women's engagement with this violence demands the attention of the audience in what I consider to be a profoundly political move. Forte contends that "[a]ll women's performances are derived from the relationship of women to the dominant system of representation... [and their] disruption of the dominant system constitutes a subversive and radical strategy *vis-à-vis* patriarchal culture."[73] A gendered reading focusing on even the most peripheral, marginalised female figures illuminates the impact that such work has in terms of a critique of the patriarchal and heteronormative settings from which the performances emerge. These women artists are claiming a space in which violated female characters can tell their own stories, thus successfully refusing "to be the 'other' in some(male)body else's story."[74]

Works Cited

Aston, Elaine and Geraldine Harris. "Feminist Futures and the Possibilities of 'We'?" In *Feminist Futures? Theatre, Performance, Theory,* edited by Elaine Aston and Geraldine Harris, 1–16. New York: Palgrave Macmillan. 2006.

Bennett, Jane. "Treating One Another Like Human Beings: South African Engendering Within the Semantics of Current Feminist Discourse." *Southern African Linguistics and Applied Language Studies* 24, no. 4 (2006): 425–435.

Blumberg, Marcia. "South African Theatre Beyond 2000: Theatricalising the Unspeakable." *Current Writing: Text and Reception in Southern Africa* 21, no. 1–2 (2009): 238–260.

Diamond, Elin. "We Keep Living." *Theatre Journal* 62, no. 4 (2010): 521–527.

Flockemann, Miki. "Facing the Stranger in the Mirror: Staged Complicities in Recent South African Performances." *South African Theatre Journal* 25, no.2 (2011): 129–141.

Foot, Lara. *Tshepang: The Third Testament.* Johannesburg: Wits University Press, 2005.

Foot, Lara. *Karoo Moose.* London: Oberon Books, 2009.

Forte, Jeanie K. "Women's Performance Art: Feminism and Postmodernism." In *The Routledge Reader in Gender and Performance,* edited by Lizbeth Goodman and Jane de Gay, 236–240. Abington, Oxon: Routledge, 1998.

Ganley, Anne L. "Understanding Domestic Violence." In *Improving the Health Care Response to Domestic Violence: A Resource Manual for Health Care Providers,* edited by C Warshaw and Anne L Ganley, 15–45. San Francisco: The Family Violence Prevention Fund, 1995.

---

73   Jeanie K Forte, "Women's Performance Art," 236.
74   Elaine Aston and Geraldine Harris, "Feminist Futures and the Possibilities of 'We'?," 5.

Gqola, Pumla Dineo. "Through Zanele Muholi's Eyes: Re/Imagining Ways of Seeing Black Lesbians." In *African Sexualities: A Reader*, edited by Sylvia Tamale, 622–629. Cape Town: Pambazuka Press, 2011.

Homann, Greg. "Landscape and Body." *South African Theatre Journal* 23, no. 1 (2009): 149–176.

Humbane, Aluta. "Black South African Visual Artist Lesbian, Zanele Muholi, in a Transparent Coffin of Love and Loss." Accessed June 19, 2017. https://inkanyiso .org/2014/02/24/2014-feb-14-black-south-african-visual-activist-lesbian-zanele -muholi-in-a-transparent-coffin-of-love-and-loss/.

Jayawardane, Neelike. "Zanele Muholi's Visual Activism 'Isibonelo/Evidence' at the Brooklyn Museum." Accessed June 10, 2017. http://africasacountry.com/2015/10/ zanele-muholis-visual-activism-isiboneloevidence-at-the-brooklyn-museum/.

Marx, Gerhard. "Designer's Note." In *Tshepang: The Third Testament*. Lara Foot, ix–xii. Johannesburg: Wits University Press, 2005.

Maufort, Marc. "Negotiating the Post-apartheid Condition: Violence, Trauma and the Realist Aesthetic in Contemporary South African Drama." In *New Territories: Theatre, Drama, and Performance in Post-apartheid South Africa*, edited by Greg Homann and Marc Maufort, 241–260. Brussels: P.I.E. Peter Lang, 2015.

Mitra, Shayoni. "It Takes Six People to Make a Mattress Feel Light...': Materializing Pain in Carry that Weight and Sexual Assault Activism." *Contemporary Theatre Review* 25, no. 3 (2015): 386–400.

Mohoto, Lieketso. "Theatrical Strategies of Storytelling, Bearing Witness and Testimony for Another: An Examination of Two South African Plays." *South African Theatre Journal*, 28, no. 1 (2015): 78–87.

Muholi, Zanele. "I Have Truly Lost a Woman I Loved." In *Reclaiming the L-Word: Sappho's Daughters Out in Africa*, edited by Alleyn Diesel, 11–25. Athlone: Modjaji, 2011.

Muholi, Zanele. *African Women Photographers number 1*. Granada: Casa Africa, 2011.

Murray, Jessica. "Stitching a Female Corporeal Archive: Representations of Gender, Violence and Resistance in *To the Black Women We All Knew*." *Current Writing* 29, no. 1 (2017): 16–25.

Rapoo, Connie. "Theatre, Place and Privation: Staging Silence and Precarious Existence in Lara Foot Newton's *Tshepang*." *Theatre and Performance Studies* 25, no. 2 (2015): 66–79.

Rich, Adrienne. *On lies, secrets and silence: selected prose 1966–1978*. New York: W.W. Norton, 1979.

Schuhmann, Antje. "Shooting Violence and Trauma: Traversing Visual and Social Topographies in Zanele Muholi's Work." In *Gaze Regimes: Film and Feminisms in Africa*, edited by Jyoti Mistry and Antje Schuhmann, 55–80. Johannesburg: Wits University Press, 2015.

"South Africa Convicts Man in Baby Rape Case." *VOA – Voice of America*. July 26, 2002. https://www.voanews.com/a/a-13-a-2002-07-26-9-south-67572562/388612.html.

CHAPTER 15

An Unfinished Homecoming: Postmemory, Place and New Practices of Politicisation in the Plays of Nadia Davids and Amy Jephta

Ksenia Robbe

Abstract

One of the main aspirations of the early post-apartheid period was the idea of home-coming, which involved hopes for restoring peace and rebuilding communities, restitution and healing. Thus, engagements with cultural archives and performances of memory have become an inherent part of communities' struggles for repossessing land and homes. One of the iconic sites of such performances has become District Six with its history of forced removals and its former residents' intense social and aesthetic preoccupations with different layers of the past. This essay focuses on two recent plays that reimagine home spaces through innovative strategies of remembering – Nadia Davids' *Cissie* and Amy Jephta's *All Who Pass*. By analysing the plays' temporalities and reconfigurations of space through postmemorial practices, this essay explores their strategies of working with archives.

1   Introduction: The Impossibility of Return

One of the main aspirations of the early post-apartheid period was the idea of homecoming, which involved hopes for restoring peace and rebuilding communities, for restitution and healing. The "rainbow nation" was to become home for all. Yet two decades after, the number of homeless and destitute people has not diminished, and the narrative of the "new" South Africa reveals multiple cracks. The problem of reclaiming spaces within the new country has appeared more complex than it seemed, involving not simply legal rights but also issues of heritage and social justice. Thus, engagements with cultural archives and performances of memory have become an inherent part of communities' struggles for repossessing land and homes.

Cape Town, having been one of the most multicultural places in South Africa prior to the forced removals during the 1950–70s and having turned as a

© KONINKLIJKE BRILL NV, LEIDEN, 2020 | DOI:10.1163/9789004414464_016

result into the most segregated city by 1985,[1] has become one of the major sites of critical inquiry and symbolic contestation since the end of apartheid. At the same time, it became the place of most aggressive commodification of space, with the city bowl and western seaboard turned into luxurious residential areas and tourist-oriented sites. After all, with the racially segregated areas remaining "relatively unchanged," "most people in Cape Town continue to live segregated lives and continue to be ignorant of the lives of people in other parts of the city."[2] According to the dot maps that show current racial distribution in South African urban areas, Cape Town appears to be the most unequal place in the country, its ghettos being "most crammed" with non-white people.[3]

Reflection on this lack of meaningful transformation, despite the ongoing efforts of intellectuals, artists and entire communities, has led to what I consider in this chapter a new turn/stage in artistic and critical engagements with questions of space and memory in post-apartheid culture. Writing about new public arts projects of the late 1990-early 2000s (such as District Six Museum, District Six Sculpture Project, PTO, Y350, Returning the Gaze and In Touch Poetry Bus Tour), Cape Town-based curator Zayd Minty considered these works as carrying out the project of symbolic reparations, initiated by the Truth and Reconciliation Commission, and "making a particular connection in Cape Town with contested urban space and the fraught terrain of national heritage."[4] Later examinations of public art in Cape Town, while similarly emphasising the significance of such projects for transforming the city's racialised geography, have been markedly less optimistic. One of the turning points in the recent history of civic and artistic engagement in the city was the case of Prestwich Place, an area adjacent to the tourist centre. In 2003, an eighteen-nineteenth century burial ground with the remains of over 3000 humans, most of them slaves and the underclasses, was discovered beneath the ground designated for private-sector development. Debates around the appropriate ways of dealing with the remains led to a confrontation between the developers and the archaeologists appointed by them, and the Hands Off Prestwich Place Ad Hoc Committee who were resisting the planned exhumations. The result of the conflict's mediation by the South African Heritage and Resource Agency was

---

1   Catherine Besteman, *Transforming Cape Town* (Berkley, Los Angeles, London: University of California Press, 2008), 47.

2   *Ibid.*, 48.

3   Jared Sacks, "Mapping Neoliberalism," *Africa is a Country*, Sept. 24, 2013. http://africasacountry.com/2013/09/mapping-neoliberalism/.

4   Zayd Minty, "Post-Apartheid Public Art in Cape Town: Symbolic Reparations and Public Space," *Urban Studies* 43, no. 2 (2006): 438.

that the bodies were exhumed and removed to a memorial site created in the vicinity. This utilitarian solution which supported the gentrification process and disregarded the community's plea for time to mourn and make sense of the "forgotten" histories[5] signified a serious challenge for the project of symbolic reparation. Other historical points of realising the impasses in earlier post-apartheid projects of restoration included forced relocations in the run-up to the World Cup 2010, the Marikana massacre of 2012, and the student protests of 2015–16. During the past decade, this challenge has been addressed by a number of critical and creative projects and has resulted in reconsidering the vocabulary and methodology of working with archives as part of public memory interventions, some examples of which I will examine here.

One of the key realisations has been the "impossibility" of adequate restoration and return. The 2015 documentary *An Impossible Return* by Siona O'Connell, former director of the Centre for Curating the Archive at the University of Cape Town, encapsulates this realisation perhaps in the most direct and acute ways. The film features several former residents of Cape Town's central districts who have returned to the places and sometimes houses which they were forced to leave three decades ago as well as those who had never gotten the opportunity to return. It reflects on whether and how their longing for home can ever be publicly recognised as an unhealed psychological wound and addressed not as part of a bureaucratic process but as a step towards countering "the unfinished business of apartheid."[6] Calling return an "impossible" project, here, is not a sign of defeat, but a rhetorical gesture meant at articulating a critique and forging a resistant consciousness. It invokes an aporetic impossibility, entwining the desire and necessity of return with a recognition that no complete redress is ever achievable – one can only aim to engage as sensitively as possible with the archives, treating them as open-ended structures that connect past and present, and that open into the future.

These are the processes which this chapter will trace in two plays, Nadia Davids' *Cissie* (2008) and Amy Jephta's *All Who Pass* (2015), which, similar to

---

5   According to Heidi Grunebaum, "exhuming the bodies performed a material delinking of the historically aggressed from the moral and historical grounds of claim: for mourning, for reckoning, for social, spiritual and political regeneration and for the modes of enumeration that proclaim, 'This happened here. Here and not there. This is the place and it happened here.'" Heidi Grunebaum, *Memorializing the Past: Everyday Life in South Africa after the Truth and Reconciliation Commission* (New York: Transaction Publishers, 2011), 139.

6   "Coming Soon: *An Impossible Return* – An Exhibition and Documentary Directed by Dr. Siona O'Connell." *Centre for Curating the Archive*, 12.06.2015, http://www.cca.uct.ac.za/coming-soon -an-impossible-return-an-exhibition-and-documentary-directed-by-dr-siona-oconnell/.

O'Connell's films,[7] re-open archives – through the media of oral history and photography – to speak to the present in a consciously active and activist way. Both plays engage with the processes of spatialisation in Cape Town, and particularly with the spaces of District Six, an iconic site referring to the history of forced removals and its former residents' intense social and aesthetic preoccupations with different layers of the past. These plays' engagement with issues of spatial injustice in Cape Town (and, by extension, in South Africa at large as well as other postcolonial places) is defined by their performances of (post) memory (more on this term below); it is, I will argue, at the interfaces of their work with imaginations of space and time/memory that they propose new approaches to restoration and "homecoming."

While the outlined above crisis of imagining restoration in South African city and other social spaces has engaged artists and writers working in different genres and media, recent theatre productions preoccupied with the spaces and places of Cape Town, and their theorisation of memory and archival work, have been at the forefront of devising new methodologies of representation. Discussing the production of his play *Cargo* as a response to the crisis signified by the Prestwich Place case, Mark Fleishman reflects on the possibilities of theatre performance to intervene into the problems of remembering in the postcolony. In particular, he focuses on the paradox of the postcolonial situation: it "demands remembering" while the particularities of the postcolony (defined in Achille Mbembe's terms of multiplicity, excess, hysteria and super-fluity[8]) "render remembering highly problematic, if not impossible."[9] While "set[ting] out in search of coherence, of new ways of being together," forms of historiographical productions in the postcolony "tend towards disruption and discontinuity and ultimately dissolve back into fragments."[10] He, then, discusses *Cargo* – the play he directed, which engages with the fragmentary archives of slaves' lives at the Cape – as an example of alternative remembering that temporarily assembles a vision of the past only to let it fall apart into fragments.

---

7   Among O'Connell's other films and exhibitions engaging with similar issues and intervening into current practices of public memory are *The Wynberg 7* (2015) and *Promises and Lies: The ANC in Exile* (2016).

8   In his reference to Mbembe's theorisation of the postcolony, enlisting the above-mentioned terms, Fleishman summarises the concept as "the multiple, contradictory moments of everyday life in Africa read against the persistent accretions of slavery, colonialism, apartheid and neo-liberal forms of democracy" Mark Fleishman, "Cargo: Staging Slavery at the Cape," *Contemporary Theatre Review* 21, no. 1 (2011): 8.

9   Mark Fleishman, "Cargo: Staging Slavery at the Cape," 10.

10   *Ibid.*, 19.

This methodology of archival recreation departs from the idea that historiographical productions can ever restore what is absent, but this does not suggest a deadlock. Rather, it leads us to understanding performative historiography as a situational process of interaction between performers and audiences – a "history of the present" that "must be worked at, brought into being, creatively imagined, re-invented, collectively sustained, argued over each and every time."[11] In a similar vein, Nadia Davids,[12] reflecting on the production of *Cissie* and its later version, *This Woman is not for Burning* (2011), defines her search for the most poignant form of representing the life of the early twentieth-century woman activist from District Six in terms of testing "the efficacy and limitations of *restorative* archiving and historiography" and critically exploring "the potential seductions of hagiography."[13]

Fleishman and Davids' engagement with the issue of restoration after a catastrophe can be read in terms of distinction, suggested by Ernst van Alphen, between different strategies, and hence different effects, of archival work in visual and performative art.[14] Elements of what the playwrights refer to as "restorative" archiving comes close to van Alphen's discussion of works that reflect the intensified "memory crisis":[15] trying to recreate (private) histories with the aim of setting the record straight, such practices tend to have additive rather than transforming effects. On the other hand, works that recover certain details that allow for "actively engaging this past into our political present"[16] reveal more productive historiographical engagements. This practice of "reanimating the archive" produces difference by "turning memory into an almost literal re-calling that makes the past more present than those moments that are contemporaneous to the viewer's time."[17]

When reading texts and performances which engage with memory in the postcolony, it is hardly possible to dismiss the restorative, "homecoming" imperative, as the above discussion attests. Taking this into account and considering the meanings attached to the places of District Six, the "lost" home, my discussion will focus on the dynamics of restorative and reanimating

---

11   *Ibid.*

12   Davids collaborated with Fleishman on several occasions, e.g. in staging the play *Önnest'bo* (2002) as well as *This Woman is not for Burning* at the Magnet Theatre he directs, thus one can definitely speak about cross-pollination of ideas between the two researchers and playwrights/directors.

13   Nadia Davids, "'This Woman is Not for Burning': Performing the Biography and Memory of Cissie Gool," *Social Dynamics* 38, no. 2 (2012): 255, my emphasis.

14   Ernst van Alphen, *Staging the Archive: Art and Photography in the Age of New Media* (Chicago: U of Chicago Press, 2014).

15   *Ibid.*, 247–250.

16   *Ibid.*, 265.

17   *Ibid.*, 266.

approaches to this archive in Davids' and Jephta's plays. This dynamic, I suggest, is facilitated by the structures of postmemory – an imaginative investment of "generations after" into the past experienced by their (grand)parents
and the stories spun around that past.[18] Postmemory here works as a way of
interrelating different histories and memories that concern the same historical
place and the problems of belonging associated with it. But, even more importantly, it enables a dialogue between different *strategies* of archiving – those
performed by the plays within the present-day context *and* those, recalled in
the plays, that were used during the 1980 and 1990s within anti-apartheid
movements. This interlacing of memories and strategies of remembering is
staged as a work of comparison, which is also a work of learning, situating and
imagining future strategies.

My reading will proceed as an analysis of postmemory – focusing on the
plays' reanimations of photographic images from District Six, and what can be
understood as their "watching"[19] through performance, and discussing the
feminist aspects of this postmemory. Drawing on this analysis, it will discuss
the plays' innovative methodologies of recollecting the past. The last section
will consider these methodologies as creating new practices of politicising historiography. I will conclude my reading with some observations of Davids'
most recent production *What Remains*, the European première of which within the Afrovibes festival in the Netherlands was presented by Jephta in October
2017, considering how the described strategies of comparative remembering
might point at new horizons of imagining restitution, beyond the aporia of
impossibility.

2   Performing Postmemory of District Six: "Watching Photography"

Among the reasons for comparing the two plays are the biographical affinities
between their authors. Nadia Davids and Amy Jephta both come from District
Six families; born a decade apart, but both after their families had been relocated, they grew up in Walmer Estate and Mitchell's Plain, respectively. They
both graduated from the University of Cape Town's Drama department and
became internationally renowned playwrights in their twenties. Both combine
the practice of playwriting and academic work that engages similar historical

18   Marianne Hirsch, "The Generation of Postmemory," *Poetics Today* 29, no.1 (Spring 2008):
      103–128.
19   Ariella Azoulay, *The Civil Contract of Photography*, trans. Rela Mazali and Ruvik Danieli
      (New York: Zone Books, 2008).

and theoretical issues – among them, the past and present of Cape Town Coloured communities, Muslim identity and womanhood in South Africa, and transnational and local migration and belonging. Davids' doctoral thesis both staged and examined practices of "inherited memory" of District Six; both authors have written on the *Kaapse Klopse*[20] as a tradition of resistance to apartheid spatialization.[21]

Furthermore, in their creative and academic work, both authors continuously reflect on their experience of (non)belonging and their search for identity in post-apartheid South Africa *in relation to* the somewhat similar entrapments and transgressions of earlier generations that were part of the Coloured and Muslim communities. In exploring the inscription of this relationality in their plays I rely on Marianne Hirsch's conception of postmemory as "describ[ing] the relationship that the generation after those who witnessed cultural or collective trauma bears to the experiences of those who came before, experiences that they "remember" only by means of the stories, images, and behaviors among which they grew up."[22] This is not exactly a memory but a type of recollection that "approximates memory in its affective force."[23] In contrast to the Holocaust postmemory practiced by the generations who were not direct victims of violence (yet often claimed victimhood), the nature of trauma and hence postmemory in the (post)apartheid society is different in that the violence of dispossession directly affects the "generations after" who are still barred from the areas and institutions of privilege. But their relationship to District Six as one of the ghost-like places that signifies the privilege of return is still mediated by stories and images.

Both Davids and Jephta, like most descendants of District Six families, grew up in the environments that were full of stories entwining family and community, biography and auto-biography, the real and the fantastical. Jephta's

---

20   *Kaapse Klopse* is a yearly Carnival, practiced since the nineteenth century by Cape Town's multicultural population most of whom were termed under apartheid as "Cape Coloured." *Klopse* is the Afrikaans word for "club" or "troupe." Although the festival has been officially renamed "Cape Town Minstrel Carnival," the colloquial name is still very popular.

21   Amy Jephta, "On Familiar Roads: The Fluidity of Cape Coloured Experiences and Expressions of Migration in the Performances of the Kaapse Klopse in Cape Town," in *Performing Migrancy and Mobility in Africa: Cape of Flows*, ed. M. Fleishman (New York: Palgrave Macmillan, 2015), 164–179; Nadia Davids, "'It's Us': An Exploration of 'Race' and Place in the Cape Town Minstrel Carnival," *TDR: The Drama Review* 57, no. 2 (Summer 2013): 86–101.

22   Marianne Hirsch, "The Generation of Postmemory," 106.

23   *Ibid.*, 109.

grandmother,[24] just like the older character in the play, would recall the traumatic events through fairy tales and supernatural characters: only those houses where jinns lived were to be demolished by bulldozers.[25] Davids foregrounds
anecdote as a form of witnessing and transmission of memory that has shaped
her own vision of District Six, and she uses it as a strategy of recollecting the
figure of Cissie Gool, a prominent anti-apartheid community activist who was
part of several socialist movements in the 1930–60s and a strong opponent of
government's appropriation of District Six, and who died just before the removals commenced. Davids' and her autobiographical narrator's second-hand
memory of Cissie is, then, made up of anecdotes which typically conflated
family and community in acts of affective storytelling. She recalls:

> When I was little, *I just assumed that Gool was a relative.* Partly because
> my community tends to stretch its familial connections beyond the al-
> ways explicable: "He is your uncle – he's your father's half-brother's
> father-law's cousin – so he's family," and partly because her name was
> spoken with such familiarity.[26]

In both plays, the process of postmemory is initiated by the authors' engagement with photographs of District Six. The script of Jephta's play is preceded by
four photographs providing central images that structure the scenes of the play
taking place in 1974 and involving the main character's mother as a ten-year
old, together with other family members and neighbours. According to Davids,
her re-imagining of Cissie was guided by two main archival sources – the samples of her own oral history research from the early 1990s (representing Cissie
in very contradicting ways, these contradictions showing how vital her image
has been for shaping later generations' identities) and a selection of seven photographs from different periods of Cissie's life.[27] The photographs signified for
Davids a series of choices on the part of Cissie and turning points in her personal and political life, which is reflected in the play's structure as a sequence
of seven episodes narrating a history of community through the story of Cissie's life. In the later version of the play, she revised the linear structure and
supplemented it with a series of monologues *about* Cissie by her contemporaries, performed by the same actress. This structure represents biography as a
puzzle, rather than a conventional historical narrative, that can be assembled

---

24   Amy Jephta, personal communication with author, Cape Town, January 2017.
25   Amy Jephta, *All Who Pass* (Unpublished playscript, 2015), 24.
26   Nadia Davids, "This Woman is Not for Burning," 257. My emphasis.
27   *Ibid.*, 253–276.

and re-assembled by the viewers. Such fragmentary form induces a process of reading similar to what Ariella Azoulay has called "watching photography" – an act that, in contrast to "looking at," involves the dimension of time and movement in the creation of a relationship between the image, the photographed and the viewer.[28] Following Azoulay, reading a photograph that represents a person who has suffered some sort of injury "becomes a civic skill" as it "reconstructs the photographic situation and allows a reading of injury inflicted on others."[29]

Hirsch regards photography as "a primary medium of transgenerational transmission of trauma"[30] since it creates an embodied connection that implies affiliation beyond family lines. Self-reflective engagement with photographs initiates postmemorial working through traumas – which, in the post-apartheid context, are continuing and multiple. In opening "a window to the past," photographs connect positionalities of past and present[31] and, according to Azoulay, create a "civil contract" that temporarily establishes a citizenship-like equality between the photographer, the photographed and the viewer, and thus create a larger community.[32] Significantly, this act of implicating a different community "deterritorializes citizenship, reaching beyond the conventional boundaries and plotting out a political space" of democratic participation.[33] Relating the two positions – of bringing together different temporal positionalities and of constructing a democratic relationship – in her reading of Jansje Wissema's photographs of District Six on the verge of destruction, Kylie Thomas argues that such images can make visible forms of resistance that were previously not recognised and can re-actualise them for the future.[34]

Similar to the act of "watching photography," Jephta and Davids' plays *reanimate* past futures by enacting them through performance. Engaging with the iconic images of children playing in the streets of District Six, often among the rubble from demolished houses, *All Who Pass* imagines the way the children (represented by the ten-year old Aziza and nine-year old Sam) coped with the reality and anticipation of loss by collecting and cherishing old broken objects and creating a treasure map (as Aziza does) out of an eviction notice. These flashbacks from 1974 intermingle with episodes from the present of 2013 when

---

28   Ariella Azoulay, *The Civil Contract of Photography*.

29   *Ibid.*, 14.

30   Marianne Hirsch, "The Generation of Postmemory," 103.

31   *Ibid.*, 117.

32   Ariella Azoulay, *The Civil Contract of Photography*, 25.

33   *Ibid.*

34   Kylie Thomas, "Photography and the Future in Jansje Wissema's Images of District Six," *Safundi* 15, no. 2/3 (2014): 283–305.

Nadira, the twenty-nine-year old main character who grew up in Britain after her mother Aziza (the girl appearing in the flashbacks) emigrated from South Africa, visits Cape Town to receive the keys from one of the newly built houses granted to her mother after fifteen years of waiting. Meanwhile, her mother is on her deathbed; she asks Nadira to travel to the place of her childhood and do as she feels fit. Nadira travels together with her British boyfriend who is trying to offer her moral support, but the longer she stays in the house, the more she experiences his presence as interfering the development of a new relationship with the place and her mother. She starts seeing visions of her mother and family and even speaks to them, emerging in her present, neither she nor they realising that timelines have merged and that they are now able to communicate across the temporal divide.

Another moment of re-invoking past resistances takes place when Nadira meets her uncle Farooz dressed as a "coon" for the parade in District Six, having travelled all the way from Hanover Park (the district to which the family was relocated). The encounter compares him to the present-day carnival procession which Nadira witnesses and enjoys, but it does not assimilate him into the present. His speech and attitudes are represented as distinctly from the 1970s, and it is this difference that alerts Nadira to the resistance that was practiced in District Six through lifting its (male) inhabitants above the ordinary existence of segregated spaces and limited possibilities. The play ends with Nadira and Aziza, as a ten-year old, in the last minutes before relocation, chatting and watching the sun rise over the mountain. These encounters – between Nadira and Farooz and Nadira and Aziza – create a representational equality between the differential social positions of the two generations, their injuries, and their quests for belonging, along the lines of Azoulay's civil contract. While not conflating the two temporal planes, they stage a dialogue across them. Thus, they "respond to the photographed future"[35] (the ways in which the future was imagined in the past) and implicitly deliberate possible constructions of future in the present.

3   Feminist Performances of Postmemory

Similar dialogues take place in Davids' *Cissie*, in the opening and closing scenes, when the autobiographical narrator Sara attempts to "remember" District Six by gazing at its gaping spaces. At the beginning of scene 4, she transforms into Cissie – an act that represents the effects of embodiment in the

---

35   Ariella Azoulay, *The Civil Contract of Photography*, 16.

work of postmemory. In the later version, Davids abandons this fusion and represents Cissie through the stories of others, without the figure of the mythologised woman appearing on the scene (in a sense, this performance is more "photographic" as it is structured as an assemblage of stories not connected by a narrative). But back to the earlier version, its structure juxtaposes two temporal planes from the past: Sara as a high-school student in 1993, trying out the role of an academic by conducting archival research on Cissie Gool, and Cissie, expecting her third child and struggling to complete a degree at the University of Cape Town during the 1930s. In the latter part of the scene, we witness the heated arguments between Cissie and her parents (her father Dr. Abdurahman, leader of the anti-segregationist movement African Political Organisation, and her mother, Helen Potter who was part of the suffragist movement in Scotland). In an uncompromising way, Cissie criticises her father's accommodationist politics, claiming that only by protest and complete defiance of government policies can equality be achieved. Part of her radical critique is her decision to oppose the university system which, even though allowing her access to education formally, in practice bars her from equal participation, as a woman, mother, activist, and a black person. In the dialogue with her mother, she undermines the idea of an easy affiliation between them, arguing that her mother is unable to understand how she feels at a "white" university. In response, the mother expresses an intersectional vision saying that "oppression has many faces" and that she is able to relate to the experience of being racialised through her struggles as a feminist.[36] She supports an ideological link through a memory of embodied connection by recalling: "The first time I held you, our eyes locked, and I knew then that you were like me. You looked a little like me, I thought, but it was much more than that. You felt like me. You and I – we don't walk the easiest paths."[37] This episode, similar to the cross-generational dialogues in Jephta's play, juxtaposes experiences of oppression and resistance at different historical moments but in the same space of racialising practice; it problematises what we think of as "exceptional" (the story of a non-white woman in the early twentieth-century South Africa) by rendering it in the context of continuing "ordinary" violence of racism and sexism. Similarly, these conversations make visible the particular tensions, practices of resisting as well as visions of future from the past while making us think about their implications in the present.

As can be seen from these intimate conversations between mothers and daughters, both plays exemplify what Hirsch calls "feminist postmemory"

---

36   Nadia Davids, *Cissie: The Playscript* (Oxford: Oxford University Press, 2008), 36.
37   *Ibid.*, 37.

which is "defined by a particular mode of knowledge about the other, a particular intersubjective relation of 'allo-identification.'"[38] In an opening scene of *All
Who Pass*, the women of three generations appear to be almost physically
drawn together: *"the muezzin's call weaves around the three figures, binding
three generations together across space and time: mother (AZIZA), daughter
(NADIRA), grandmother (NAZREEN)."*[39] Throughout the play, Nadira is only
able to speak to her mother when male characters (Ben, Salim) are absent (at
the beginning, Salim's appearance "breaks the spell"[40]); moreover, her pushing
Ben out of the house and almost breaking up with him is a result of Nadira's
growing connection with her mother – both in the present (calling and thinking about her dying mother) and past (talking to the little Aziza).

The practice of postmemory, however, is not easily initiated: the connection
between women of different generations is not given, but has to be forged
through self-introspection and intersubjective translation. It proceeds through
silences, myopia, and misunderstanding. At the beginning, Nadira is struggling
to relate to the place of District Six and the new home: "I'm as much of a stranger here as you are, Ben"[41] and "These aren't my memories, Ben. All the stories
about this place are hers. The same recycled anecdotes, the fantastical myths
with no foothold in reality. None of them are mine. I have to look really hard to
see where the edges are."[42] But in a later dialogue with Ben she objects to his
suggestion that she should return to her mother's deathbed as soon as possible:
"What if Cape Town is where she wants me. … Then explain why I've never felt
closer to her than when I'm walking through the District, on my own. Or when
I hear the noon gun, or the call to prayer in the morning. Everything in this
place is starting to feel like a piece of her."[43] She develops this affinity even
while being confronted with many silences as her mother "rarely talks about
any of that. She rarely talks about the things she lost."[44] In a similar vein, in the
opening scenes of *Cissie*, Sara's quest of "remembering" takes place in a twi-
light zone between day and night, against the vast expanse of District Six. As
she "feel[s] [her] feet walk and pick out a path [she has] no map for,"[45] she
recalls:

---

38   Marianne Hirsch, "The Generation of Postmemory," 98.
39   Amy Jephta, *All Who Pass*, 6.
40   *Ibid.*, 7.
41   *Ibid.*, 11.
42   *Ibid.*, 29.
43   *Ibid.*, 52.
44   *Ibid.*, 65.
45   Nadia Davids, *Cissie: The Playscript*, 15. This reference to embodied memory representing
      one's exploration of the place through walking and feeling is echoed by Nadira's

That stretch of road –
  I remember passing it
  when I was very young
  (always on the way to town)
  and whispering to my mother
  in an undertone
  that it would make a lovely playground
  ...
  My mother was quiet
  her gaze trained forward
  her face a tight profile[46]

But, years after, the mother's melancholic silence becomes a departure point for the daughter in her post-memorial exploration. Thus, both plays, while staging solidarity through embodied and located encounters between mothers and daughters, along the lines of Hirsch's description of feminist postmemory, "d[o] not absorb the other, but grant the pastness and the irretrievability of the past, the irreducibility of the other, the untranslatability of the story of trauma."[47]

4   New Practices of Politicisation: Dialogues of Situated Resistance

In my reading of the plays, so far, I have stressed the moments of juxtaposition without assimilation – between different "placed" practices of resistance and different types of "situated'" (gendered, raced) knowledge. In what follows, I will argue that postmemory which works through such juxtapositions involves new forms of politicisation through reanimations of the archive. Looking at the history of reclaiming District Six in theatre productions, we can trace different types of representation and remembering which reflect particular politics of societal engagement. The famous *District Six – The Musical* (1987) by Taliep Petersen and David Kramer is an example of what can be called a vindicatory mode: the major thrust behind this powerful performance that re-created an affective community was to defy representations of the District as a slum and a place of crime, and to re-assert it as a place of humanity. It did so by, among

experience in *All Who Pass*, when she states at the beginning that she does not know the place since "the ground doesn't know [her] feet." Amy Jephta, *All Who Pass*, 7.

46   Nadia Davids, *Cissie: The Playscript*, 13.
47   Marianne Hirsch, "The Generation of Postmemory," 99.

other means, rehabilitating the figure of the gangster and cultivating pride in being "local"; however, the performance itself did not not raise any questions regarding the ethics and politics of recollecting life in District Six during the 1960s during the politically tense moment of the late 1980s. Debunking apartheid myths and setting record straight became, then, a leading impetus during the 1990s, involving reconstruction and recuperation of "forgotten" histories.

Davids' play captures this moment by including Sara's oral history project of recovering the figure of Cissie in 1993 (the project the author herself undertook as a high-school student). In her later reflection on the play and its reception, Davids critiques her biographical method which through the representation of Sara's archival effort inflected the performance with an idea of restoring a "truth" (even though the author tried to avoid it).[48] She based her newer version of the play on the interviews from 1993 being performed as an archive while neither Cissie nor Sara appear on the scene. Thus, the interviews serve not as a key to a story to be re-created, but as a story in its own right, the whole performance becoming a process of remembering the memories of Cissie by those who knew her as well as those who only heard of her (the latter group staging the process of postmemory). *All Who Pass* involves a similar consciousness of memory's situatedness. The play, similarly to *Cissie*, recalls the moment of intensified struggle and transition already in its title: as the audience enters the theatre, they see a projection of the plaque from St. Mark's Anglican Church, one of the remaining buildings in District Six, with an inscription dated 1989:

> ALL WHO PASS: Remember the thousands of people who lived for generations in District Six and were forced by law to leave their homes because of the colour of their skins. Remember St. Mark's Church and the community who resisted the destruction of District Six.
>   Hands Off District Six Campaign, 11.2.1989[49]

This invocation of a document from the time of radical resistance to the annihilation of District Six and its memory – supported by the two epigraphs to the play, with quotes from Czeslaw Milosz' and Don Mattera's[50] poems, dated 1974

---

48   Nadia Davids, "This Woman is Not for Burning," 253–276.
49   Amy Jephta, *All Who Pass*, 3.
50   Czeslaw Milosz, a Polish exiled writer who live and worked in France and the USA since the 1950s, is considered among most important Eastern European dissidents. Don Mattera was a prominent anti-apartheid activist, journalist and writer, much of whose work focused on preserving and engaging the memory living in multicultural communities in South Africa.

and 1987 respectively – is akin to the role of Sara's interviews. Towards the end of the play, Nadira meets Salim's mother, Rayda, in her fifties, when she enters the new house, accusing its young inhabitants of stealing it from the real owners. Rayda's timeline of 1995, when she together with many others expected their houses in District Six to be rebuilt, intersecting with Nadira's present, is another reminder of discourses and practices of community-based resistance from the 1980-early 1990s transitional period.

Thus, in both plays the representations of archival practices from the late 1980s – early 1990s serve as a "bridge" connecting the struggles for ownership and belonging during the time of District Six (as it existed up to the 1970s) and nowadays. These "bridging" representations invoke the moment of politicisation, heightened hopes and revisionism; the moment when an activist discourse was developed with its celebratory practices of remembering (casting Cissie as Joan of Arc) which later morphed into discourses of disillusionment (Cissie as an authoritarian).[51] It establishes a dialogue between the contemporary moment, with its disillusionments and renewed struggles for restitution engaging the spaces of Cape Town city centre, and the earlier struggles at the hand of an oppressive regime. This connection created also through the autobiographical characters and their memory of the past raises questions of how resistance today should be similar to or different from yesterday.

Cissie, particularly its later version, reflects on the problems of biographical recuperation. *All Who Pass* ruminates on the difficulties of returning and repairing, by representing how the displacement has scarred or destroyed the lives of the older generation and how much effort it will take to repair the damage and get over the loss. A similar feeling that comes with "knowing the place" is invoked in the last stanzas of Sara's final monologue:

> I turn to the sea
>   and watch the ships pass
>   Turn from the place I know now
>   Is the Architecture of Loss.[52]

But the knowledge gained produces more than an experience of loss; it invokes hopeful anticipation and a sense of new engagement that takes more self-reflective and embodied forms. Nadira's reclaiming of the new/old house through a newly built connection with her mother serves as a metaphor of her re-gaining of herself and developing a new agency in her relationship with Ben. Sara, in her discovery of Cissie, starts seeing political activism as a deeply

---

51   Nadia Davids, "This Woman is Not for Burning," 260.
52   Amy Jephta, *All Who Pass*, 62.

gendered matter: she comes to perceive Cissie's entire life as an embodiment of her political principles and her fight with the regime as a "a corporeal struggle."[53] This politicised engagement is facilitated by the work of postmemory that functions as a vehicle for transcending historical revisionism by staging inheritance and "homecoming" as a fraught, but open-ended and thus promising process.

5   Memory as "a Space of Reckoning"

In the above discussion of *Cissie* (together with the author's reflection on the play's revised version) and *All Who Pass* – as two recent examples of symbolic reclaiming of District Six as a space for remembering – I hope to have demonstrated how their practices of postmemory facilitate new methodologies of historical representation through performance. I have argued that these practices convey meanings beyond restoration of a (mythologised) past, which some representations of District Six have been criticised for;[54] that they embark on *reanimating* family and community archives, to use Van Alphen's term, by engaging practices of resistance from the past in their critiques of the political present. In the South African context, this political present involves the accelerating processes of spatial and social inequality in Cape Town, among other urban centres. Among the methods of historiographical representation that are central to both plays, the chapter discussed their employment of District Six photography within the performative acts of "watching" which make the audiences reconstruct, re-imagine and relate to the injuries experienced by the inhabitants. Further, it argued that the acts of feminist postmemory explicitly staged in these plays foreground situatedness and encourage intersectional and translation-based approaches to understanding and interrelating past and present struggles of women in (post)colonial contexts.

In a similar vein, the plays intersect present-day archival engagements and the approaches that were practiced during the period of intense resistance and the transition. Without assimilating earlier experience and practice into the contemporary, they put the two in a dialogue, which can lead to revisions. By representing the story of Cissie through the ways she was/is remembered by other District Six inhabitants (thus, stressing their situated visions and agency)

53   Nadia Davids, "This Woman is Not for Burning," 273.
54   Richard Rive, "District Six: Fact and Fiction," in *The Struggle for District Six Past and Present*, ed. Shamil Jeppie and Crain Soudien (Cape Town: Buchu Books, 1990), 110–116.

and by including the voices of Farooz and Rayda as connecting to those of the community and Hands Off District Six activists, the plays "remember" them and grant them a due place in the present.

An important aspect of both plays' performances of (post)memory, as my reading has indicated, is their embodied character (the knowledge of/belonging to a place is articulated in terms of bodily memory; memory is preserved and transmitted through material objects like maps created out of eviction notices; social knowledge and memory are circumscribed by gendered and raced bodies). Together with these practices of embodiment, elements of magic and imaginative transformation (transformation of Sara into Cissie and time travelling, intersection of timelines and stories of jinns) play a key role in forging new imaginations of the past. According to Yvette Hutchison, "[t]he non-realistic form is important as a methodology for interrogating an historical narrative, as it highlights the potential for multiple readings of the narratives, and thus highlights rather than obfuscates the ambiguities associated with historiography."[55] It also links to Fleishman's theorisation of remembering in the postcolony as "putting together of the fractured body" and requiring forms of fragmentation and assemblage for reconstructing and re-engaging a sense of the past.[56]

As I was finalising this chapter, I got the chance to see the European premiere of Davids' most recent play, *What Remains*, which was presented and opened to a public discussion in Amsterdam and Rotterdam by Amy Jephta. The play, based on the story of the Prestwich Place, centres upon the conflict between an archaeologist and a representative of the District Six community – which are figurations of the clash between "scientific research" and "social accountability," "development" and "memory."[57] It certainly deserves a separate discussion, but an important aspect to observe within this reading is that it further activates and intensifies the practices of memory and methodologies of representing the past that this chapter has discussed in relation to the earlier plays. To mention a few, the play continues activating photographic images (now projected on the scene), representing memory as embodied practice (through the centrality of dance in the performance) and stressing

---

55   Yvette Hutchison, *South African Performance and Archives of Memory* (Manchester and New York: Manchester UP, 2013), 185.

56   Mark Fleishman, "Cargo: Staging Slavery at the Cape," 8.

57   Nick Shepherd and Christian Ernsten, "The World Below: Post-Apartheid Urban Imaginaries and the Bones of the Prestwich Street Dead," in *Desire Lines: Space, Memory and Identity in the Post-Apartheid City*, ed. Noëleen Murray, Nick Shepherd and Martin Hall (London and New York: Routledge, 2007), 221–224.

the importance of indigenous knowledge (through the role of imagination and affect in the plot and performance). The centrality of the figure of a young descendent of District Six inhabitants as the narrator and her role in the final scene, representing her ability to revolt against the ongoing social injustice by virtue of sensing the experience and inheriting the memory of past generations, speaks to the very recent histories of the 2015–16 student protests against colonial practices of education and the 2017 "Reclaim the City" campaign against spatial segregation in Cape Town. This confirms the politicising function of the new methodologies of relating memory, identity and place described in this chapter.

It is this change in perspectives and methods of remembering and representing that Davids speaks about in her reflection on her practice:

> The contemporary political landscape of South Africa is so full of immediate urgency that the question of revisionism itself has changed: it is no longer about the importance of recognising those who have come before for their own sake (remembering the dead, after all, serves no one but the living), but rather finding ways in which we can place them in conversation with the present.[58]

In this context, the politics of memory becomes that of critical intervention into the historical injustices of the present – "brokering a dialogue between then and now, between past struggles and present failures [...] then we could use performance as not just a means of exploring identity, active memorialisation and historicising, but also, crucially, as a space of reckoning."[59]

Works Cited

Azoulay, Ariella. *The Civil Contract of Photography*. Translated by Rela Mazali and Ruvik Danieli. New York: Zone Books, 2008.

Besteman, Catherine. *Transforming Cape Town*. Berkley, Los Angeles, London: University of California Press, 2008.

"Coming Soon: *An Impossible Return* – An Exhibition and Documentary Directed by Dr. Siona O'Connell." *Centre for Curating the Archive*, 12.06.2015, http://www.cca.uct.

---

58   Nadia Davids, "This Woman is Not for Burning," 273.
59   *Ibid.*

ac.za/coming-soon-an-impossible-return-an-exhibition-and-documentary-directed-by-dr-siona-oconnell/ (last accessed 29.10.2017).

Davids, Nadia. *Cissie: The Playscript*. Oxford: Oxford University Press, 2008.

Davids, Nadia. *This Woman is not for Burning*. Unpublished play, 2011.

Davids, Nadia. "'This Woman is Not for Burning': Performing the Biography and Memory of Cissie Gool." *Social Dynamics* 38, no. 2 (2012): 253–276.

Davids, Nadia. "'It's Us': An Exploration of 'Race' and Place in the Cape Town Minstrel Carnival." *TDR: The Drama Review* 57, no. 2 (Summer 2013): 86–101.

Davids, Nadia. *What Remains*. Directed by Jay Pather. Unpublished play, 2017.

Fleishman, Mark and Jennie Reznek, directors. *Önnest'bo*. Unpublished play, 2002.

Fleishman, Mark. "Cargo: Staging Slavery at the Cape." *Contemporary Theatre Review* 21, no. 1 (2011): 8–19.

Grunebaum, Heidi. *Memorializing the Past: Everyday Life in South Africa after the Truth and Reconciliation Commission*. New York: Transaction Publishers, 2011.

Hirsch, Marianne. "The Generation of Postmemory." *Poetics Today* 29, no.1 (Spring 2008): 103–128.

Hutchison, Yvette. *South African Performance and Archives of Memory*. Manchester and New York: Manchester UP, 2013.

Jephta, Amy. *All Who Pass*. Unpublished playscript, 2015.

Jephta, Amy. "On Familiar Roads: The Fluidity of Cape Coloured Experiences and Expressions of Migration in the Performances of the Kaapse Klopse in Cape Town." In *Performing Migrancy and Mobility in Africa: Cape of Flows*, edited by M. Fleishman, 164–179. New York: Palgrave Macmillan, 2015.

Mbembe, Achille. *On the Postcolony*. Berkley: University of California Press, 2001.

Minty, Zayd. "Post-*Apartheid* Public Art in Cape Town: Symbolic Reparations and Public Space." *Urban Studies* 43, no. 2 (2006): 421–440.

O'Connell, Siona, director. *The Wynberg 7*. Centre for Curating the Archive, University of Cape Town, 2013. (DVD).

O'Connell, Siona, director. *An Impossible Return*. Centre for Curating the Archive, University of Cape Town, 2015. (DVD).

O'Connell, Siona, director. *Promises and Lies: Fault Lines in the ANC*. Centre for Curating the Archive, University of Cape Town, 2016. (DVD).

Petersen, Taliep and David Kramer. "District Six – The Musical." In *District Six and Other Plays*, compiled by M. William, 16–65. Oxford UP Southern Africa, 2005.

Rive, Richard. "District Six: Fact and Fiction." In *The Struggle for District Six Past and Present*, edited by Shamil Jeppie and Crain Soudien, 110–116. Cape Town: Buchu Books, 1990.

Sacks, Jared. "Mapping Neoliberalism." *Africa is a Country*. September 24, 2013. http://africasacountry.com/2013/09/mapping-neoliberalism/ (last accessed 29.10.2017).

Shepherd, Nick and Christian Ernsten. "The World Below: Post-Apartheid Urban Imaginaries and the Bones of the Prestwich Street Dead." In *Desire Lines: Space, Memory and Identity in the Post-Apartheid City*, edited by Noëleen Murray, Nick Shepherd and Martin Hall, 215–232. London and New York: Routledge, 2007.

Thomas, Kylie. "Photography and the Future in Jansje Wissema's Images of District Six." *Safundi* 15, no. 2/3 (2014): 283–305.

van Alphen, Ernst. *Staging the Archive: Art and Photography in the Age of New Media*. Chicago: U of Chicago Press, 2014.

PART 4

Creolization: From the Cape to Transnational Vistas

∵

"Dis Nie Myne Nie, Dis Nie Joune Nie" or Kramer and Petersen's *Ghoema*: Inscribing the Past, Claiming the Present?

Paula Fourie

Abstract

In 2005, musical theatre co-writers Taliep Petersen and David Kramer brought *Ghoema* to the stage. This musical engages with the early history of the Cape to demonstrate the unacknowledged contribution of slaves to the cultural life of Cape Town. In this, it relies heavily on a body of Afrikaans folk songs shared by both coloured and white Afrikaans-speakers. Like Afrikaans, these songs are the result of processes of creolization, created in the painful and violent encounter between slave and slave master in colonial Cape Town. This essay is concerned with examining whether what is regarded as a staging of creolization can contribute to exploring the contemporary identities of slave descendants, the vast majority of whom were classified as "coloured" or "Cape Malay" during apartheid and marginalized by the ruling government.

∙ ∙ ∙

In the opening scene of *Ghoema*,[1] David Kramer and Taliep Petersen's last musical, its two young male narrators, Hot and Tot, immediately break the fourth wall, drawing the audience in by rapping:

Hot   Word wakke, word wakke
            Jull's almal annie slaap
            O's is hip hop brasse
            Gebore innie Kaap
            Sy naam is Tot
            En my naam is Hot

---

1   "Dis nie myne nie, dis nie joune nie" is the title of a *ghoemaliedjie* that translates as, "It's not mine, it's not yours."

Ons issie brasse

Hot en Tot

[...]

Tot   Ja o's is twee laaities

O's kom vannie Kaapse Flats

O's is so-called coloureds

But there's more to us than that

So sit back, relax

Switch af jou sel

Issie storie vannie ghoema

Wat o's nou gaan vetel.[2]

With these opening words, the agenda of *Ghoema* is unequivocally estab-lished: to explore the past of South Africa's coloured population with all eyes focused firmly on their present. More specifically, in the words of one of its co-writers, Kramer, it would do so by attempting "to re-imagine the fact and the fiction, to rewrite the history of early Afrikaans music and to acknowledge the nameless people who created and contributed to it."[3] Central to this agen-da is the evocation of the ghoema drum and its eponymous rhythm, unique South African musical creations formed in the cultural melting pot that was colonial Cape Town. Considered characteristic of much Western Cape folk music, the ghoema beat, whose rhythmical formation can be reproduced on a wide range of instruments, has been theorized by Denis-Constant Martin as the most recognizable musical signifier of Cape Town, even as its "unifying creole pulse."[4]

In keeping with the instruction to "sit back, relax," *Ghoema* tells its story in 120 minutes of song and dance, interweaving spoken dialogue and humor-ous sections of rap with a number of original compositions and a large body of folk songs. From the perspective of a present-day New Year's Eve, it tells of

---

2   "Wake up, wake up/ You're all asleep/ We are hip hop *brasse*/ Born in the Cape/ His name is Tot/ And my name is Hot/ We are the *brasse*/ Hot and Tot [...] Yes, we are two *laaitjies* [South African slang for young boys], we come from the Cape Flats/We are so-called coloureds/But there's more to us than that/ So sit back, relax/Switch off your cell/ It's a story of the ghoema/ That we are going to tell." All the translations in this essay are by the author. To avoid doing damage to Kaaps by forcing it to adapt to the spelling conventions of so-called "standard Af-rikaans," I have written down spoken and sung text phonetically as I have heard it.

3   Qtd. In: Percy Zvomuya, "Singing History from the Cape of Sorrows," *Mail & Guardian* (Johan-nesburg), June 21, 2007. https://mg.co.za/article/2007-06-21-singing-history-from-the-cape -of-sorrows.

4   Denis-Constant Martin, *Sounding the Cape: Music, Identity and Politics in South Africa* (Som-erset West: African Minds, 2013): 353.

Portuguese and Dutch oceanic trade leading to the establishment of a refresh-
ment station at the Cape of Good Hope, the importation of slaves by the Dutch
and the growth of a slave society at the Cape, replete with a large body of folk
songs that developed on its farms. It tells of eventual British rule, slave emancipation in 1834, and the impact of visiting figures such as Frans de Jonge from
the Netherlands and Orpheus McAdoo from the USA on the growth of the
present-day Cape Coon Carnival and Cape Malay Choir traditions.[5] Throughout, even during the sections of rap, the use of acoustic instruments such as
the ghoema drum, tambourine, guitar, banjo and piano-accordion combine to
create a folk-music tapestry. Musically as well as thematically, Afrikaans folk
songs occupy a prominent place in the musical.

At the outset, I had intended my research on *Ghoema* to focus on the musical's combined use of two anachronistic musical idioms. I conceived of these
as, on the one hand, an established body of Afrikaans folk songs, and on the
other, the vibrant tradition of Western Cape rap with its historically "strongly
activist orientation."[6] I was excited by the thought that these idioms, separated
by different historiographical narratives, could inscribe the past and simultaneously claim the present. Put differently, in asserting a new place in the national memory for coloured South Africans through the combined use of these
musical genres, *Ghoema* could also enable the articulation of new present-day
identities for those designated "coloured" by the apartheid government. In this
way, the lines given to the narrators Hot and Tot in *Ghoema* would echo the
message rap associated with hip hop nationalism in the United States in the

---

5 Although the word "coon" has its origins in the United States as a racist reference to African-
   Americans, members of the South African *klopse* (literally "clubs") that partake in this tradition generally use it with an entirely different set of connotations. For this reason, it is
   employed in this essay rather than the term "minstrel" that has more recently entered the
   discourse for the sake of political sanitization. This is a deliberate strategy aimed at acknowledging the power of words and concepts to travel and to be reinscribed with new
   meanings. I also take my cue from Taliep Petersen, who not only started his musical career
   in the Cape Coon Carnival, but who remained active as a coach for the rest of his life. "The
   Americans come and they don't want us to use the word 'coon' because it's derogatory," he
   explained to Denis-Constant Martin in 1994. "For the people here, 'coon' is not derogatory, in
   our sense, for us, the minute you talk coon he sees New Year's Day, he sees satin, and the
   painted ... white around the eyes, black around the rest, the eyes and mouth with circles in
   white, the rest of the face was in black like the American minstrel, or, it's easy to understand,
   like Al Jolson." Taliep Petersen, Interview with Denis-Constant Martin, 15 November 1994.
6 Ncedisa Nkonyeni, "Da Struggle Kontinues into the 21st Century: Two Decades of Nation-
   Conscious Rap in Cape Town," in *Imagining the City: Memories and Cultures in Cape Town*, ed.
   Sean Field et al (Cape Town: HSRC Press, 2007), 154.

1990s (the origin of the Western Cape rap aesthetic), concerned as it was with a "rethinking of the past in an effort to empower the present struggle for black liberation."[7]

Yet as soon as I began researching these idioms and their history, I realized first of all that to call them "anachronistic" was fundamentally misleading. Doing so would deny the place of these practices in the present soundscape of South Africa. The *ghoemaliedjies, nederlandsliedjies* and other Afrikaans folk songs that form the backbone of *Ghoema* are very much alive, continually being reinvented as "tradition" finds ways of asserting its importance in the here and now. Furthermore, as I watched the musical over and over again, I also began to question the most basic assertion that I had wanted to make, namely that by inscribing the past, *Ghoema* was also claiming the present. From the vantage point of present-day South Africa, this gradually seemed to constitute a grossly exaggerated claim, one based on a false and fast-dissipating sense of national optimism. It is one I no longer wish to make. Instead, *Ghoema* became a catalyst for fundamental questions about the performance of creolization or, as Zimitri Erasmus has described this dynamic process in the context of South Africa, of "cultural creativity under conditions of marginality."[8]

• • •

Ghoema!, as the first manifestation of this musical was titled, opened at the *Klein Karoo Nasionale Kunstefees* (KKNK) in March 2005 as a seventy minute stage piece that explored the origins of Afrikaans as well as the contribution of former slaves to Afrikaans folk music. After a successful staging at the festival, it was reworked, extended to two hours and renamed *Ghoema.* Under the direction of David Kramer and the musical direction of Taliep Petersen, this reworked version opened in Cape Town's Baxter Theatre on 16 November 2005, starring Loukmaan Adams, Munthir Dullisear, Zenobia Kloppers, Gary Naidoo, Carmen Maarman and Danny Butler, and with a band consisting of Butler, Gammie Lakay, Howard Links, Solly Martin and Charlie Rhode.[9] The set design

---

7 Jeffrey Louis Decker, "The State of Rap: Time and Place in Hip Hop Nationalism," *Social Text* 34 (1993): 55.

8 Zimitri Erasmus, "Introduction: Re-Imagining Coloured Identities in Post-Apartheid South Africa." in *Coloured by History, Shaped by Place: New Perspectives on Coloured Identities in the Cape,* ed. Zimitri Erasmus (Kwela and South African History Online, 2001), 16.

9 This is the version that will be discussed in this essay, specifically a performance filmed at the Baxter Theatre and brought out on DVD in 2009.

was by Kramer, lighting design by Kramer together with Gert du Preez, and costume design by Jesse Kramer.[10]

Ghoema was the seventh and final musical by lyricist and librettist Kramer and composer and arranger Petersen, two men whose working relationship served as an all-too rare example of interracial collaboration during the apartheid years. Kramer, an English-speaker originally from Worcester, was designated white by the apartheid government, while Petersen was an Afrikaans-speaker from Cape Town's infamous District Six designated "Cape Malay," a category subsumed under the broader category of "coloured." Over the previous twenty years, starting with *District Six: The Musical* in 1987, they had written six musicals together – *Fairyland* (1990), *Poison* (1992), *Crooners* (1992), *Kat and the Kings* (1995) and *Klop Klop* (1996) – all which were in some way rooted in the musical idioms, social contexts or landscapes associated with South Africa's coloured population.[11] *Ghoema* was no exception. In fact, it could be called the musical that most directly grappled with past and present realities of being coloured, placing center-stage the cultural products – language, music and food – embraced by large sections of this community.

As a racial construct eventually codified in the apartheid government's Population Registration Act, the term "coloured" has always been a notoriously nebulous one, even to the hegemonic powers themselves. During apartheid, it was used to lump together into a single racial category (albeit one that later acknowledged several subgroups) diverse individuals that included persons of mixed race; the native Khoikhoi and San, the descendants of political convicts exiled to the Cape by the Dutch East India Company, and a significant number of slaves brought mainly from the Indonesian Archipelago. Although the term "coloured" has outright derogatory connotations elsewhere, in South Africa it has a complex history that has included both its rejection as a racist label and its claiming as a self-referential term.[12] I employ it here without any qualifying appendages, both to emphasize personal agency in identity creation and from the perspective that the use of politically sanitized terminology has the

---

10   Mariana Malan, "'Ghoema' Stuur Jou Met Lied in die Hart Huis Toe," Die Burger (Cape Town), Nov. 18, 2005; Gerrit Brand, "'Ghoema' Kraai Koning by Fleur du Cap-Teaterpryse," *Beeld* (Johannesburg), March 8, 2006.

11   For more information about the Kramer/Petersen collaboration and a discussion of these individual musicals, see Paula Fourie, "'Ghoema vannie Kaap': The Life and Work of Taliep Petersen (1950–2006)," Dissertation: University of Stellenbosch, 2013.

12   For an overview of the changing perspectives on South African coloured identity in the twentieth century, see Mohamed Adhikari, "From Narratives of Miscegenation to Post-Modernist Re-Imagining: Toward a Historiography of Coloured Identity in South Africa," *African Historical Review* 40, no. 1 (2008): 77–100.

potential to undermine restitutive work precisely because it strips words of those connotations that inform the contexts of such work. Moreover, while the continued use of racial signifiers in contemporary South Africa is lamentable from the perspective of what was fought for in the name of non-racialism, I take the stance that an artificial levelling of experiences through language in contemporary post-post-apartheid South Africa is at least equally problematic (if not more so), considering the continuities of apartheid-era deprivations and patterns of privilege.

The complexity of these issues is underlined in an interview that I conducted with jazz pianist and composer Paul Hanmer who played in Petersen's dance band of the early 1980s, Sapphyre. Speaking in the context of the historical visibility of Cape Coon Carnival practices in Cape Town, Hanmer remembers that his father regarded this popular portrayal of people of colour as "derogatory" and expected him to "step away from that." As he muses on what he had been taught in his family context, telling perspectives emerge on what it might mean to be coloured:

> You know, just because we find ourselves behind the coloured fence it doesn't mean we're a tribe with any special attributes. You know, it's just a collection of people who are mixed, you know, from other people who do have a tribal history or can trace their whatevers. But we're this motley collection of almost anybody. And that therefore it's simpler to try and think of us as people, and that we should try and do our best as people, rather than as coloured people or... But I mean it's kind of, it's quite a strange kind of... Because it cannot be an absolute. And I realised that there's a lot of things [laughs] about me and where I come from and the people that have shaped me that, that are still a part of me, you know, and if that means being, growing up in a coloured community, going to a coloured school, going with coloured friends, and you know, falling in love with coloured girls, whatever, it means a whole hell of a lot, you know? It's more than just, um, any one thing. So, there is, there is a lot of people's culture in what I've grown up with, and the cultures could be admixtures of any number of people from Europe and from South Africa, and other parts of Africa, and in lots of cases St Helena island and you know ... and intermarriage between Muslim and Christian people.[13]

Since those early years when the word "coloured" was viewed in essentialist terms, it has since evolved – as is so eloquently articulated by Hanmer – to

---

13   Paul Hammer, personal interview, Nov. 29, 2011.

describe a diverse group of people with a heritage that is at once transformed and transforming through processes of creolization. In invoking creolization, I refer specifically to that "unpredictable energy of overcoming," as Martin translates the Caribbean poet Édouard Glissant's "dépassante imprévisible,"[14] to that limitless mixture of cultural mixtures that becomes more than the sum of its parts, "its consequences unforeseeable."[15] A process understood by Glissant as affecting the entire world, creolization is also a manifestation of his Poetics of Relation, "in which each and every identity is extended through a relationship with the other."[16] Yet to evoke creolization is also to acknowledge one of its fundamental conditions – conflict. To speak of creolization in this context is also to stress the term's origins – in the writing of Kamau Brathwaite and others – as a means to understand cultural processes in a society with a history of colonialism, slavery and dominion, where the confrontation between different and unequal cultures is "not only cruel, but also creative."[17]

Several writers, including Shell, Erasmus, Martin, Adhikari and Willemse, have enlisted creolization as a way to speak about the coloured population of South Africa. To do so is to identify the slaves of the Cape Colony and their descendants as people "transformed elsewhere into another people," as a community that has entered into processes of creolization by virtue of not having brought with it "the methods of existence and survival, both material and spiritual, which it practiced before being uprooted."[18] This invariably resulted in the creation of new cultural forms, new mixtures made from the old; not to be seen as derivative, but as powerfully more than the sum of their parts. In his history of slavery at the Cape of Good Hope, Robert Shell lists one of its legacies as "the as yet unexamined creole culture of South Africa, with its new cuisine, its new architecture, its new music, its melodious, forthright, and poetic language, Afrikaans, first expressed in the Arabic script of the slaves' religion and written literature."[19] It is precisely this legacy that the musical *Ghoema* sets out to explore, with particular emphasis – as the medium of musical theatre suggests – on both language and music.

---

14   Denis-Constant Martin, *Sounding the Cape*, 62.
15   Édouard Glissant, *Poetics of Relation*, trans. Betsy Wing (Ann Arbor: University of Michigan Press, 2010), 34.
16   *Ibid.*, 11.
17   Denis-Constant Martin, *Sounding the Cape*, 61.
18   Édouard Glissant, *Caribbean Discourse: Selected Essays,* trans. J. Michael Dash (Charlottesville: University of Virginia Press, 1989), 15.
19   Robert C.-H Shell, *Children of Bondage: A Social History of the Slave Society at the Cape of Good Hope, 1652–1838* (Johannesburg: Witwatersrand University Press, 1994), 415.

Yet it is not only slave descendants who are party to the intimate and violent entanglements of creolization. One of the acknowledgements of this in *Ghoema* is the evocation of the stereotype, "Hottentot," in the combined names of its hip-hop narrators. Applied by Europeans since the 17th century to refer to the native Khoikhoi, evoking this name on stage is a reminder to the audience that, as indentured labourers often treated no differently to slaves, South Africa's earliest inhabitants share the legacy of slavery and oppression. A pejorative term, "Hottentot" is also a reminder of the negative stereotyping and loss of dignity that South Africa's coloured population have had to endure from the time of early Dutch settlement, throughout the apartheid years, and beyond. Still others contributed the riches of their cultures of origin to the creolization process. This included other indigenous African people by way of the Bantu-speaking individuals who settled in Cape Town and joined the mix. Also party were political convicts from Dutch "possessions" in the Southeast Indies, individuals who played a role in establishing Islam at the Cape and whose descendants, together with slave descendants who had converted to Islam, eventually began to be regarded as constituting the Cape Malay community.

In emphasizing the contribution of coloured individuals to the rich cultural heritage of South Africa, *Ghoema* brought an alternative history to the stage. It was a history that sought to trounce one of the most brutal stereotypes that colonialism and apartheid had attached to the coloured population: that as essentialized products of miscegenation they had no culture, and no history of their own. That *Ghoema* sought to historicize the coloured experience is made apparent when, after Hot and Tot's first lines, the two female narrators, Minnah and Dina, introduce the audience to the traditions of a Cape Town New Year as they know it, all the while emphasizing its "oldness."

Dina	Dis ou traditions dié.
Minnah	Kom al 'n langpad.
Dina	Nou Minnah, Minnah, hoe het dié goed hie in die Kaap in gebeur?
Minnah	Ko sit. Ko sit lekkertjies.
Dina	Ko sit lekkertjies.
Minnah	Dan sal o's vi julle vetel wat hie honderde jare terug gebeur het.[20]

---

20   "These are old traditions, these." "They've walked a long road." "Now Minnah, Minnah, how did all these things happen here in the Cape?" "Come sit. Come sit nicely." "Come sit nicely." "Then we will tell you what happened here hundreds of years ago."

If an audience were to take *Ghoema*'s history lesson seriously, it would no longer be possible to entertain the debilitating myth that coloured South Africans possessed no history or culture. This implausible construction of a historical void can perhaps best be explained as an attempt on the part of white South Africans, and in particular Afrikaners, to deny creolization altogether in a strategy to safeguard their own imagined racial purity. Creolization has always taken as its premise that there is no such thing as purity, proceeding from the premise that everything is always already gloriously mixed. Moreover, creolization involves both slave *and* master. Its main stage is there where the most intimate exchanges take place, in the slave master's home. The denial of creolization, the historic disavowal of the Afrikaners' involvement in anything that would have involved them in racial intermingling, is integral to the purist identity that they sought to construct for themselves during the first half of the twentieth century.

This notion is powerfully underlined in that oft-quoted passage spoken by the Afrikaner poet Breyten Breytenbach during a speech delivered at the University of Cape Town in 1973:[21]

> Ons is 'n bastervolk met 'n bastertaal. Ons aard is basterskap. Dis goed en mooi so. Ons moet kompos wees, ontbindend om wéér in ander vorme te kan bind. Net, ons het in die slagyster getrap van die baster wat aan bewind kom. In daardie gedeelte van ons bloed wat van Europa kom, was die vloek van meerderwaardigheid. Ons wou ons mag regverdig. En om dit te kon doen, moes ons ons gewaande stamidentiteit stol. Ons moes áfkamp, bekamp, verkramp. Ons moes ons andersheid verskans en terselfdertyd behóú wat ons verower het. Ons het van ons andersheid die norm, die standaard gemaak – en die ideaal. En omdat die handhawing van ons andersheid *ten onkoste* van ons mede-Suid-Afrikaners – en ons Suid-Afrikaansheid – is, het ons ons bedreig gevoel. Ons het mure gebou. Nie stede nie, maar stadsmure. En soos alle basters – onseker oor hul identiteit – het ons die begrip van *suiwerheid* begin aanhang. Dit is apartheid. Apartheid is the law of the bastard.[22]

---

21   Breyten Breytenbach, *Parool/Parole: Versamelde Toesprake/Collected Speeches* (Cape Town: Penguin, 2015), 12.

22   "We are a bastard people with a bastard language. Our nature is one of bastardy. It is good and beautiful thus. We must be compost, disintegrating to once more integrate into other forms. Only, we have stepped into the snare of the bastard who has come into power. In that part of our blood that comes from Europe was the curse of superiority. We wanted to justify our power. And to be able to do that, we had to congeal our imagined tribal identity. We had to fence off, fight off, cramp up. We had to entrench our otherness and

Referring to Ronald Radano's analysis of the racialization of American music in the wake of the Civil War, Martin identifies a similar turn of events in
South Africa.[23] In the United States, a denial of interracial commingling (including with regard to musical practices) on the part of the white population
led to the classification of music – even though it was already more or less
mixed – as either "white" or "black," and thus resulted in African-Americans
being inadvertently given the "gift" of the latter.[24] Martin, who has described
the musical history of Cape Town as "largely the result of a process of creolization that has been devalued and rejected by the ruling sections of the population but never wiped out," suggests that a denial of creolization in South Africa
served similarly to fracture its legacy.[25] This is a convincing explanation of why
certain creolized and creolizing cultural forms – like the language Afrikaans
and certain folk songs – were claimed as "pure" by white Afrikaners, while still
others – a number of *ghoemaliedjies* for example – were rejected, and "gifted"
to coloured South Africans.

It is this very terrain that *Ghoema* traverses. The musical contains a number
of *ghoemaliedjies* and *nederlandsliedjies,* but also original compositions influenced by these song forms, such as "Blue Sky" (based on an old *nederlandslied-
jie*). Sharing its name with both the ghoema drum and its eponymous rhythm,
the *ghoemaliedjie* or *piekniekliedjie* (literally "picnic song"), originated as a repertoire sung by slaves during times of leisure. Thought to contain influences
from both Dutch comic songs and from the Indonesian repertoires of *kront-
jong* and *pantun, ghoemaliedjies* were originally dancing songs with Afrikaans
lyrics, "on the caustic side," used to poke fun at people or situations.[26] *Nederlandsliedjies,* on the other hand, are slower songs sung to a Dutch text altered

---

simultaneously retain what we had conquered. We made of our otherness the norm, the
standard – and the ideal. And because the maintenance of our otherness is at the expense
of our fellow South Africans – and of our South Africanness – we felt ourselves threatened. We built walls. Not cities, but city walls. And like all bastards – uncertain about their
identity – we began to cling to the notion of purity. That is apartheid. Apartheid is the law
of the bastard."

23   Denis-Constant Martin, *Sounding the Cape,* 87.
24   Ronald Radano, *Lying a Nation, Race and Black Music* (Chicago: U of Chicago P, 2003),
     114–115.
25   Denis-Constant Martin, "Cape Town: The Ambiguous Heritage of Creolization in South
     Africa," in *Popular Snapshots and Tracks to the Past: Cape Town, Nairobi, Lubumbashi,* ed.
     Danielle de Lame and Ciraj Rassool (Royal Museum for Central Africa, 2010), 184; Denis-
     Constant Martin, *Sounding the Cape,* 67–68.
26   Denis-Constant Martin, *Sounding the Cape,* 112.

by oral transmission that often takes a romantic theme as its subject. Thought to have evolved from old Dutch songs and influenced by expressive forms absorbed from Islam (in particular the *adhan*, or Muslim call to prayer), *neder-landsliedjies* are responsorial with elements that sound both eastern and western: a soloist singing a melody characterized by melismatic ornamentations, and a choir answering in four-part harmony.

Both *ghoemaliedjies* and *nederlandsliedjies* are considered traditional music repertories of coloured and Cape Malay South Africans. Yet *Ghoema* also contains several folk songs that belong to an overlapping repertoire shared both by coloured and white Afrikaans-speakers, even if not always explicitly acknowledged by the latter. Part of *Ghoema's* power lies in demonstrating that a number of these songs were created by the slaves themselves who embedded hidden messages, often of a sexual nature, in the lyrics. These include "Vanaand gaan die volkies koring sny" (Tonight the folk will cut corn), "Die trane die rol oor jou, bokkie" (The tears are rolling over you, darling), and "Solank as die ri-etjie in die water lê" (As long as the reed is lying in the water). By way of an example, these three songs are all included in the *Federasie van Afrikaanse Kul-tuurereninginge* (FAK) *Sangbundel,* a collection of folk songs published by an institution historically associated with white Afrikaner nationalism.[27] There, these songs are each listed as a "S.A. Volkswysie" (South African Folk Song), arranged by either S.H. Eyssen or Dirkie de Villiers, both white Afrikaans composers. Taliep Petersen's stance to this perceived cultural appropriation is illustrated by comments he made in 2006, suggesting that the problem is not just with how these songs are presented, but with their very inclusion in the FAK-*Sangbundel*:[28]

> Baie van ons goete (Kaaps-Maleise liedjies) is daarin. Ons het dit niks gelaaik nie. Dis die hele ding van vat wat nie aan jou behoort nie. Ek het al boeke gesien met die naam Bóére sangbundel, dan wemel dit van Ma-leise musiek. My mense het wég gevoel daarvan. Ons is nié FAK nie.[29]

Part of *Ghoema's* subversion, then, is located in the rehabilitation of these folk songs by demonstrating that they are just as much the cultural "property" of

---

27   Dirkie De Villiers, et al, *Nuwe F.A.K.-sangbundel* (Cape Town: Nasionale Boekhandel Beperk, 1961), 463, 468, 483.

28   Hanlie Retief, "Afrikaans deur dik en dun," *Rapport* (Johannesburg), Feb. 26, 2006.

29   "A lot of our things (Cape Malay songs) are in it. We didn't like it at all. It's that whole thing of taking what doesn't belong to you. I have seen books before with the name, Boere song-book, then it crawls with Malay music. My people felt away from that. We are not FAK."

coloured South Africans. Related to this is another important way through which *Ghoema* attempts to right cultural misappropriation – through the use of Kaaps in its spoken and rapped text. "There is a huge misconception among people that Afrikaans is the oppressor's language," Petersen explained to a journalist shortly before the musical's opening at the Baxter Theatre. "But they don't understand that the slaves also used the language and they made a major contribution to this country."[30] Accordingly, one of the most important messages in *Ghoema* is that the Afrikaans language is one of the legacies of creolization at the Cape of Good Hope, and that slaves and slave descendants played a vital role in its creation. This message wasn't a fanciful political ploy, but the staging and popularization of established research. As Achmat Davids has established, already in the early nineteenth century the Cape Malay religious community used the language that would later be known as "Afrikaans" as a medium of instruction in their schools, and some of the first books written in this language were published in Arabic script.[31]

Ghoema's narrators, Minnah and Dina, explain the creole origins of Afrikaans simply, emphasizing as they do so those words that have their origin in the Southeast-Asian languages spoken by the slave population in the early years of the Cape Colony:

Minnah Die hele jaar werk die slawe oppie plaas. Hulle bou die huise, melkie koeie, pas die boer se kinnes op. Dra water aan, kap hout, vang vis innie see. Hulle werk oppie skippe en hulle werk innie kombuis.

Dina En daar tussen waar die sailors is, en waar die kos gekoek word, kom 'n nuwe taal na vore. 'n Taal wat almal kon vestaan. Met woorde soos baadjie, baie, baklei, blatjang, bredie, koejawel, kantoor, piering, piesang, soebat, tronk, rottang en sambok.[32]

---

30 Igsaan Salie, "A New Take on the History of Our Liedjies," *Saturday Weekend Argus* (Cape Town), Nov. 5, 2005.

31 Achmat Davids, *The Afrikaans of the Cape Muslims: From 1815 to 1915*, eds. Hein Willemse and Suleman E Dangor (Pretoria: Protea, 2011), 84–87.

32 "The whole year the slaves work on the farm. They build the houses, milk the cows, take care of the farmer's children. Carry water, chop wood, catch fish in the sea. They work on the ships and they work in the kitchen." "And there in-between where the sailors are, and where the food is cooked, a new language emerges. A language that everyone can understand. With words like jacket, much, fight, chutney, stew, guava, office, saucer, banana, beg, jail, cane and whip."

Simply put, *Ghoema* stakes a claim for Afrikaans as belonging to all who speak it, whether coloured or white. But in using that contested variant of Afrikaans long denied legitimacy by the white minority who claimed a "standardized" version of the language as core component of their own, exclusive identity, it goes a step further to lay claim to Kaaps as an equally legitimate form of the language. In this, it would join other artistic efforts, such as the work of hip-hop crews Brasse vannie Kaap and Prophets of da City, or the popular *Joe Barber* comedy shows. To these, years later, the 2010 stage show *Afrikaaps* would be added.

Exploring the roots of Western Cape folk music had long been a keen interest of Kramer's. As he explains, "For me, Ghoema was what I had wanted to do right from the beginning and which is what led me to District Six in the first place. It took twenty years for Taliep and I to amalgamate properly to have the same vision."[33] Petersen, who started his career as a six-year-old soloist in the Cape Coon Carnival, had grown up surrounded by the music presented in *Ghoema*, and speaking the language it showcased on the stage. Even though, as Kramer remembers, his writing partner had not been interested in pursuing a musical about slavery in the early years of their collaboration, Petersen, himself a slave descendant, had over the years gradually become more and more committed to exploring this part of his heritage. Besides actively claiming a slave heritage from the early 1990s onward, he also claimed to have traced his own ancestry to both Malacca and Indonesia.[34] Seven years before *Ghoema* was staged, he proudly addressed the audience of the concert *Two Worlds – One Heart,* held in Malaysia in 1998, as follows:

> I happen to be the ninth generation of Malay slaves. It took me exactly ... it took us three-hundred-and-seven years to come back home. My forefathers were taken from here as slaves, exactly three-hundred-and-seven years ago. I came in search of my roots in the year 1994, because as you know, we could not come to your country before that, nor could you come to my country. I was very proud and honoured to discover that, from my father's side, are we from an area called Malacca, and my father's surname, the family surname is Boeganoedien. From my mother's side, we're from an area in Indonesia, and their surname is Boerhaan. So, I can say proudly, I'm fully-fledged Malayu.[35]

---

33 David Kramer, personal interview, Nov. 1, 2012.
34 Paula Fourie, "Ghoema vannie Kaap," 275–280.
35 *Ibid.*, 277.

By 2005 Petersen was heavily invested in this aspect of his personal history, and increasingly interested in exploring the origins of the folk music with which he had grown up. Compared to the vast majority of coloured South Africans, this made him something of an anomaly. Kramer remembers that at the time, the history presented in *Ghoema* was as unknown to their company of coloured actors and musicians as it was to their audiences. In an e-mail, he explained as follows:

> It had an enormous impact on the way people saw themselves and their place in this South African story. My experience of developing this piece in rehearsal was that, although the musicians and singers had been deeply involved in their traditions (for example the 'Malay' choirs, *klopse*, *nagtroepe* etc.), they were completely in the dark about the history and origins of these traditions. Their personal family histories were also limited. Almost all the research that was brought into the rehearsal room was a revelation to them. And this is probably what the reaction was for most of our audiences [...] The connection to historical events and the syncretic process of creolization was completely absent. The ghoema drum is a good example of this. They were all very familiar with this drum, how it looked, how it was played and when and where it was used. So my question to them was: Why did they think it was constructed from plywood panels? Why was it different to a djembe drum? Why this drum and not a djembe? When I presented them with the historical connection to the wine vats found on farms and that the ghoema drum had evolved from these early farm instruments they began to understand how unique it is to the Cape and the part their forefathers and previous generations had played in most aspects of this creole culture.[36]

• • •

Given Kramer and Petersen's intentions with the piece, its content and its use of the ghoema drum as its central symbol, it readily presents itself to a reading through the lens of creolization theory. One such a reading has been performed by Afrikaans literary scholar, Hein Willemse.

Willemse touches on several of the aspects of *Ghoema* that I have discussed in this essay, highlighting in particular its strategy of claiming a history for

---

36   David Kramer, Email to author, April 23, 2017.

coloured South Africans, its demonstration of "métissage" in Cape musical forms, and its presentation of folk music as subversive in the Bakhtinian sense of the word.[37] Willemse finally reads *Ghoema,* with its continued emphasis on the uniqueness of Cape creole culture, as a declaration of a unique contemporary identity that runs the risk of – and indeed succumbs to – becoming a search for authenticity.[38] Ultimately, as Willemse cautions, this runs counter to creolization's central thesis. The claiming of a fixed identity is always incompatible with the ever-transformative power of creolization, a process which can lead to nothing other than, in Glissant's words, "a never ending change."[39] Said another way, there is no such thing as a creole identity, only a creolizing one.

This seems to be, at least for Willemse, the point at which *Ghoema* unintentionally forsakes the possibilities of creolization. Yet in reaching this conclusion, he also betrays a fundamental ontological bias towards Kramer's script. As a literary scholar, he seems to treat the musical as a fixed literary text; not as a performance, and not as music, both of which are ontologically fluid. Regarding *Ghoema* as the manifestation of a fixed identity, I would argue, is to deny its performative aspect, to forget that with every performance of *Ghoema,* meanings are generated anew between actors, musicians and audience. It is to forget that the future-orientated words of its final anthem, "Ghoema vannie Kaap," would ring out differently each night, each time it was performed.

> In die Kaap van Goeie Hoop
> Groei daar 'n blom
> Kan jy dit hoor?
> Daar's iets aan die kom!
> Dis die ghoema
> Die ghoema drom
> Hoor hoe slaan die ghoema
> Hoor hoe slaan die ghoema
> Die ghoema
> Die ghoema vanie Kaap[40]

---

37 Hein Willemse, "Kreolisering en Identiteit in die Musiekblyspel, Ghoema," *Stilet* 19, no.1 (2010): 34–38.

38 *Ibid.,* 38.

39 Qtd. in Denis-Constant Martin, *Sounding the Cape,* 63.

40 "In the Cape of Good Hope/ A flower is growing/ Can you hear it?/ Something is coming!/ It's the ghoema/ The ghoema drum/ Listen to the beat of the ghoema/ Listen to the beat of the ghoema/ The ghoema/ The ghoema of the Cape."

Reading *Ghoema* as a staged representation of creolization, my qualms were different to those of Willemse. For me, a fundamental aspect of creolization was conceptually missing (not ontologically contradicted) from the very start. This missing essence is the violence that ripped slaves and indentured labourers from their worlds, the cruelty that led them finally, in the words of Martin, to "on the one hand, bring together every faintest trace that could have been preserved from their own cultures and, on the other, to 'borrow' from the master's culture whatever could be used towards the reconstruction of their humanhood."[41]

This absence of violence in the musical is not confined to a theoretical understanding of creolization. The continued effects of South Africa's history of trauma and dispossession are very much present in the fabric of its every-day life. Testament to the importance of *Ghoema* is that the work makes it possible to ask fundamental questions about the performance of historical violence and trauma on a twenty-first century South African stage, particularly as it is performed through music. To do so is not to negate the brave and ground-breaking efforts of Kramer and Petersen in creating *Ghoema*. They took the history of violence against coloured South Africans seriously in their presentation of a new "truth" about the origins of creolized cultural practices. Rather, it is to question the nature of and the reasons for the domestication of violence in musical theatre. It is also to question whether staging a "truth" in this way in itself amounts to a form of restitution, or just its pale reflection. Put differently, could this particular inscription of the past really facilitate a claiming of the present?

After the run of *Ghoema!* at KKNK, the musical's reworking into *Ghoema* and its subsequent opening at the Baxter Theatre, it played at the University of Johannesburg's Arts Centre and in Stellenbosch's HB Thom Theatre. It also toured to the Netherlands and to London. In response to a question from me about the audience response to *Ghoema,* Kramer answered in an e-mail:

> The reaction at KKNK was very positive and enthusiastic which is what encouraged us to bring it to the city. Ton Vosloo said to me after seeing it in Oudtshoorn, 'Jy't die mense op 'n mooi manier vertel waarvandaan die taal kom [You told the people in a nice way where the language comes from].' Difficult for me to say what people thought. My impression was that our version of the roots of Cape creole (Afrikaans) and the

---

41   Denis-Constant Martin, *Sounding the Cape*, 86.

introduction of the contribution that was made by slaves was shocking for some and hugely liberating for others. It's possible that a few whites were uncomfortable with this perspective. But the general reaction was enthusiastic. It was a huge box office success and travelled internationally. For coloured audiences it conveyed a secret history. It was reaffirming. That it celebrated a topic and a history which people had suppressed and felt shameful about, was liberating.[42]

Kramer's easy equation here of the efficacy of *Ghoema* in conveying its "secret history" to its success as a commercial endeavor points to the meaning of such a domestication of violence in this performance. Had more whites been uncomfortable with its message, had it not been presented in a "mooi manier" [nice way], would *Ghoema* still have been a box office success? The history that *Ghoema* presents to its audiences can only be described as a painful one. Yet any vestige of pain is lost in the energetic playing and dancing on stage, in the exaggerated gestures of its actors that steer their performances dangerously close to caricature. To take us back to that opening instruction of "sit back, relax," erasure of the discomfort resulting from violence seems like a precondition to creating a piece with entertainment and commercial value.

Music means different things to different people. It also means different things to different people at different times. *Ghoema*'s musical landscape brims with toe-tapping, tonal celebrations of Cape culture. To many, this provided a positively uplifting experience, as is evident from the title of Mariana Malan's review in *Die Burger*: "'Ghoema' stuur jou met lied in die hart huis toe" ["Ghoema" sends you home with a song in the heart]. To what extent does music dull the pain of apartheid's violence in *Ghoema*? Judging from Malan's review in a newspaper with an overwhelming white Afrikaans readership, in no small measure. It did so precisely by emphasizing communality – through Afrikaans and this shared body of folk songs – between Afrikaners and formerly oppressed South Africans. Finding communality has become one way in which the former ruling class and their descendants can justify existing in privilege in the disfigured country of their birth. The reality of contemporary Afrikaans language politics is such that white denial of creolization has been replaced by an emphasis on a shared cultural heritage with formerly oppressed South Africans, if only in the interests of preserving said cultural heritage. The ease with

---

42   David Kramer, Email to author, April 23, 2017.

which this transition has been made begs the question of whether the music in *Ghoema* fulfils the function of diffusing trauma, of servicing the amnesia craved by the beneficiaries of apartheid and of lulling through easy-listening aesthetics the restless collective consciousness of white shame.

To what extent, finally, did *Ghoema* succeed in claiming the present for coloured South Africans? How has the "enormous impact" that Kramer speaks of translated into everyday life? *Ghoema*'s history lesson stops short just before the traumatic years of apartheid. There is a period of historical amnesia, if you will, that separates the musical's past from its present. In the painfully fractured environment of contemporary South Africa, it is hard to think of a purposefully didactic piece such as *Ghoema* as having taught its lesson in the way it really needed to have been heard. Fifteen years after it graced the stage to enthuse audiences and critics alike, the victims of its story are still very much on the margins, many of them living in poor conditions on the Cape Flats – apartheid's dumping ground – without access to all the opportunities promised to them after 1994.

Ultimately, *Ghoema* can productively be read as one of the many artistic projects that performed identity claims in Desmond Tutu's Rainbow Nation, with individuals and groups seeking to reconfigure their identities in a context where cultural pluralism and heritage were seen as key components in the nation building agenda.[43] This was before the politics of reconciliation began to give way so dramatically to the politics of decoloniality that inform this particular reading. Seen from the perspective of post-post-apartheid, *Ghoema*'s failure to translate its inscription of the past into a meaningful claiming of its present becomes an illustration of the fault lines in the geology of reconciliation that ultimately made the seismic shift towards decoloniality inevitable. Yet it also posits *Ghoema* as a performance "out of time," as it were. It suggests that the politics of meaning-making in post-post-apartheid South Africa have overtaken the horizons of possibility inherent in *Ghoema*. Socio-politically, the country moves to a different rhythm from its creolizing language and repertoire. Right now, at least, the pulsating and energetic ghoema beat is simply too slow.

---

43   Heike Becker, "A Hip-Hopera in Cape Town: The Aesthetics, and Politics of Performing 'Afrikaaps,'" *Journal of African Cultural Studies* 29, no. 2 (2017): 246, http://repository.uwc .ac.za/xmlui/bitstream/handle/10566/3042/Beker_A-hip-hopera_2017.pdf?sequence=3& isAllowed=y.

Works Cited

Adhikari, Mohamed. "From Narratives of Miscegenation to Post-Modernist Re-Imagining: Toward a Historiography of Coloured Identity in South Africa." *African Historical Review* 40, no. 1 (2008): 77–100.

Becker, Heike. "A Hip-Hopera in Cape Town: The Aesthetics, and Politics of Performing 'Afrikaaps.'" *Journal of African Cultural Studies* 29, no. 2 (2017): 244–259. http://repository.uwc.ac.za/xmlui/bitstream/handle/10566/3042/Beker_A-hip-hopera_2017.pdf?sequence=3&isAllowed=y.

Brand, Gerrit. "'Ghoema' Kraai Koning by Fleur du Cap-Teaterpryse." *Beeld* (Johannesburg), March 8 2006.

Breytenbach, Breyten. *Parool/Parole: Versamelde Toesprake/Collected Speeches*. Cape Town: Penguin, 2015.

Davids, Achmat. *The Afrikaans of the Cape Muslims: From 1815 to 1915*. Edited by Hein Willemse and Suleman E Dangor. Pretoria: Protea, 2011.

De Villiers, Dirkie et al. *Nuwe F.A.K.-sangbundel*. Cape Town: Nasionale Boekhandel Bpk, 1961.

Decker, Jeffrey Louis. "The State of Rap: Time and Place in Hip Hop Nationalism." *Social Text* 34 (1993): 53–84.

Erasmus, Zimitri. "Introduction: Re-Imagining Coloured Identities in Post-Apartheid South Africa." In *Coloured by History, Shaped by Place: New Perspectives on Coloured Identities in the Cape*, edited by Zimitri Erasmus, 13–28. Kwela and South African History Online, 2001.

Fourie, Paula. *"Ghoema vannie Kaap": The Life and Work of Taliep Petersen (1950–2006)*. Dissertation, University of Stellenbosch, 2013.

Glissant, Édouard. *Poetics of Relation*. Translated by Betsy Wing. Ann Arbor: University of Michigan Press, 2010.

Glissant, Édouard. *Caribbean Discourse: Selected Essays*. Translated and with an introduction by J. Michael Dash. Charlottesville: University of Virginia Press, 1989.

Hanmer, Paul. Personal Interview. 29 November 2011.

Kramer, David and Taliep Petersen. *Ghoema: Die Storie van Kaapse Musiek*. DVD, Blik, 2009.

Kramer, David. Email Correspondence. 23 April 2017.

Kramer, David. Personal Interview. 1 November 2012.

Malan, Mariana. "'Ghoema Stuur Jou Met Lied in die Hart Huis Toe." *Die Burger* (Cape Town), Nov. 18, 2005.

Martin, Denis-Constant. *Sounding the Cape: Music, Identity and Politics in South Africa*. Somerset West: African Minds, 2013.

Martin, Denis-Constant. "Cape Town: The Ambiguous Heritage of Creolization in South Africa." In *Popular Snapshots and Tracks to the Past: Cape Town, Nairobi,*

Lubumbashi, edited by Danielle de Lame and Ciraj Rassool, 183–202. Royal Museum for Central Africa, 2010.

Nkonyeni, Ncedisa. "Da Struggle Kontinues into the 21st Century: Two Decades of Nation-Conscious Rap in Cape Town." In *Imagining the City: Memories and Cultures in Cape Town*, edited by Sean Field et al, 151–172. Cape Town: HSRC Press, 2007.

Petersen, Taliep. Interview with Denis-Constant Martin. 15 November 1994.

Radano, Ronald. *Lying a Nation, Race and Black Music.* Chicago: University of Chicago Press, 2003.

Retief, Hanlie, "Afrikaans deur dik en dun." *Rapport* (Johannesburg), Feb. 26, 2006.

Salie, Igsaan. "A New Take on the History of Our Liedjies." *Saturday Weekend Argus* (Cape Town), Nov. 5, 2005.

Shell, Robert C.-H. *Children of Bondage: A Social History of the Slave Society at the Cape of Good Hope, 1652–1838.* Johannesburg: Witwatersrand UP, 1994.

Willemse, Hein. "Kreolisering en Identiteit in die Musiekblyspel, *Ghoema.*" *Stilet* 19, no.1 (2010): 30–42.

Zvomuya, Percy. "Singing History from the Cape of Sorrows." *Mail & Guardian* (Johannesburg) June 21, 2007. https://mg.co.za/article/2007-06-21-singing-history-from-the-cape-of-sorrows.

CHAPTER 17

Shakespeare versus Shakespeare: Notes on Theatre-Making from Belgium to South Africa

Chris Thurman

Abstract

This essay explores both the material conditions and the historical-political contexts for theatre-making in South Africa by focusing on recent Shakespearean productions. To this end, the author pursues some transnational comparisons. His starting-point is *Ten Oorlog*, Tom Lanoye and Luk Perceval's 1997 rendering of Shakespeare's history cycles for a Belgian audience, later translated into German as *Schlachten!* (1999). The creation and reception of this work has echoes, twenty years later, in discussions around modernising, translating and adapting (or "tradapting") Shakespeare in South Africa. The title's reference to "Shakespeare versus Shakespeare" carries various implications: the insights that connecting Shakespeare in Belgium to Shakespeare in South Africa might bring, as well as the boldness of attending to the local without shying away entirely from the permutations of "universality."

In this essay I want to argue with myself – or, at least, I want to explore a contrary position to one I have up until now adopted regarding Shakespeare in/ and South Africa. Shakespeare is a relatively marginal concern when it comes to South African theatre; yet, as I hope to show, those considerations that apply to staging Shakespeare can also be applied in trying to understand the undercurrents and crosscurrents of theatre-making more generally in our national context. I am thus concerned here with Shakespeare in performance, rather than Shakespeare in the classroom or a more "literary" approach to Shakespeare-as-text, although inevitably these three phenomena overlap and intersect in numerous ways.

I have previously been a strong opponent of invocations or manifestations of Shakespearean "universality" in a (South African) postcolonial or decolonial context.[1] I have argued for specificity, or "singularity," in producing Shakespeares:

---

1 See Thurman, "From Shakespearean Singularity to Singular Shakespeares"; "Multilingual Shakespeare"; "After Titus"; "Generation S."

attentiveness to local context, to the consequences of South Africa's political and socio-economic history for the relationship between members of an audience (or perhaps readers) and "Shakespeare" – whether that appellation is used to refer to a Shakespearean play, to the Shakespearean canon, to Shakespeare as an historical figure or to Shakespeare as a symbol. This does not mean turning every Shakespeare production into a national allegory or a contrived commentary on current affairs (a well-intentioned impulse that nonetheless carries its own perils). But if theatre makers want to avoid repeating colonial or apartheid tropes, they have to work hard to resist the imperial remnants that shaped (and still shape) the ways in which South Africans of all stripes think about Shakespeare. This has implications for every decision from casting to costuming, from marketing to stage-managing, and indeed – prior to these – to the treatment of the text: translation, modernising, adaptation.

"Universality" is, of course, also not a word with a fixed meaning. In recent years, scholars such as Kiernan Ryan and Ewan Fernie have both presented impassioned defences of Shakespeare's significance on the grounds that his work gives expression to an egalitarian impulse, to the eternal human cry for freedom.[2] Whereas Ryan sees in this impulse the grounds of a truly liberating Shakespearean universality – "the profound commitment of Shakespeare's drama to the emancipation of humanity"[3] – Fernie is more uncomfortable with the ambiguity of the term: he is disdainful of "the myth that Shakespeare is deathless and universal"[4] but is drawn to those who have recruited Shakespeare to their fight for "universal suffrage."[5] The South African Shakespeareans Laurence Wright, David Schalkwyk and Natasha Distiller each make a convincing case for redeeming the notion of universality as it pertains either to "ethical universals … the universal freedoms increasingly visible on history's far horizon"[6] or to Shakespeare not as "*the* voice of humanity," but as "*a* voice that captures something which might be universally human" in the context of

2 One might see this as a resurgence of the felt need to vindicate Shakespeare as a "radical" figure, a view that has receded somewhat since the heyday of cultural materialism and new historicism in the 1980s and early 1990s – and one that risked being replaced, in the years building to the 2016 quatercentenary, by effusive Shakespearean "criticism" approaching a kind of Bardolatry.

3 Kiernan Ryan, *Shakespeare's Universality: Here's Fine Revolution* (London: Bloomsbury/Arden, 2015), 5.

4 Ewan Fernie, *Shakespeare for Freedom: Why the Plays Matter* (Cambridge: Cambridge UP, 2017), 18.

5 *Ibid.*, 20.

6 Laurence Wright, "'Thinking with Shakespeare': The Merchant of Venice – Shylock, Caliban and the dynamics of social scale," *Shakespeare in Southern Africa* 29 (2017): 22.

the cognitive turn in the arts and humanities.[7] There remains nonetheless a stubborn and influential version of universality that, as I have repeatedly claimed, perpetuates a model in which cultural capital is held in the metropolitan (neo-colonial) "centre" and distributed for consumption in the "periphery" of the global south; and this is, more often than not, still tied to a pseudo-historicist and almost hagiographical celebration of "the man Shakespeare," as well as of the society that produced him.

Imagine my surprise, then, at finding myself cheering on a production of *Shakespeare in Love* in Cape Town: a piece of theatre shipped over from the West End, itself derived from a Hollywood film and owned by Disney, that seems to depend heavily on a pre-existing audience fascination with the much-mythologised Shakespearean biographical subject. So much for opposing universality!

•••

To explain my about-turn, a stalking horse of sorts is required – a way of getting at this Shakespearean paradox from a different angle. It is only appropriate, given that the present volume owes its existence to a Belgian / South African collaboration (the "New Stage Idioms" conference on South African drama, theatre and performance held in Brussels in 2017), that my starting point is a transnational one: *Ten Oorlog*, Tom Lanoye and Luk Perceval's 1997 rendering of Shakespeare's history cycles for a Belgian audience, later translated into German as *Schlachten!* (1999). This epic undertaking, first performed in the Flemish city of Ghent, became a landmark production in terms of European – arguably, global – Shakespeare. Even though there is a small but substantial body of scholarship and critical writing about *Ten Oorlog* in English, however, it is not widely known among anglophone Shakespeare scholars and theatre makers. Certainly, it is not a work that has any purchase on the South African theatre scene.

Yet Lanoye's connection to the country is a significant one. He began visiting South Africa in the early 1990s, during the transition to democracy; nowadays, he divides his time between homes in Antwerp and Cape Town. South Africa does not feature prominently in his work, although there are notable traces. In a story like "Johannesburg, Le Bain (Een Reisverhaal)," from the 1994 collection *Spek en Bonen*, the travelogue mode allows both for reflection on the city and its residents, and for a turn inwards – towards memories of

---

7   Natasha Distiller, "On Being Human," in *South African Essays on "Universal" Shakespeare*, ed. Chris Thurman, (Burlington: Ashgate, 2014), 19–20.

childhood in Flanders, one of the author's abiding preoccupations. Lanoye has also collaborated with South African writers and performers, most notably Antjie Krog, who translated his *Mamma Medea* into Afrikaans in 2001 and subsequently joined him on stage for installments of the *Geletterde Mensen* series. In 2019, Lanoye's rendition of *King Lear*, *Koningin Lear* (2015), was translated into Afrikaans – again by Krog – and directed by Marthinus Basson, with Antoinette Kellerman in the title role. Lanoye's relationship to South Africa and South Africans is, however, probably best captured in an interview he gave soon after one of his early visits to the country, in which he professed a certain admiration for (perhaps even envy of) the urgent sense of political engagement among South African writers and artists. This was "totally different" to the paradigm he typically encountered in Belgium, which was "the absolute task of the absolute writer": a responsibility to be concerned first and foremost with one's own craft.[8] Insofar as such a version of *l'art pour l'art* (where the criteria for relevance are primarily, if not purely, "formal and aesthetic") "does not exist" in South Africa, Lanoye found this "liberating"; although he does not believe that political engagement should be every artist's priority, he is temperamentally inclined "to evolve with the zeitgeist."[9]

There is no doubt that Belgian current affairs of the 1990s informed the conceptualising and writing of *Ten Oorlog* – but to what degree, and to what effect, is a contested matter. The ambitious project started when Perceval, planning a production of *Richard* III, came to the conclusion that the play would make no sense to a Belgian audience unless they were familiar with its "prequels": *Richard* II, *Henry* IV parts one and two, *Henry* V, and the three *Henry* VI plays. That is, they would need to know enough about the Wars of the Roses to understand what it means for Richard III to be a Yorkist and Henry Tudor / Henry VII to be a Lancastrian. But did they need to be subjected to a "chaotic" storyline, "a baffling set of conspiracies, marriages, murder, and battles; a pandemonium of forty acts, two hundred scenes and three hundred characters"?[10] Perceval thought not, and thus invited Lanoye to pen a translation and adaptation that would condense the material and make it accessible to a contemporary audience. The result was the division (or redistribution) of eight Shakespeare plays into a three-part cycle, sometimes performed separately and sometimes

---

8   Jos Joosten, *Tom Lanoye: De ontoereikendheid van het abstracte* (Amsterdam: SUN / Kritak, 1996), 15. Here and where necessary throughout this chapter, I have translated from Flemish/Dutch into English.

9   *Ibid.*

10   Ton Hoenselaars, "Two Flemings at war with Shakespeare," in *Shakespeare's History Plays: Performance, Translation and Adaptation in Britain and Abroad*, ed. Ton Hoenselaars (Cambridge: Cambridge UP, 2004), 245.

sequentially in a ten-hour theatrical marathon: 1. "In de Naam van de Vader en de Zoon" ("In the Name of the Father and the Son"), 2. "Zie de Dienstmaagd des Heren" ("Behold the Handmaid of the Lord"), and 3. "En Verlos Ons van het Kwade" ("And Deliver Us from Evil").

Much scholarship on *Ten Oorlog* cites Lanoye's quip[11] that names like Richmond and Kent are known to Belgians not as historical figures, or as characters in the history plays, but rather as cigarette brands. Although this assertion of the "foreignness" of the Shakespearean material in Belgium is pithy, it is not entirely accurate. Firstly, the history plays are concerned not only with English but also with European history, albeit from an English perspective; as Ton Hoenselaars observes, having a character like John of Gaunt / Jan van Gent in *Richard* II / *Richaar Deuzième* speaking in Flemish on a stage in the city from which he actually took his name troubles the notion of "foreign history": "Appropriation here was really a case of reappropriation."[12] Secondly, the "European" dimensions of Shakespeare's histories have multilingual implications – so a polyglot play like *Henry* V makes for interesting case studies of numerous French and Dutch translations.[13] Thirdly, while Richmond and Kent may be familiar geographical place names to people in England, it is something of an overstatement on Lanoye's part to declare that this "grounding in historical truth" automatically makes figures from medieval English history more familiar to contemporary audiences in Britain than to those in Belgium.[14]

Nonetheless, *Ten Oorlog* was very much aimed at the latter. The primary feature of this aim was, obviously, linguistic. In the opening scenes of Part One, we are presented with what seems (for the most part) a curtailed but "straight" translation of *Richard* II into a somewhat archaic and formal Flemish/Dutch, interrupted by Richard and his courtiers' occasional affected French. The language power battle alluded to here can only be properly appreciated in the context of Belgium's "language wars," with French-speaking Wallonia and Brussels historically maintaining the economic and political upper hand. This has changed in recent decades, however, and the Vlaams of Flanders is no longer "secondary" (indeed, writers and cultural practitioners like Lanoye and Perceval have contributed to a form of Flemish language activism). As Belgium has changed, so have its languages; by the time we get to Part Three, culminating not in *Richard* III but in *Risjaar Modderfokker den Derde* – the moniker

---

11   Jozef De Vos, "Jozef de Vos in gesprek met Tom Lanoye en Luc Joosten," *Documenta: Tijdschrift voor theater* 16, no. 2 (Special volume, 1998): 116.

12   Ton Hoenselaars, "Two Flemings at war with Shakespeare," 252.

13   See: Dirk Delabastita, "A Great Feast of Languages: Shakespeare's Multilingual Comedy in King Henry V and the Translator," *The Translator* 8, no. 2 (2002): 303–340.

14   Jozef De Vos, "Jozef de Vos in gesprek," 116.

needs no translating – the fragmenting of Shakespeare's plays is echoed in linguistic heterogeneity, a kind of hip-hop "street" Dutch infused with bursts of English that could variously be described as scat, patter or patois.

Other examples of Belgian "localising" include such adjustments as turning Henry v's victory at Agincourt in 1415 into an earlier moment of French defeat: Guldensporenslag, the Battle of the Golden Spurs at Courtrai/Kortrijk in 1302, when a rebellious army of Flemish foot soldiers defeated the cavalry of the ruling French nobles. (This also, incidentally, speaks to an historical connection between England and Belgium; from the early modern period through to the nineteenth century, many Flemish leaders took the side of the English in conflicts with France.) It would be impossible to sustain such local references, or to apply them consistently, if Lanoye and Perceval were attempting to stay true to the Shakespearean storyline. Never mind that Henry was the invader at Agincourt, as opposed to the Flemish who revolted at Kortrijk against French occupation; the Battle of the Golden Spurs took place almost a century before the Wars of the Roses began. But, as becomes clear mid-way through Part One of *Ten Oorlog*, Lanoye and Perceval neither wished simply to depict Shakespeare's version of medieval English history in Flemish, nor did they wish to depict a specifically Flemish (or, for that matter, French) medieval history. Rather, their interest was threefold: to address a very particular local context – a *now*; to sketch a broad historical trajectory stretching towards this present from a distant past – a *then*; and to meditate on certain archetypal, or "universal," truths about human beings and the exercise of power – an *everywhen*. The question of whether or not these three contradict and undermine each other is of central importance here.

• • •

Lanoye's writerly instinct to respond to the national zeitgeist meant that *Ten Oorlog* was framed in terms of high-profile issues in Belgian politics of the 1990s. Crammed between the momentous events in greater Europe following the fall of the Berlin Wall in 1989 and the postcolonial reckoning that Belgium would face at the end of the decade – a matter to which I shall return – were two key developments of national concern. Hoenselaars summarises these neatly:

> In many interviews and press statements Lanoye and Perceval went out of their way to stress the contemporary relevance of their Shakespearean adaptation. On one level, Shakespeare's troubled sequence of English kings was said to rehearse the Belgian apprehension over the monarchy

at the sudden death in 1993 of the childless and pious dreamer King Bau-
douin ... the production [also] appealed to a series of interrelated concerns about the political, juridical as well as moral rule and misrule of the
Belgian nation following, among other things, the discovery in the mid-
1990s of a network of child abuse centring on Marc Dutroux.[15]

The analogy between Baudouin/Boudewijn and Henry VI was there, Lanoye
and Perceval felt, for all to see; both were figures of *le roi triste*, "The errant king
full of self-pity, unable to father a child. 'Why did I have to become king at such
an early age?' ... utterly alienated from the realities of the world."[16] The child
abuse scandal, which exposed various high level cover-ups and revealed numerous shortcomings in the Belgian legal system, did not have such a ready
correlative in Shakespeare's history plays. This resonance was created in *Ten
Oorlog* by changing the ages and stage presences of a handful of characters:
Richard II's queen, Anne, is a young child; Henry VI is a boy who never quite
grows up; the princes killed in the tower by Richard III are presented as half-
eaten corpses on which the butcher-king gorges himself; and Henry Tudor,
supposed bringer of peace and reconciliation, is a naked toddler reciting a
nursery rhyme.

Another "abused" child is Henk (Prince Hal); Lanoye and Perceval turned
Bolingbroke/Henry IV into the cruel and homophobic father of a son who is
uncertain of his sexual orientation. Henk takes refuge in genderqueer La Falstaff, by turns surrogate mother and lover. As in *Henry V*, when Hal takes the
crown he rejects Falstaff – but in this case, as Hoenselaars explains, he does so
"with a right-wing rigour that glorifies virility, male authority and reactionary
views of the family":

> Ten Oorlog appropriates the troubled relationship between Henry IV, La
> Falstaff and Hal, in order to position right-wing rule and sexual licence as
> the twin poles of a socio-political conflict. The carnal excesses and crimes
> of the Dutroux affair were by many seen as the political and juridical fail-
> ure of the Christian Democrats. This climate of opinion worked in favour
> of the Flemish right-wing party which launched a renewed assault on the
> permissive society which accepted pornography and homosexuality.[17]

---

15   Ton Hoenselaars, "Two Flemings at war with Shakespeare," 260.
16   *Ibid.*
17   *Ibid.*, 250–251.

If this was art reflecting life, then life reflected art when *Ten Oorlog* prepared for its German debut as *Schlachten!* at the Salzburger Festspiele in Austria two years later. Prior to opening night, the powers-that-be in Salzburg put an age restriction on the production; this was understood to be an act of censorship in a country "increasingly marked by extreme right-wing tendencies."[18] The ban was lifted, but the irony was largely missed – and the brief controversy also had the effect of drowning out the play's pertinence to Belgian socio-political concerns.

Schlachten! subsequently transferred to Hamburg, where it was tremendously popular; it has since taken on various incarnations on German and Austrian stages, most recently in Freiburg in 2016. The shift from Belgium to Germany is interesting for historical reasons – if one compares the scope and scale of Shakespeare in the Low Countries to the German Shakespeare industry[19] – but, for present purposes, the more important consideration is the nature of the production's initial reception in Germany. Hoenselaars judges German reviewers to have "missed what might be termed a serious and explicit political engagement"; at best, "some reviewers admired the bleak power struggles taken over from Shakespeare, struggles conducted not for a specific purpose but pursued for their own sake."[20] Others, however, denied the play's political credentials. Veteran German Shakespearean Maik Hamburger went so far as to declare that "Politics as a social category, as the totality of decision-making mechanisms through which public interests are coordinated, has been severely alienated from [*Schlachten!*]. One would almost think that there is more political material in every single history play ... than in the entire trilogy."[21] Hoenselaars proposes that German critics valued Lanoye and Perceval's "iconoclastic

---

18   *Ibid.*, 253.
19   Shakespeare in the Low Countries is not a marginal concern, but placed against Shakespeare in Germany it is inevitably a more modest phenomenon. Although Shakespeare was probably first translated for performance into German in the early decades of the seventeenth century, his work was first published in translation in Dutch in 1621. Yet while German Bardolatry was in full swing in the eighteenth and nineteenth centuries, the first Flemish Shakespeare production only took place in 1884. Surveying "Shakespeare on the Flemish Stage of Belgium" in 1952, D. De Gruyter and Wayne Hayward were at pains to defend Flemish theatre to an international readership; thirty to forty years later, leading Flemish Shakespeare scholar Jozef de Vos would be in a position to send regular updates on "Shakespeare in Belgium" to *Shakespeare Quarterly*, as a generation of translators and directors (including, along with Lanoye and Perceval, "postdramatic" theatre makers like Jan Decorte, Jan Lauwers and Peter Verhelst; see Stalpaert) tackled Shakespeare's work. Nonetheless, in quantitative terms, Germany still outdoes Belgium – as it does every other country in the world – when it comes to Shakespeare on stage.
20   Ton Hoenselaars, "Two Flemings at war with Shakespeare," 253.
21   *Ibid.*

verve" and their "bold representation of language, sex and gender,"²² but lacked
the frame of reference to properly appreciate their politics.

This is, however, only part of the story. While the relationship between *Ten Oorlog* and contemporary Belgian politics was presented in author interviews and other publicity material both before and after the premiere season, this was not the sole paradigm provided by the creators. Much of their discussion of the trilogy emphasised history in a very broad sense. As Jürgen Pieters observed at the time, "Perceval and Lanoye want less history, but ironically enough they simultaneously want more history. In place of a hundred year War of the Roses they want 'an impression of seven hundred years of humanity.'"²³ Jozef de Vos writes that Lanoye and Perceval's desire to "transcend" the medieval English material was matched by a desire to "record nothing less ambitious than the evolution of Western society."²⁴ *Ten Oorlog*, according to its creators' notes in the original production programme, should be understood as "beginning in the autumn of the feudal period and ending in the brackish pool of war and pollution that the world is today." This undermines the notion that nuances were lost when *Ten Oorlog* crossed the border as *Schlachten!*; with such a broad historical-political purview, there would be little difference between German and Belgian audiences.²⁵ But Lanoye and Perceval were also looking beyond a putatively 'Eurocentric' history – in addition to the *now* and *then*, as I have suggested, they also saw the trilogy as playing out in an *every-when*: a geographical and temporal "theatrical no-man's land."²⁶

Pieters notes that such a vision is in line with the "universalist" discourse of Perceval in particular, who had consciously presented previous theatrical work in terms of "the universal search for meaning ... humans, tormented by their demons, searching for peace, harmony and balance."²⁷ This "search for salvation" is not concerned with "singular, unique individuals" but with "mythical figures" and "Jungian archetypes," with rituals that "surpass history."²⁸ Such language, you would think, ought to set alarm bells ringing for a politically committed writer such as Lanoye who wishes to attend to the "singular" conditions

---

22   *Ibid.*

23   Jürgen Pieters, *Die Honden van King Lear* (Groningen: Historische Uitgeverij, 1999), 64.

24   Jozef De Vos, "Shakespeare's History Plays in Belgium: Taken Apart and Reconstructed as 'Grand Narrative,'" in *Four Hundred Years of Shakespeare in Europe*, ed. A. Luis Pujante and Ton Hoenselaars (London: Associated University Presses, 2003), 213.

25   Wouter Hessels (18) identifies a different "European trajectory" beyond the play's "Belgian roots": "The conflicts in the Balkans were certainly present ... and the Yugoslav crisis, erupting into war in the very heart of Europe, gave it a very explicit context."

26   Jozef De Vos, "Jozef de Vos in gesprek," 117.

27   Jürgen Pieters, *Die Honden van King Lear*, 54.

28   *Ibid.*

that prevail in his country. But an impasse is avoided because, it appears, Shakespeare's work can accommodate both approaches. One the one hand, *Ten Oorlog* replaces Shakespearean references with Belgian references: Pieters lists, in addition to the Guldensporenslag, allusions to the Ijzertoren (a First World War memorial and a symbol of Flemish nationalism); to Belgian poets Guido Gezelle, Alice Nahon and Paul Snoek; to a very British rallying cry being transformed into "Everything for Flanders, and Flanders for Christ."[29] On the other hand, "an aspect of history is retained that *is* found in Shakespeare and that is not local ... this history is universal, and therefore also ours":

> That this is perfectly possible with Shakespeare's work is, according to Perceval and Lanoye, easily declared: somewhere under the layer of dust of specific history sits, if you blow and polish long enough, "a general story about the war for power, fed by conflict, faithlessness and betrayal."[30]

This is the *everywhen*, the "universal" history in *Ten Oorlog* – below the *now* of Belgium in the 1990s, below the *then* of seven centuries of European history. It would seem to match a cyclical concept of time – not the casual use of "cycles" to describe Shakespeare's two tetralogies of history plays, but something closer to eternal recurrence. The thematic treatment of the three parts of *Ten Oorlog* is thus appropriate; first we see the archetypal conflict based on fathers and sons, then conflict between the sexes, then the war against the self. Ultimately, the struggle is for nothing – after witnessing ten hours of violent confrontation, we end with something we have seen before: a child-king who is presumably going to make the same mistakes as the child-kings who came before him.

The traditional approach to Shakespeare's history plays (one that had "had its day" by the time *Ten Oorlog* came along;[31]) affirmed that, while they were not written or performed in an order matching the historical timeline on which they depend, there is an implied trajectory: the mess started in *Richard* II is eventually resolved eighty years later at the end of *Richard* III, ushering in the Tudor era. But what about all the sub-plots and sub-sub-plots, the vast array of characters, the digressions – precisely the material that Perceval and Lanoye chose to cut because it was deemed too confusing or distracting? This is where Shakespeare's portrayal differs from the chroniclers' accounts that were his source material, with their narrative of a divinely ordained progression from medieval past to early modern present. It is evidence, for Pieters, of

---

29   *Ibid.*, 64.
30   *Ibid.*
31   See: Jozef De Vos, "Shakespeare's History Plays in Belgium," 212.

Shakespeare's interest in "the heterogeneity of the past"; and it is opposed to, or at least complicates, "the one big story" that follows "the great line of universal history,"[32] which is what Perceval and Lanoye present in *Ten Oorlog*. "It is at least a remarkable and somewhat paradoxical phenomenon," observes De Vos, that a "radical adaptation" like *Ten Oorlog* "seems to take apart the two-fold cycle in order to construct a new and even more comprehensive 'grand narrative,' as if the authors wanted to counter the fragmentation of postmodern culture."[33]

Instead of fragmentation, what we have is a "rising" plot, even if it is one that reaches "a climax of violence and loneliness" and rather bleakly confirms "the more things change, the more they stay the same."[34] Ultimately, Pieters suggests, there may be a "strictly contemporary message" for audiences of *Ten Oorlog*, but this requires them to look askance – like a viewer studying a perspectival painting – so that they can see past the "undisguised universalism" expressed by Lanoye and Perceval in the publicity material.

•••

Another way of approaching the conundrum of *Ten Oorlog*'s simultaneous commitment to "local politics" and "universal history" – with the latter, as Pieters presents it, overwhelming the former – is to think about the production in the context of postdramatic theatre. As a critical term and as a conceptual category, "postdramatic" has perhaps become somewhat overworn and, consequently, too broad in its application.[35] Still, Hans-Thies Lehmann's coinage retains some purchase; Christel Stalpaert, for one, has applied it productively to the work of contemporary Flemish theatre practitioners like Jan Decorte, Jan

---

32   Jürgen Pieters, *Die Honden van King Lear*, 64–65.

33   Jozef De Vos, "Shakespeare's History Plays in Belgium," 213.

34   Jozef De Vos, Jürgen Pieters and Laurens de Vos, *Shakespeare: Auteur voor alle seizoenen* [e-book] (Tielt: Lannoo Maulenhoff, 2016), n.p.

35   There is also a changing geopolitical context to consider. What Hans-Thies Lehmann observed in the decade prior to the publication of his book *Postdramatisches Theater* (1999) was a move away from the socio-political engagement that had characterised theatre (particularly in divided Germany) from the late 1960s to the 1980s. Arguably, postdramatic theatre is not politically committed in the same way that Brechtian theatre is, even if both "disrupt" the audience-performer contract of suspended disbelief. Lehmann has, however, subsequently observed that global developments in the early years of the twenty-first century have driven postdramatic theatre makers back to socio-economic and political questions (see Lehmann, "'Postdramatic Theatre,' a Decade Later"; see also Jürs-Munby, Carroll and Giles' *Postdramatic Theatre and the Political*).

Lauwers and Peter Verhelst (see Stalpaert, "Something is Rotten" and "Enter Ghost").

It is telling that Stalpaert doesn't mention Lanoye and Perceval in this company – especially insofar as the postdramatic entails an emphasis on the visual rather than the textual, the meta-dramatic rather than narrative and character.[36] However subversive, playful and provocative *Ten Oorlog* may be, its creators remain committed to story and sense-making, to dialogue between characters in a self-contained and more or less coherent fictional universe.[37] They are, moreover – Lanoye in particular – committed to text: to the play-script as the basis of performance and as its artifact, as well as a "literary" work in its own right. De Vos and Pieters remind us that the published text of *Ten Oorlog* (which has been through numerous editions, from collectors' box sets to paperback volumes) is as much of a theatrical landmark as the staging itself. Hoenselaars notes that the translation of the text into German, in which it was "edited and annotated to preserve and protect Lanoye and Perceval's intellectual property," further demonstrated how "*Ten Oorlog*, lauded for its iconoclastic zeal vis-à-vis the literary canon, was eventually, under the pressure of Western market forces and the rule of copyright to which Shakespeare himself is not entitled, endowed with canonical status in its own right."[38]

This brings us to Lanoye's much-touted "oedipal relationship with Shakespeare"[39] – the notion that, with *Ten Oorlog*, he enacted a Bloomian killing-off of his strong precursor. But Hoenselaars has also called this "a combined case of Shakespearomania and bardophobia":[40] for *Ten Oorlog* is equally an act of tribute, of careful and sustained engagement with the plays. Lanoye's war with Shakespeare is "a paradoxical battle in which the Fleming simultaneously vents his destructive, iconoclastic urge and must acknowledge the creative energies that are released by killing Shakespeare"; thus, "a profound urge to subvert the playwright's almost inescapable hegemony in order to find a personal voice" is matched by "a desire for cultural identification with one of

---

36   Ironically, postdramatic theatre's interest in the "tableau" is perhaps not that far off from early twentieth century Shakespearean experiments in Flanders, which – using "Rembrandt lighting" – sought to make each scene "more like a Flemish painting than a stage set" (De Gruyter and Hayward 108).

37   An argument for analysing *Ten Oorlog* in a post-dramatic paradigm may nonetheless be made; see Van Den Abbeele. For further comparisons between *Ten Oorlog* and other contemporary Belgian/Dutch Shakespeare (the histories in particular), see De Vos and Pieters.

38   Ton Hoenselaars, "Two Flemings at war with Shakespeare," 255.

39   *Ibid.*, 258.

40   *Ibid.*

western literature's most popular icons."[41] Or perhaps, Hoenselaars has hinted elsewhere, it works the other way around: perhaps sincere "admiration for Shakespeare" is actually what "produces a need to destroy the sacrosanct image that Shakespearomaniacs have been constructing" for centuries.[42]

Either way, if the success of *Ten Oorlog* was partly dependent on, but also further entrenched, Lanoye's cultural status – part of a decades-long shift from "bad boy" to eminent figure in Flemish literature and theatre – the production also had the effect of revivifying Shakespeare.[43] Arguably it paved the way for later epic productions from the low countries like Ivo van Hove's combined Dutch "cycle" of Roman plays, *Roman Tragedies* (2007), which has had a greater impact in the anglophone theatre world. In its own right, however, *Ten Oorlog* was (and remains) a landmark in Belgian theatre history: "the major theatre event over two seasons" when it premiered, "an artistic and commercial success" whose popular and critical reception was echoed in Germany and other European countries, and followed over the next fifteen years by "a series of sell-out revivals and spectacular sales of the printed text."[44]

···

What might all of this mean for South Africans who have an interest in the staging of Shakespeare's plays? The best way to pursue this transnational comparison is to consider again the challenges and opportunities presented by multilingual contexts. In his introduction to *Shakespeare and the Language of Translation*, Ton Hoenselaars identifies two main strands in Shakespearean "tradaptation" around the world. On the one hand, there are the postcolonial concerns of translators, playwrights and directors in Africa, Asia and South

---

41   Ton Hoenselaars, ed. *Shakespeare and the Language of Translation* (London: Bloomsbury/Arden, 2012), 17.

42   Ton Hoenselaars, "There is Tremendous Poetry in Killings: Traditions of Shakespearean Translation and Adaptation in the Low Countries," in *Translating Shakespeare for the Twenty-First Century*, ed. Rui Carvalho Homem and Ton Hoenselaars (Leiden: Brill/Rodopi, 2004), 96.

43   In this way, *Ten Oorlog* fits the model described by Dirk Delabastita: when translators "hold a canonised position in the target literature or theatre, which is taken to entitle them to the privilege of a more 'personal' response to Shakespeare," they do not feel the need to be "faithful" to the source text; instead, "their commitment to revitalising Shakespeare for the modern stage implies a rejection of the 'museum theatre' they feel is the outcome of philological orthodoxy in translation" ("Bird's Eye View" 105).

44   Wouter Hessels, "Theatre Wars Great and Small: Apt Metaphors of Belgium and Flanders," in *The World of Theatre: Edition 2000*, ed. Ian Herbert and Nicole Leclercq (London: Routledge, 2014), 18.

America – or even in countries typically identified as part of the "global north," such as Canada or Scotland – that constitute a "major incentive" for new translations and adaptations.[45] By contrast, there is that form of "translation-*cum*-adaptation of Shakespeare that is not so easily measured against any explicit political predicament past or present" but that is "best appreciated in the light of the daunting cultural position that Shakespeare has acquired worldwide": it "primarily subverts the canonical status of Shakespeare," which may in many instances overlap with, but is never quite coterminous with, Shakespeare's position as a symbol of certain colonial legacies (it is in this latter category that Hoenselaars places *Ten Oorlog*).

Similarly, Dirk Delabastita distinguishes between Shakespeare translations that are more determined "by the private poetics of individual translators" and those that are part of a wider cultural-political project, as in "politically sensitive contexts" such as "emergent postcolonial cultures."[46] In South Africa, where translators of Shakespeare have been too few and too far between – a consequence of heavily anglophone Shakespearean educational and staging traditions – the line between these two categories has always been blurred. In the case of Afrikaans, the language most strongly associated with the apartheid state, this is further complicated by the conflicting political stances of different translators. If the work of a poet-translator like Eitemal (W.J. du Plooy Erlank) was co-opted into Afrikaner Nationalism, that of L.I. Coertze and Anna Neethling-Pohl consciously set out to contribute to it. By contrast, Afrikaans "rebels" such as André Brink, Breyten Breytenbach and Uys Krige used their translations of Shakespeare's plays to challenge the racism and hypocritical Calvinism of the state. Yet the "private poetics" of these translators differ widely.

The first formal translator of Shakespeare's plays into an African language, Sol Plaatje, presents a different kind of challenge. Plaatje's political credentials are well established – even if their "imperial" framing is contested – and the connection between his work as an activist and his practice as a translator into Setswana is a significant one (see Willan). But the only two translations that survive, *Diphosho-phosho* (*Comedy of Errors*) and *Dintshontsho tsa bo-Juliuse Kesara* (*Julius Caesar*), also attest to Plaatje's idiosyncratic "private poetics." Plaatje's seminal translations represent something of a lost opportunity: not simply because his other translations have been lost or were not completed, but because they could have been the beginning of a rich and diverse tradition

---

45   Ton Hoenselaars, ed. *Shakespeare and the Language of Translation*, 16.

46   Dirk Delabastita, "Shakespeare in Translation: A Bird's Eye View of Problems and Perspectives," *Ilha do Desterro* 36, no. 1 (1999): 112.

of translating Shakespeare into South African languages. Certainly, translations into isiZulu, isiXhosa and other African languages exist; ironically, the apartheid government's attempts to "tribalise" black South Africans through Bantu education led to the printing and distribution, for a period, of translations by B.B. Mdledle and others. Apart from outliers such as *SeZaR!* (2000) and *uVenas noAdonisi* (2012), however, there has been precious little Shakespearean translation in post-apartheid South Africa – either on the page or the stage.

It was a potentially significant moment, therefore, when *Julius Kesara* was billed for a run at the Artscape Theatre in Cape Town in September 2017. A multilingual adaptation of Plaatje's translation, this six-woman piece directed by Sia Sikawuti promised to be exactly the kind of production that I have hoped for: attentive to the contemporary (local) moment but acknowledging (local) Shakespearean histories, attuned to the politics of language and gender and class and race. Sadly, however, it was canned before opening night. The all-too-familiar reason? Money. Sikawuti would not be able to pay his actors unless the publicly-funded Artscape could provide more financial support. They could not.

Such banal details are rarely recorded in written accounts of theatre practice. Critics, scholars and theatre historians tend to emphasise creative vision or popular reception, aesthetics or ideology, stage-craft or cast and audience dynamics, socio-political context or sometimes just gossip. We tend not to dwell on the material conditions under which plays take to the stage – or, as in the case of *Julius Kesara*, don't make it to the stage. The dearth of arts funding in South Africa is an old saw by now. One may debate the allocation of state resources in a country beset by poverty and facing perpetual health and education crises; one may decry the corruption and misspending that has come to be expected from the government; one may complain about the identification of "preferred" projects that do receive support from the Department of Arts and Culture, the National Arts Council, the Lottery Distribution Trust Fund and other entities. The point is that those in the arts sector have become increasingly – in many cases exclusively – dependent on private rather than public money. This works better in some fields than others. In the visual arts, wealthy benefactors and corporate collectors purchase works as an investment but are generally happy to make these available for public viewing or even to loan them to public art galleries that have no acquisitions budgets. With theatre, such patrons are much less likely to see a return – which is why business sponsorship of theatre productions, for instance, tends to fall under a marketing budget or "Social Responsibility" spending.

There are, each year, big-name productions that are commercial successes for large and small theatres alike. As often as not, however, theatre in South

Africa is a loss-making endeavour: audiences don't fill auditoria, and sometimes even sold-out shows only just manage to cover their expenses and break
even. Theatre needs to be subsidised. But who will do the subsidising? These
mercenary and mercantile considerations are central to theatre-making in
South Africa, and therefore to staging Shakespeare. It is no coincidence that
some of the most interesting and experimental work in and with Shakespeare's
texts in recent years has happened in educational contexts – mostly student
productions conceived and directed by teaching academics who also have professional experience, with university resources and "underwriting" to secure
some financial independence; or, less often, productions aimed primarily at
school audiences that are ambitious for more than the utilitarian bums-on-
seats contract of "helping learners prepare for exams" and undertake innovative staging strategies.

So where does this leave independent theatres and theatre-makers who
don't receive state funding and want to do Shakespeare?

• • •

A few weeks after *Julius Kesara* failed to open, Capetonians had the chance to
see a very different Shakespearean beast: the Fugard Theatre's *Shakespeare in
Love*, directed by Greg Karvellas. The success of the 1999 Oscar-winning film
and its place in popular culture is such that I will assume readers' familiarity
with it. I suspect, on this basis, that the prospect of comparisons between the
stage version of *Shakespeare in Love* (adapted by Lee Hall for its London première in 2014) and *Ten Oorlog* may seem outlandish to many readers. I hope to
show, however, that they share certain key elements – and that these, taken
together with the considerations I have noted about the practicalities of theatre-making in South Africa, suggest some future prospects for staging Shakespeare in our particular national context.

Executive Director at the Fugard, Daniel Galloway, describes the production
as an attempt "to test the waters, to gauge the appetite for Shakespeare":

> Everything we put on stage must not only suit an artistic agenda, but also
> give itself a chance of being commercially viable. This was a piece which
> we thought would be a very appealing introduction to Shakespeare. As
> the season continued, we saw more and more young people coming to
> watch the show. Teenagers were excited about being at the theatre! We
> had an attractive young cast, speaking contemporary language but with

period music and costumes. Audiences responded with enthusiasm – it was not something that they regularly get to see.[47]

I will return shortly to questions of the appetite for Shakespeare's plays, of commercial viability, of audiences and of casting. First, however, I want to focus on a key feature of *Shakespeare in Love* mentioned by Galloway: contemporary language.

Fragments and strands of various Shakespearean plays find their way into the script: *Romeo and Juliet*, most obviously, but *Shakespeare in Love* also becomes a prefatory fable to introduce *Twelfth Night*; there are dozens of throwaway lines from other plays, references to titles of works already written by young Will and suggestions of plot lines, characters and settings he is yet to write. Galloway recalls:

> In the rehearsal process, the Shakespearean references were very apparent to a cast trained in Shakespeare. But we were uncertain how much emphasis to place on the allusions and in-jokes. In performance, there were widely divergent responses from audiences night by night; many audience members didn't "get" the references – and that's also fine. *Shakespeare in Love* is ultimately a romantic comedy, filtered through various prisms, recognisably Shakespearean, but still just a love story. Audiences don't need a Shakespearean "background" or education, or even to be familiar with the any of the plays.[48]

Here one can readily discern echoes of Lanoye's comments about his approach to Shakespearean material when writing *Ten Oorlog* – in particular, Belgian audiences' lack of familiarity with the "history" of and in the history plays. But we are still skirting the question of language. *Ten Oorlog* as "tradaptation" fits into a four-centuries-old European tradition of translating Shakespeare. How can it be compared, linguistically, to *Shakespeare in Love*? This is possible if we think about the latter film/play as a "tradaptation" of *Romeo and Juliet*; in other words, the combination of Shakespearean and contemporary language, which is a form of "modernising" Shakespeare, must be understood as an act of translation.

In light of Shakespeare's global status – a status that could only be attained by the translation of his work into the globe's many language – there is something slightly comical about the anxiety of "native" English speakers over the

47 Daniel Galloway, Interview with the author, 22 November 2017.
48 *Ibid.*

pros and cons of rendering Shakespeare in modern English. Dirk Delabastita
gives a useful overview of the modernising "controversy" in an article assessing
a selection of modern versions of *Romeo and Juliet*.[49] Delabastita explores the
difference between viewing the process of modernising Shakespeare as a kind
of "intralingual" translation (following Roman Jakobson) between two dialects
of English – Early Modern and Modern – and pursuing the possibility that
these two may indeed be considered distinct languages. If they are so different,
then modernising is in fact "interlingual" translation, or translation as it is more
commonly understood. And if those English teachers, actors and critics who
are so protective of Shakespeare's "original" text (the term is a dubious one, as
scholars of the history of editing Shakespeare can attest) don't mind Shakespeare being translated into contemporary Flemish or German, then they
shouldn't mind him being translated into contemporary English. The implication for the South African context is that, while the translation of Shakespeare's
plays into African languages – as instantiated by the Plaatje-to-Sikawuti
trajectory of *Julius(e) Kesara* – must be a priority for theatre makers who want
to stage Shakespeare, translation into modern English can be seen as a complementary process.

• • •

The cultural cachet of the translator-adapter is, of course, a significant factor.
Hoenselaars writes of *Ten Oorlog*: "Audiences came to see not Shakespeare, but
Lanoye and Perceval."[50] When *Shakespeare in Love* hit the big screen, it was
widely understood that the script's wit and Shakespearean nuance was chiefly
the work of playwright Tom Stoppard rather than of Marc Norman, the screen-
writer who wrote the early drafts before Stoppard was brought in by director
John Madden. Yet Stoppard's status was not what brought audiences flocking
to cinemas – that phenomenon was more attributable to the names in the cast.

If the Fugard Theatre wished to draw young audiences to its *Shakespeare in
Love*, however, it could not rely on the brand of a film made twenty years ago;
Gwyneth Paltrow and Joseph Fiennes found their next-generation equivalents
in Roxane Hayward and Dylan Edy. For older Capetonians, a different sort of
star appeal was offered by radio talk show host and sometime actor John May-
tham in the part of financier-turned-apothecary Hugh Fennyman – perhaps
not the same scale of celebrity casting as Jude Law or David Tennant playing

---

49   Dirk Delabastita, "'He shall signify from time to time': Romeo and Juliet in modern Eng-
      lish," *Perspectives* 25, no.2 (2017): 189.
50   Ton Hoenselaars, "Two Flemings at war with Shakespeare," 256.

Hamlet, but a strategic choice nonetheless. Ultimately, as with the film, what makes the stage version of *Shakespeare in Love* "work" is a vividly-portrayed group of secondary characters (the Fugard production had the experience of Robyn Scott, Nicholas Pauling, Theo Landey, Jason Ralph, Mark Elderkin, Darron Araujo and the rest of a strong ensemble to draw on). One could go so far as to say that it is the dynamic of the collective – of busy public life, of competing and collaborating theatre makers, of crowds in taverns and courts and streets – that saves *Shakespeare in Love* from Bardolatry.

I have argued elsewhere that, particularly in the wake of the quatercentenary celebrations of 2016, it is as necessary as ever to resist "the biographical impetus that is ultimately behind the notion of universality: the obsession with a specific man, in a specific country, at a specific time, whose significance is such that it overshadows and constrains every other man or woman, in every other place and every other time, who engages with his work."[51] *Shakespeare in Love* may appear to be precisely the kind of depiction of "The Bard of Avon" that reinforces this obsession. In fact, for most audience members, quite the opposite occurs: it becomes all too clear that the clever interweaving of an embellished and largely imagined biography with *Romeo and Juliet* – the putative intersection of life and art – is a fable, a fantasy and a farce. The farcical aspects are vital: *Shakespeare in Love*'s refusal to take itself seriously means that it could never become confused with the kind of "detailed historicist and materialist account" of the Jacobean theatre scene that can inadvertently bolster "the dangerous discourse of universality: Shakespeare as an historical figure who was uniquely placed to produce the work that he did becomes indistinguishable from Shakespeare the universal genius – the Shakespeare promoted in Jonson's terms ('not of an age...')."[52] Presenting Shakespeare among his fellows, emphasising his dependence on – and friction with – Christopher Marlowe and Richard Burbage and Ned Alleyn, mocking his weaknesses and shortcomings as an aspirant writer, *Shakespeare in Love* betrays an iconoclastic impulse that counterbalances the celebration and tribute. Here again, even if the tone, style and content of the two productions are worlds apart, we are in similar terrain to *Ten Oorlog*: the intention, you might say, is both to bury Shakespeare and to praise him.

What we see from the writers and performers of *Shakespeare in Love* is also, of course, a gentle self-parody. There is another kind of universality embedded in the script, best captured in Philip Henslowe's exchange with Fennyman

---

51   Chris Thurman, "From Shakespearean Singularity to Singular Shakespeares: Finding New Names for Will-in-the-world," *Shakespeare in Southern Africa* 30 (Special volume, 2017): 9.

52   *Ibid.*, 6.

about the theatre business: "The natural condition is one of insurmountable obstacles on the road to imminent disaster," explains Henslowe, but "Strangely enough, it all turns out well." Asked how this serendipitous outcome is brought about, he can only shrug: "I don't know. It's a mystery." The plight of Will and co, making stage magic against all odds, is recognisable to all theatre makers, everywhere – even those who are well funded, assured of an audience and not at risk of censorship or imprisonment. Features of the material conditions of playmaking in contemporary South Africa and Elizabethan England are not entirely dissimilar: constantly seeking both public and private funding, aiming for popularity alongside prestige, navigating the state's love-hate relationship with its artists.

As was the case with European audiences of *Ten Oorlog*, then, there may have been a "strictly contemporary message" for South African audiences of *Shakespeare in Love*, but this likewise required them to look askance – like a viewer studying a perspectival painting, if we apply Jürgen Pieters' conceit again – so that they could see past the play's "universalism."[53] This message is that "Shakespeare" is a malleable substance. It (rather than he) can be torn apart and reconstituted. It doesn't need to be respected. Above all: it can be entertaining.

• • •

I have suggested that, beyond the achievement of simultaneously updating and lampooning Shakespeare, the two most important things about *Shakespeare in Love* at the Fugard – trite though this may seem – are that it was brought to the stage and that people came to see it. *Shakespeare in Love* might not have been at the level of *Ten Oorlog* in terms of its commercial success and its impact on the national theatre scene, but it was popular enough to sell out a six-week run and it was, as Wouter Hessels wrote of *Ten Oorlog*, "a real feast for eye and ear, even for those who know little about Shakespeare."[54] Pieters and others have pointed out that perhaps *Ten Oorlog* was a little too enthusiastically received; that theatre critics, raving about the production, abandoned their critical role. On a smaller scale, this applies to the reception of *Shakespeare in Love* in Cape Town. But does one really want to complain about well-attended theatres?

As it happens, despite the full houses, the Fugard Theatre lost money on *Shakespeare in Love*. Between the rights and the cast size ("twenty actors and a

---

53   Jürgen Pieters, *Die Honden van King Lear*, 65.
54   Wouter Hessels, "Theatre Wars Great and Small," 17.

dog") it's an expensive show from the outset, and in this case the sets and the ridiculously expensive costumes brought to Cape Town from London and Stratford-upon-Avon pushed the production over budget to the tune of a few hundred thousand rand. The Fugard had made a financial success of big budget shows before, but for this to happen audience members in their thousands, rather than in their hundreds, were required each night – as was the case with *West Side Story*, which the Fugard had produced the previous year but which played to the huge auditoria at Artscape in Cape Town and the Joburg Theatre in Johannesburg. The Fugard Theatre spaces are much more intimate; architecturally, the buildings (which used to house a clothing wholesaler and a church hall) are striking, but there are limitations on how many patrons can be squeezed in.

The Fugard can afford not to take any shortcuts in terms of production costs because it is underwritten by founder Eric Abraham, who has acquired a substantial fortune since leaving South Africa for Britain in the 1970s (he was a student activist and journalist, and was forced to flee the country after being placed under house arrest). Abraham's commitment to theatre in the country of his birth could be seen as the country's sole performing arts equivalent of the private visual arts collectors mentioned earlier. He is, you could say, a replacement for a state subsidy; his aim since founding the Fugard has been to reduce his contribution as the theatre becomes a going concern, but his arts philanthropy is based on a belief that financial constraints should not hold back talented South African theatre makers. The Fugard is thus an anomaly, and hardly a model that could easily be replicated; but it does point the way to what could be done if independent funding were matched with a more parsimonious approach to production costs, and a theatre culture in which bums-on-seats is not a nightly source of anxiety.

As Galloway asserts, "The South African theatre landscape entails constant undercutting":

> You could buy a ticket for our *Shakespeare in Love* for under R300; for a similar production almost anywhere else in the world, people would pay at least R1000. Sure, you can factor in exchange rates and higher expenses overseas. But the fact is that South Africans aren't willing to spend money on theatre. Those who have the means will pay R1000 for dinner, but not for a show![55]

---

55   Daniel Galloway, Interview with the author, 22 November 2017.

Speculation about theatre audiences in a South African context is inevitably inflected by the country's severe inequality, which is still a "raced" phenomenon. Even with the undercutting Galloway describes, it is difficult for an establishment like the Fugard to make theatre that is truly "for the people" and still balance the books.

Ironically, the political commitment that Lanoye so admired in South Africa's artists and writers – a consequence of the ethical imperatives of making art under apartheid – is linked to unreasonable public expectations of theatre makers. "For decades," Galloway observes,

> South Africans have looked to theatre to "solve" political and socio-economic problems. That can be a constructive pressure. But theatre makers can't "fix" the fact that most South Africans can't afford to pay for tickets. And most of those who can afford to, prioritise their spending elsewhere. If we were to charge what we could or "should" charge in terms of the value of what we put on stage, we wouldn't sell enough tickets. It doesn't help that there is limited leisure capital available in families, etc. It's "hard work" to go to the theatre compared to other forms of entertainment, even if there is money. So at the Fugard we want to make sure that the whole theatre experience, from front of house to chatting at the bar after the show, entices people to come back. They may or may not enjoy the specific theatrical "product" they came to see, but the visit is a memorable one. Many, if not most, South African theatres overlook that.[56]

Anyone who has watched a performance at the Fugard can attest to its success in this regard. When it comes to Shakespeare, then, is the greater priority not creating a culture of theatre-going – a brand, such as the Fugard, that draws audiences in its own right? Having Shakespeare on the billing (next time, not *Shakespeare in Love*, but *Julius Caesar* or *Julius Kesara*, say) in such an environment minimises the weight of association, positive or negative, with "Shakespeare."

There remains the problem, Galloway admits, of "*Who* comes, from *where*, and how often." Emphasising its location on the edge of the historically significant District Six – a symbol of contestation over land ownership, of the apartheid government's forced displacement of "non-white" citizens, and of belated or incomplete restorative justice – the Fugard is cognisant of the need to stage work that speaks to black (or, given Cape Town's demographics, "coloured") history and contemporary experience. This is a vital part of the racial

---

56   *Ibid.*

transformation of the South African theatre industry; connected to it are difficult questions about casting and audience development. While a production like the Fugard's *Kat and the Kings* might have a creative team, cast, crew and audience that is racially representative, there is no question that the demographics of *Shakespeare in Love* – both on stage and in the auditorium – were predominantly white. This, certainly, cannot be the future for Shakespeare in South Africa.

It is worth noting, then, that when the Fugard decided to bring *Shakespeare in Love* back to the stage in August 2018, Daniel Mpilo Richards was cast in the role of Will. Richards has a cachet of his own, particularly from his work in a series of one-man political satires penned by Mike van Graan – he also has Shakespeare under his belt and played Chino in the Fugard's *West Side Story* – so he was, in light of the earlier discussion about "star appeal," good looks and ticket sales, an obvious choice. But given the Fugard management's appropriate anxiety about the intersections of race and class (or geography and history) in its production choices as well as in its audiences, Richards' identity as an actor of colour is significant. This was not directly remarked upon by any reviewers of the 2018 production, which arguably attests to a curiously persistent reticence in the Cape Town and, more broadly, the South African theatre sector to foreground discussions about race and casting when it comes to Shakespeare – notwithstanding the impossibility of "colourblind" casting in our context. So it fell to John Kani's *Kunene and the King*, which opened at the Fugard in April 2019 after premiering in Stratford-upon-Avon (it was co-produced by the Royal Shakespeare Company), to make race the explicit subject matter of a "Shakespearean" experience for Cape Town audiences. The play, starring Kani as the nurse of an ageing and terminally ill actor – portrayed by Antony Sher – makes heavy-handed use of *King Lear* and, not incidentally, *Julius Caesar* (in Mdledle's isiXhosa translation). *Kunene*, too, helped to develop an appetite among Fugard audiences for a South African Shakespeare.

The Fugard Theatre has since announced that it will be staging a production of *Hamlet*, to be directed by Neil Coppen, in 2020.

• • •

Jürgen Pieters notes – by turns earnestly and wryly – that 1997, the year in which *Ten Oorlog* made its debut on the Belgian stage, was associated with various endings and farewells.[57] The Blauwe Maandag Compagnie, an influential presence in Flemish theatre for over a decade, would soon merge with the

---

57   Jürgen Pieters, *Die Honden van King Lear*, 51–53.

Royal Dutch Theatre in Antwerp to become ToneelHuis. Earlier in the year, one prominent cultural commentator had already pronounced the death of the il-lusion that theatre could be truly "contemporary" and keep up with the affairs of the day. Another (in response to the effusive reviews received by *Ten Oorlog*) took it upon himself to declare that theatre criticism, too, was dead. More gen-erally, the passing of an era seemed to be marked by the passing of famous figures like Princess Diana, Mother Teresa and Gianni Versace.

There is another (and indeed more important) sense in which this was a watershed period in Belgium. Given the child abuse scandal and the political-juridical faultlines that were exposed, it may sound odd to describe 1997 as the end of an "age of innocence" – in fact an age of ignorance, or rather of denial – but authors such as Martin Ewans (2003) argue convincingly that this was the experience of many, if not most, Belgians.[58] 1998 saw the appearance of Adam Hochschild's book *King Leopold's Ghost*, which was translated for publication in Belgium in 1999. In the same year came Ludo de Witte's *De Moord op Lu-mumba* (*The Assassination of Lumumba*). Together the books caused outrage across Belgium, signaling the beginning of the end of what Hochschild had called "The Great Forgetting."[59] For most of the twentieth century, Belgians had been encouraged to dismiss any hint of colonial guilt. Indeed, according to such views, Belgium had never really seen itself as an imperial nation; Leopold II had made it clear from the outset that the Congo Free State belonged to him, and the Belgian parliament was loath to bail him out and annex the territory. It reluctantly administered the Belgian Congo from 1908 until independence in 1960, despite the suffering of the Belgian people during two world wars in which their country was mostly flattened.

That narrative could no longer be sustained in the wake of *King Leopold's Ghost* and *De Moord op Lumumba*. If Hochschild provided a damning account of cruelty and exploitation (much of what he said was not new, but previous historians of the Congo had not managed to spark a similar global public out-cry), as well as of the benefits that continued to accrue to Belgium after Leop-old's demise, then De Witte provided incontrovertible evidence that the Bel-gian government had acted maliciously and duplicitously in replacing Lumumba with the villainous Mobutu. The early 2000s were marked by com-missions of enquiry into the assassination and official acknowledgement that it was time to correct the false glorification of Belgium's role on the African

58   Martin Ewans, "Belgium and the Colonial Experience," *Journal of Contemporary European Studies* 11, no. 2 (2003): 167–180.

59   Adam Hochschild, *King Leopold's Ghost: A Story of Greed, Terror and Heroism in Colonial Africa* (New York: Houghton Mifflin, 1998), 295.

continent by institutions such as the Royal Museum for Central Africa. During this period, belated international attention on the Rwandan genocide of 1994 was a further spur for Belgians to reflect on their colonial legacy. The Great Forgetting was replaced by the Great Reckoning – a process that is still underway, but one that has been complemented by a necessary coming-to-terms with a shifting set of racial and cultural "national" Belgian identities.

What all this means for Belgian theatre, and Belgian Shakespeare, remains to be seen. Lanoye's novel *Het Derde Huwelijk* (2013) is an indication of his desire to tackle the questions that this new Belgium poses – Elleke Boehmer and Sarah De Mul describe it as part of "a localised body of literature" that "reflects and contributes to the heightened discursivity of multiculturalism in Flemish society in transition across the past two decades."[60] Lanoye's subsequent pair of translations/adaptations, *Hamlet versus Hamlet* (2013) and *Koningin Lear* (2015), do not depart from their precursors quite as radically as *Ten Oorlog* but nevertheless innovate, "intervene" and reinterpret Shakespeare's texts. Perhaps, some two decades after *Ten Oorlog*, a very different political moment in Belgium is waiting for expression in a new Shakespearean idiom.

What, then, about Shakespeare in South Africa? Belgium came late to the European imperial game; then there was the near-century of the Great Forgetting. There has never been a time in South Africa's history, by contrast, in which cultural production – like staging Shakespeare – could be separated from our status as a colony, or a neo-colony, or a not-yet-postcolony. Nor is this possible with a work such as *Shakespeare in Love*. The Fugard Theatre team that staged *Shakespeare in Love* were all too aware of the shortcomings that would be visible if the show were viewed through a "decolonising" lens, in terms of the show's origins as well as in terms of the whiteness of both the cast and the audience they performed to each night. A single theatre cannot be held responsible for the broad socio-economic, political, cultural and even geographical dynamics that shape its audiences, or (as Galloway notes) curate its theatrical offerings solely towards "solving" these problems. This applies equally to staging Shakespeare. Nevertheless, it is worth asking: how can the features of the Fugard's approach to theatre-making that I have discussed be applied to "making Shakespeare" in other South African theatre contexts? Is there a third way, a golden mean between *Shakespeare in Love* and the ideologically appealing but unstaged *Julius Kesara*? Perhaps.

Two months after the Fugard *Shakespeare in Love* completed its first run, a production of *The Taming of the Shrew* headlined the 2018 summer season at

---

60   Elleke Boehmer and Sarah De Mul, *The Postcolonial Low Countries: Literature, Colonialism and Multiculturalism* (Plymouth: Lexington, 2012), 2.

Cape Town's Maynardville Open-Air Theatre. It was directed by Tara Notcutt who, at 31, was the youngest person to take the reins at Maynardville; she was also only the fifth woman to direct a play in Maynardville's sixty-two year history. Notcutt was acutely aware of the barriers that women face when it comes to staging Shakespeare: there is the problem of "parts for women" in orthodox approaches to casting Shakespeare's plays, of course, but beyond this there is a theatre industry – global and local, with Cape Town as an acute example – in which producing and directing opportunities for women are still comparatively rare.[61] Her *Shrew*, therefore, sought to intervene directly in and to disrupt these gendered patterns by employing an all-woman cast, crew and creative team.

The choice of *The Taming of the Shrew* was significant beyond the play's gender dynamics, its staging history and its potential either to subvert or to reinforce patriarchal conditions. This was an opportunity to engage more meaningfully with the gender-based violence in the play than when it was last staged at Maynardville, in 2011, under Roy Sargeant's direction (see Young for a critique of that production in light of South Africa's epidemic of violence against women). It was also a statement about the history of Maynardville; *Shrew* was the first play performed there, in 1956, and by offering it in 2018 Notcutt was simultaneously acknowledging the theatre's history and announcing a new beginning.

For decades, the annual production at Maynardville was the most important – or, at least, the most prominent – South African Shakespeare in any given year. Having celebrated its fiftieth anniversary, however, it increasingly became a source of controversy. Aside from accusations of favouritism in the appointment of directors and in casting, there were fierce arguments over whether public funds should be spent on what some perceive as a neo-colonial indulgence and others ardently defend as a Capetonian institution and an educational boon (after all, hordes of schoolchildren are taken to Maynardville each February). The sustainability of Maynardville had come to depend heavily on funding and resources from Artscape, but it was increasingly clear that this would no longer be feasible. The opportunity to direct *Shrew*, then, came to Notcutt with the appeal of independence but with limited financial backing (Artscape and the Maynardville Open-Air Theatre Trust would be "venue partners" and provide technical support). Fortunately she found a co-producer in comedian Siv Ngesi; significantly, this was also the first time a black theatre maker invested in Shakespeare at Maynardville.

---

61   Tara Notcutt, Interview with the author, 29 November 2017.

The 2018 *Taming of the Shrew*, I want to suggest, demonstrates that the "third way" referred to above is possible. It represents the inevitable move away from state support towards independent funding, but with a co-production model lacking the largesse of an Eric Abraham. Maynardville has traditionally placed emphasis on scale and spectacle; Notcutt's trimmed-down *Shrew* had a cast of ten and was of necessity "leaner and meaner" (the set could collapse into a portable box). Shakespeare was also only one of various offerings at a re-launched 2018 Maynardville Festival, which included music, dance and comedy – while the *Shrew* asked tough questions about misogyny and violence in contemporary South Africa, Shakespeare as part of the Maynardville line-up was thus offered as a form of popular entertainment rather than as "difficult" and "inaccessible."

Notcutt and colleagues made relatively few textual changes beyond cuts necessary to reduce running time; translation and modernising of the text was limited to interjections and occasional stage business. This was not a tradaptation. Yet it responded to Shakespeare's play with a tradaptor's spirit, and it situated the *Shrew* within its temporal and geographical or "national" context – Cape Town, South Africa, 2018 – without contrivance. There was no attempt to allegorise, nor was it necessary to say, "This is a production about the present moment"; that much was self-evident, even as sustained musical and fashion references to the 1990s introduced a form of anachronism (the effect of which was both comic and thematically serious, pointing audiences to the unquestioned misogyny of "innocuous" popular culture from that period). The cast members' multiracial, multilingual identities infused their performances. Notcutt's *Shrew* was a "South African Shakespeare" that took as a given the prerogative to navigate between the local and the global.

• • •

In this essay I have tried to construct an unusual transnational framework for aspects of the study of Shakespeare in South Africa, a subject that in the past I have tended to approach (*mea maxima culpa*) from a somewhat parochial perspective. If South Africans have, reluctantly, come to accept that our national story is not as "exceptional" as we once hoped, then South African Shakespeareans such as myself must likewise unlearn our own version of exceptionalism. As postcolonial or "global south" Shakespeareans more generally, we also have to acknowledge that – while undoubtedly our context *is* different to that of Shakespeareans in the global north, or the former imperial centre, or the "developed" world – it is not always different in the ways that we assume, or for the reasons that we expect.

The relationship between the local and the universal is not, after all, one of opposition but one of intersection. I have sought to identify echoes, shadows, resonances and parallels between two very specific and contrasting contexts for theatre-making, in the hope that such an enterprise reinforces the collaboration between European, North American and South African theatre scholars represented by this book. "Shakespeare versus Shakespeare" thus comes to mean: the insights that connecting Shakespeare in Belgium to Shakespeare in South Africa might bring, the boldness of attending to the local without shying away entirely from the permutations of "universality": the contrast between ideas of how Shakespeare could/should/might be performed and the material conditions that limit these possibilities; and, finally, the argument with oneself that is the basis of all scholarship, writing and theatre.

Works Cited

Boehmer, Elleke and Sarah De Mul. *The Postcolonial Low Countries: Literature, Colonialism and Multiculturalism*. Plymouth: Lexington, 2012.

Delabastita, Dirk. "'He shall signify from time to time': *Romeo and Juliet* in modern English." *Perspectives* 25, no.2 (2017): 189–213.

Delabastita, Dirk. "*Henry* v in the Low Countries." In *Shakespeare and the Low Countries*, edited by Ton Hoenselaars and Holger Klein, 233–250. Lewiston, NY: Edwin Mellen Press, 2005.

Delabastita, Dirk. "A Great Feast of Languages: Shakespeare's Multilingual Comedy in *King Henry* v and the Translator." *The Translator* 8, no. 2 (2002): 303–340.

Delabastita, Dirk. "Shakespeare in Translation: A Bird's Eye View of Problems and Perspectives." *Ilha do Desterro* 36, no. 1 (1999): 15–27.

Delabastita, Dirk and Ton Hoenselaars. *Multilingualism in the Drama of Shakespeare and his Contemporaries*. Amsterdam: John Benjamins, 2015.

De Gruyter, D. and Wayne Hayward. "Shakespeare on the Flemish Stage of Belgium, 1876–1951." *Shakespeare Survey* 5 (1952): 106–110.

De Vos, Jozef. "Discussing *Ten Oorlog*: an interview with Tom Lanoye." In *Shakespeare and the Low Countries*, edited by Ton Hoenselaars and Holger Klein, 315–328. Lewiston, NY: Edwin Mellen Press, 2005.

De Vos, Jozef. "Shakespeare's History Plays in Belgium: Taken Apart and Reconstructed as 'Grand Narrative.'" In *Four Hundred Years of Shakespeare in Europe*, edited by A. Luis Pujante and Ton Hoenselaars, 211–222. London: Associated University Presses, 2003.

De Vos, Jozef "Jozef de Vos in gesprek met Tom Lanoye en Luc Joosten." *Documenta: Tijdschrift voor theater* 16, no. 2 (Special volume, 1998): 111–128.

De Vos, Jozef, Jürgen Pieters and Laurens de Vos. *Shakespeare: Auteur voor alle seizoenen* [e-book]. Tielt: Lannoo Maulenhoff, 2016.

Distiller, Natasha. "On Being Human." In *South African Essays on "Universal" Shakespeare*, edited by Chris Thurman, 19–37. Burlington: Ashgate, 2014.

Ewans, Martin. "Belgium and the Colonial Experience." *Journal of Contemporary European Studies* 11, no. 2 (2003): 167–180.

Fernie, Ewan. *Shakespeare for Freedom: Why the Plays Matter*. Cambridge: Cambridge UP, 2017.

Galloway, Daniel. Interview with the author, 22 November 2017.

Hessels, Wouter. "Theatre Wars Great and Small: Apt Metaphors of Belgium and Flanders." In *The World of Theatre: Edition 2000*, edited by Ian Herbert and Nicole Leclercq, 17–22. London: Routledge, 2014.

Hochschild, Adam. *King Leopold's Ghost: A Story of Greed, Terror and Heroism in Colonial Africa*. New York: Houghton Mifflin, 1998.

Hoenselaars, Ton, ed. *Shakespeare and the Language of Translation* [2004]. London: Bloomsbury/Arden, 2012.

Hoenselaars, Ton. "Two Flemings at war with Shakespeare." In *Shakespeare's History Plays: Performance, Translation and Adaptation in Britain and Abroad*, edited by Ton Hoenselaars, 244–261. Cambridge: Cambridge UP, 2004.

Hoenselaars, Ton. "There is Tremendous Poetry in Killings: Traditions of Shakespearean Translation and Adaptation in the Low Countries." In *Translating Shakespeare for the Twenty-First Century*, edited by Rui Carvalho Homem and Ton Hoenselaars, 79–98. Leiden: Brill/Rodopi, 2004.

Hoenselaars, Ton and Holger Klein, eds. *Shakespeare and the Low Countries*. Lewiston, NY: Edwin Mellen Press, 2005.

Joosten, Jos. *Tom Lanoye: De ontoereikendheid van het abstracte*. Amsterdam: SUN / Kritak, 1996.

Jürs-Munby, Karen, Jerome Carroll and Steve Giles (eds). *Postdramatic Theatre and the Political: International Perspectives on Contemporary Performance*. London: Bloomsbury, 2014.

Lanoye, Tom. *Koningin Lear*. Amsterdam: Prometheus, 2015.

Lanoye, Tom. *Hamlet versus Hamlet*. Amsterdam: Prometheus, 2014.

Lanoye, Tom. *Mamma Medea*. Amsterdam: Prometheus, 2001.

Lanoye, Tom. *Spek en Bonen*. Amsterdam: Prometheus, 1994.

Lanoye, Tom and Luke Perceval. *Ten Oorlog*. Amsterdam: Prometheus, 2016.

Lanoye, Tom. *Mamma Medea*. Translated by Antjie Krog. Cape Town: Queillerie, 2002.

Lehmann, Hans-Thies. *Postdramati c Theatre* [1999]. Translated by Karen Jürs-Munby. Abingdon: Routledge, 2006.

Lehmann, Hans-Thies. "'Postdramatic theatre,' a decade later." In *Dramatic and Postdramatic Theater Ten Years After: Conference Proceedings*, edited by Ivan Medenica, 31–46. Belgrade: Faculty of Dramatic Arts, 2011.

Notcutt, Tara. Interview with the author, 29 November 2017.

Pieters, Jürgen. *Die Honden van King Lear*. Groningen: Historische Uitgeverij, 1999.

Ryan, Kiernan. *Shakespeare's Universality: Here's Fine Revolution*. London: Bloomsbury/Arden, 2015.

Schalkwyk, David. "Foreword." In *South African Essays on "Universal" Shakespeare*, edited by Chris Thurman, xiii–xxi. Burlington: Ashgate, 2014.

Stalpaert, Christal. "Something is Rotten on the Stage of Flanders: Postdramatic Shakespeare in Contemporary Flemish Theatre." *Contemporary Theatre Review* 20, no. 4 (2010): 437–448.

Stalpaert, Christal, Bram van Oostveldt and Jaak van Schoor. "Enter Ghost…: The Linguistic, Theatrical and Post-dramatic 'Afterlife' of Shakespeare's *Hamlet* in Flanders." In *Variorum Hamlet Project: Annexes*. Cambridge, MA: MIT Press, 2005.

Thurman, Chris. "From Shakespearean Singularity to Singular Shakespeares: Finding New Names for Will-in-the-world." *Shakespeare in Southern Africa* 30 (Special volume, 2017): 1–13.

Thurman, Chris. "Multilingual Shakespeare: A South African Reflects on Translation and Performance in Germany." In *Translation Studies beyond the Postcolony*, edited by Kobus Marais and Ilse Feinauer, 94–129. Newcastle: Cambridge Scholars Publishing, 2017.

Thurman, Chris. "'After Titus': Towards a Survey of Shakespeare on the Post-apartheid Stage." In *New Territories: Theatre, Drama, and Performance in Post-apartheid South Africa*, edited by Greg Homann and Marc Maufort, 75–103. Brussels: Peter Lang, 2015.

Thurman, Chris. "Generation S: 'Southern' Shakespeares across Time and Space." In *South African Essays on "Universal" Shakespeare*, edited by Chris Thurman, 1–18. Burlington: Ashgate, 2014.

Van den Abbeele, Lien. "Men moet naar de sterren reiken, ook al vermoedt men dat ze er niet zijn: De poëtica van Perceval en Lanoye in *Ten Oorlog* en Verhelst en Simons in *Richard* III: twee hedendaagse Shakespeare-adaptaties in het licht van het postdramatisch tragische." MA thesis, University of Ghent, 2013.

Willan, Brian. "'A South African's Homage' at One Hundred: Revisiting Sol Plaatje's contribution to the *Book of Homage to Shakespeare* (1916)." *Shakespeare in Southern Africa* 28 (2016): 1–19.

Wright, Laurence. "'Thinking with Shakespeare': *The Merchant of Venice* – Shylock, Caliban and the dynamics of social scale." *Shakespeare in Southern Africa* 29 (2017): 17–26.

Young, Sandra. "A Charming, Troubling Circus." *Shakespeare in Southern Africa* 23 (2011): 81–83.

Index of Names and Literary Works